Democratic Transit

MW01109231

In the wake of the unprecedented uprisings that swept across North Africa and the Middle East in late 2010 and 2011, observers widely speculated that these events heralded the beginning of a new age of democratic transition across the region. The result of a four-year research project, this book offers a cross-country analysis of the dynamics of democratic transition and of the state of democracy and authoritarianism from Tunisia, Sudan and Egypt to Syria, Kuwait and Lebanon.

Ibrahim Elbadawi and Samir Makdisi identify specific economic, political and social conditions influencing the transition across the region and in each of the individual countries, as well as the requisite conditions for consolidating democracy once the process is initiated. This volume examines the struggling, halted and painful transitions, where these have for the time being failed, as well as instances in which democratic consolidation can be seen.

This is a unique and wide-ranging examination of Arab development and democracy for those investigating the fate of authoritarian regimes.

Ibrahim Elbadawi is Research Fellow, The Economic Research Forum, Cairo, Egypt. He is the co-editor of two recent volumes: with Samir Makdisi, *Democracy in the Arab World: Explaining the Deficit* (2011); and, with Hoda Selim, *Understanding and Avoiding the Oil Curse in Resource-Rich Arab Economies* (2016).

Samir Makdisi is Professor Emeritus of Economics and Founding Director of the Institute of Financial Economics at the American University of Beirut (AUB). He is the author of *The Lessons of Lebanon, the Economics of War and Development* (2004) and co-editor (with Ibrahim Elbadawi) of *Democracy in the Arab World: Explaining the Deficit* (2011).

Democratic Transitions in the Arab World

Edited by

Ibrahim Elbadawi and Samir Makdisi

CAMBRIDGE
UNIVERSITY PRESS

CAMBRIDGE
UNIVERSITY PRESS

University Printing House, Cambridge CB2 8BS, United Kingdom

Cambridge University Press is part of the University of Cambridge.

It furthers the University's mission by disseminating knowledge in the pursuit of education, learning and research at the highest international levels of excellence.

www.cambridge.org
Information on this title: www.cambridge.org/9781107164208

© Cambridge University Press 2017

First published 2017

Printed in the United States of America by Sheridan Books, Inc.

A catalogue record for this publication is available from the British Library

Library of Congress Cataloging-in-Publication data
Elbadawi, Ibrahim, editor. | Makdisi, Samir A., editor.
Democratic transitions in the Arab world / edited
by Ibrahim Elbadawi, Samir Makdisi.
Cambridge, United Kingdom : Cambridge University
Press, [2017] | Includes bibliographical references and index.
LCCN 2016047813 | ISBN 9781107164208 (hardback)
LCSH: Democracy – Arab countries – 21st century. | Arab countries –
Politics and government – 21st century. | Arab Spring, 2010–
LCC JQ1850.A91 D464 2017 | DDC 320.917/4927–dc23
LC record available at https://lccn.loc.gov/2016047813

ISBN 978-1-107-16420-8 Hardback
ISBN 978-1-316-61578-2 Paperback

To all those who believe in and continue to struggle for democracy in the Arab world

Contents

Figures

Tables

Contributors

IBRAHIM ELBADAWI is Research Fellow at the Economic Research Forum, Cairo, Egypt. He is the co-editor of two recent volumes, with Samir Makdisi, *Democracy in the Arab World: Explaining the Deficit* (2011); and, with Hoda Selim, *Understanding and Avoiding the Oil Curse in Resource-Rich Arab Economies* (2016). He has a PhD in economics and statistics from North Carolina State University and Northwestern University.

SAMIR MAKDISI is Professor Emeritus of Economics and Founding Director of the Institute of Financial Economics at the American University of Beirut (AUB). He is the author of *The Lessons of Lebanon, the Economics of War and Development* (2004) and the co-editor (with Ibrahim Elbadawi) of *Democracy in the Arab World: Explaining the Deficit* (2011). He has a PhD in economics from Columbia University.

ABDELWAHAB EL-AFFENDI is Professor of Politics and Head of the Politics and IR Program at the Doha Institute for Graduate Studies. He is the author of *Genocidal Nightmares: Narratives of Insecurity and the Logic of Mass Atrocities* (2015) and *Darfur: A Decade in Crisis* (in Arabic, 2013).

MONGI BOUGHZALA is Professor of Economics at the University of Tunis-El Manar. He is co-editor of *Inflation Targeting in MENA Countries: An Unfinished Journey* (2011), and has written numerous papers in the areas, among others, of macroeconomic and monetary policy, labour issues and inflation targeting with special reference to the Middle East and North Africa regions.

SAOUSSEN BEN ROMDHANE is Assistant Professor of Economics at the University of La Manouba-Tunisia. She has published academic papers on trade, development policy and democracy in the Arab world and is the author of *Regional Integration in North Africa* (2013).

NOHA EL MIKAWY is Regional Representative at the Ford Foundation. Noha has written two books on the politics of reform in Egypt and one comparative book on the processes of economic reform, participation and legislation in Egypt, Jordan and Morocco.

MOHAMED MOHIEDDIN is Professor of Sociology at Menoufia University, Egypt. He has published numerous papers on social inequality and poverty in the Arab world, social exclusion and the socio-economics of water resources, and he is the author of a textbook on *Demography* (2012).

SARAH EL ASHMAWY is Research Analyst on the Middle East desk at KPMG's Corporate Intelligence team in London.

RAED SAFADI is the executive director of the Research and Policy Directorate in Dubai's Department for Economic Development. He is co-author of *Inclusive Global Value Chain* (2016) and numerous publications on, among other subjects, trade and development, regional trading arrangements and the world trading system.

SIMON NEAIME is Professor of Economics at the American University of Beirut and associate editor of the *Journal of International Financial Markets, Institutions, and Money*, among other journals. His publications include *Money and Finance in the Middle East: Missed Opportunities or Future Prospects?* (2005) and *The Macroeconomics of Exchange Rate Policies, Tariff Protection and the Current Account: A Dynamic Framework* (2000).

ATIF KUBURSI is Emeritus Professor of Economics at McMaster University, Canada. His publications include *The Economic Consequences of the Camp David Accords* (1981) and *Oil, Industrialization & Development in Arab Gulf States* (1984 and 2015), and he has published numerous papers in academic and professional journals and many technical reports.

YOUSSEF EL KHALIL is Executive Director of the Financial Operations Department at the Bank of Lebanon, a part-time lecturer in economics at the American University of Beirut and the author of numerous publications on the Lebanese economy.

ATTA ELBATTAHANI is Professor of Political Science at the University of Khartoum. He is the author of *Crisis of Governance in Sudan* (2011) and of many publications on, among other subjects, ethnic and religious conflicts in African societies; governance and state institutional reform; gender politics; and peripheral capitalism and political Islam.

Acknowledgements

For the past eight years, the editors of this volume have been managing two major research projects, housed at the Institute of Financial Economics (IFE) at the American University of Beirut, that have focused on issues of democracy and development in the Arab region. Both projects were based on a combination of conceptual and empirical cross-country work, as well as on case studies of individual countries. The first project concentrated on factors underlying the lagging democratic development in the region, while the second, which we initiated shortly before the Tunisian uprising in 2010, diagnosed the dynamics of Arab democratic transitions, the limitations thereof and the necessary conditions for a stable democracy.

In undertaking these projects we were fortunate to enlist the collaboration and support of distinguished colleagues, inside and outside the Arab world. Their full cooperation helped us greatly in achieving our set targets. The outcome of this collaborative research was two publications, the first titled *Democracy in the Arab World, Explaining the Deficit* (Routledge, 2011). This volume is the second.

We should like to acknowledge a number of debts. From the beginning the International Development and Research Centre (IDRC) provided grant support for our research endeavours. When at times unforeseen delays in meeting agreed deadlines had to be faced, IDRC proved understanding of our requests for extensions. Our special thanks to Roula El-Rifai for her support and counsel throughout the project. To the IFE we owe a great debt for its hospitality, congenial work environment and administrative and research support that greatly facilitated our work. The Office of Contracts and Grants at AUB efficiently managed our IDRC grants, as well as provided the requisite administrative support.

As part of our research efforts, a number of open workshops were held at AUB to discuss work in progress by members of the research team. We also had the opportunity to present our ongoing research at conferences in the region and abroad. The feedback we received was invariably most helpful.

We wish to thank Ali Abdelgadir Ali, Wafic Grais, Ali Kadri and Raimondo Soto for providing insightful comments on earlier drafts of Chapters 1, 2 and 3 of this volume, and also Youssef El Khalil and Michael Ross for their perceptive comments on Chapter 1.

For excellent research support we are grateful to Dhuha Fadhel, Vivian Norambuena and Layal Wehbe, who throughout have been most helpful.

To Isabel Miller we extend our great appreciation for her excellent editorial work and patience with our repeated editorial requests.

Our thanks are due to Rima Shaar, secretary of the IFE, who throughout has provided excellent secretarial support. Over the years a good number of research assistants at the IFE efficiently provided requested research support. Our thanks go out to each one of them.

Samir Makdisi would like to acknowledge his enormous debt to his wife, Jean, for reading and in the process significantly improving drafts of papers she had been requested to read. Her incisive comments and intellectual insights always helped clarify issues under discussion and greatly improved the readability of the text. He also would like to acknowledge his debt to his three scholar sons, Saree, Ussama and Karim, for the vibrant intellectual discussions he often had with them on major issues facing the Arab world, Arab–Western relationships and of course Lebanon; and to Layal Wehbe for assisting him in various tasks with great efficiency and a cheerful spirit.

Ibrahim Elbadawi would like to thank his wife, Enayat, for her encouragement, patience and support during the past eight years since the project began. He would also like to extend his appreciation and gratitude to his three children, Lina, Elsadig and Khalid, for their challenging and intellectually stimulating and sometimes sceptical arguments on issues of development and democracy reflecting the perspective of their generation.

Introduction and Summary

Ibrahim Elbadawi and Samir Makdisi

In a previous work, based on both cross-country research and case studies of individual Arab countries (Elbadawi and Makdisi 2011), the editors of this volume explored various economic, political, social and historic factors that may explain the persistence of a general democracy deficit in the Arab region. Taking it as a framework for analysing long-term cross-country differences in the standards of democracy, rather than as a theory of political transition the modernisation hypothesis was deployed as a benchmark model for analysing the Arab democracy deficit relative to the counterfactual consistent with its level of development, as well as for testing hypotheses that might explain the persistence of this deficit.

Very briefly summarised, the evidence from the cross-country model (for details refer to Elbadawi and Makdisi 2011) showed that for the Arab region as a whole, while the extended 'modernity' variables (e.g. income, education, neighbour polity, female participation in the labour force) are important determinants of democracy in the long run, they fail to explain why the Arab democracy deficit persisted relative to other regions. Other possible explanatory factors included past colonial rule, ethnic fractionalisation and religion. Colonial rule has certainly had a negative impact (a preponderance of Arab countries became authoritarian immediately after independence), but does not furnish evidence for the entrenchment of Arab autocracy. Ethnic fractionalisation increases regime instability, whether autocratic or democratic. However, the results imply that ethnic fractionalisation does not seem to have influenced to any substantial degree the democratisation process in the Arab region. It is noteworthy that religion did not emerge as a factor promoting autocracy in the Arab world.

What in large measure seemed to explain the entrenchment of Arab authoritarianism, as a region-wide phenomenon, was the twin emergence of abundant oil wealth in a region that is not yet democratic (the oil curse effect) and a highly conflictual environment (frequent home and regional wars as well as the persisting Arab–Israeli conflict) with all their attendant disruptive foreign imperial interventions. At the level of individual countries, the effects of these two variables were dependent on further supplementary factors that helped to explain the durability of particular autocratic regimes. To illustrate, the extent to which oil wealth might facilitate the trade-off between economic welfare and political freedom is contingent on the specific socio-political history of the country concerned. Similarly, the Arab–Israeli conflict has had a much stronger impact on domestic political developments in countries nearer to the theatre of the conflict. In recent years, foreign military interventions (e.g. Iraq) and the rise of Islamist fundamentalism (encouraged by such interventions) have also acted, in one way or another, to bolster authoritarianism in the region.

The case studies revealed that, whatever the specific explanation for the lagging democratisation in each one of them, they shared common explanatory factors (e.g. historical legacies, co-option of business elites and so on). And as El-Affendi (2011) put it succinctly: 'What stands out is that the post-independence Arab rulers continued to arrogate to themselves the same privileges and powers that the colonial state had enjoyed, thus alienating themselves from their societies as much as the colonial powers had done before them.'

In December 2010, this alienation was finally manifested in the successful Tunisian uprising that toppled the prevailing autocratic order. The knocking of history at the bolted door of autocracy in the Arab region was loud, albeit delayed, but it was soon followed during 2011 by uprisings in Egypt, Yemen, Libya and Syria. Whatever the immediate triggers for the Tunisian and other uprisings, a gamut of interacting factors, economic, political and others underlying them, have been building over the years towards a push for democracy in the region.

However, the ray of hope for democracy to which the initial uprisings gave rise soon faded away. More than five years after the initial uprisings, the door of autocracy is only very slightly ajar. Of the five countries where uprisings have taken place, only Tunisia appears to be forging its way successfully through a democratic transition which, however, facing important socio-economic challenges and occasional acts of terrorism, is yet to be firmly established (Boughzala and Ben Romdhane, Chapter 3). Egypt's progress along a path of social justice, liberties and freedoms has not so far taken hold (El Mikawy, Mohieddin and El Ashmaouy, Chapter 4), while the other three countries have been suffering from vicious civil conflicts intertwined with foreign intervention. The case of Syria, where the conflict has drawn in external armed interventions, both regional and international, in support of opposing sides in the conflict, has been especially tragic (Safadi and Neaime, Chapter 5).

Of the other Arab countries, since independence, Lebanon (Makdisi and El Khalil, Chapter 7), with its consociational democracy, has throughout constituted an exception to the general trend of autocracy in the region, though it has not been spared the pains of civil war. Iraq progressed politically after the fall of Saddam Hussein (with its Polity score rising to 3 in 2010–14), but political rights and civil liberties have remained restricted (with Freedom House scores ranging between 5 and 6 for this period), while the Economist Intelligence Unit (EIU) democracy index placed Iraq in 2014 at the bottom of the so-called hybrid regime category.[1] The political process has been plagued by sectarian politics, which reduced the democratic opening to a 'winner take all' electoral system controlled by the governing majority; and, since mid-2014, when vast areas were lost to Daesh militarily, the country has been witnessing an ongoing war between Daesh and government forces. Sudan (Elbattahani, Chapter 8) and the Gulf countries remain highly autocratic, except for Kuwait whose political system allows for a measure of political participation via parliamentary elections (Elbadawi and Kubursi, Chapter 6). In 2003, Algeria introduced some reforms to the executive authority which helped raise its polity score from –3 for that same year to 2 subsequently. However, its freedom scores for political rights and civil liberties continue to reflect significant restrictions (6 and 5 respectively for 2014), and the EIU index for 2014 classified it as an autocracy. Similarly in the wake of the uprisings of 2011, reforms in the executive branch of Morocco improved its polity score for that year a little, from –6 to –4. Again its political rights and civil liberties scores continue to demonstrate restrictions (5 and

---

[1] Various measurements of democracy have been constructed, the Polity and Freedom House indices being among the longest standing and most widely used in empirical work. According to the authors of Polity, its scores reflect a spectrum of governing authority that spans from fully institutionalised autocracies through mixed, or incoherent, authority regimes (termed 'anocracies') to fully institutionalised democracies. The Polity score captures this regime authority spectrum on a twenty-one-point scale that ranges from −10 (hereditary monarchy) to +10 (consolidated democracy). The Polity scores can also be converted into regime categories in a suggested three-part categorization of 'autocracies' (−10 to −6), 'anocracies' (−5 to +5), and 'democracies' (+6 to +10). Freedom House carries out annual comparative assessments of political rights and civil liberties in the world. Each country is assigned two numerical ratings – from 1 to 7 – for political rights and civil liberties respectively, with 1 representing the most free and 7 the least free. The more recent EIU index of democracy is based on four categories: electoral process and pluralism, civil liberties, functioning of government, political participation and political culture. It classifies countries into five categories: authoritarian (score of 0–3.9); hybrid regime (4–5.9); flawed democracy (6–7.9) and full democracy (8.1). It should be added, of course, that all these indices have their inherent limitations (e.g. see Munck and Verkuilen 2002, and Paxton 2000). A full appreciation of the attributes of the political system of any country can be achieved only through an in-depth study of the country concerned.

4 respectively for 2014), though to a lesser degree than Algeria. In turn the EIU index for 2014 classified it at the top of the autocracy category.

Thus, as of mid-2016, with a few exceptions – among them Lebanon and Tunisia – autocracy continues to reign in the Arab region, though in varying forms and to different degrees from one country to another. Only slightly ajar, the doors of autocracy have taken some battering; when they will open wide only time will tell.

A primary objective of this volume is to shed light on the dynamics of transition in the Arab world and the conditions for its success, as revealed by select Arab case studies, but not on the particular form of democracy that might arise. In the concluding chapter, we touch on the emerging resistance to transition.[2] Again we combine cross-country work and country case transitions. The cross-country work, divided into two chapters, sets the framework of analysis: the first is based on an elaborate econometric analysis that focuses on the region-wide and global factors that underlie democratic transitions, while the second is a conceptual polemical analysis elucidating the requirements for stabilising the democratic transition or at least for transforming autocratic regimes in democratic directions. With this framework as a background, six case studies identify specific economic, political and social conditions influencing the transition in each of them, as well as the requisite conditions for consolidating democracy once the process is initiated. They reflect varying Arab experiences that not only highlight specific factors associated with each country's transition trajectory, but also reflect common explanatory factors that tally with major findings of the cross-country work. Given the emergence of strong resistance to democratic change in the aftermath of the initial uprising, this volume concludes with remarks on the underlying reasons for this resistance and the prospects for democratic transition that lie ahead.

---

[2] In a recent study by Mukand and Rodrik (2015) on the political economy of liberal democracy, the authors distinguish between three political groups (elite, majority and minority) and three kinds of rights: property (elite interest), political (majority interest) and civil (minority interest). They point out that a liberal democracy requires all three rights, whereas an electoral democracy generates only the first two. They then explain why in the West liberal democracies came to be established while in the developing world most democracies that emerged are electoral democracies that provide property and political rights but not civil rights. Earlier, Schmitter (2010) noted that in countries that had democratized since 1974 their evolving regimes came to be regarded as poor-quality regimes, i.e. defective, partial or only electoral democracies.

The Thematic and Cross-Country Analysis: Main Results and Issues

Elbadawi and Makdisi (Chapter 1) employ an empirical multi-year index of 'sustainable' democratic transition, based on a widely used global indicator of the standard of democracy (Polity). Using this index they analyse an extended 'rentier' model emphasising the role of resource rents and conflicts, while accounting for modernisation and other traditional controls analysed in the received literature. They find that rents from oil and other minerals are a hindrance to democracy when managed by less than fully democratic regimes and that their corrosive influence is subject to threshold effects. Their results also suggest that home wars, including civil wars and the Arab–Israeli conflict, have impeded democratic transition throughout the Arab world. Testing for two causative mechanisms that might explain how resource rents might constitute a drag on democratisation, they show that resource rents are an effective deterrent when they are deployed to create jobs. On the other hand, compared to resource transfers, political repression does not seem to be the first, best option, especially for highly resource-endowed countries.

Finally, they find negative neighbourhood externalities exist for democratic transitions when a resource-endowed country is located in a non-democratic or conflictive region. Based on their evidence concerning the adverse regional externalities affecting the region, together with the prevailing regionalisation and even internationalisation of the conflicts in the Arab world, and the looming re-entrenchment of regional autocracy, they conclude that the prospects for democratic transition appear highly uncertain.

In Chapter 2, El-Affendi analyses the challenges of stabilising democracies in the aftermath of the Arab Spring. In this context he reviews the arduous trajectory of the struggle for democracy, starting with the rise and failure of early post-colonial democratic experiments in several Arab countries, which gave way to the rise and eventual entrenchment of authoritarianism in the Arab world. In line with the empirical analysis of Elbadawi and Makdisi, El-Affendi's conceptual analytic narrative also emphasises the role of oil and conflicts in facilitating the ascendency of authoritarian rule and the capacity of autocratic regimes to maintain their grip on power. However, he draws attention to the point that the role of oil and conflicts in shaping the evolution of the political landscape in the region is rather complex, in view of the feedback effects between oil and conflicts on one hand and between autocracy and conflicts on the other.

According to El-Affendi, the arrival of the Arab Spring was made possible when the accumulated economic and political failures of the

Arab political order led to a convergence of visions on the part of the Islamist and secular elements in society, notably in Tunisia and Egypt. However, despite the apparent success of moving towards democracy in Tunisia, as uncertain as it may be, the failure to maintain consensus on a common platform of a viable social contract between these forces and the flaring up of sectarian and sub-national anxieties in the societies of the Arab Spring have all paved the way for an authoritarian counter-revolution. He argues that the most potent weapon the counter-revolution has used has been 'induced violence', unfortunately with remarkable success, to restore social cleavages along lines of ideology and identity and thus to undermine the case for democracy. The ongoing authoritarian counter-revolution, contends El-Affendi, threatens to force a post-Arab Spring relapse into the 'democratic deficit' phase, where 'stabilising democracies' becomes an endeavour the success of which is difficult to visualise, and much less 'consolidating democracies'.

The Case Studies: Main Results and Issues

The case studies taken up in this volume may be classified as of three categories. The first category includes three autocracies where uprisings have broken out, namely Tunisia, Egypt and Syria. The second comprises two countries which traditionally have had partial democracies, albeit partial to varying degrees: Lebanon with its long-standing consociational democracy, and Kuwait where the political system allows for a measure of participatory governance; both countries have so far failed to establish fully fledged democracies. The third category includes one country, Sudan; with the exception of short-lived democratic experiences in the 1950s, 1960s and 1980s, it has throughout been subject to autocratic rule and is yet to re-initiate any moves towards democracy. These case studies reflect variations in the political experiences of the Arab world but, as already noted, autocracy continues to prevail generally.

While the respective politico-economic trajectories that led to the uprisings in Tunisia, Egypt and Syria differ, the case studies amply demonstrate that they do share common elements. In the economic domain, these include rising unemployment, over the years, reaching very high levels especially for the young, and the persistence of economic inequality as well as significant disparities between urban centres and rural regions. Concretely, the benefits of growth went in large measure to the ruling elites and favoured groups in society. In the political domain, highly exclusive governing bodies alongside a popular desire for greater freedom bred increasing resentment, with civil society organisations pressing ever harder for political reform, a state of affairs that eventually turned into full-blown civil uprisings.

Boughzala and Ben Romdhane (Chapter 3) draw attention to the relatively rapid economic growth and rising per capita income as well as improved levels of education that Tunisia experienced prior to 2011. They argue that, as the country developed economically and socially, its social structure became more complex, with a highly educated salaried workforce becoming the main social category and civil society, as a whole, developing rapidly. These developments carried with them the seeds of change in line with the modernisation hypothesis. Economic openness also gradually took hold, becoming increasingly incompatible with restrictive political institutions. This growing incompatibility eventually helped to bring about the overthrow of the regime. But while democratic institutions have been taking root since the uprising, their consolidation will require not only effective leadership and more political cohesion but above all a new, participative and inclusive economic strategy focusing on society's expectations and the aspirations of the youth whose economic and political frustrations played a major role in triggering the uprising.

In the case of Egypt, as El Mikawy, Mohieddin and El Ashmaouy point out (Chapter 4), the factors underlying transition were multifaceted. They included structural drivers of economic and social exclusion (e.g. unemployment and informalisation, impoverishment of the middle class, pronounced poverty); institutional drivers, that is, political exclusion that, among other things, meant a captured state – as they put it, the marriage between capital and politics; exclusion of minorities and women from effective political participation – and finally the declining regional role of Egypt, awareness of which exacerbated popular resentment of the regime. The authors caution that, unlike Tunisia, Egypt is undergoing a protracted transition process. While progress at the constitutional level has been achieved (a more liberal constitution was adopted in 2014), the consolidation of democracy remains a goal to aspire to, requiring guarantees of freedoms, the accountability of governmental institutions and social justice. Equally imperative will be to put in place an inclusive and progressive social justice agenda. The authors also bring to mind the importance of elite choices, especially with respect to how they define the role and the accountability of the institutions of religion and security.

The Syria uprising may be traced, as Safadi and Neaime (Chapter 5) explain, to gross economic mismanagement and a harsh authoritarian and clientalist political system which have combined to thwart any move towards freedom and equality in the country. The uprising turned civil war (now five years old) has pitted an amalgamation of opposition groups, with fundamentalist parties effectively in the lead and attempting to expand their control of the country, against regime forces that are trying to re-establish governmental authority. The conflict has invited international and regional interventions in support of one side or the other. The final outcome remains uncertain. The authors believe any future settlement will, and indeed should, bring in its wake profound political change leading to a pluralistic, democratic Syria. They emphasise the point that as democracy is restored, a new socio-economic model of development, based on inclusive socio-economic policies and the promotion of good governance, should emerge. Genuinely democratic and accountable governance in Syria will be able to implement such a model.

The Kuwait case, taken up by Elbadawi and Kubursi (Chapter 6), exhibits features of partial democracy, a state of affairs unique among the monarchies of the Gulf. Kuwait has an elected parliament, regular elections and a constitution that guarantees basic human rights and the powers of the parliament. In contrast to the countries that have witnessed uprisings, the main challenge facing Kuwait, as the authors point out, is how to sustain the march towards more advanced forms of democratic governance. The authors explain that Kuwait's early democratic experience had much to do with its geographic location, positioned apart from the trade route to India controlled by the British. This led to an inclusive and equitable relationship between the Emir and the Kuwaiti trading families who, in the past, used to finance the ruling family and also enjoyed access to footloose sources of income. However, this pioneering democratic experiment has been partially derailed by the advent of oil, which altered the initial political equilibrium in Kuwaiti society. Therefore they argue that, among other factors, economic diversification and the expansion of the non-oil economy are likely to have positive implications for democracy in the country, since they would weaken the oil-driven authoritarian bargain. However, the authors also recognise that Kuwait's autocratic neighbourhood and the region-wide sectarian conflicts constitute a serious threat to its social cohesion and democratic consolidation.

The Lebanese case is unique in the Arab region. Lebanon's political system has been based on a consociational democracy model: an arrangement for power-sharing between its multiple religious communities that was intended to guarantee freedom of expression and stability. Furthermore, the national economy has throughout been open and dominated by the private sector. However, as Makdisi and El Khalil point out (Chapter 7), in practice the intended objectives of this political model have only been partially realised. It allowed for plural political activity and parliamentary elections, but also encouraged the emergence of weak political institutions that fostered corruption and nepotism and did not ensure political stability or equal political and civil rights. And despite robust economic growth, the political system could not prevent the outbreak of a civil war. The authors argue that only a transition to a fully fledged secular and democratic system with accountable political institutions will guarantee stability and allow for the promotion of a more equitable structure at both the economic and social levels.

Analysing the Sudan case, El Battahani outlines the elements that have allowed autocratic rule to prevail following the overthrow of a democratically elected, multi-party government in 1989. The leaders of the ruling party have utilised their monopoly of the instruments of power to control soft and hard rent sources. Over time, various repressive measures were implemented with a view to undermining opposition groups, while violent conflicts in marginal regions have rendered traditional political parties increasingly less effective at leading any confrontation with the ruling autocracy. There was a brief and limited opening up to democracy (2005–11), but with South Sudan going its own way in 2011, autocracy in Sudan re-asserted itself under the leadership of al-Bashir, seizing more power via constitutional amendments. The author argues that prospects for transition in Sudan are uncertain. New politicised groups, among the youth for instance, have emerged as potential agents of change. Yet despite harsh economic conditions and a fiscal crisis, the autocracy of Sudan has managed to survive, thanks to favourable regional and international circumstances, by concluding authoritarian bargains with rival elites and running a strong authoritarian state underpinned by durable coercive institutions.

Outline

Accordingly, this volume is divided into four parts: first the introduction and summary, then Part I, on the dynamics of transition, sets the framework of analysis. It comprises two chapters: Chapter 1 explains the dynamics of democratic transitions in the Arab world, and Chapter 2 considers existing obstacles to democratisation, the means by which they may be overcome and the stabilisation of the democratic process. Part II comprises six case studies (Chapters 3–8), which reflect the variations in the experiences of the Arab countries under study. These case studies include three countries where uprisings have taken place: Tunisia, Egypt and Syria, which respectively have been experiencing a successful, protracted and painful transition; two countries with halted democracies, Kuwait and Lebanon; and one country, Sudan, where since 2011 an autocratic regime has been trying, under extremely uncertain conditions, to prevail against the winds of change. Part III (Chapter 9) concludes with remarks on the resistance to and prospects for democratic change and consolidation in the region.

Part I

Conceptual and Cross-Country Perspectives

1 Explaining Democratic Transitions in the Arab World

Ibrahim Elbadawi and Samir Makdisi[1]

1.1 Introduction

The recent Arab uprisings have forced the opening up of a new trajectory for transitions to democracy from the long-reigning autocracies that have dominated this region. This chapter analyses the factors that underlie this transition, where we code 'democratic transitions' as a multi-year phenomenon. We find that rents from oil and other minerals are a hindrance to democracy when managed by less than fully democratic regimes, and that their corrosive influence is subject to threshold effects. Our results also suggest that home wars, including civil wars and the Arab–Israeli conflict, have impeded democratic transitions. We tested for two causative mechanisms that potentially explain how resource rents constitute a drag on democratisation. We show that resource rents are an effective deterrent when they are deployed to create jobs. On the other hand, compared to resource transfers, political repression does not seem to be the first-best option, especially for highly resource-endowed countries. We also find that negative neighbourhood externalities exist for democratic transitions when the resource-endowed country is located in a non-democratic or conflictive region. Therefore, in view of the prevailing regionalisation and even internationalisation of the conflicts in the Arab world, and the looming existence of entrenched regional autocracy, the prospects for democratic transition appear highly uncertain.

The recent Arab uprisings constitute a belated awakening. Save for some short-lived and disconnected democratic spells in the two poor and politically unstable countries of Sudan and Mauritania,[2] the Arab region

---

[1] The authors are indebted to participants in a workshop on 'The Arab World in the Wake of the Uprisings: Transition to Democracy vs. Regeneration of Autocracy' held at the American University of Beirut, 8–9 November 2014, for very helpful comments. They are also grateful to anonymous referees for their beneficial remarks. They would also wish to acknowledge the excellent research support of Dhuha Fadhel, Vivian Norambuena and Layal Wehbe.

[2] For example, Sudan experienced two popular uprisings against military regimes in 1964 and 1985, which led to elected but short-lived governments in 1965–69 and 1986–89, both of which were followed by long-lasting military regimes.

13

has remained unaffected by the successive democratic waves that transformed other developing regions, despite its notable socio-economic development in the past five decades.[3]

The political trajectory of the Arab region was shaken by the uprising in Tunisia in late 2010, which was quickly followed by a similar one in Egypt in January 2011; in turn subsequent uprisings were unleashed in Syria, Libya and Yemen. But while these uprisings may have shaken the foundations of autocracy in parts of the Arab world and have produced a glimmer of hope for regional democratic change, their outcome remains highly uncertain. As of late 2015, Tunisia appeared to be forging ahead with establishing democratic governance,[4] but Egypt's democratic course looked uncertain, while in the other three countries the uprisings turned into armed conflicts, with confessional and/or ethnic overtones, that are yet to be resolved. In particular, the massive violence the regime deployed against the initial uprising in Syria eventually led to its militarisation and the ensuing vicious civil war that has attracted armed fundamentalist groups and transnational sectarian militias. The emergence of the so-called Islamic State of Iraq and Syria (ISIS or Daesh), which managed to control large segments not only of Syria but also of Iraq, has, in turn, triggered overt foreign armed (areal) interventions by international powers, initially by the United States in support of the Kurds in their fight against Daesh, but a year later (beginning 30 September 2015) much more actively by Russia in support of the regime.

Nonetheless, it remains a fact that the Arab uprisings have opened up a new area of research on the dynamics of transition from autocracy to sustained democracy in the Arab region. They call for a better understanding of the dynamics of this regional transition from autocracy to democracy and of the necessary conditions for sustaining it. Building on the received literature, this chapter seeks to contribute to this endeavour.

---

[3] It is interesting to note that historians have referred to the creation of the first Ottoman parliament (March 1877 to February 1878) as the first Ottoman experiment in democracy, not of course in the sense of today's established democracies. Rather it embodied the concept of having elected representatives (though with very limited powers) to defend the interests of a constituency, negotiate taxation and attempt to control the budget. The election process was indirect and restricted to certain strata of the male population: the deputies were elected in their respective constituencies, albeit under the influence of the governors of the various provinces (for more details, see Herzog and Sharif 2010).

[4] As attested by the approved constitution of January 2014, the free parliamentary elections of 26 October and the presidential elections of 22 December of the same year, and generally the relatively peaceful transfer of power between its major political contestants. Attempts at destabilising the domestic situation (e.g. the terrorist attack on the Bardo National Museum in Tunis that killed twenty-one people on 18 March 2015) have been unsuccessful, and possible similar future attempts will hopefully not succeed in derailing this process.

There is already a vast literature on democratic transitions, spanning varied – if not contrasting – hypotheses or theories explaining these phenomena. They include the impact of cultural factors, negotiated transitions by political elites and instrumentalisation of identity cleavages or ideology. A review of this literature lies outside the purview of this chapter.[5] For the purposes of our own analysis, we take the influential modernisation hypothesis advanced by Lipset (1959) that occupies a major place in this literature, as the benchmark analytical framework for explaining democratic transition in the Arab region and go on to identify additional factors that are salient to the Arab world, and therefore might have also influenced this transition.

Simply put, the modernisation hypothesis argues that democracy is secreted out of dictatorship by economic development. As countries develop, social structure becomes complex, labour more active, technological advances empower producers, civil society is also empowered, and thus dictatorial controls become less effective. This interpretation essentially characterises the Lipsetarian modernisation view as the framework for understanding the process of transition from autocracy to democracy (e.g. Barro 1999).

To the extent that the modernisation hypothesis is expressed as a causal positive effect from development to democracy, it remains a contested issue.[6] To illustrate this debate, we selectively review the critical strands of the literature followed by those in support of the hypothesis. Przeworski (2004; 2009) investigates a probability model for political regime transition in which authoritarian regimes in relatively high-income societies are likely to make the transition to democracy not because of the modernisation effect related to high income levels, but because income is highly associated with past regime instability. Moreover, he also finds that authoritarian regimes in growing economies are less, not more, likely to experience democratic transition. On the basis of these findings, Przeworski went on to argue that, empirically speaking, the modernisation theory does not offer a convincing explanation for democratic transitions: development makes democracies endure, but it does not make them more likely to emerge.[7]

---

[5] For instructive reviews, see for example, Brumberg (2014) and Munck (1994).

[6] The contrasting empirical outcomes, it should be added, may be related to the differing empirical methodologies that have been employed: countries selected, statistical methods applied, selection of socio-economic indicators, democracy measure chosen and the form of the relationship being tested.

[7] This is in line with the transitions paradigm, which holds that no level of economic, social or cultural development constitutes a necessary prerequisite for the initiation of a transition. Instead, transitions are governed by political 'pacts' through which opposition forces or parties guarantee the property rights of regimes in return for formal political rights, thereby mitigating social tensions that otherwise could prevail (for example, see Brumberg 2014).

However, in defence of the modernisation hypothesis, and in response to Przeworski's critique, Boix and Stokes (2003) argue that one needs to 'push back' his entire sample (1950–90) to a point in time when no country was democratic, that is, 1850–1950. They then show that the endogenous effect (i.e. the positive impact of development on democracy) applies not only to the 1950–90 period Przeworski and colleagues analysed, but that it is even stronger for the pre-1950 period. For their part, Epstein and colleagues (2006) question Przeworski's interpretation of the role of income. Instead, they argue that higher per capita incomes significantly increase the likelihood of democratic regimes, both by enhancing the consolidation of existing democracies and by promoting transitions from authoritarian to democratic systems. Moreover, they classify countries into autocracies, democracies and partial democracies, and find that the latter were much more susceptible to democratic transition, as these countries tend to be more volatile than either democracies or autocracies and are characterised by a largely unpredictable polity. Based on these findings, they argue that partial democracies should be the point of focus of transition analysis.

Another critical perspective of the modernisation hypothesis is put forward by Acemoglu, Johnson, Robinson and Yared (2008; 2009), who take a long historical view and focus on the relationships between economic, political and historical factors. They argue that, although income and democracy are positively correlated (over long periods of time), no evidence emerges of a causal effect. Instead, omitted factors – most probably historical – appear to have shaped the divergent political and economic development paths of various societies, leading to the positive association between democracy and economic performance. Thus, they call for a re-evaluation of the modernisation hypothesis with much greater emphasis on the underlying factors that influence the political and economic paths which developing societies have followed.

Defending the modernisation hypothesis, Barro (2015) challenges Acemoglu and colleagues' critique and argues that, at the empirical level, their rejection of the modernisation theory hinges on the insignificance of income and education as determinants of democracy in fixed-effects panel regression systems with a moderate time dimension. Instead, he contends that estimating fixed-effects regressions for a smaller number of countries for which data are available throughout a century lends strong support to the modernisation hypothesis (this debate is further taken up in Section 1.4.4).

The modernisation hypothesis has also met with further wide-ranging critiques from some strands of the political science literature. For example, Gleditsch and Choung (2004) argue that economic factors influence the stability of autocracies and the likelihood of crises in general, but do not make transitions to democracy more likely; and Gleditsch and Ward (2006) stress the importance of the geographic neighbourhood and argue that there is a tendency for transitions to democracy to cluster regionally. In a similar vein, Ulfelder and Lustik (2005) emphasise the role of past experiences with democracy in such transitions, for both resource-rich and other countries, while saying that economic recessions increase its likelihood. Furthermore, they argue that in countries where they prevail, higher levels of civil liberties and non-violent collective action help to initiate such transitions. Therborn (1977) argues that European countries became democratic as a result of wars rather than modernisation.

Finally, Inglehart and Welzel (2009) emphasise differentiating between two distinct phases of modernisation: industrialisation and post-industrialisation. Whereas industrialisation is accompanied by bureau-cratisation, centralisation, rationalisation and secularisation, people in post-industrial societies display an increasing emphasis on autonomy, choice, creativity and self-expression. Both processes have changed the way people relate to authority. Emancipation from authority takes place only during the post-industrialisation phase, when the focus shifts from external authority to greater individual autonomy and human choice.

This brings up the question of religious practices in the transition to democracy, specifically as they concern the Arab region. Rothstein and Broms (2011) have focused on how these practices are financed. In the Christian West, they argue, religion has been financed from below, which has followed semi-democratic representation, transparency and account-ability. They claim that in the Arab-Muslim countries religion has been financed from above instead, thereby hindering the development of semi-democratic representation as well as systems for transparency and accountability in public affairs. Chaney (2012) makes a similar claim in that he links Arab autocracy to the long-running influence of a 'control structure' that evolved under the Islamic empires in the pre-modern era (see Section 1.5). Of course earlier writers (e.g. Huntington 1991; Kedourie 1994) have invoked Islamic religious practices and/or tradi-tions, as being conducive to non-democratic governance.

However, others, for example, Maseland and van Hoorn (2011), van Hoorn and Maseland (2013), Kuru and Stepan (2012) and Elbadawi and Makdisi (2011), do not find that religion is a significant element in this regard. In rejecting religion (specifically Islam) as an explanatory factor for the lack of democracy, Kuru instead focuses on the influences of the rentier state as a region-wide phenomenon. This, in his view, should help to explain the persistence of authoritarianism in Muslim-majority coun-tries in the MENA and Central Asia, in contrast to the democratic experience of Muslim-majority countries in other regions where the democratisation process has taken place. But, as Aldashev, Platteau and Sekeris (2013) have pointed out, religion can be employed as an instrument to promote authoritarian rule: clerics beholden to the ruler, especially in oil-rich countries, have and continue to present themselves as defenders of the status quo. Indeed, it can be said today's fundamentalist groups have advanced the instrumentalisation of religion to much higher (not to say brutal) levels in an attempt to achieve their political (autocratic) goals.

What the foregoing review of the literature suggests is that whether the influential Lipsetarian thesis is taken as a framework for analysing long-term, cross-country differences in the standards of democracy or as a theory of political transition, it should be empirically tested in an extended model that accounts for other potentially competing factors.

Along the lines of this interpretation, we have deployed the Lipset hypothesis in our earlier work (Elbadawi and Makdisi 2007; Elbadawi, Makdisi and Milante 2011) as a useful benchmark model for analysing the Arab democracy deficit relative to the counterfactual level of democracy consistent with its level of development, as well as for testing the two fundamental hypotheses on the additional role of oil and conflicts. They show that for the Arab region as a whole, while the traditional 'modernisation' variables remain important determinants of democracy in the long run, they fail to explain the Arab democracy deficit relative to other regions. Rather, oil and conflicts and their interactions appear to explain this persistent deficit and more generally the politico-economic trajectory of the Arab region, at least in the post-World War II period.[8] Certain writings have referred to the particular features or identities of the region as illustrating the limitations of the global approach of the modernisation hypothesis or transition theory in identifying the factors that underlie the transition process of any given country or region. It is contended there is a need to focus on endogenous forces that shape political preferences or dictate a particular transition course.[9] Indeed, what this chapter and the following case studies clearly reveal is that the unfolding

---

[8] We would like to note here earlier studies, notably by El Beblawi and Luciani (1987), that have analysed the impact of oil revenues on the nature and functions of oil-exporting countries such as the Gulf countries. They describe them as allocation states or rentier economies, i.e. states that derive their income from abroad and can spend without having to collect domestic taxes. Important, with no taxation, citizens are far less demanding in terms of political participation, let alone the negative impact of the rentier nature of state on work ethics.

[9] See Brumberg (2014) for a critique of transition and post-transition theories and Waterbury (1994) for an earlier analysis of specific features of Arab regimes that accounted for the lag in their democratic development.

Arab transition cannot be explained simply by general hypotheses of transition, specifically the modernisation hypothesis. Analysis of the specific socio-economic or institutional conditions that have influenced these transitions is equally crucial. As already noted, the modernisation framework provides a good starting point for our focus on the particularities of the Arab transition.

This chapter complements our earlier longer-term analysis of the Arab democracy deficit and contributes to the literature by estimating the probability of democratic transition, using a multi-year index of 'sustainable'[10] democratic transition, based on the Polity score. We analyse an extended 'rentier' model emphasising the role of resource rents and conflicts, while accounting for modernisation and other traditional controls analysed in Przeworski's (2009) benchmark model. In view of the fact that the democracy deficit is a related, albeit different phenomenon, it is natural that we account for these two pivotal variables that have essentially shaped the Arab political and economic landscape post-independence.[11] Our model also accounts for other potential determinants discussed in the recent literature, including neighbourhood democracy and neighbourhood conflicts, as well as the initial standard of democracy.[12]

This chapter's model, we would argue, addresses the weaknesses of the benchmark modernisation model discussed in the literature and attempts to introduce policy content and institutional structure to the largely empirically oriented Przeworski approach. Moreover, in our quest to address the foregoing critique through specifying and estimating an encompassing democratic transition model, we also attempt to make novel contributions to the literature in the following seven dimensions.

First, we analyse democratic transitions using a more appropriate empirical concept than the ones adopted in earlier literature. According to our concept, a country is coded as having experienced a democratic transition during a half decadal period if its Polity score jumped by three points at the beginning of the period and the average rate of change of the

---

[10] The term 'sustainable' is meant to stress the distinction between the multi-year (decade and half decade) approach to coding democratic transitions and the year-on-year concept adopted in the received literature. However, although we don't use this term on a consistent basis, it is implicitly assumed.

[11] Our model, however, does not account for the indirect effect of rents on democracy in the case of the non-oil-producing Arab countries, which depend on oil through remittances and aid. The relative paucity or accuracy of remittances and FDI data precluded extension of the model to account for this potentially important effect.

[12] The model, however, abstracts from other traditional idiosyncratic factors that, in the received literature, were not found to be robustly associated with democracy, such as colonial history, religion and social cleavages (see, for example, Elbadawi and Makdisi 2007 and Elbadawi, Makdisi and Milante 2011).

score was non-negative during the period. Unlike the other measures used in the received literature, ours accounts for the fact that democratic transition is a process that might take several years to come to completion. Also this index allows for the likely possibility that during the transition phase a country's democratic standing might experience a degree of setback for a year or more while pursuing a rising multi-year democratic trend.

Second, our model assesses not only the impact of oil, other resource rents and conflicts on democratic transitions, but also whether they explain regional fixed effects, most notably the Arab dummy (for oil and non-oil-producing Arab countries), that is whether they render the Arab and other regional dummies insignificant in a model that controls for developing countries' regional effects. The insight behind this test is that, unlike in developed countries, the process of democratisation in developing countries is likely to be more susceptible to the corrosive effects of resource rents and conflicts.

Third, as theory predicts (e.g. Ali and Elbadawi 2012), our empirical model controls for the threshold effects of resource rents per capita.

Fourth, we also test for the recent hypothesis that partial democracies are more susceptible to regime change than either autocracies or complete democracies (e.g. Epstein et al. 2006).

Fifth, we discuss the channels through which resource rents might hinder democratisation. In this context, we test the effects of political repression and public employment as possible channels.

Sixth, in view of the unfortunate predicament of the Arab world being plagued by a high frequency of wars and lingering conflicts, such as the Arab–Israeli conflict, we unpack the Arab wars and test the impact on democratisation of the types and intensity of such wars.

Seventh, finally we undertake an assessment of the prospects of democracy in the Arab world in the aftermath of the Arab Spring by assessing the impact of two negative regional externalities on the probability of democratic transition: the increasing regionalisation and internationalisation of conflicts in the Arab world and the weak standard of democracy at the regional level.

In Section 1.2 we present the definition of the democratic transitions index and highlight preliminary associations and trends for pivotal variables used in the analysis. Section 1.3 presents the empirical model and outlines the econometric strategy for estimating it. Section 1.4 contains the core econometric results and tests a set of hypotheses concerning the role of resource rents, home wars and partial democracy, as well as Arab and non-Arab regional dummies. This section revisits the empirical debate on the modernisation hypothesis, as well as undertakes extensive robustness checks of our extended rentier model, and the associated hypotheses, against three alternatives. First, we re-estimate the model using a sample of ten-year periods, where the coding of the transition index is based on ten-year periods rather than five-year ones. Second, we split the five-year sample into two sub-samples – before and after 1990 – and estimate the model for each of the two sub-samples, in order to test whether the results concerning the effects of resource rents were driven by the end of the Cold War and the emergence of several new states following the breakup of the Soviet Union in 1990. Third, similarly we test for the claim that resource rents became a hindrance to democratic transition only after the 1970s, when the oil-producing developing countries managed to capture the oil rents that were previously expropriated by multinational companies (Andersen and Ross 2014).

Section 1.5 revisits the question of how resource rents, the most important factor from the Arab world perspective, might hinder democratic transitions, and we analyse the role of public employment and political repression. Section 1.6 unpacks the Arab wars and re-assesses the unique impact of the Arab wars in slowing democratic transitions, especially the lingering Arab–Israeli conflict, a widely held view in the Arab world that has been the subject of a recent critique in the literature (e.g. Chaney 2012). Section 1.7 analyses the prospects for democracy in the Arab world in the aftermath of the Arab uprisings, emphasising the negative externalities of the conflictive and non-democratic neighbourhood. Section 1.8 concludes.

1.2   Democratic Transitions Inside and Outside the Arab World

In assessing democratic transitions we rely on the widely used Polity IV Index as a measure of democracy.[13] The Polity IV Index is based on two concepts: 'institutionalised democracy' (DEM) and 'institutionalised autocracy' (AUT). The DEM score is coded according to four measures of regime characteristics: competitiveness in executive recruitment; openness in executive recruitment; constraints on the chief executive; and competitiveness in political participation. These measures, along with regulation of participation, form the basis for calculating the AUT score. The Polity score (POL) is computed by subtracting the AUT score from the DEM score, resulting in a score ranging from −10

---

[13] This measure is somewhat more objective than the Freedom House Index because it uses objective questions with a wider range of measurement. However, Elbadawi, Makadisi and Milante (2011) showed that the FH index, as well as the 'Democracy and Development classifications' (Przeworski et al. 2000), strongly corroborates the findings based on the Polity Index.

(strongly autocratic) to 10 (strongly democratic). Using the Polity data set we define the following index:

Democratic transition. A country is coded as having witnessed a democratic transition during the period (t_0, t_0+N), provided that it experienced a jump of three points in the Polity scale at time t_0 and that the average log change in this index is non-negative during the period between t_0 and t_0+N. The transition period (N) should be long enough to allow the process to play out. In particular, we define democratic transitions over ten- and five-year periods.

Other recent empirical research on democratic transitions was built around the dichotomous democracy-autocracy index, due to Przeworski and colleagues (2000) and updated by Cheibub and Gandhi (2004). In this data set, political regimes are classified as democracies if they meet all of the following conditions: the chief executive and the legislature are elected; there are at least two political parties; and at least one incumbent regime has been defeated in elections. In addition to Przeworski and his research associates, Ross (2009), for example, uses this data set and codes the incidence of democratic transition by a dummy variable that takes the value of 'one' in the year that a country changes from authoritarian to democratic rule and 'zero' otherwise. However, he also uses Polity IV to fill the gaps for countries not included in their data set.[14]

The year-on-year indices, however, do not account for the fact that democratic transition is a process that might take several years, even decades, to come to completion. Moreover, during the transition phase a country's democratic standing might experience some degree of setback for a year or more although pursuing a rising multi-year democratic trend. Our proposed multi-year measure is precisely intended to account for this key feature of democratic transitions.

The Arab world missed out on the recent democratic wave that has swept the developing world since the mid-1970s. For forty-five years (1960–2004) it was ruled by extremely autocratic regimes, which averaged −7 or less in the Polity score, improving to about −4 in 2010 (Table 1.1). The wave started in the Latin American region (LAC), which achieved a Polity score of 3 in the second half of the 1980s decade and steadily democratised to reach a score of 8 in the 2000 decade. A similar, but weaker trend was also experienced by East Asia (EA), which achieved a Polity score of more than 4 in the first half of the 2000 decade, but appears to have suffered an autocratic relapse in the second

---

[14] Instead, Ulfelder (2007) develops his own dichotomous year-on-year autocracy-democracy index.

Table 1.1: *Democracy across the Developing World*

	1960–64	1965–69	1970–74	1975–80	1981–84	1985–90	1991–94	1995–99	2000–04	2005–09
Arab	−7	−7	−8.35	−8.4	−8.2	−8	−7.4	−7	−6.7	−4
Sub–Saharan Africa	−6	−6.6	−7	−7	−7	−7	−5.4	−1.5	0	2.5
Latin America	−1.7	−2.6	−6	−6	−4	3	6	7	8	8
Southern & Central Asia	−9.4	−8	−8	−7.4	−6	−5.7	−3	−3.8	−5.2	−2.25
East Asia	−6	−6.4	−4.8	−7	−7	−2	2.5	1.4	4.125	2.25

Source: Polity IV Data Set

half of the decade. The worldwide democracy trend was further consolidated following the collapse of the former Soviet Union, and when Sub-Saharan Africa (SSA) also joined the democratisation club in the second half of the 1990s. The average Polity score in this region achieved a significant jump in this period, from less than −5 to −1.5, then reaching 2.5 in the second half of 2000. However, in addition to the Arab region, Southern and Central Asia (SCA) also constitutes an exception.

Samuel Huntington (1991) suggests that global patterns of democratisation and 'reverse' democratisation come in waves. He notes that following the first pro (1810–1920) and reverse waves (1920–40) of democratisation, the 'second wave' of democratisation began in 1943 and ended in 1962. He argues that this led to a second reverse wave that started in 1958 and ended in 1975, followed by a third wave of democratisation beginning in 1974. While the debate continues on the validity of these claims, the evidence cited earlier suggests that these waves do exist, albeit only weakly synchronised across regions. In addition to the pro-democracy waves discussed previously, there was evidence of reverse waves in LAC and EA during 1970–80 and 1975–84, respectively. Moreover, though SSA and the Arab world were already autocratic in the 1960s, both regions experienced what amounts to an even deeper autocratic wave in the following two decades during 1970–90. However, as discussed earlier, SSA managed to achieve a major transition thereafter. Should, as expected, the current popular uprisings in the Arab world usher in a wide-scale democratic transformation in the region, it would certainly qualify as a new democratic wave.[15]

The evidence on the frequency of 'sustainable' democratic transitions strongly coheres with this story (Figure 1.1). As expected, such frequency is the lowest in the Arab region, where only seven such transitions have happened in half a century. Prior to 2011, most Arab countries had not experienced positive jumps in the Polity scale, and in those that had done so as a result of popular uprisings that ended long-reigning military rule, such as Sudan and Mauritania, the nascent democratic regimes soon fell victim to another military coup.[16] This record pales when compared to the seventy-nine transitions for Latin America, fifty-two for Sub-Saharan Africa and forty-one for East Asia. Again, in tandem with the level

[15] For example, Haseeb (2013), p. 15, argues that the emergence of the Arab democracy wave hinges on a set of four factors that 'when co-incident are *decisive*, and these are: breaking the "barrier of fear"; non-violent resistance; sufficient national cohesion and popular sentiment; and the stance of the armed forces vis-à-vis uprisings'.

[16] For example, since its independence Sudan has been ruled by three short-lived democratic regimes (1956–58; 1965–69; 1986–89), with a total duration of ten years. On the other hand, the three military regimes that toppled them (1958–64; 1969–85; 1989–present) have so far ruled the country for more than forty-five years.

democracy data, the other exception outside the Arab world was Southern and Central Asia, which recorded an equally disappointing record of only thirteen transitions.

For the remainder of this section and before we formally estimate the process of democratic transition, we take a preliminary look at the core correlates of democratic transitions and highlight the key contrasts between the Arab world and other developing regions.

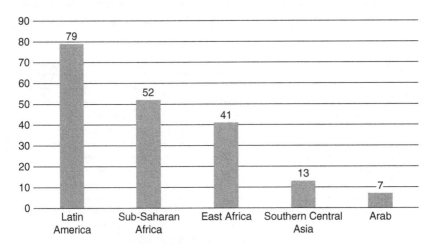

Figure 1.1: Frequency of 'Sustainable' Democratic Transition in Developing Regions (1960–2009)
Source: Authors' calculation based on Polity IV Index

1.2.1   The Core Correlates

The resource rents per capita. Mostly due to data availability, the received literature has commonly measured natural resource rents using the share of oil and mineral exports in GDP. However, as Ross argued, this measure is flawed because it does not account for the share of resource rents spent in the domestic economy. Moreover, GDP is not the appropriate scale variable because the democracy impact of rents/ GDP is subject to multiple sources of biases, since third factors (such as civil wars, corruption, etc.) are likely at work, affecting both democracy and growth, and hence the rents/GDP ratio. Instead, Ross proxies oil rent by the total value of the resource income divided by population. He contends that his oil income per capita valuation can be used to 'test the starkest version of the "oil hinders democracy" claim, i.e. that the value of a country's geological endowment – regardless of how well it is managed, and how it influences the rest of the economy – affects the accountability of government' (2008, pp. 3–4).

However, the gross natural resource income measure tends to overstate the influence of resource rents because they do not account for the production cost. Fortunately, we can avoid this problem thanks to new global data on natural resource rents.[17] This new resource rents variable, based on the World Bank's 'genuine' saving database, adjusts income from oil and other minerals to the cost of production and transfers to non-government investors, such as the oil and mining companies.

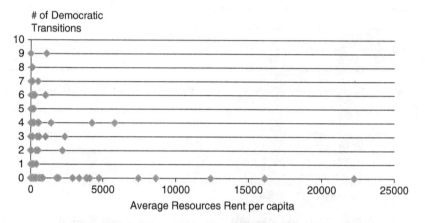

Figure 1.2: Resource Rents and Democratic Transitions (1960–2009)
The x-axis: country's average resource rent per capita during
1960–2009
The y-axis: number of democratic transitions in 1960–2009 per country

As expected, a strong negative association occurs between resource rents and the frequency of democratic transition (Figure 1.2). The figure depicts a country's total number of democratic transitions in the period 1960–2009 (y-axis) against a country's average resource rents per capita during 1960–2009 (x-axis). The figure also suggests that the potential corrosive effect on democracy of resource rents is likely particularly strong in the case of the Arab world, given that oil looms so large in this region. For example, out of the top ten countries that collected the highest resource rents per capita during 2005–09, seven were Arab oil and gas exporters – all from the oil-rich, population-scarce GCC plus Libya; and the following

[17] The resource rents data series we have used is obtained from the World Bank database (WDI), and the methodology used for computing the rents is based on Hamilton and Ruta (2008).

fifteen countries include six Arab oil and mineral exporters, including oil-rich but populous Algeria and Iraq (Figure 1.3).

Evidence from the received literature suggests that the observed robust negative association between resource rents and democracy is in fact causative (e.g. Ali and Elbadawi 2012; Elbadawi, Makdisi and Milante 2011; Ross 2008; 2009). Therefore, it has been argued that the immense oil resources controlled by several Arab countries have facilitated the emergence of repressive militaristic regimes or protected un-democratic, traditionally authoritarian regimes. The theoretical literature proposes several channels through which resource rents might complicate the transition to democratic rule. Furthermore, the concentration of the largest share of global oil reserves in the Arab region, in a handful of small countries, has led to the presence of a tremendous amount of foreign influence, as well as occasional direct intervention, all of which by and large has not favoured democratisation.[18]

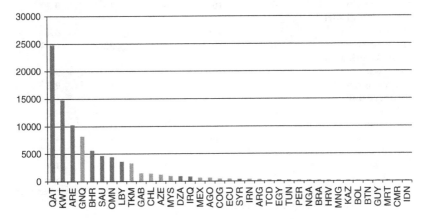

Figure 1.3: Average Resource Rent per Capita (2005–2009)

Home wars. A further examination of Figure 1.1 reveals that the Arab countries as a whole have by far the smallest number of democratic transitions, including those with limited or no oil and mineral resources. This suggests that other factors may be at work in shaping the democratic outcome in this region. As argued earlier, the proclivity of the region to conflict strongly suggests this is likely to be an additional explanatory factor. The Arab world is second only to SSA in terms of incidence of 'home

---

[18] For example, the three major Gulf wars (1980–88, 1991 and 2003), linked to the interests of global powers in this oil-rich region, not only have failed to stimulate a democratic process in the region at a time of positive changes in global democratisation, but in some ways have tended to promote sectarian and/or ethnic divisions.

wars', where a country-year is coded as 1 if the country was party to an external war or has experienced a civil war during the given year; a peaceful year is coded instead as 0 (Table 1.2). According to this index, any Arab country experienced an average of more than five incidences of home war per decade during the last forty years of the twentieth century (1960–99); and its immediate neighbourhood was affected by nine incidences of war per decade during the same period. The neighbourhood war index for a country is given by the average incidence of war experienced by its immediate neighbours.

Table 1.2: *Average Number of Wars (1960–1999)*

	1960–69	1970–79	1980–89	1990–99	Average
Arab					
Home war	4.5	5.5	5.5	5	**5.1**
Neighbour war	6.5	10	9	10.5	**9**
Sub-Saharan Africa					
Home war	2	6.5	8	9	**6.4**
Neighbour war	10.5	18	22.5	22	**18.3**
Latin America					
Home war	2.5	3	5.5	4	**3.8**
Neighbour war	5	7	14	12	**9.5**
Southern and Central Asia					
Home war	1.5	2	3	3	**2.4**
Neighbour war	2.5	2.5	3	4	**3**
East Asia					
Home war	2	3	5	3.5	**3.4**
Neighbour war	2	5.5	6.5	6.5	**5.1**

Source: Correlates of War (CoW) Data Sets

However, contrasting the Arab world with other regions in terms of the incidences of war, as we did, understates the arguably far more devastating impact of the lingering Arab–Israeli conflict and the perceived adversarial global power interventions in the region, which has provided potent arguments for an authoritarian brand of Arab nationalism for most of the past fifty years or so. Moreover, the large-scale regional Gulf wars that involved major external powers, as well as the surge of sectarian civil wars in a few Arab countries (e.g. Algeria and Sudan), are likely to have had much more dire consequences for democracy than the traditional ideological insurgencies that have occurred in other parts of the developing world, most notably Latin America.

Modernisation controls: income per capita and growth. The Arab world experienced high growth for some twenty-four years during 1960–84, with per capita GDP increasing at an annual average rate of 2.5 per cent in the median Arab country, including spectacular growth in some oil-producing economies. However, following the collapse of oil prices in the early 1980s, per capita growth in the Arab world declined to about 1 per cent. Nonetheless, income per capita remains relatively high in most Arab countries. The median income per capita in 2000–09 for the high-income GCC group (at almost $32,000) was second only to the OECD countries, and some (e.g. Qatar, Kuwait and the UAE) have recently surpassed many others in the latter group; while the income per capita for the Arab countries that comprise the other oil and diversified non-oil economies was only slightly below $4,000, which was more than twice the median income for the developing world. Even the primary-producing poor Arab countries of Mauritania, Sudan and Yemen had an average per capita income of about $1,450, which was higher than the median income level for SSA.[19]

However, despite its sustained economic and social development lasting almost two and a half decades since 1960, the region failed to join the 1980s democratic waves that transformed Latin America and East Asia (Table 1.1). The divergence between Arab and East Asian countries over the period 1960–2010 is perhaps most revealing, because East Asia in the 1960s seemed to be a reasonable comparator group. Despite the initial similarities in their level of development, the average polity score of East Asian countries in 2003 was −0.25, whereas the Arab countries had a mean of −3.7; and for 2010 the gap between the two regions remained almost the same at more than three points in the Polity scale.

Therefore, while the modernisation variables are likely to be relevant controls for the analysis of democratic transitions generally, the Arab world presents a notable example where they may be necessary but not sufficient to explain the phenomenon.

Past political instability: STRA. In addition to initial income per capita and economic growth, this is the third control variable analysed in Przeworski's (2004) benchmark model. It is given by the number of times a country experienced a transition from democracy to autocracy and goes with the mnemonic STRA (the sum of transitions to authoritarianism). STRA is motivated by pure empiricism, in that the transition probability

---

[19] Moreover, most Arab countries were able to effectively exploit their initial extended economic success to achieve considerable gains in the area of human development. The increased wealth was distributed throughout society, leading to an increase in average schooling years by 100 per cent between 1960–84 and 1985–98. Similarly, life expectancy increased by an impressive ten years. Average income per capita in 1985 ($5,300 in purchasing power parity) was almost five times the income level of 1960 (Shafik 1995).

from autocracy to democracy (P_{AD}) or vice versa (P_{DA}) tends to exhibit a strong degree of path dependence. This phenomenon, however, turns out to have important policy implications for the role of initial income in the probability of democratic transition. Using a global sample of types of regime in a conditional Markovian transition probability model, Przeworski finds that in a country which has never experienced the death of a democratic regime in the past (i.e. STRA = 0), a current dictatorship has an expected future life span of eighty-three years. In contrast, a history of only one transition from democracy to autocracy would shorten the expected life of the present authoritarian regime to only fourteen years.

Controlling for STRA in a democratic transition probability (P_{AD}) probit model along with initial income and growth, Przeworski finds that initial income is no longer significant. The same variable is both positive and highly significant in the pure modernisation model that excludes STRA. He interprets this important finding to mean that a dictatorship that assumes power in a high-income society is also likely to have inherently high political instability, which, in turn, tends to increase levels of instability for the incumbent regime. This finding has important implications for the Arab world as it provides a plausible explanation for the fact that the region's relatively high income has not been a factor in promoting democratic transitions in the past.[20] The average STRA per an Arab country was a minuscule 0.09, compared to 0.15 for SSA; 0.21 for SCA; 0.35 for EA; and 1.09 for LAC (Figure 1.4).

To the extent that higher initial income affects current regime instability by having bred political instability in the past, the apparently weak association between the two variables in the case of the Arab world should be an interesting issue for future research, in particular, when assessing whether resource-based income has had different implications for political instability in the past from those of non-resource income.

1.3   Modelling Democratic Transitions

The empirical model of Przeworski (2009) suggests that the transition probability from authoritarian (A) to democratic (D) regimes is characterised by four empirical regularities that survive extensive empirical testing:
- First, authoritarian regimes that assume power in relatively rich societies are likely to experience a greater frequency of mortality (i.e. higher probability of transition to democracy: P_{AD}).

---

[20] The Arab region has experienced a very low level of STRA, being ruled by long-reigning autocracies for most of its post-independence history. The sole exception was Sudan, which has experienced the death of three democracies since 1956; however, it has so far also experienced two popular uprisings that toppled two dictatorships.

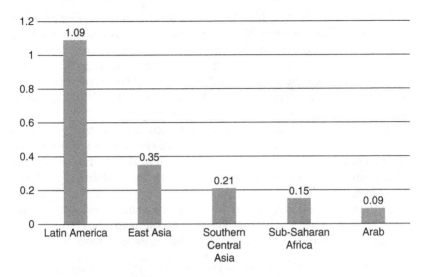

Figure 1.4: The Sum of Transitions to Authoritarianism (STRA) (1960–2009)

- Second, autocracies in countries with a history of political instability in terms of frequent transitions from democracy to autocracy are likely to experience a high frequency of democratic transition in the future: that is, past political instability (STRA) matters.
- Third, autocracies in historically high-income societies tend to experience a greater frequency of mortality because high income also breeds high levels of instability, hence controlling for STRA renders the income effect insignificant as a determinant of (P_{AD}).
- Fourth, however, even after controlling for STRA, given initial income, authoritarian regimes that achieve higher growth are less, not more, likely to die (i.e. lower P_{AD}).

In view of our interest to explain the 'halting' democratisation process in the Arab world, we use an extended version of this benchmark model to sequentially test for the two pivotal factors of resource rents, most notably oil rents, and then wars. As discussed earlier, both are strongly emphasised by recent econometric and case study literature on the Arab democracy deficit.[21]

---

[21] Ross (2008: 2009) and Ulfelder and Lustik (2005) analyse the role of oil as a hindrance to democratic transitions in general; Elbadawi and Makdisi (2011) and Makdisi (2011) contain global and country-specific research on the role of oil and conflicts as two overarching factors that affect the entire Arab world and possibly provide an explanation for the region's democracy deficit.

We should like to note here that while there is ample evidence on the association of oil rents with the prevalence and persistence of autocratic rule, relatively little systematic empirical analysis has been conducted of the causal link between the two. A few exceptions include Ross (2008; 2009), who tested the impact of oil income on democratic transition in a Przeworski 'benchmark' model. Ulfelder and Lustik (2005) tested the impact of resource rents in a variant of a similar model, though more focused on political and human development controls than on overall income per capita and growth as in the Przeworski model. Both studies find that natural resource rents (specifically oil wealth for the case of Ross) were robustly and negatively associated with the probability of democratic transition.

To formalise the exposition and systematically develop our main hypothesis, we posit a rentier model that accounts for the resource rents per capita in addition to the controls of the Przeworski model:

$$P_{AD}(i, T + S) = F_{AD}(1 = yes, 0 = no) = f(\beta, \delta_{Re\ nt}, \delta_{Dum},$$
$$\times u_i | x_{i,T}, Re\ ntpc_{i,T}, Re\ gDum) \qquad (1.1)$$

Where for country i, time T is an initial year at the start of the democratic transition, S is the time the process takes before the democratic transition is complete at time T+S. However, to avoid reverse endogeneity, we only include the explanatory variables at the beginning of the period. P_{AD} (T+S) is the transition probability from A to D in time T+S; $x_{i,T}$ is a vector containing Przeworski's three control variables: $logGDPpc_{i,T}$, the log of per capita income in time T; $Growth_T$, average per capita growth at the beginning of the transition period; and STRA (i, t < T), the measure of past political instability, given by the sum of transitions to authoritarianism prior to time T. The resource rents per capita ($Rentpc_{i,T}$), the central focus of this analysis, is the ratio of the resource rents per population at the beginning of period. Finally, RegDum stands for regional dummies covering Sub-Saharan Africa (SSA); Latin America and the Caribbean (LAC); Southern and Central Asia (SCA); East Asia (EA); and the Arab world (Arab).

The parameters β, $\delta_{Re\ nt}$ and δ_{Dum} are the corresponding coefficients, and u_i refers to a country-specific random effect. Empirical analysis in the received literature has mostly relied on pooled or fixed-effects regressions. The problems with the former are well known; however, applying the fixed-effects estimator to models with qualitative dependent variables based on panel data is also problematic. Though the conditional fixed-effects logit model seems to be the preferred choice, it requires very strong assumptions, including strict exogeneity of the regressors and stationarity over time. Because these conditions are frequently violated in economic data, the random-effects estimator is an attractive alternative. In the panel data context, the probit model is computationally tractable while the logit model is not. The only limitation of probit models is that they require normal distributions for all unobserved components, a feature that may characterise most unobserved, random components, but which is notoriously absent in cases where variables are truncated (e.g. prices must be positive).[22] Therefore, on balance we follow Elbadawi, Schmidt-Hebbel and Soto (2011) and choose the discrete choice random-effects probit for estimating the probability of democratic transition (P_{AD}).

Next we consider adding 'home wars' to account for the combined effects of civil and external wars, hence we have:

$$P_{AD}(i, T + S) = f(\beta, \delta_{\text{Rent}}, \delta_{\text{wars}}, \delta_{\text{Dum}}, u_i | x_{i,T}, \text{Re } ntpc_{i,T},$$

$$\times \, HomeWars_{i,T}, \text{Re } gDum) \qquad (1.2)$$

Where δ_{wars} is the coefficient of home wars (HomeWars), and as for the other explanatory variables, to avoid reverse causation, the war dummy was coded at the beginning of the period.[23]

These two models allow for testing several interesting hypotheses regarding the potential roles of these two factors in halting democratic transitions, some of which have not been considered before in the literature. In particular, we test for whether oil and conflicts combined account for the two negative sub-Arab dummies for oil and non-oil countries.

Finally, the third core model is a further extension of Equation 1.2:

$$P_{AD}(i, T + S) = f(\beta, \delta_{\text{Rent}}, \delta_{wars}, \delta_{Pdem}, \delta_{\text{Dum}}, u_i | x_{i,T}, \text{Re } ntpc_{i,T},$$

$$\times \, HomeWars_{i,T}, PartialDemoc_{i,T}, \text{Re } gDum) \qquad (1.3)$$

where δ_{Pdem} is the coefficient of the partial democracy variable (PartialDemoc).

This model is designed to test the hypothesis that partial democracies[24] are more susceptible to democratic transition, as some scholars claim in the recent literature. For example, Epstein and colleagues (2006) argue

---

[22] See Elbadawi, Schmidt-Hebbel and Soto (2011) for a more detailed discussion of the econometric properties of logit and probit estimators in panel data estimation in respect of qualitative dependent variables.

[23] Collier and Rohner (2008), for example, argue that democracy reduces the incentive for armed rebellion because it promotes accountability. On the other hand, by restraining government repression, it might also make rebellion less costly for rebels. In this context they developed a theoretical model to guide an empirical assessment of the two channels and find that nascent democracies will likely face more conflicts and wars because the second channel tends to dominate.

[24] To be more precisely defined in Section 1.4.

that partial democracies should be the point of focus of transition analysis, as these counties are more volatile than either democracies or autocracies and their transitions are largely unpredictable. Moreover, to the extent that regions outside the Arab world appear to be dominated by partial democratic regimes, we also test for whether this effect might also explain non-Arab regional dummies.

Next we estimate these three core models and discuss the results in the context of explicit hypotheses on the role of resource rents, wars and partial democracy.

1.4   The Core Econometric Results

We estimate the probability model using a panel data set of 449 half-decadal country periods between 1960 and 2009 and covering 118 countries, including 55 that generated annual average per capita (net) revenues of at least $50 (real PPP) from oil and other point-source minerals during 2005–09, of which 14 are from the Arab world. Appendix Table A.1 presents the overall summary statistics for all regression variables.

1.4.1   *The Resource Rents Effect*

We consider three hypotheses on the role of resource rents as a hindrance to democratic transition:

H1: Controlling for initial income, growth and the legacy of past political instability, natural resource rents *hinder* democratic transition.

H2: However, the impact of resource rents on democratic transition is subject to *threshold* effects (i.e. below a certain threshold, resource rents have no impact).

H3: Moreover, resource rents are an impediment to democratic transition only in societies governed by *autocracies or partial democracies*.

Table 1.3.A includes the results of random probit regressions, based on the model of Equation 1.1. To begin with, the results of regression 1 suggest that economic growth is negatively and highly significantly associated with the probability of democratic transition, while past political instability (STRA) is positively and robustly associated with democratic transition. On the other hand, initial income is not found to have any statistically or quantitatively significant impact. These results hold not only in a model that controls for the level of resource rents, but also when we extend the analysis to account for the threshold effects of the resource rents (regression 2), and the interaction between resource rents and initial autocracy or partial democracy (regression 3).

Table 1.3.A: *Probability of Democratic Transition – An Extended Rentier Model*

Explanatory Variables	Random Effect Probit [1]	Random Effect Probit [2]	Random Effect Probit [3]	Random Effect Probit [4]
Log REAL GDP per capita_Initial	−0.35(0.4)	−0.35(0.4)	−0.33(0.5)	−0.30(0.3)
REAL GDP_pc Growth	−9.73***(3.0)	−9.73***(3.0)	−9.81***(3.1)	−6.91**(2.9)
Top_Log Rentpc			−0.37***(0.1)	
Med_Log Rentpc			−0.41***(0.1)	
Low_Log Rentpc			−0.25(0.2)	
STRA	1.65***(0.4)	1.65***(0.4)	1.77***(0.4)	0.79***(0.3)
Arab	−7.38***(1.8)	−7.38***(1.8)	−7.94***(2.1)	−5.12***(1.4)
SSA	−5.03***(1.5)	−5.03***(1.5)	−5.48***(1.7)	−3.78***(1.1)
LAC	−3.70***(1.2)	−3.70***(1.2)	−4.02***(1.3)	−2.74***(0.9)
SCA	−5.26***(1.5)	−5.26***(1.5)	−5.67***(1.6)	−3.96***(1.2)
EA	−3.60***(1.3)	−3.60***(1.3)	−4.01**(1.5)	−2.41**(1.0)
Log Rentpc	−0.41***(0.1)	−0.41***(0.1)		0.01(0.1)
Log Rentpc* Dum_Polity<6				−0.43***(0.1)
Constant	7.04*(3.9)	7.04*(3.9)	6.88(4.2)	5.66**(2.8)
Observations	441	441	441	441

Table 1.3.A: *(cont.)*

Explanatory Variables	Random Effect Probit [1]	Random Effect Probit [2]	Random Effect Probit [3]	Random Effect Probit [4]
Number of id	93	93	93	93
LR statistic	36.58	36.58	38.61	8.116
Log likelihood	−140.8	−140.8	−139.4	−118.6

Notes:

1. *: for 0.05 < p-value ≤ 0.10;

   **: for 0.01 < p-value ≤ 0.05;

   ***: for p-value ≤ 0.01

2. Definition of Regressors:

   - Log Real GDP pc: natural logarithm of initial GDP per capita in each period
   - Real GDP_pc Growth Rate: Real GDP pc growth rate in each period
   - Ln Rentpc: Natural logarithm of resource rents per capita
   - Ln Rentpc* Dum_Polity < 6: interaction between Rent pc and the dummy for countries with initial polity below 6
   - Top_Log Rentpc: interaction between Log Rent pc and Dum$_{Top}$, where Dum$_{Top}$ equals 1 if the Rentpc is equal to or larger than $1400 (in 2005 fixed dollars) and zero elsewhere
   - Med_Log Rentpc: interaction between Log Rent pc and Dum$_{Med}$, where Dum$_{Med}$ equals 1 if the Rentpc is equal to or larger than $100 but less than $1400
   - Low_Log Rentpc: interaction between Log Rent pc and Dum$_{Low}$, where Dum$_{Low}$ equals 1 if the Rentpc is less than $100 and zero elsewhere
   - Arab: Dummy variable = 1 if country is in the Arab region, 0 otherwise
   - SSA: Dummy variable = 1 if country is in Sub-Saharan Africa, 0 otherwise
   - LAC: Dummy variable = 1 if country is in Latin America and the Caribbean, 0 otherwise
   - SCA: Dummy variable = 1 if country is in Southern Central Asia, 0 otherwise
   - EA: Dummy variable = 1 if country is in East Asia, 0 otherwise

Therefore, in this baseline model, we corroborate Przeworski's two fundamental findings: first, authoritarian states witnessing lower growth in the previous period and having a history of political instability are more likely to become democratic; second, initial wealth has no impact when past political instability is accounted for. Przeworski's model argues that autocratic regimes in initially relatively wealthy societies are likely to lose power to new democracies not because of the modernisation effect of wealth but rather because the latter has bred political instability in the past. On the other hand, other researchers (e.g. Ross 2008) find that the income effect is positively and strongly associated with democratic transition once they control for oil, implying that modernisation has a positive impact on this transition. Since the relevance, or lack thereof, of modernisation to democratic transition has been a subject of a major recent debate in the received literature, and the evidence we have obtained so far pertains to a relatively basic baseline model leading only to a preliminary finding, we revisit this issue in a context of a more encompassing model to draw out more definitive implications.

For now, our main interest is focused on the resource rents effect, which we find to be negatively correlated to the probability of democratic transition and highly statistically significant at the 1 per cent confidence level. Therefore, we accept the central hypothesis H1, in that authoritarian regimes in resource-endowed societies are less likely to become democratic. This finding confirms earlier results in the literature, including those of Ulfelder (2007) and Ross (2008). Moreover, because we use a broader concept of rent, our finding extends their earlier results to all point-source natural resources, not just oil.[25]

Next, we test for the two more complementary hypotheses (H2 and H3). These two hypotheses are not adequately analysed in the literature, though they both have strong theoretical appeal. For example, in a theoretic game model Ali and Elbadawi (2012) argue that authoritarian regimes in oil-rich countries with small populations have an advantage that is not available to other oil-rich authoritarian or partially democratic regimes with relatively large populations. In contrast to both latter groups of countries, the small population oil-rich countries command sufficient resources (per capita), which they can redistribute to effectively remove the incentive to revolt. In addition, they argue that the public sector is the mechanism of choice for governments seeking to effect this redistribution. Therefore, public sector jobs essentially become funnels for channelling

---

[25] While the 'oil curse' effect, the trade-off between economic welfare and political rights associated with the relative abundance of oil resources, appears to be well established in the literature, it is not necessarily universally agreed upon (e.g. Haber and Menaldo 2011).

income to the citizens of the said countries. Hence at the theoretical level, the use of resource rents to effectively fend off regime change, democratic or otherwise, is premised on the country not having democratic elites (H3), and the fact that the rent-sharing strategy is not likely to be an optimum choice from the perspective of these elites, unless they have control over a sufficiently high amount of rent per citizen above a given threshold (H2).

Regression 2 of Table 1.3.A provides the test for H2, where we replace the resource rents variable of regression 1 by three threshold variables defined as interaction terms with the resource rents:

- Top_Resource Rents = Log Rentpc* Dum_{Top}
- Med_Resource Rents= Log Rentpc* Dum_{Med}
- Low_Resource Rents = Log Rentpc* Dum_{Low}

Where, Dum_{Top} is a dummy variable that equals 1 if the Rentpc is equal to or larger than \$1400 (in 2005 fixed dollars) and zero elsewhere; Dum_{Med} is a dummy variable that equals 1 if the Rentpc is equal to or larger than \$100 but less than \$1400 and zero elsewhere; and Dum_{Low} is a dummy variable that equals 1 if the Rentpc is less than \$100 and zero elsewhere. This typology is based on the profile of the average of non-overlapping half-decadal Log Rentpc during 1970–2009. The distribution of rents broadly approximates to a tri-modal pattern of average half-decadal values.

We find that the two top resource rents groups (Top_Resource Rents and Med_Resource Rents) are negatively and strongly significantly associated with transition probability, while the lowest group (Low_Resource Rents) has a negative but insignificant effect. Hence, we accept H2 in that, when resource rents are too low, they are not likely to have a negative influence on democratic transition.

Finally, we test for H3 in regression 3, which adds an interactive term: Log Rentpc*Dum_Polity below 6, where the dummy is set equal to 1, if initial Polity is less than 6; and zero elsewhere. We find that the level effect (Log Rentpc) is no longer significant, while the interaction term was negative and highly statistically significant. It is interesting to see that the interaction effect (at −0.43) is essentially equal to that of the level effect in regression 1 (at −0.41). This suggests that the estimated corrosive effect of resource rents on democratic transition is fully accounted for by the strategic choices of the ruling elites in autocracies and partial democracies. This is consistent with the experiences of most countries. Indeed, it is fairly safe to reckon that incumbent elites in Norway or Chile will not, in fact in all likelihood cannot, use oil or copper rents to remain in power. Therefore, we accept H3.

1.4.2 Explaining the Regional Dummies: 'Home Wars'

However, although resource rents enter highly significantly and our evidence strongly supports all three hypotheses associated with the resource role as a hindrance to democracy, the resource-augmented model could not explain the regional dummies, most notably the 'aggregate' Arab dummy. Very important, it should be noted that all regional dummies enter with negative and highly significant signs. This suggests that, controlling for resource rents and other systematic determinants in the model, the developing world is likely to be less open to democratic transition relative to the excluded group of developed countries (regressions of Table 1.3.A). Hence, we conclude that other factors appear to be at play in explaining the lacklustre democratic transition experiences of developing countries. Based on the propensity of many developing countries, most notably resource-dependent ones, to experience conflicts, we conjecture that, among other plausible factors, war could be a major explanatory one.

Therefore, we pursue the quest to explain these regional effects – especially the so-called Arab dummy, which could be interpreted as an epitome of the so-called Arab World exceptionalism – by estimating a set of two more encompassing models that account for the home wars effect (Table 1.4.A). In this context we analyse the possible impact of wars by testing for the two following hypotheses:

H4: *Wars* <u>impede</u> democratic transitions, after controlling for resource rents and other traditional controls.

H5: The extended model that includes *resource rents and the incidence of wars* <u>explains</u> *the Arab dummy and other regional effects* in an extended rentier model.

The first two columns of Table 1.4.A (regressions 7 and 8) report the estimation results of the war-augmented model (the two regressions are, respectively, extensions of regressions 2 and 3 of Table 1.3.A). The home war effect is negative and significant at a 5 per cent level for the threshold-based model (regression 7), and has a much greater negative and statistically stronger impact (at a 1 per cent significance level) for the initial polity-based model (regression 8). The estimated war coefficients of the two regressions suggest that the probability of successful democratic transition in a war-affected country accounts for 34 {= exp (-1.07)*100%} to 27 {= exp (-1.30)*100%} per cent of the transition probability for a war-free country with identical characteristics. Wars, therefore, are strong hindrance to democratic transitions, as H4 predicted. Moreover, now having controlled for the war effect, the developing countries dummies, including the infamous Arab dummy, are all no longer statistically significant. Therefore, we accept H5 as well.

Having established that wars do hinder democratic transitions and also that an extended war and rents model fully explains the Arab and other regional dummies, it is pertinent to assess the robustness of the earlier results of regressions 2 and 3 (of Table 1.3.A) under the war-augmented model of Table 1.4.A. It is rather remarkable that almost all the results continue to hold. However, though both the top and medium rents per capita variables remain significant, the latter is now only weakly significant at 10 per cent. This is a more realistic finding, and is more consistent with countries' experiences.[26]

1.4.3   *Assessing the Partial Democracy Thesis*

As discussed earlier in this chapter, Epstein and colleagues (2006) show that, relative to full democracies and autocracies, partial democracies tend to be volatile and characterised by unpredictable polity; hence they are likely more susceptible to democratic transition than autocracies. Based on their finding, they argue that partial democracies should be the point of focus of transition analysis. Save for the two regions of the Arab world and Southern and Central Asia, countries in the developing regions have made major strides in terms of democratic transition from hitherto autocratic regimes, though most have not as yet consolidated such transitions sufficiently to be able to join the club of mature democracies (Table 1.1). Therefore, though the regional effects are no longer significant in the home war-augmented model, the status of being a partial democracy should be considered as a further possible instrument for explaining the regional effects specifically associated with developing regions.

We define partial democracy (PartialDemoc) as follows:
- PartialDemoc = Polity*Dum(PartialDemoc),
  where,
- Dum (PartialDemoc) = 1 for 0 < Polity < 6; 0 elsewhere

Adding this variable to account for the marginal impact of the partial democracy effect, we generate perhaps the most encompassing core democratic transitions model in the literature. This model allows testing for the following hypothesis:

---

[26] For example, Ali and Elbadawi (2012) present evidence suggesting that the resource rents in the highly resource-endowed and sparsely populated GCC appear to be an effective tool for the authoritarian bargain, while ruling elites in other populous Arab oil countries, with much lower resources per capita, have not been as successful.

H6:   Compared to autocracies and full democracies,[27] *Partial democracies (0 < Polity < 6)* are *more susceptible* to democratic transition.

The results of the estimation of the two versions of the model are reported in regressions 9 and 10 of Table 1.4.A. We find partial democracy to be positively and significantly (at a 5 per cent significance level) associated with democratic transitions, as H6 predicted. Therefore, we corroborate Epstein and colleagues' thesis regarding the higher propensity of a partial democracy to experience further democratic transition, compared to mature democracies as well as to autocracies. Moreover, all regional effects continue to be insignificant. Again, all the results regarding the marginal impact of resource rents and home wars remain valid under the more encompassing model of regressions 9 and 10.

1.4.4   Revisiting the Modernisation Hypothesis

Though Przeworski's claim that it is past political instability rather than wealth that is likely to be the cause of the death of autocracies seems to be corroborated by our evidence so far, we pursue this matter further by investigating the extent to which the lack of significance of lagged income might in fact be a statistical artefact of the limited within-country variation of income per capita. In this case, the income effect is likely to be confounded with those of the regional dummies. This argument is different but is not unrelated to the Acemoglu and colleagues–Barro debate referred to in Section 1.1 regarding the robustness of modernisation as a viable theory for explaining democratic transition. For example, Acemoglu and colleagues (2005; 2008) argue that modernisation is not empirically supported once country fixed effects are accounted for in democratic transition models. However, Barro (2015) shows that the fixed-effects procedure in a relatively short time period tends to inflate the standard errors of the time-varying explanatory variables, the so-called Hurwicz bias (Hurwicz 1950). Barro shows that, instead, estimating fixed-effects regressions for a smaller number of countries for which data is available over a century lends strong support to the modernisation hypothesis. This is because this particular fixed-effects bias becomes less severe for very large T and disappears when T approaches infinity (Nickell 1981).

Other contributors to this debate include Faria and colleagues (2014), who suggest that the modernisation hypothesis should 'survive' Acemoglu and colleagues' critique; and Idzalika and colleagues (2015), who re-estimated the data of Acemoglu and colleagues using a flexible distributional approach to explaining democracy as a response variable

---

[27] Since we eliminate from the sample all country years with Polity scores of more than 8, the 'full' democracy group will be those countries with Polity scores equalling 6, 7 or 8.

and, contrary to the latter's evidence, found support for modernisation. However, Paleologou (2015) assesses the relationship between democracy and income by employing panel count data models and finds that, though positive association exists between the two variables, the estimated coefficients are so small as to suggest no causal effects; and that, once income endogeneity is controlled for, the estimated effect becomes insignificant.

In the absence of extended time series as is the case in most panels in this literature, Barro recommends estimating linear regression models without fixed effects in order to avoid the Hurwicz bias. Furthermore, he argues that, insofar as a model is sufficiently encompassing, such as the ones estimated in Table 1.4.A, it is likely that the misspecification bias that might happen due to the removal of the country effects will be negligible.[28] Subscribing to Barro, especially since the regional dummies are no longer significant in the extended model that includes home war and partial democracy, we re-estimate the regressions of Tables 1.3.A and 1.4.A without the regional dummies. The results are reported in regressions 4–6 of Table 1.3.B and regressions 11–16 of Table 1.4.B.

The estimated income effect is found to be positive and significant in all the regressions of the two tables. It is remarkable that, despite the differences in the measure of democratic transition and the empirical model, our results mirror those of Barro. Therefore, we would argue, our findings lend strong support to the modernisation hypothesis. This evidence is important for understanding democratic transitions in the Arab world analysed in this book. It suggests that modernisation is a key factor in explaining why Tunisia's popular uprising, whatever its underlying factors, appears on course to a stable democratic transition, in contrast to other Arab countries where uprisings have taken place (see Boughzala and Ben Romdhane, Chapter 3, this volume).

Save for some variations, such as the relative lack of robustness of growth,[29] home war and partial democracy effects, the other main findings stay largely intact. If anything, the rents effect in societies under autocracies and partial democracies, or in those endowed with very high resource rents (top rents pc), have become even more appreciable and more significant. Moreover, in the model that controls for the rents and

[28] Notwithstanding the Hurwicz bias, to the extent that there are unobserved or missing country-specific factors that are important for democracy, it might be useful to include country fixed effects in the regression to account for these effects.

[29] The lack of robustness of the growth effect as a hindrance to democratic transition coheres with the evidence that, compared to democracies, autocracies are less capable in sustaining long-term economic growth (e.g. Rodrik and Wacziarg 2005). In a similar vein pointing out the important positive link between good economic governance and growth, certain researchers have argued that democracy can lead to better governance, and therefore, better economic policies and credible reforms (e.g. Nabli 2007).

Table 1.3.B: *Probability of Democratic Transition – An Extended Rentier Model*

Explanatory Variables	Random Effect Probit [4]	Random Effect Probit [5]	Random Effect Probit [6]
Log REAL GDP per capita_Initial	0.54*	0.65**	0.40*
	(0.288)	(0.31)	(0.21)
REAL GDP_pc Growth	−7.8**	−7.7**	−4.44
	(3.05)	(3.11)	(2.97)
Top_Log Rentpc		−0.34***	
		(0.10)	
Med_Log Rentpc		−0.31***	
		(0.11)	
STRA	2.30***	2.41***	1.18***
	(0.36)	(0.39)	(0.30)
Log Rentpc	−0.37***		0.41
	(0.09)		(0.10)
Log Rentpc*Dum_Polity<6			−0.44***
			(0.06)
Constant	−4.26**	−5.68**	−2.83**
	(1.99)	(2.26)	(1.44)
Observations	441	441	441
Number of id	93	93	93
LR statistic	92.39	85.59	23.99
Log likelihood	−158.11	−156.42	−135.19

polity interactions, the home war and partial democracy effects have become highly significant, although they lost their significance in the threshold model. In view of the high incidence of wars and the various types of wars the Arab region experiences, we further investigate the war effect in Section 1.6.

1.4.5   Robustness Checks

First, we test the robustness of our extended rentier model and the associated hypotheses using a ten-year sample, where democratic transition was coded over ten-year rather than five-year periods. Second, we assess the robustness of the rents effect before and after the demise of the Soviet Union in 1990 and the onset of the ensuing democratic wave that swept the developing world. We do this by re-estimating the basic rentier model using two five-year sub-samples: 1960–89 and 1990–2009. Third, we also test for the robustness of rents effects before and after 1980, when the oil-producing developing countries managed to expropriate the oil rents, by splitting the five-year data and estimating the model for two sub-samples of

Table 1.4.A: *Probability of Democratic Transition – Partial Democracy and Home War*

Variables	Random Effect Probit [7]	Random Effect Probit [8]	Random Effect Probit [9]	Random Effect Probit [10]
Log REAL GDP per capita_Initial	−0.14	−0.06	−0.23	−0.23
	(0.6)	(0.4)	(0.5)	(0.4)
REAL GDP_pc Growth	−14.39***	−12.43***	−14.38***	−12.90***
	(4.9)	(4.6)	(4.5)	(4.3)
Top_Log Rentpc	−0.30**		−0.24*	
	(0.1)		(0.1)	
Med_Log Rentpc	−0.34*		−0.28*	
	(0.2)		(0.2)	
Low_Log Rentpc	−0.21		−0.18	
	(0.2)		(0.2)	
STRA	1.38**	0.33	0.93*	0.09
	(0.6)	(0.3)	(0.5)	(0.2)
Arab	−24.74	−18.56	−20.69	−16.27
	(13,080.3)	(7,116.0)	(10,602.7)	(4,472.0)
SSA	−14.59	−11.48	−12.62	−10.45
	(10,310.6)	(6,072.3)	(7,494.8)	(3,729.5)
lta	−12.74	−9.61	−10.73	−8.45
	(10,310.6)	(6,072.3)	(7,494.8)	(3,729.5)
SCA	−13.18	−9.90	−11.32	−8.97
	(10,310.6)	(6,072.3)	(7,494.8)	(3,729.5)
EA	−12.50	−9.20	−10.83	−8.47
	(10,310.6)	(6,072.3)	(7,494.8)	(3,729.5)

	(1)	(2)	(3)	(4)
Homewar	-1.07**	-1.30***	-1.13**	-1.33***
	(0.5)	(0.5)	(0.5)	(0.4)
Log Rentpc		0.04		0.09
		(0.1)		(0.1)
Log Rentpc*Dum_Polity<6		-0.49***		-0.45***
		(0.1)		(0.1)
Partial Democ			0.94**	1.02**
			(0.5)	(0.4)
Constant	14.79	12.13	13.50	11.95
	(10,310.6)	(6,072.3)	(7,494.8)	(3,729.5)
Observations	324	324	324	324
Number of id	78	78	78	78
LR statistic	13.21	3.669	4.644	0.374
Log likelihood	-90.73	-69.39	-88.82	-66.68

Notes:

- Partial Democ: Polity multiplied by a dummy for Partial Democracy, where the latter = 1 if Polity falls in the open interval: 0<Polity< 6
- Homewar: dummy that equals 1 if a country experiences civil or external wars during the period; 0 elsewhere

Table 1.4.B: *Probability of Democratic Transition – Partial Democracy and Home War*

Explanatory Variables	Random Effect Probit [11]	Random Effect Probit [12]	Random Effect Probit [13]	Random Effect Probit [14]	Random Effect Probit [15]	Random Effect Probit [16]
Log REAL GDP per capita_Initial	0.80*	0.80*	0.71**	0.72*	0.72*	0.63**
	(0.42)	(0.42)	(0.30)	(0.40)	(0.40)	(0.29)
REAL GDP_pc Growth	−11.87**	−12.05**	−5.73	−12.31**	−12.41**	−6.22
	(5.29)	(5.20)	(4.69)	(5.21)	(5.11)	(4.59)
Top_Log Rentpc	−0.28*	−0.27***		−0.25*	−0.24**	
	(0.14)	(0.10)		(0.14)	(0.09)	
Med_Log Rentpc	−0.26	−0.24**		−0.23	−0.22**	
	(0.18)	(0.10)		(0.18)	(0.09)	
Low_Log Rentpc	−0.04			−0.02		
	(0.27)			(0.27)		
STRA	2.72***	2.75***	1.02***	2.49***	2.51***	0.86**
	(0.56)	(0.54)	(0.36)	(0.56)	(0.55)	(0.35)
Homewar	−0.80	−0.81	−1.12**	−0.82	−0.82	−1.16**
	(0.65)	(0.64)	(0.55)	(0.63)	(0.63)	(0.53)
Log Rentpc			0.01			0.05
			(0.12)			(0.12)
Log Rentpc*Dum_Polity<6			−0.52***			−0.51***
			(0.09)			(0.09)
Partial Democ				0.93	0.93	1.01**
				(0.59)	(0.59)	(0.51)
Constant	−7.09**	−7.23**	−4.25**	−6.58**	−6.66**	−3.90**
	(3.04)	(2.95)	(1.90)	(2.96)	(2.87)	(1.82)
Observations	324	324	324	324	324	324
Number of id	78	78	78	78	78	78
LR statistic	55.63	55.66	20.38	44.55	44.57	13.15
Log likelihood	−107.32	−107.33	−87.30	−106.03	−106.03	−85.23

1960–1979 and 1980–2009. In the two latter cases we focus on the basic rentier model because of the rather limited variations of the war and partial democracy variables in the shorter sub-periods.

The ten-year sample. The decadal and half-decadal frequencies have similar shapes, though, as expected, the number of countries achieving democratic transition during a ten-year period tends to be larger than during a half-decade period (see Appendix Figure A.1). The estimation results for the ten-year democratic transitions lend support to our extended rentier model, especially with regard to the core hypotheses on the corrosive effects of resource rents and wars on democratisation (regressions 17–22 of Table 1.5). We find that, overall, resource rents have had negative impact on democratic transition (H1) and that the impact of resource rents is, however, subject to a scale effect (H2). Moreover, we corroborate hypothesis H4, in that home wars hinder democratic transition. On the other hand, we cannot corroborate our earlier evidence on the susceptibility of partial democracies to democratic transitions (H6). And, surprising, we could not support the hitherto fairly robust findings for the argument that resource rents constitute a hindrance to democratic transition (or consolidation) only in autocracies or partial democracies (H3). Finally, the lagged income effect was found to be positively associated with democratic transition, albeit with relatively weak significance (at 10 per cent). Nonetheless, we cannot reject the modernisation hypothesis, which continues to attain a measure of significance despite the fact that we control for Przeworski's instability effect (STRA), which is associated with past income.

Before and after the collapse of the Soviet Union: 1960–89 and 1990–2009. Extensive documentation in the literature demonstrates the fact that major democratic waves have occurred in the aftermath of global systemic shocks, such as international wars. Furthermore, scholars have argued that these waves were associated with the creation of new states that usually followed the conclusion of major conflicts. For example, the breakup of the Austro-Hungarian and Ottoman Empires, the decolonisation following the end of World War Two, and the end of the Cold War and the breakup of the Soviet Union have all resulted in the creation of new states. To the extent that these new states were relatively democratic because they were likely to emulate the democracy of the victors or their former colonial masters, if clustered together in terms of time, their emergence should have given rise to democratic waves (Strand et al. 2012).

Subscribing to this view we estimate the model using the two subsamples (before and after 1990). The estimation results (regressions 23–26 of Table 1.6.A) suggest that resource rents hindered democratic transition after, but not before, 1990. However, in societies governed by autocracies or partial democracies, the resource rents effect remains

Table 1.5: *Probability of Democratic Transition: Robustness Checks – Ten-Year Periods/Democratic Transitions*

Explanatory Variables	Random Effect Probit [17]	Random Effect Probit [18]	Random Effect Probit [19]	Random Effect Probit [20]	Random Effect Probit [21]	Random Effect Probit [22]
Log REAL GDP per capita_Initial	0.46*	0.73*	0.73*	0.54*	0.70*	0.71*
	(0.25)	(0.43)	(0.44)	(0.34)	(0.43)	(0.44)
REAL GDP_pc Growth	-6.41	-13.92	-14.29*	-12.49*	-13.39	-13.99*
	(4.19)	(9.26)	(8.20)	(7.15)	(9.14)	(8.11)
Log Rentpc	-0.33***			-0.12		
	(0.07)			(0.14)		
Log Rentpc_po16				-0.08		
				(0.10)		
Top_Log Rentpc		-0.20	-0.19**		-0.20	-0.18**
		(0.13)	(0.08)		(0.13)	(0.08)
Med_Log Rentpc		-0.26	-0.25*		-0.26	-0.23
		(0.24)	(0.13)		(0.24)	(0.14)
Low_Log Rentpc		-0.2			-0.04	
		(0.36)			(0.35)	
STRA	2***	2.56***	2.57***	1.94***	2.44**	2.46**
	(0.41)	(0.87)	(0.86)	(0.62)	(0.94)	(0.98)
Partial Democ					0.18	0.16
					(0.76)	(0.75)
Homewar		-2.59**	-2.6**	-2.11**	-2.50*	-2.52**
		(1.23)	(1.23)	(0.97)	(1.23)	(1.25)
Constant	-3.53*	-6.49*	-6.59*	-4.40*	-6.17*	-6.34*
	(1.8)	(3.47)	(3.28)	(2.39)	(3.51)	(3.38)
Observations	321	210	210	210	210	210
Number of id	96	79	79	79	79	79
LR statistic	33.38	20.34	20.44	13.09	12.21	12.21
Log likelihood	-122.9	-69.62	-69.62	-70.45	-69.60	-69.61

Table 1.6.A: *Probability of Democratic Transitions – Robustness Checks for before and after the Demise of the Soviet Union (1990)*

EXPLANATORY VARIABLES	Random Effect Probit [23] 1960–89	Random Effect Probit [24] 1991–2009	Random Effect Probit [25] 1960–89	Random Effect Probit [26] 1991–2009
Log REAL GDP per capita_Initial	1.68*	0.30	3.93*	0.05
	(0.95)	(0.30)	(2.29)	(.0.15)
REAL GDP_pc Growth	−13.23	4.67	1.52	2.56
	(10.29)	(6.40)	(13.70)	(4.13)
STRA	3.17***	2.17***	2.20	0.72***
	(0.84)	(0.59)	(1.47)	(0.17)
Log Rentpc	−0.40	−0.29*	0.44	0.49***
	(0.32)	(0.15)	(0.50)	(0.13)
Log Rentpc*Dum_Polity<6			−1.66**	−0.67***
			(0.66)	(0.11)
Constant	−14.63**	−2.92	−29.59*	−1.10
	(6.05)	(2.09)	(15.95)	(1.06)
Observations	177	182	177	182
Number of id	68	93	68	93
LR statistic	42.82	17.34	20.25	8.1e–06
Log likelihood	−39.37	−79.45	−26.73	−56.98

negative and highly significant before and after the demise of the Soviet Union. Finally, there was another notable result concerning the income effect, which was found to be positive and significant before, but not after, 1990. This result seems to corroborate the literature (e.g. Strand et al. 2012), in that after the demise of the Soviet Union, democratisation took place regardless of the initial level of incomes due to the creation of the new states that were bent on breaking away from their authoritarian past.

Before and after the nationalisation of the oil industry: 1960–79 and 1980–2009. Andersen and Ross (2014) claim that oil wealth became a hindrance to democratic transition only after the expropriations of the 1970s, which enabled the governments in oil-producing developing countries to 'capture the oil rents that were previously siphoned off by foreign-owned firms'. Their evidence is further supported by Wright and colleagues (2014), who find that 'higher levels of oil wealth deterred democratic transitions between 1980 and 2007 but not between 1947 and 1979' (Ross 2015, p. 247). We lend partial support to these findings. We find the unconditional resource rents effect to have hindered democratic transition only in the post-1980s period. However, we also find the rents effect to be a deterrent to democratic transition before and after 1980 alike in resource-rich societies that happened to be governed by autocratic or partial democratic regimes (regressions 27–30 of Table 1.6.B).

To recapitulate, the robustness checks suggest that the core hypotheses regarding the role of resource rents and wars as hindrances to democratisation remain robust against the choice of the duration of the democratic transition (five versus ten years). Moreover, in societies ruled by autocratic or partially democratic governments, resource rents are likely to have corrosive effects on democratic transition in all sub-periods, including before and after the collapse of the Soviet Union and the unleashing of the 1990s democratic wave, or before and after the post-1980s nationalisation of the oil and mineral industries.

1.5   How Do Resource Rents Hinder Democratic Transitions?

Having corroborated and extended the evidence from the received literature on the central role of resource rents in hindering democratic transition, especially oil in the case of the Arab world, the next question is, naturally, how does this phenomenon manifest itself?

This would require identifying 'causal' links or intervening variables between resource rents and the 'halting' of democratic transitions. The received cross-country literature identifies several such variables reflecting authoritarian bargain effects (Ali and Elbadawi 2012; Desai et al. 2009; Ross 2009); political repression (Ross 2009); and corruption

Table 1.6.B: *Probability of Democratic Transitions – Robustness Checks for before and after the Expropriation of Oil Rents by Producing Countries (1980)*

EXPLANATORY VARIABLES	Random Effect Probit [27] 1960–79	Random Effect Probit [28] 1981–2009	Random Effect Probit [29] 1960–79	Random Effect Probit [30] 1981–2009
Log REAL GDP per capita_Initial	1.41	0.47*	1.72*	0.15
	(5161.47)	(0.27)	(0.96)	(0.15)
REAL GDP_pc Growth	9.34	-7.17**		-2.77
	(34103.99)	(3.42)		(2.78)
STRA	-0.48	1.96***	-0.60	0.72***
	(1785.65)	(0.37)	(1.02)	(0.20)
Log Rentpc	-0.42	-0.34***	0.50	0.27***
	(1545.37)	(0.10)	(0.40)	(0.10)
Log Rentpc*Dum_Polity<6			0.83*	-0.51***
			(0.45)	(0.07)
Constant	-9.68	-3.53*	-14.20**	-1.37
	(35362.96)	(1.86)	(6.09)	(1.01)
Observations	51	332	51	332
Number of id	51	93	51	93
LR statistic	1.4e-14	53	3.0e-14	4.41
Log likelihood	-12.81	-135.58	-7.93	-113.00

(Fish 2005). Other factors, widely discussed in the literature, are those associated with interventions by external powers in support of resource-rich authoritarian regimes (e.g. arms sales, foreign aid and outright military intervention, etc.). However, while shown to be highly relevant to the Arab world in the case-study literature,[30] these plausible causative channels are not found to be significant in the empirical cross-country literature, mainly due to the difficulty of constructing good global empirical proxies to account for them.[31] Moreover, external and domestic wars, including the long-standing Arab–Israeli conflict, might also be among the causative mechanisms, provided they can be linked to the presence of revenue from natural resources. Of course, as our results suggest, conflicts are impediments to democratisation in their own right regardless of whether natural resources exist.

The other set of potential causative factors associated with the corrosive impact of resource rents on democracy, especially with regard to the Arab world, has centred on the social aspects of modernisation, such as female labour force participation, fertility and so forth. However, the whole cultural-societal approach to explaining the lacklustre performance of democracy in the Arab world and other lagging regions has been widely critiqued in the vast polemical social science and historical literature as irrelevant (e.g. see El-Affendi 2011, for an extensive review). Moreover, perhaps due to poor data quality, Ross (2009), for example, could not find robust cross-country evidence linking social modernisation to the impact of oil rents on democratic transitions.

With this in mind, we reconsider this issue by examining two potential causative mechanisms: the effect of employment, as an instrument for the rentier-authoritarian bargain strategy, and the effect of political repression. These two, we would argue, are the most important mechanisms from the perspective of the Arab world.

The rentier-authoritarian bargain effect: the employment channel. Recent game theoretic literature links extensive public sector employment, financed by resource rents, to a bargain the ruling autocratic elites proffer in their attempt to evade a revolution mounted by the population they rule over (e.g. Ali and Elbadawi 2012). Similarly, other work in this literature models economic transfers and political influence as joint outcomes of non-democratic politics in resource-rich economies (e.g. Desai, Olofsgard and Yousef 2009). These authors use their

---

[30] See, for example, the Arab countries case studies included in Elbadawi and Makdisi (2011).

[31] For example, Ross (2009) fails to find a significant impact for most of the intervening instruments which he considers in the context of his cross-country study such as repression, social modernisation, foreign support and corruption.

theoretical model to motivate a simultaneous system for the joint estimation of 'welfare', the empirical proxy for the authoritarian bargain; and Polity, the proxy for political rights. They measure welfare by total expenditure on social policies for education, health, housing, unemployment benefits, pensions and so forth.

Subscribing to the theoretical literature, and drawing on evidence regarding the frequent incidence of instability in the political regimes of developing countries with high unemployment, including resource-rich ones, we ask whether resource rents are less effective in halting the transition to democracy in economies with high unemployment. We formally test for this potential unemployment effect in the first three regressions of Table 1.7, where we control for both the linear and quadratic unemployment effects in an extended model, based on regression 11 (of Table 1.4.B). Regressions 31 and 32 of Table 1.7 lead us to consider the more parsimonious model of regression 33, which eliminates the highly insignificant medium and low rents pc as well as the war and partial democracy variables. The evidence of regression 33 allows us to conclude that, by introducing unemployment to the threshold-based rentier model, three important results obtain. First, the resource rents effect is no longer significant for the cases of the low- and middle-rents pc groups (Med_Lnrentpc and Low_Lnrentpc). Second, unlike the lower pc levels, the resource rents effect for the top rents per capita group (Top_Lnrentpc) remains highly negative and significant, despite controlling for unemployment. Third, unemployment enters with highly significant and non-monotonic effect (regressions 2 and 3). According to these estimates, unemployment rates higher than the threshold of about 10 per cent {approximately equal to $(83.08/2 \times 407.75)100\%$} help to motivate democratic transition in the low- and middle-rents pc group?[32]

It is interesting to note that the unemployment story in the Arab world perfectly reflects the dichotomy between the highly resource-endowed GCC and the other lower resource-dependent Arab countries. For example, during 2000–09, unemployment was very low in the GCC (4 per cent in UAE, 0.5 in Qatar and 5.6 in Saudi Arabia), which was well below the 10 per cent threshold level. By contrast, it reached more than 16 per cent in Algeria and more than 10 per cent in Egypt, Morocco, Syria and Tunisia. Even when making comparisons with other regions, only East Asia managed to achieve rates comparable to that of the GCC

---

[32] It is remarkable that the unemployment threshold was equal to 10 per cent for all first three regressions of Table 1.7, even when the unemployment effect was only marginally significant in the, obviously, overextended model of regression 31.

Table 1.7: *Probability of Democratic Transition: How Does Resource Rent Hinder Democratic Transitions? – The Employment and Political Repression Channels*

Explanatory Variables	Random Effect Probit [31]	Random Effect Probit [32]	Random Effect Probit [33]	Random Effect Probit [34]	Random Effect Probit [35]
Log REAL GDP per capita_Initial	4.34**	3.48**	3.59***	0.78*	0.54
	(2.19)	(1.40)	(1.37)	(0.46)	(0.39)
REAL GDP_pc Growth	−44.67	−43.77*	−43.56**	−7.82	−9.67
	(34.41)	(23.31)	(23.57)	(7.56)	(7.26)
Top_Log Rentpc	−0.94	−0.77	−0.84*	−0.37*	−0.27**
	(0.68)	(0.69)	(0.49)	(0.19)	(0.12)
Med_Log Rentpc	−0.05	0.13	—	−0.19	—
	(0.78)	(0.49)		(0.23)	
Low_Log Rentpc	−0.63	0.01	—	0.03	—
	(1.29)	(0.74)		(0.34)	
STRA	5.22***	5.48***	5.48***	1.90***	1.85***
	(1.92)	(1.63)	(1.35)	(0.68)	(0.62)
Partial Democ	−1.02	—	—	1.09	1.04
	(1.97)			(0.72)	(0.66)
Homewar	−4.36	—	—	−1.81	−1.75*
	(3.19)			(1.10)	(0.98)
Pol Repress_p25	—	—	—	−8.46**	−6.92**
				(3.66)	(3.25)
Pol Repress_p25_75	—	—	—	−5.62***	−5.16***
				(1.90)	(1.73)
Pol Repress_p75	—	—	—	−2.17*	−2.04*
				(1.20)	(1.13)

Unemp Rate	−103.98	−80.73*	−83.08*	—	—
	(71.72)	(46.46)	(47.23)	—	—
Unemp Rate_sq	498.44*	394.28**	407.75**	—	—
	(279.83)	(187.61)	(198.31)	—	—
Constant	−25.83**	−23.82**	−24.17**	−4.55	−3.31
	(13.41)	(10.84)	(9.70)	(3.33)	(2.80)
Observations	82	121	121	213	213
Number of id	35	43	43	77	77
LR statistic	9.39	15.77	16.01	19.57	21.39
Log likelihood	−23.90	−36.19	−36.26	−74.81	−77.23

Notes:

- Unemployment rate (source ILO): the number of unemployed divided by the labour force (employment + unemployment)
- Political Repress_25: Political Repression index multiplied by a dummy for countries in the lowest quartile of political repression distribution (where the Political Repression index is increasing in terms of the degree of repression and ranges between 0 (repression free) to 1 (most repressive))
- Political Repress_25–75: Political Repression index multiplied by a dummy for countries in the two middle quartiles of the political repression distribution
- Political Repress_75: Political Repression index multiplied by a dummy for countries in the top quartile of the political repression distribution

56   *Ibrahim Elbadawi and Samir Makdisi*

Table 1.8: *Average Decadal Rate of Unemployment Rate by Region (2000–2009)*

Arab	8.94
UAE	4.00
Qatar	0.52
Saudi Arabia	5.63
Algeria	16.60
Egypt	10.20
Morocco	10.12
Syria	10.13
Tunisia	14.38
Sub-Saharan Africa	**16.08**
Latin America	**9.26**
Southern Central Asia	**10.28**
East Asia	**4.88**

Source: World Bank:World Development Indicators

(Table 1.8). However, the key difference is that unlike the former, the GCC countries rely primarily on oil-financed public sector employment to absorb the rising numbers of their national working-age populations (Ali and Elbadawi 2012).

The evidence can be reformulated in the following two succinct hypotheses:

H7: High *unemployment*, beyond a certain threshold (U > 10%), *promotes* democratic transition.

H8: However, employment *does not fully* account for the authoritarian bargain in the highly resource-endowed societies.

These findings (hypotheses) could be interpreted in the context of the reviewed game theoretic literature as suggesting that, for most resource-dependent countries, the resource rents can only be an effective hindrance to democratic transition in a *functioning* authoritarian bargain when they are used to create employment opportunities in undemocratic societies. However, because resource-dependent economies are likely to suffer from the consequences of the Dutch Disease, this would limit the capacity of the private sector to generate enough jobs in the non-resource sectors, and so the public sector has had to bear the brunt of the employment expansion. As the country and regional unemployment data suggest (Table 1.8), only ruling elites in highly resource-endowed societies have control over sufficiently large amounts of resources to allow the financing of such a process in the longer term. In fact, at the theoretical level,

Ali and Elbadawi (2012) argue that autocratic elites in lower resource-endowed societies might have a greater preference for political repression as an alternative strategy for remaining in power (see further discussion later).

Moreover, the (ex post) hypotheses also suggest that the authoritarian bargain would continue to hold in highly resource-rich societies even under high levels of unemployment. This finding could be explained by the fact that incumbent elites in societies richly endowed with resources possess enough resources to further promote social welfare through other means, such as direct cash transfers, generous pension programmes, subsidised mortgage loans and so forth.

Therefore, the unemployment channel, we would argue, is particularly relevant to explaining recent Arab uprisings in the low to medium resource-endowed countries, such as Egypt, Tunisia and Yemen; those in the making, such as Syria; or that are ripe for change, such as Algeria and Sudan.[33] Whereas relatively low unemployment, in addition to various social welfare programmes, is relevant for explaining why the Arab Spring is yet to reach the GCC and may not do so for some time to come.

The political repression effect. As discussed earlier, the incumbent autocratic elites in resource-rich countries would use the resource rents to increase the employment and general social welfare of their citizens in their attempt to remain in power, in lieu of extending the franchise. However, for the purpose of pre-empting or quelling incipient or unfolding revolts, the elites might also find it necessary to supplement their public sector employment strategy, by using their resource rents to build an apparatus of political repression.

Ample evidence is available on the large share of the budget in authoritarian oil- and other resource-rich countries which is devoted to military and security spending, though such spending might also reflect other considerations, such as external threats. To avoid this ambiguity, we follow Ross (2009) by using a direct measure of government repression that is available in the Cingranelli-Richards data set (2008)(http://www.humanrightsdata.com/p/data-documentation.html). This measure, called *Physical Integrity Rights*, constructs an annual variable that ranges from 0 (repression free) to 1 (worst repression) and accounts for

---

[33] Diwan (2012) points out that in order to understand the transition in the Arab world, we should account for the role of the middle class, which, he suggests, appears to have been decisive, not so much because its ranks have significantly swelled in the periods prior to the uprisings, but more because the middle class, a significant part of which had supported the ruling autocratic coalition in the past, switched sides to the democracy camp. He suggests that the improved democratic aspirations of the middle class in these societies might be linked to increased unemployment and inequality.

incidences of torture, extrajudicial killing, political imprisonment and disappearances that are attributable to the government.[34]

We formally test for the political repression effect in the last two regressions of Table 1.7 by including the index of political repression in the threshold-based rentier model, where we distinguish between degrees of political repression, constructed as three quartile-based sub-indexes:
- Political Repression_Q1 = Physical Integrity Rights index * DumQ1
- Political Repression_Q2–3 = Physical Integrity Rights index * DumQ2–3
- Political Repression_Q4 = Physical Integrity Rights index * DumQ4

DumQ1 is equal to 1 if political repression was below the first quartile of the data, and is equal to 0 elsewhere; DumQ2–3 is equal to 1 if political repression fell between the second and third quartiles, and is equal to 0 elsewhere; and DumQ4 is equal to 1 if political repression was higher than the third quartiles, and is equal to 0 elsewhere.

We find that political repression at all three levels is negatively and significantly associated with democratic transitions. We also find that the resource rents effect is no longer significant for the cases of the low and middle quartile resource-dependent groups though, as in the case of unemployment, the resource rent effect for the high resource-dependent group remains highly negative and significant (regressions 34–35 of Table 1.7). We present these findings in terms of the following two ex-post hypotheses:

H9:   Political repression *impedes* democratic transition.
H10:   However, political repression *does not* account for the rent effect in highly resource-endowed societies.

We interpret these findings to suggest that in high-resource but population-scarce countries the ruling elites are likely to rely more on expanding public employment and less on political repression. In contrast, our results suggest that the opposite is likely to happen in moderately endowed but populous countries. The Gulf Cooperation Council (GCC) member countries provide the most notable example of the former, while the other oil-rich but populous Arab economies epitomise the latter.

First, according to data analysed by Ali and Elbadawi (2012), the median oil rent per capita in the GCC during 2000–07 stood at an annual

[34] The original index decreases in degree of repression, where the most repressive cases are coded as 0; while repression-free cases receive a code equal to 8. For ease of exposition we inverted the index and rescaled the variables so that it increases in degree of repression and is contained in the [0,1] interval.

average of $11,898 (in real PPP dollars), which is twenty times more than the average rent for the median country from the populous Arab oil economies. In a similar vein, the median annual public sector wage bill per capita in the GCC, about $6000 (in real PPP dollars), was fifteen times the wage for the populous Arab oil economies.

Second, the cross-country data on the 'physical integrity rights' reveals that the resource-rich countries constitute one of the leading repressive groups. However, again, as in the case of unemployment, a significant difference appears between the highly endowed and the other countries dependent on lower levels of resources. For example, during 2005–09, the GCC group had a median score of only 0.29, which is second only to the developed countries' score of 0.18. On the other hand, the median populous oil-dependent Arab country scored 0.69, coming close to the scale of 1 (worst degree of repression). The other resource-dependent region of Southern and Central Asia, with a median index at 0.63, also came close to the worst repression level (Figure 1.5).

Our findings on employment and political repression in the context of the contrast between the GCC and the other moderately endowed oil-dependent Arab countries suggest two fundamental conclusions. First, it is clear that ruling autocratic elites in resource-rich societies might rely on political repression only as a supplementary means of forestalling

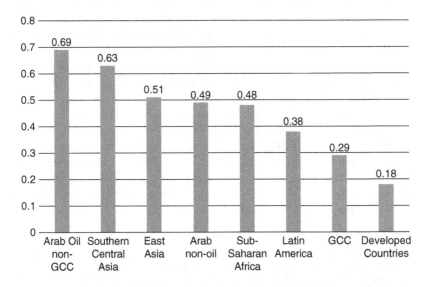

Figure 1.5: Political Repression by Region (2005–2009)

democratic transitions. Second, political repression is also likely to be a less efficient strategy for fending off democratic transitions than policies for promoting public employment. In this context, it is pertinent to stress that, these findings cohere with the fact that, while the populous Arab oil group has been susceptible to democratic forms of regime change, especially after the outbreak of the Arab uprisings, the GCC countries seem relatively unaffected so far.

1.6   Modernisation, Resource Rents and Arab Wars

In Section 1.4, the role of home wars as a hindrance to democratic transition was confirmed for alternative periods of transition and for before and after the end of the Cold War. Moreover, it has also been shown to account for any plausible idiosyncratic effects associated with the largely conflictive oil and non-oil Arab countries as well as other regional groupings. However, given the emphasis in the received literature on wars as an impediment to democratisation in the Arab world, it is important to test the war effect in regressions using alternative measures of Arab war to confirm that they are not driven by our initial specification, given by the aggregate incidence of wars experienced by a country in every half decade.

In this context we are interested in deconstructing this unique feature of Arab states. To disaggregate the effect of conflict and determine which type of Arab conflict affects democratisation, we follow Elbadawi, Makdisi and Milante (2007) and introduce four measures of Arab battle deaths, weighted by distance:[35] battle deaths from the Israeli–Palestinian conflict; from Arab civil wars; from international wars fought wholly or partly in Arab countries; and from all three types of war. We employ data on battle deaths from the Uppsala/PRIO Armed Conflicts Database. Additionally, these battle-death data are weighted by the distances between Arab states in a fashion similar to a gravity model, using data on distances from Centre D'Etudes Prospectives et d'Informations Internationales (CEPII; the French Centre for Research on International Economics). Lagged values of these measures are employed to avoid endogeneity, and the natural log of the variable is used to reflect the diminishing effect of large-scale violence. The distance-weighted battle deaths variables are contained in Figures 1.6–1.8 for the three

---

[35] For example, for a civil war in Algeria, the number of battle deaths for Algeria will be the actual numbers, while the regional impact of the Algerian civil war for Kuwait will be measured by the battle deaths from the Algerian civil war weighted by a scale variable reflecting the distance between Algiers and Kuwait City.

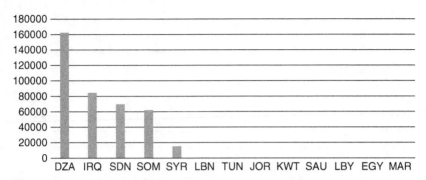

Figure 1.6: Total Battle Deaths in Arab Civil Wars in 1960–2009
(weighted by distance from the country of violence)

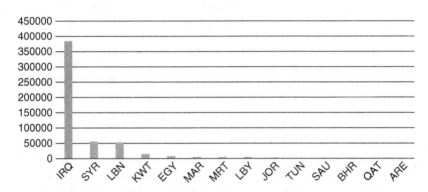

Figure 1.7: Total Battle Deaths in Arab International Wars in
1960–2009 (weighted by distance from the country of violence)

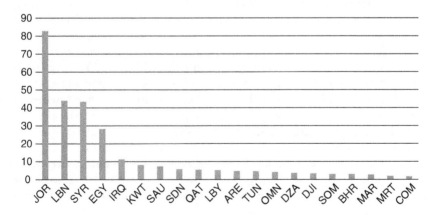

Figure 1.8: Total Battle Deaths (in thousands) in Arab–Israeli Wars in
1960–2009 (weighted by distance from the country of violence)

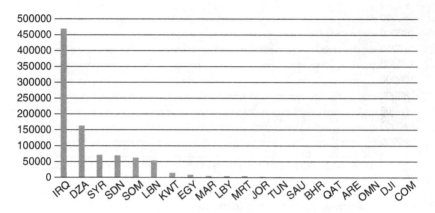

Figure 1.9: Total Battle Deaths in Major Arab Wars in 1960–2009
(Weighted by distance from the country of violence)

types of Arab wars, respectively, civil, regional and Arab–Israeli wars; and
Figure 1.9 presents the corresponding variable for all major Arab wars
combined.

To shed more light on the type and intensity of Arab wars and, hopefully, glean more nuanced evidence on their role as hindrance to democratic transitions in the Arab world, we replace in regression 14 (of
Table 1.4.B), our baseline 'home war' variable with Arab-specific war
measures, based on the number of battle deaths. The results of estimating
this model are included in Table 1.9. We find that the battle deaths from
civil wars have had a significant and negative effect on democratic transition, proportional to the scale of the civil strife (regressions 36 and 37).
However, proximity to large international conflicts is not found to be
significantly associated with Arab democratisation (regressions 38 and
39). This is rather surprising since large-scale interventions such as the
occupation of Iraq and conflicts like the Gulf Wars are likely to have
contributed to the resistance to democratisation in the Arab world, especially in countries bordering these conflicts. On the other hand, when all
Arab battle deaths are summed up and weighted by distance, the effect of
local and regional large-scale violence is negative and significant (regressions 42 and 43).

Finally, the battle deaths from the Arab–Israeli conflict are negatively and highly significantly associated with democratic transitions
in the Arab world (regressions 40 and 41). This finding suggests that

Table 1.9: *Probability of Democratic Transition – Modernisation, Resource Rents and Arab Wars*

Explanatory Variables	Random Effect Probit [36]	Random Effect Probit [37]	Random Effect Probit [38]	Random Effect Probit [39]	Random Effect Probit [40]	Random Effect Probit [41]	Random Effect Probit [42]	Random Effect Probit [43]
Log REAL GDP per capita_Initial	0.68**	0.68**	0.62**	0.62**	0.67**	0.67**	0.69**	0.69**
	(0.29)	(0.29)	(0.27)	(0.27)	(0.27)	(0.27)	(0.28)	(0.28)
REAL GDP_pc Growth	−7.98***	−7.88***	−7.68***	−7.61**	−7.58***	−7.50***	−7.73***	−7.64***
	(2.95)	(2.95)	(2.95)	(2.95)	(2.88)	(2.88)	(2.91)	(2.91)
Top_Log Rentpc	−0.27***	−0.23***	−0.26***	−0.23***	−0.25***	−0.22***	−0.26***	−0.23***
	(0.09)	(0.07)	(0.09)	(0.07)	(0.09)	(0.07)	(0.09)	(0.07)
Med_Log Rentpc	−0.26**	−0.20***	−0.23**	−0.19***	−0.23**	−0.19***	−0.25**	−0.20***
	(0.11)	(0.07)	(0.11)	(0.06)	(0.10)	(0.06)	(0.11)	(0.06)
Low_Log Rentpc	−0.10		−0.07		−0.08		−0.09	
	(0.16)		(0.16)		(0.15)		(0.15)	
STRA	1.97***	1.99***	1.94***	1.95***	1.83***	1.84***	1.90***	1.92***
	(0.38)	(0.39)	(0.38)	(0.39)	(0.36)	(0.37)	(0.37)	(0.38)
Partial Democ	0.67**	0.70**	0.73**	0.75**	0.71**	0.74**	0.69**	0.72**
	(0.31)	(0.30)	(0.31)	(0.30)	(0.30)	(0.30)	(0.30)	(0.30)
Ln CivilWars_bddist_1	−0.80**	−0.78**						
	(0.34)	(0.33)						
Ln IntArabWars_bddist_1			−0.29	−0.29				
			(0.23)	(0.23)				
Ln ArabIsraelWars_bddist_1					−7.56*	−7.49*		
					(4.24)	(4.22)		
Ln MajArabWars_bddist_1							−0.67**	−0.66**
							(0.28)	(0.28)

Table 1.9: *(cont.)*

Explanatory Variables	Random Effect Probit [36]	Random Effect Probit [37]	Random Effect Probit [38]	Random Effect Probit [39]	Random Effect Probit [40]	Random Effect Probit [41]	Random Effect Probit [42]	Random Effect Probit [43]
Constant	−5.61***	−5.94***	−5.47***	−5.70***	−5.61***	−5.89***	−5.63***	−5.93***
	(2.09)	(2.04)	(2.02)	(1.96)	(1.99)	(1.94)	(2.06)	(2.00)
Observations	441	441	441	441	441	441	441	441
Number of id	93	93	93	93	93	93	93	93
LR statistic	51.81	51.44	50.88	50.78	47.96	47.71	50.43	50.13
Log likelihood	−148.19	−148.39	−152.90	−153.00	−150.56	−150.70	−148.25	−148.41

Notes:

- Ln CivilWars_bddist$_{-1}$ = lagged log of battle deaths from Arab civil wars in 1960–2009, weighted by distance from the Arab countries directly involved in the conflicts
- Ln IntArabWars_bddist$_{-1}$ = lagged log of battle deaths from Arab international and regional wars in 1960–2009, weighted by distance from the Arab countries directly involved in the conflicts
- Ln ArabIsrealWars_bddist$_{-1}$ = lagged log of battle deaths in Arab–Israeli wars in 1960–2009, weighted by distance from the Arab countries directly involved in the conflicts
- Ln MajArabWars_bddist$_{-1}$ = lagged log of battle deaths in all major Arab wars in 1960–2009, weighted by distance from the Arab countries directly involved in the conflicts

the Arab countries close to Israel and Palestine are especially resistant to democratisation following periods of large-scale Israeli–Palestinian conflict.[36] And, we would argue, this reflects a special significance in that it provides direct evidence corroborating the widely held view in the scholarship on contemporary Arab politics that this lingering conflict has in fact greatly influenced Arab political discourse since the late 1940s.[37]

In his 2012 paper referred to earlier, Chaney claims that oil and the Arab–Israeli conflict do not explain the Arab democracy deficit. Though he does not directly analyse democratic transition, nevertheless, his results merit some discussion in this context as well. He presents results, based on a cross-country empirical model of historical institutions, suggesting that the Arab democracy deficit can be explained by the share of a country's land mass that the Arab armies conquered in the centuries following the death of the Prophet Muhammad. As already noted, he links his results to the long-running influence of the 'control structure' that evolved under the Islamic empires in the pre-modern era. Moreover, he claims that his results are robust against the two factors of oil and the Arab–Israeli conflict, because when oil countries and those that are in close geographic proximity to Israel are removed from the sample, his results remain unchanged.

In our view, Chaney's approach flies against fairly established evidence and accumulated country experiences. First, the role of oil as a hindrance to democracy has been firmly established in the literature. This thesis, of course, reflects global evidence that is not necessarily confined to the Arab region and, therefore, is not a compelling answer as to why the Arab region is different. However, the uniqueness of this region in terms of the dominance of oil, coupled with the other evidence on the diffusion of democratic transitions in the form of waves across countries in a geographic space, which until recently did not include the Arab world, provides, in our view, a viable explanation for the peculiar democratic discourse in the Arab world. Second, the evidence presented in this chapter regarding the negative impact of wars on democracy suggests

---

[36] Indeed, in support of this suggestion, national survey findings of the Arab Barometer on impediments to reform in the Arab countries point out that 'Citizens in countries that border Israel overwhelmingly perceive the Arab–Israeli conflict as a significant obstacle to political reform in their country', see Jamal and Robbins (2015), p. 21.

[37] By contrast, in other regions of the contemporary world, with no experience similar to the Palestinian one, civil conflicts have mostly been followed by a process towards democracy, noted reversals notwithstanding (Jai Kwan Jung 2008).

that conflicts that have a regional reach not only directly impede democratic transition but are also likely to be a causative channel for the hindering impact of oil and resource rents. The view that the lingering Arab–Israeli conflict has played that role, and still does so, is widely held by the vast majority of Arabist scholars. Moreover, Chaney's approach wanders too deep into history and is egregiously abstracted from important recent historical developments that have been widely documented as having a distinct and formative impact on institutions in the Arab world.

In addition to confirming the central role of Arab wars as a major hindrance to democratic transition, the encompassing model accounting for these measures of Arab wars also delivers the most compelling evidence in support of all the hypotheses analysed in the previous sections (Table 1.9). First, we corroborate the hypotheses regarding the corrosive impact of resource rents. Second, we also lend strong support to the modernisation hypothesis. Third, we find much stronger support for the Epstein and colleagues partial democracy thesis. Fourth, we also lend support to the two Przeworski arguments that the instability effect associated with past income (STRA) promotes democratic transition, while a growing economy under an autocratic regime could help consolidate its grip on power and, hence, prevent democratic transition. However, since we find lagged income to be robustly and positively associated with the probability of democratic transition, we don't support Przeworski's claim that, once we control for the instability associated with past wealth, modernisation is no longer relevant for explaining democratic transition.

Putting in all the evidence from this extensive econometric analysis, we reckon that the democratic transition model of Table 1.9, which unpacks wars in the Arab world and accounts for their effect in terms of geographic distance and intensity (battle death), appears to be the most relevant framework for analysing democratic transitions in the Arab world.

1.7   Neighbourhood Externality and the Future of Democracy in the Arab World

Recent literature suggests that regional neighbourhood and international developments could exert external influences on the domestic democratic discourse of a country. In this context it has been argued that these externalities can influence the balance of power between actors in a society; realign their evaluation of payoffs and contest strategies; and, as argued by, among others, Gleditsch and Ward (2006), possibly ultimately lead to institutional change. They present evidence to support their argument, where in a democratic transition model they find that regional (as well as international) democracy promotes the process of democratisation at the country level, whereas a country located in a war-affected (in other words, non-peaceful) region is less likely to become democratic. In the same vein, Elbadawi and colleagues (2011a) (http://idlbnc.idrc.ca/dspace/bitstream/10625/44957/1/IDL-449 57.pdf) find neighbourhood democracy to be robustly and positively associated with the Polity index of democracy.

The observed patterns of democratisation across the developing world suggest that transitions have transpired in the form of processes of regional diffusion, as reflected in the various democracy waves. Of course the Arab world has, until the current uprisings, provided an example of a 'reverse' diffusion where, over most of the past half-century, autocracy was not only consolidated but spread as a result of the overthrow of certain unstable Arab democracies (Table 1.1).

So what are the factors at work that have differentiated the Arab world from almost all other developing regions?

As discussed, a non-democratic neighbourhood is one key factor behind the diffusion of autocracy in the Arab world. Another is the prevalence of conflictive (non-peaceful) neighbourhoods (Table 1.2). The most damaging aspect of the conflicts is that they tend to be non-localised with strong regional, even global, implications. In particular, in the post-independence Arab world, the lingering Arab-Israeli conflict has swept in a popular Arab political culture of 'resistance' to the occupation of Palestinian and Arab land. This, it has been argued, has allowed autocratic Arab regimes to exploit a just cause to fashion a potent, even popular, brand of authoritarian Arab nationalism that ruled supreme for more than three decades.[38] And by the turn of the 1980s, when the 'resistance' case for non-democratisation started to run out of steam, several autocratic regimes tried to rehabilitate themselves by switching to alternative causes such as fighting terrorism, which brought them the support of powerful external powers.

We test for the potential causative influence of neighbourhood democracy on the transition impact of resource rents through regressions 44 and

---

[38] See Elbadawi and Makdisi (2011) for a review of the debates on these issues and for analysis of several case study experiences.

45 of Table 1.10, which is an extension of the threshold model of regression 14 (of Table 1.4.B). Similarly, we test for the role of neighbourhood wars through regressions 46 and 47 (of Table 1.10). We define 'neighbourhood democracy' as the average polity in a country's immediate

Table 1.10: *Probability of Democratic Transition – Neighbourhood Externalities*

Explanatory Variables	Random Effect Probit [44]	Random Effect Probit [45]	Random Effect Probit [46]	Random Effect Probit [47]
Log REAL GDP per capita_Initial	0.37	0.38	0.58	0.57
	(0.36)	(0.36)	(0.39)	(0.39)
REAL GDP_pc Growth	−10.21**	−10.03**	−13.38***	−13.76***
	(4.86)	(4.72)	(5.28)	(5.25)
Top_Log Rentpc	−0.11	−0.13	−0.26*	−0.21**
	(0.13)	(0.09)	(0.14)	(0.09)
Med_Log Rentpc	−0.11	−0.14	−0.26	−0.19**
	(0.17)	(0.08)	(0.18)	(0.09)
Low_Log Rentpc	0.04	–	−0.12	–
	(0.25)	–	(0.27)	–
STRA	1.80***	1.77***	2.38***	2.44***
	(0.54)	(0.52)	(0.57)	(0.56)
Partial Democ	0.98*	0.97*	0.95*	0.96*
	(0.53)	(0.53)	(0.58)	(0.58)
Homewar	−0.70	−0.69	−0.72	−0.74
	(0.57)	(0.56)	(0.61)	(0.61)
Regional Polity	0.14**	0.13**	–	–
	(0.05)	(0.05)	–	–
Neighbourwar	–	–	−0.74*	−0.71*
	–	–	(0.42)	(0.42)
Constant	−4.20	−4.07	−4.75*	−5.16*
	(2.67)	(2.55)	(2.92)	(2.83)
Observations	316	316	324	324
Number of id	76	76	78	78
LR statistic	31.25	31.27	38.74	38.75
Log likelihood	−100.23	−100.24	−104.54	−104.62

Notes:
- Average Regional Polity: average polity in the immediate neighbouring countries for the country in question
- Neighbourhoodwar: the number of the immediate neighbours of the country in question that experienced war

neighbours. In coding the neighbour polity, note that island countries do not have neighbours. Since a missing variable would drop all island countries from the sample, the relevant question is: how should the neighbour polity be coded for island countries? To address this issue, the average world polity per annum is calculated and the world is used as a neighbour to all countries, ensuring that every country has at least one neighbour. The average for the period is then calculated for the country and lagged to measure the neighbour polity effect: (Median Neighbour Polity$_{t1}$). Similarly, the 'neighbourhood wars' variable is constructed in the same fashion as the average of the 'home wars' index for the immediate neighbours of a country. In turn, as described in Table 1.2, the home war for a given country year is coded as 1 if the country was involved in civil, regional or international war in that year and 0 otherwise.

We find that neighbourhood democracy enters positively and highly significantly (at a 5 per cent significance level). Moreover, very important, all the threshold effects of resource rents are now highly insignificant, including those at the top level of rents per capita. On the other hand, the neighbourhood wars effect is only moderately (at a 10 per cent significance level) and negatively associated with democratic transitions. Nonetheless, it is pertinent to note that the estimated neighbourhood effect is obtained despite the fact that we control for the domestic war effect, which is also negative but insignificant. This suggests the possible presence of multicollinearity between the two variables. Moreover, though accounting for the neighbourhood war effect marginally weakens the quantitative impact of the high- and medium-resource rents effect, both continue to be a hindrance to democratic transition (at a 5 per cent level of significance).

We recast these findings in terms of the following four hypotheses:

H11: Neighbourhood democracy _promotes_ democratic transitions.
H12: Moreover, resource rent is _not a constraint_ to democratic transition in a democratic neighbourhood.
H13: Neighbourhood wars _impede_ democratic transitions, even when controlling for the effect of home wars.
H14: Moreover, neighbourhood wars do not fully explain the resource rents effect, as high- and medium-resource rents _remain an impediment_ to democratic transition in war-affected neighbourhoods.

The first two hypotheses (H11 and H12) suggest that, should the current Arab uprisings expand and consolidate, they would generate an increasingly positive neighbourhood externality that eventually would trump the currently dominant resource endowment effect in the highly endowed societies, which has so far shielded some countries, such as the GCC and Algeria, from the spread of these uprisings. However, this might take time, depending on how the neighbourhood effect scales up. And, despite being based on less compelling evidence, the remaining two hypotheses (H13 and H14) could also be interpreted as suggesting that, should the various wars and other violent conflicts afflicting the Arab world be fully resolved, including reaching a just and sustainable resolution to the Arab–Israeli conflict, the region would be likely to become more democratic. Moreover, in a peaceful Arab region oil would also be less of a hindrance to democracy.

Perhaps a more compelling interpretation of H13 and H14 is that the weak regional democracy is a manifestation of the entrenched regional autocracy, which in turn might explain the use of 'induced' violence as a potent instrument by the authoritarian counter-revolutions which have so far succeeded in derailing the democratic agenda of the Arab awakening (see El-Affendi, Chapter 2, this volume). The regionalisation and internationalisation of these conflicts is made possible by the weakness of the regional democratic externality, or, to put it differently, exacerbated by the strength of the negative autocratic externality. To the extent that the negative regional neighbourhood effect is not countered by forces pushing for change, it would currently appear that the future of democracy in the region is highly uncertain.

At the same time, the experiences of other regions teach us that democratic breakthroughs have been followed by numerous reversals, though at a decreasing rate over the decades since 1960, and with notable variations from one region to another (Kapstein and Converse 2008). And we tend to think that, following the Tunisian experience, socio-economic and political forces pushing for change, making demands for freedom and calling for a move towards democratic governance in the Arab region will prevail. The challenge would then be to minimise the possibility of reversals. As the cases studies in this book point out, it would be of the utmost importance for the countries taking the democratic path to succeed in the implementation of inclusive socio-economic policies in parallel with political reforms aimed at establishing inclusive political institutions intended to sustain the democratic transition.

1.8   Conclusions

In an earlier work (Elbadawi and Makdisi 2011), it was amply demonstrated that the interlocking of oil wealth and regional conflicts rendered the Arab region less attuned to the democratisation process despite the notable socio-economic development it had achieved in the previous five decades. Admittedly, the effects of these factors, which varied from one country to another, were not the sole explanation for the persistence of autocracies in various Arab countries. However, they remained dominant explanatory factors of the entrenched democracy deficit in the Arab region as a whole, until the Tunisian uprising of December 2010 and the subsequent ones elsewhere in the Arab region forced a new political trajectory. As of late 2016, of the countries where uprisings have taken place, only Tunisia appeared to be transiting towards democratic governance; of the remaining four, three (Libya, Syria and Yemen) have been witnessing tragic armed conflicts, and the fourth (Egypt) has been plagued by violence and political retrenchment. Their future political course remains uncertain. Nevertheless, it is a fact that the door to democratic transition in the region has been opened. Emerging counter forces may obstruct this process for some time, but eventually, we believe, democracy will prevail in the region.

This chapter analyses the factors that underlie democratic transitions. We code such transitions as a multi-year phenomenon, which allows for the likely possibility that during the transition phase a country's Polity score might experience some degree of setback for a year or more while pursuing a rising multi-year democratic trend. This concept of transition, we would argue, is more appropriate than the year-on-year measures used in most of the received literature. Moreover, while controlling for the benchmark modernisation determinants, the model we employ permits an assessment of the marginal impacts of resource rents, home wars and the status of being a partial democracy through testing for six fundamental hypotheses associated with these key factors. Further, we follow up by testing four more hypotheses on the causative mechanisms related to the natural resource rent effect on democratic transitions.

The model is estimated by using 449 five-year country periods and is then subjected to three types of robustness checks. First, we test the robustness of the evidence by choosing an alternative period for the duration of democratic transition of ten rather than five years. Second, we test for the robustness of the resource rent effect before and after 1990, because some researchers (e.g. Ross 2015) have claimed that oil rents became a significant hindrance to democracy only after the demise of the Soviet Union in the 1990s. Third, we also test for an alternative view, viz., that the corrosive effect of oil rents on democracy materialised only after the 1970s, when the conditions in the global oil market strengthened the position of the governments of oil-producing countries vis-à-vis multinational oil companies; by allowing them to appropriate larger shares of the rents.

Having estimated the core results and performed some diagnostic tests, we revisit the recent 'empirical' debate on the modernisation hypothesis in the context of our non-linear random probit model. Second, we ask the critical question, especially from the perspective of the Arab region, of 'how resource rents might hinder democratic transitions', where we assess the role of public employment as an instrument for the rentier-authoritarian bargain strategy, and political repression as another potential channel. Third, we probe deeper into the Arab wars and disaggregate them in terms of type and intensity, as measured by the number of casualties. Fourth, and finally, we assess the potential negative externality for the future of democratic transition in the Arab world of the conflictive and non-democratic neighbourhood that characterises the region.

The key findings are summarised next.

First, we confirm a baseline result from the received literature, that natural resources impede democratic transitions. We also find that resource rent hinders democratic transition only when managed by less than fully democratic regimes, such as autocracies or partial democracies. However, the resource rent is subject to threshold effects, where the resource rent appears to be a robust deterrent to democratisation only in those societies endowed with sufficiently high resources per capita (i.e. those that belong to the top rents per capita group in the sample).

Second, we corroborate the hypothesis that home wars hinder democratic transitions. Moreover, we also find that the highly negative and significant Arab and other regional dummies are no longer significant once we account for the war effect. Hence, we conclude that the extended democratic transition model that accounts for both resource rents and wars fully explains the regional dummies, most notably the infamous Arab regional dummy. This effect might be construed as an 'empirical' epitome of the concept of 'Arab exceptionalism' that has dominated the discussion about the lacklustre performance of the region as regards democratic transition.

Third, as recently discussed in the literature, we can corroborate the thesis that partial democracies are more susceptible to democratic transition than are autocracies, though this finding does not withstand our robustness checks. Nevertheless, given the high frequency of transitions in partial democracies and the strong theoretical argument associating this phenomenon with this type of polity, we believe that the results of the robustness checks might be influenced by multicollinearity due to the smaller samples used for these checks.

Fourth, high unemployment beyond a certain threshold (about 10 per cent or more) tends to promote democratic transition, suggesting the failure of the authoritarian bargain. However, unemployment does not fully account for the resource effect in the highly resource-endowed societies, perhaps because the ruling elites in this case can provide other forms of transfers beyond the provision of public sector employment.

Fifth, political repression impedes democratic transition, though again it does not fully account for the rent effect in highly resource-endowed societies. This suggests that for the ruling elites in the latter group, political repression is not an efficient strategy. Instead direct resource transfer is the strategy of choice; in the less endowed societies, political repression might be unavoidable for lack of a better alternative in terms of resource transfer.

Sixth, societies located in democratic neighbourhoods tend to be more susceptible to democratic transition. Moreover, resource rents cease to be a constraint on democratic transition in democratic regions, even for highly resource-endowed societies. This suggests that, should the current Arab uprisings swell into a major regional phenomenon, they might have much stronger effects, even in the highly resource-endowed GCC societies that have so far remained unaffected.

Seventh, regional wars impede democratic transitions and further reinforce the corrosive effects of resource rents on democratisation. Therefore, we strongly corroborate the widely held view that the major regional Arab wars, most notably the Arab–Israeli conflicts, have constituted a hindrance to democracy in the Arab world.

These two findings also suggest that, in view of the prevailing regionalisation and even internationalisation of the conflicts in the Arab world, and the looming existence of entrenched regional autocracy, the prospects for democratic transition appear highly uncertain.

Eighth, we find the income effect to be insignificant in the baseline regressions that not only control for income per capita, resource rents and past regime instability but also account for regional fixed effects. The latter effects – proxied by dummies for the Arab world and other regional groupings from the developing world – were found to be negatively and highly significantly associated with the probability of democratic transition in this baseline model. However, they cease to be significant when wars and partial democracy were also accounted for in the extended model. Moreover, by removing the regional dummies, income per capita becomes positively and significantly associated with democratic transitions in the extended model without regional fixed effects. We therefore conclude that the income effect is likely confounded with those of the regional dummies due to the fact that both have limited internal country variations. This argument is different from, but not unrelated to, the recent debate that regards the lack of robustness of the modernisation hypothesis as a statistical artefact of the bias generated by the inclusion of the fixed effects. In our case, the regional dummies are fully explained; hence, the appropriate framework for assessing the relevance of the modernisation hypothesis should be one without these regional dummies.

We therefore regard our evidence as lending support to the modernisation hypothesis. Moreover, because we corroborate this hypothesis despite having accounted for past political instability associated with past wealth, our findings do not lend support to Przeworski's claim that the death of autocratic regimes in initially relatively wealthy societies is likely to be caused by past political instability rather than by the modernisation effect of wealth. This evidence is important, not because it contributes to the current debate on the relevance of the modernisation hypothesis, important as it may be, but also because it is relevant to the current debate about the future of democracy in the Arab world. Among other factors, the past economic success of Tunisia and its vastly superior achievements on the education front have been discussed as important factors in explaining why, unlike the other Arab countries where uprisings have taken place, Tunisia appears on course towards a stable democratic path.

To recapitulate: we submit that the findings gleaned from this chapter's analysis provide a promising initial analytic framework for understanding the potential dynamics involving transitions towards democratic governance in some countries of the Arab region as well as limitations that continue to prevent, at least for the foreseeable future, a genuine democratic transformation in other Arab countries.

We acknowledge, however, that this framework may be further refined and nuanced by accounting for additional factors including, among others, past experiences with democracy, the role and strategies of the middle class, the formation of coalitions among social groups and so forth. Linking these shifting correlates to some of the benchmark results of this chapter, such as the non-monotonic effect of unemployment on democratic transition, should be a promising strategy for future research.

2   Overcoming Induced Insecurities: Stabilising Arab Democracies after the Spring

Abdelwahab El-Affendi

In his pioneering work, *Arabic Thought in the Liberal Age, 1798–1939* (1962), Albert Hourani established the myth that an Arab 'liberal age' came and went by the early 1940s, giving way to an age of mass politics (see also Reid 1982). Many authors followed him in arguing that such a 'liberal age' had indeed flourished for 100 years, ending abruptly in the mid-1950s, mainly due to the trauma of the 1948 defeat in front of Israel (Ibrahim 2004). Others date the demise of Arab liberalism to the second and more traumatic Arab defeat in June 1967 (Osman 2006). This paradoxical view (many others, such as Ibrahim, see 1967 as the end of radical nationalism) is supported by sentiments expressed by authors such as Galal Amin, a Nasserist with nostalgia for the liberalism of the 1920s and 1930s (Amin 2011). Many did not consider radical Arab nationalism as liberal, while a few even went so far as to see both pan-Arabism and Islamism as manifestations of a totalitarian ideology, directly influenced by European fascism (Berman 2003). Proponents of a related perspective argue that the brief life of Arab democracy is in itself evidence that Arab soil (not to mention the 'Arab mind') is somehow inhospitable to democracy. Arabs do not seem to understand, let alone desire, democracy (Kedourie 1992).

2.1   Undermining Democracy

It was indeed the case that some sort of democratic system emerged in most Arab countries in the post-independence period. In fact, the democratic struggle preceded independence. The 'Urabi uprising of 1881, for example, was a revolt against both authoritarianism and foreign domination (Cleveland 2000). In some cases, as in Iraq, Bahrain, Kuwait, Egypt and Sudan, parliaments were set up before independence or during partial occupation. Arabs were also involved in the constitutional movements within the Ottoman Empire, and the Arab Revolt of 1916–18 was motivated by the desire to end Young Turk despotism. One of the first outcomes of this revolt was the convening of the Syrian National Congress in Damascus in 1919, which became the voice of the people of the region. Almost every independent Arab state started with a parliamentary system. Even Saudi Arabia established a Consultative Council in 1927, headed by Prince Faisal (Chai 2006). Other Gulf countries and the rest of the monarchies also had robust constitutional arrangements on independence, with elected parliaments and a free press.

While most of these democratic arrangements were rudimentary, with the institutions constantly subverted, as we will show, their existence was a clear signal of the acceptance, however reluctant, of democracy as the only legitimate form of government. In fact, in the current struggles, democracy activists in some countries rely on that legitimacy, with activists in Bahrain demanding the restoration of the 1975 constitution, and the Kuwaiti opposition demanding respect for the 1962 constitution.

In almost all these countries, the democratic institutions came under assault early, with parliaments disbanded, obstructed or left to lapse. Rulers also used a combination of repressive measures and exploitation of political rivalries to restrict the power of parliaments or to ban party politics (Libya, Morocco, Iraq, Jordan, Kuwait). Additionally, foreign intervention assisted the subversion of democratic politics (British intervention in Egypt in 1924 and 1942), while in others, elite infighting led to military coups (Syria, from 1949 and then in 1970; Egypt, 1952; Sudan and Iraq, 1958; Algeria, 1965; Somalia, Libya and Sudan again, 1969). In some instances, as in Egypt, Iraq, Lebanon and Jordan, a combination of foreign intervention, elite squabbles and military involvement further undermined the fledgling democratic institutions. In other countries, such as Tunisia, Algeria and Mauritania, independence leaders transformed republics into virtual monarchies, with one man and one party. All later suffered military coups.

In spite of differences in detail, interlinked underlying factors lie behind these setbacks, mostly related to either democracy or independence (and often both), being an illusion. In countries like Egypt and Iraq, foreign-backed monarchies subverted the political process and played faction against faction, while foreign meddling made the whole process largely meaningless. In almost every country, intense political rivalries and lack of trust among very insecure groups within fragile states precipitated crisis situations, leading to army or foreign interventions. Military coups in the Arab world took place soon after formal independence (two to four years) (Rustow 1963), which may tend to confirm an inherent inability to handle independence and self-government. However, this point needs qualification, for in many cases, the countries involved (e.g. Iraq, Jordan, etc.) were not really independent when the first attempted coups took place. Even Egypt was still partially occupied by British troops at the time of the 1952 military takeover, and this contributed to the intense insecurity the

Free Officers felt. This insecurity was further accentuated by other instances of foreign intervention in the region (the 1953 anti-Mossadegh coup in Iran and the 1956 Suez attack on Egypt). This was one reason Arab leaders, as Hudson put it, became 'beset by insecurity and fear of the unknown', with their behaviour appearing 'at times quixotic or even paranoid' (Hudson 1977).

Hudson saw this as part of a wider crisis of legitimacy, which manifested in the Arab case at several levels. At one level, regimes lacked authority, being regarded as corrupt, inefficient and/or beholden to foreign interests. At a more fundamental level, the identity of the political community itself remained unsettled and unstable, as states were challenged from within by ethnic/religious dissent, and from without by claims of pan-Arab nationalism. At a third level, serious ideological challenges confronted Arab regimes. At a time when the ideas of freedom, democracy and socialism became 'inextricable criteria for legitimate political order in the Arab world', most Arab regimes fell short when measured against these standards of legitimacy (Hudson 1977). And, finally, regional conflict (in particular the struggle over Palestine) and foreign meddling, accentuated by the tensions of the Cold War, contributed significantly to political instability and elite insecurity.

These factors are interlinked. The contempt regimes showed towards their own 'liberal' constitutions contributed to their loss of credibility and made the excesses of their military successors appear part of the norm. The rise of new ideologies, such as pan-Arabism and socialism, in turn contributed to de-legitimising traditional, mainly pro-Western political systems, whether monarchies or elite-dominated oligarchies, as these regimes became ever more insecure and less tolerant of the limited liberties granted in the past, and more reliant on their Western patrons. The resulting deepening external involvement led to the initiation of a local 'Arab Cold War' – in fact a series of them – as radical regimes allied with the Eastern Bloc and worked to undermine the traditional monarchies (with increasing success) (Kerr 2007). The Palestinian cause and the wars with Israel fed this confrontation and became one of its key weapons.

The resulting insecurity and instability contributed considerably to the erosion of democratic institutions, while the investment of considerable resources into these conflicts undermined development. As a result, much of the Arab world, in spite of these investments' initial promise, 'suffered poverty on levels not far removed from those of Sub-Saharan Africa and South Asia'. Even many of the Arab world's oil-rich countries continued to occupy ranks on the human development index well below comparatively endowed countries (Henry and Springborg 2001).

We can therefore discern here a type of vicious circle: regimes that enjoyed weak authority and legitimacy are forced to resort to corruption and coercion to shore up their power. In the process, they undermine themselves even further, as they disrespect their own constitutions and norms. This in turn prompted more challenges to this authority, inducing those in power to become even more repressive and reliant on foreign backers. Ironically, the ensuing militarisation (especially when associated with the deployment of the military in poorly conceived and conducted external wars, as happened in the war with Israel in 1947–48) gave armies the incentive and opportunity to intervene politically. This happened in Iraq from 1933, after the army quelled the Assyrian uprising. Rebellions in Syria (1949) and Egypt (1952) followed the disastrous war with Israel and the Cairo riots of January 1952 (Rustow 1963).

The combination of ideological mobilisation and military involvement in politics created a downward spiral of polarisation and fragmentation, which further fed instability. The problem started with the Young Turks' attempts to impose their version of nationalism on the whole Ottoman Empire, provoking an Arab revolt that Britain exploited to undermine the Ottoman state. However, in spite of the success of Arabism in creating new political communities across religious lines, the excessive trumpeting of a more radical pan-Arabism alienated non-Arab communities (Kurds in Iraq and Syria, Berbers in North Africa and non-Arabs in Sudan). Simultaneously, the military intervention in politics undermined the coherence of armies and caused them to fragment along various fault lines. The fissions were first along ideological lines, as various groups – Communists, Ba'athists, nationalists and so forth – infiltrated the military and used it to stage coups. Later, as new ideological regimes sought to impose discipline on the military, polarisations along ethnic and sectarian lines began to emerge (Cleveland 2000; see also Gellner 1994). As a result, dangerous sectarian and ethnic fragmentation came to dom- inate Arab politics.

Recent empirical explorations have shown that the resulting conflicts (exacerbated by the overarching conflict with Israel) are the most decisive hindering factor for democratisation in the region (Elbadawi, Makdisi and Milante 2011). We will elaborate on this important insight later in this chapter.

2.2   Entrenched Authoritarianism: Monarchies, Republics, Hybrids

The wholesale collapse of democratic systems in the Arab world in the 1950s and 1960s was, in part, a reflection of a pattern that affected most of the Third World, and even parts of southern and eastern Europe. But even here, an Arab specificity could be discerned. To start with, apart from a couple of partial exceptions (mainly Sudan, but also Syria in the early 1960s), the regimes toppled in this process were hardly democratic in any meaningful sense. That is why military coups often enjoyed significant popularity, at least initially. Some military leaders, like Egypt's Nasser, continued to enjoy mass popular support for a long time, and well beyond Egypt's borders. Equally interesting, however, was the way in which traditional monarchies managed to survive, and even to consolidate power, after an initial period when they looked extremely vulnerable. Threatened by both internal dissent and the apparently unstoppable tide of radicalisation and modernisation, monarchies seemed well on their way to extinction. In Egypt, Iraq and Yemen, they succumbed in quick succession, while the Libyan monarchy held out until 1969. The smaller Gulf monarchies were shielded first by direct British protection and then by protection from their bigger neighbours, mainly Saudi Arabia (but also Iran under the Shah, which helped put down the Dhofar rebellion in Oman [1962–76]).

By the late 1970s, with radicalism in retreat in Egypt and elsewhere, and with the oil boom in full swing, the monarchies looked comfortably secure. Even the beleaguered Hashemite monarchy of Jordan began to look fairly robust, having managed to see off multiple challenges from a disgruntled military, disaffected elite, Palestinian guerrillas and a few unfriendly neighbours as well. The Moroccan monarchy also began to look fairly secure by the late 1970s, having survived numerous serious challenges and threats, including attacks from the king's own inner circle. This singled out the Arab world as the only region on Earth where absolute monarchies believed they had a future, especially after 1979, which saw the remaining Muslim monarchies in Iran and Afghanistan swept away by a revolutionary tide. From then on, only small isolated pockets of monarchical absolutism existed elsewhere, as in Nepal (until 2008).

Even more significant were the alliances these monarchies struck, externally and internally. All aligned themselves with the West, relying largely on Britain and France first and then on the United States for protection. Internally, most joined with the traditional religious authorities, tribal aristocracies and the merchant class. Most also struck alliances with the rising tide of Islamism, an alliance that looked 'natural' in a sense, since the conservative monarchies were attached to traditional religiosity anyway. In particular, the Saudi–Wahhabi alliance embodied militant 'Islamism', with its combination of reformism and active preaching, long before the term came into use.

The traditionalist–Islamist alliance became one feature of the 'Arab Cold War' due to shared hostility to radical leftist or nationalist movements. The expertise of the seasoned Islamist activists and intellectuals became indispensable for the traditionalist monarchies, whose religious establishments were ill equipped to fight the growing threat of nationalist radicalism. Sections of the rising generation in the Gulf, including some royals and the military, were seduced by radical ideologies. Gulf states were thus happy to host the thousands of Islamists forced to flee their countries, and enlist them as crash troops in the struggle against secular radicalism. Jordan also struck a strong and long-standing alliance with its own local Islamists.

From 1979, when the Iranian revolution began to pose another threat, the Gulf monarchies deployed a combination of oil money and Islamist/ sectarian rhetoric, as well as media campaigns, to counter the revolutionary propaganda emanating from Tehran. During the same period, the Gulf monarchies, now closely allied with Egypt, also encouraged the youth to flock to the 'Afghan Jihad', both in order to help Western allies in their fight against the 'Evil Empire', and to offer the young an outlet for their zeal and energies away from avenues of internal dissent. The West was more than happy about this tripartite Cold War alliance. After all, it was mainly in Islamic countries that the 'domino effect' of communist expansion was stopped, whether in Malaysia (1948) or Indonesia (1966), in volatile South-East Asia, or in Egypt, Sudan and Somalia, which became the sites of a significant about-turn from pro-Soviet to pro-American alignment in the 1970s. Authors like Ali Mazrui went so far as to argue that it was Afghanistan and its Mujahedin who won the Cold War for the West (Mazrui 1993).

These alliances were not without problems. For example, in spite of the heavy reliance on Islamists, most Gulf monarchies (with the partial exception of Kuwait and Bahrain) did not permit them to operate legally within Gulf countries, and their secret and informal networks suffered periodic crackdowns, as happened in UAE and Oman in recent times. Jordan permitted the Islamists to form a party as part of its reform package in the early 1990s, while Morocco, relying on the religious legitimacy of the king as 'Commander of the Faithful', was unique among the monarchies in maintaining hostility towards Islamists until recently.

Nevertheless, the 'Islamic Resurgence' from the late 1970s appeared to bolster monarchies, at least by putting radical secular republics on the defensive. Egypt under Sadat had anyway abandoned the Nasserite policy of 'exporting revolution', and struck its own peace with Islamists at home, at least during its early years. However, Syria and Iraq found themselves on the receiving end of Islamist insurgencies, aggravated in the case of

Iraq by the conflict with Iran. This forced these regimes to be more reliant on their erstwhile Gulf rivals, again strengthening the latter. Libya continued to push a radical agenda, but it actually undermined the radical camp by adopting a quasi-Islamist and certainly anti-left agenda, and by competing for the sponsorship of radical (in particular Palestinian) groups.

By the turn of the century, Arab regimes appeared to stabilise around two broad categories: rentier monarchies and populist authoritarian regimes. The former were 'the outcome of a special combination of oil and tribalism ... a hybrid of tradition and modernity virtually unique to the Middle East region'. They survived mainly in countries

where traditional forms of patriarchal and religious legitimacy retain credibility and where rent from oil revenues is used to revitalize pre-existing 'traditional' structures around which the state is consolidated. Large extended royal families substitute for the ruling parties of the republics and tribal networks are the equivalent of corporatist associations. (Hinnebusch 2006)

The durability of the monarchies cannot thus simply be explained by oil and rentier income, but one has to look into how the rentier income was used, in addition to other factors and tactics, such as appeal to sectarianism (Tétreault 2011). In particular, ruling families constituted themselves a 'ruling class which has a mechanism to regulate its own internal conflict, which dominates a modern state, and which can attract at least some support within society', thus making these models 'extremely hard to overthrow' (Herb 1999). One should add here the alliance with the business class in the context of a largely free market economy.

Populist authoritarian regimes, by contrast, 'issued from revolutionary coups, originating in the heart of society and expressive of revolt by nativist plebeians against cosmopolitan oligarchs entrenched under Western tutelage'. They mobilised a middle-class–peasant alliance against entrenched oligarchies and instituted socio-economic reforms, such as land reform and nationalisation, which 'simultaneously demolished the power of the oligarchy and the bourgeoisie while giving workers and peasants a stake in the system through guarantees of socio-economic entitlements' (Hinnebusch 2006).

However, this distinction is usually made in conjunction with the observation of regime-type convergence between the erstwhile populist republics (which have morphed into 'post-populist autocracies') and their erstwhile rivals. Long before the end of the Cold War, most 'radical' regimes (starting with Egypt and followed by Iraq, Algeria, Sudan, Somalia, Syria and Libya) retreated from their 'socialist' policies towards various forms of market economy. They also improved their relations with the West (and the monarchies) at the expense of the Eastern Bloc, toned down their populist and 'radical' rhetoric and became more pragmatic. Many even adopted the hereditary principle for succession. Similarly, the monarchies took a leaf from the book of their populist rivals, appropriating the nationalist rhetoric and some populist and social welfare policies (Hinnebusch 2006).

As the ascendancy of the radical camp gave way to Gulf hegemony, some analysts spoke of a new 'Saudi Era' supplanting the 'Egyptian Era' from 1967. This hegemony was consolidated with the oil boom from 1973 (Ḥammūdah 1995), helped by Egypt's isolation following the Camp David Accords of 1978. Iraq's increasing dependence on Gulf financial and political support following its disastrous war with Iran from 1980 also enhanced this trend. Many republics (including Egypt, Sudan and Yemen), and even the PLO, became reliant on Gulf largesse.

We will return later to this interesting conjunction of oil and conflict, and how the end of the Cold War impacted the region, where

> in contrast to other regions the authoritarian states . . . did not see their sources of international patronage evaporate with the end of the cold war or with America's subsequent reanimation with democracy, because western interest in the region has been driven by multiple security concerns that survived the cold war. (Bellin 2004)

Dependency on the region's oil supply, as well as concerns for stability and Israel's security and worries about the 'terror threat', all coalesced to increase external interest in the region rather than decrease it as the Cold War came to an end. Thus, as 1990 saw the withdrawal of Soviet troops from Eastern Europe, a massive influx of Western troops was taking place under Operation Desert Shield (later Desert Storm), in reaction to Iraq's invasion of Kuwait in August that year. Interestingly, it is about this time that the discussion started about why the Arab world in particular, and the Muslim world in general, appeared to stand out as a region that was resistant to democracy. Prior to that period, the region did not appear to have distinct trends from the rest of the Third World, and the collapse of early democratic experiments was 'attributed partly to still insufficient levels of modernization (high mass illiteracy, low income agricultural economies), hence of political consciousness' (Hinnebusch 2006). However, from the early 1990s, a flood of literature began to address Muslim and Arab 'exceptionalism', offering various explanations for the 'democratic deficit' in the region (Bellin 2004; Hinnebusch 2006; Salamé 1994).

2.3   Beyond Authoritarianism

We have summarised and critically evaluated this debate elsewhere, and there is no need to go into it in any detail again here (El-Affendi 2010; 2011). Recent major studies have also sought to add new insights in this area (Elbadawi and Makdisi: chapter 1).

However, scholars may need to revisit the subject in the light of the recent reversals the Arab revolutions have suffered. In particular, our claims regarding the revolution's practical refutation of the 'culturalist' thesis need to be looked into again. When we embarked on the current project, our guiding assumption was that we have now moved beyond the 'democracy deficit' problematic into the consolidation challenge. But do recent reversals (including the virtual 'election' of the *ancien regime* in Tunisia) indicate that we are back into deficit mode?

Recent developments have also brought into focus and have laid bare the actual mechanisms used to maintain the despotic systems in place. Understanding these mechanisms is crucial for dealing with the debilitating legacy of the authoritarian regimes, and thus for sustaining democracy. These mechanisms can be divided into two categories: the use (and abuse) of state institutions on one hand, and the manipulation of society on the other. The two are often interlinked. The use of the repressive apparatus of the state to maintain despotic rule may be standard across systems. In this regard, the intelligence services (often multiple competing ones) have become the pivotal instrument of control, subordinating other institutions, including the army, the police and paramilitary forces, to their control. The maintenance of an extensive and effective repressive apparatus required the allocation of considerable resources, and so the Arab regimes diverted a significant proportion of resources to this area. Oil revenues and helpful foreign allies contributed to this, making expenditure on security in the region amongst the highest internationally (Bellin 2004).

The states also used the resources at their disposal to co-opt elites into the service of the despotic system, and to penalise those who challenged it. In addition to direct repression and bribes, autocracies resorted to manipulating societies: encouraging and even manufacturing social and political cleavages as a deterrence to challenges to their authority. This manipulation took various forms, depending on regime type. The monarchies relied more on inducement and co-optation, while the republics leaned heavily towards coercion, coupled with populist mobilisation. This prompted the authors of a recent survey to conclude that the monarchies were 'less repressive, provide greater economic and press freedoms, and improve quality of life relative to the [populist] republics'. This meant they were more likely to engage in meaningful liberalisation (Spinks, Sahliyeh and Calfano 2008). Optimism about gradual reform in the monarchies increased following the accession to power in one year (1999) of three young kings (in Bahrain, Morocco and Jordan) who promised reform and appeared to embark on it (Ibrahim 2004).

However, the 2004 *Arab Human Development Report* (AHDR) found this distinction less pronounced, as the two regime types have converged significantly towards a pathologically dysfunctional model the Report dubbed the 'Black Hole State'. In contrast to the common argument which saw the Arab state as having adapted to its environment and successfully mobilised important sectors of society, the AHDR saw the authoritarian state as an alien and increasingly isolated entity, shrinking into a tiny core pitted against the rest of society (AHDR, p. 125–28). This argument was later developed to explain the revolutionary explosion of the Arab Spring, positing the increased isolation of the 'Black Hole State' as its Achilles heel. Having alienated most forces in society, it succeeded in uniting the major forces against it, thus making mass mobilisation of the opposition possible. Almost around the same time (in the period 2002–05), regimes in Syria, Yemen, Egypt and Tunisia began to lose internal allies as they became repressive, erratic and increasingly a 'family affair'. Secular liberal forces deserted these regimes after years of alliance against what both sides saw as an 'Islamist threat'. Umbrella opposition groups, such as *kefaya* in Egypt (2004) and the 18 October alliance in Tunisia (2005), began to form on the basis of a new joint commitment to democracy by liberals, Islamists and socialists (El-Affendi 2011). In Yemen, it was the Islamist allies of the regime who broke off and formed (with the socialists and liberals) the alliance of the Joint Meeting Parties in 2003 to fight for democracy. In Sudan, the opposition National Democratic Alliance was set up in 1991, while a common platform between Algerian parties was brokered by the Community of Sant'Egidio in Italy in 1994.

2.4   Varieties of Liberalism

This rapprochement was born out of deep transformations impacting key political forces: nationalists, Islamists and liberals. The liberals have been the weakest of these groups, having been displaced by radical nationalists as the hegemonic intellectual and political force by the 1960s, before Islamists from 1970s overshadowed them both. During the early post-independence phase, liberalism was discredited through association with corrupt elites deemed too close to imperialist powers. By the start of this century, the liberals appeared a dying breed, 'increasingly aging, increasingly isolated, and diminishing in number . . . losing a battle for the hearts and minds of their countries, and populations are increasingly driven toward younger and more disaffected personalities'. They were also accused of a 'remarkable passivity', tending to 'either throw up their hands or hope that the U.S. will deliver their countries to them'. In contrast, their Islamist rivals managed to 'conduct an active, creative, and impressive array of activities and services that affect peoples' daily lives' (Alterman 2004). Liberals were also faulted for lacking a compelling vision or the actual networks to promote their ideas. Their closeness to the West at a time of deep popular disaffection with Western policies deepened the schism separating them from the masses. More damaging was their 'deviations from liberal first principles', and their betrayal of liberal values, either by backing despots or by 'their mimicry of Islamist discourse' (Ahmari 2012).

On the eve of the Arab revolutions, a number of significant political and ideological shifts appeared to change the fortunes of liberalism. To start with, what could be dubbed a 'liberal Islamic' trend began to emerge in Iran, where the election of Muhammad Khatami as president in 1997 inaugurated a kind of *perestroika* and unprecedented openness, and in Turkey, where the Justice and Development Party's (AKP) accession to power under Recep Tayeb Erdogan in 2002 inaugurated a Turkish *perestroika*. Both developments were found inspiring by Arab public opinion, in particular the way they indicated possibilities about reconciling Islam and democracy. During the same period, a rapprochement began to occur between Islamist and radical Arab nationalist trends after a long period of bitter conflict of murderous proportions (in Nasserist Egypt, Ba'athist Syria and Iraq, South Yemen, etc.). The immediate cause was the common opposition to the Western intervention against Iraq after the invasion of Kuwait in 1990. But disillusionment among Arab nationalist trends with incumbent regimes, and the emergence of more 'moderate' Islamist thinkers and groups, including a number of prominent thinkers who crossed over from the left to the Islamist camp, helped this convergence (al-Marzouqi 2008). Concomitantly, a new type of young activist began to emerge under the influence of new media (satellite television, mobile technology, the Internet, social media, etc.) and major socio-economic and political shifts (increased literacy, expanded education, a larger middle class, disillusionment with regimes and old ideologies, increased globalisation) (Khondk 2011). These activists were committed to more inclusiveness, democracy, freedoms and more tolerance for diversity and political difference. They were not Islamists in any traditional sense, but they were not anti-Islamists either. Some observers spoke of what they called a post-Islamist phenomenon, more evident in Iran during the Khatami era, when many former hard-line Islamists became advocates of liberty without completely abandoning the Islamist foundations of their thinking (Bayat 2007; Soroush 2000). This author has argued, alternatively, that these developments, culminating in the Arab Spring, should rather be seen as a 'trans-Islamic revolution'. In this new context, Islam is no longer an issue of contention, not because it has been 'left behind' in a post-Islamist era, but rather due to the evolution of a consensus about the role of Islam in public life which made the debate largely redundant. Liberals no longer insist on excluding religion from the public debate, while Islamists no longer insist on the strictest inter-pretations of Islamic doctrine (El-Affendi 2012). This view was corro-borated by other authors who argued that the mass re-Islamisation of Arab societies has contributed to the diversification and the individua-lisation of the religious field, which in turn led to 'the inability to reconstruct religion as a political ideology. When religion is everywhere, it is nowhere' (Roy 2012). One manifestation of this development is the good showing of 'liberals' in the Libyan elections of July 2012, where the 'liberals' are in fact more supportive of Shari'a than Islamists in Morocco or Tunisia, for example (Sajoo 2012). In Egypt, the second article of the constitution, which stipulates that Shari'a is the main source of legislation, was not contested by anybody during the post-revolutionary wrangling over constitution making.

It was this emerging consensus, and the other developments surround-ing it, which made it possible to mobilise the protests which led to the Arab Spring uprisings. However, important though this consensus is, it remained precarious because it was based on disillusionment with both the 'liberal' despotism regimes (a contradiction in terms, in spite of the recommendations of some 'liberal' theorists) (Zakaria 1997). Also a factor was disillusion with Islamist experiments, such as those of Iran and Sudan, not to mention the radical nationalism of the Ba'athist and similar parties. However, these new attitudes have not evolved into a coherent and theologically and ethically elaborated doctrine, as some analysts had predicted or hoped (Binder 1988). However, the consensus was nevertheless a good start, and sufficed to mobilise and unite the pro-democracy forces. In fact, it can be argued that a 'liberal Islamic' trend is already taking shape in countries such as Tunisia and Morocco. Even in Egypt, the Islamists during the aborted Morsi presidency adopted an essentially 'liberal' programme, prompting analysts like Oliver Roy to argue that some of these groups 'can no longer even be called Islamists; they are conservatives analogous to the religious right in the US' (El Amrani 2012).

However, as we shall see, this consensus fractured disastrously in many countries, leading to a descent back into despotic systems that are much worse and more brutal than their predecessors. The 'moderate middle' (Islamist, liberal and nationalist) is now being squeezed by vicious sectarian regimes on one side and by violent radical 'Islamist' groups on the other.

2.5   Deciphering Regime Structures

The way the multi-layered regime survival mechanisms kicked in and operated in reaction to the protests was both revealing about the nature and structure of the regimes, and indicative of the problems any future transition would face. Interestingly, the first line of defence the regimes erected, in addition to the habitual and ubiquitous *mukhabarat,* was the media. The state-controlled media organs were mobilised to sow discord among the protesters, warning of chaos or 'extremist' takeover, while promising reforms to appease sections of opinion. The media was also used to mobilise, reassure and rally supporters. In Libya, a combination of threats by the leader and cajoling and pleading by his son put the nation in front of stark choices: either accept our promised 'reforms' or prepare for a destructive civil war. In most other countries, a similar line was adopted, where pro-regime media portrayed protesters as 'disruptive forces' made up of 'unemployed thugs, foreign conspirators, and delinquent and violent youth who did not have the national good at heart'. The protests were also depicted as economically disruptive and highly damaging to the country's national security (Hamdy and Gomaa 2012). Some of the techniques were rather hilarious, with an alleged 'protester', claiming to have 'escaped' from Tahrir Square, appearing on TV to announce that 'everybody there spoke English' (implying that they were all aliens), while free luxury food was lavishly available. Simultaneously, claims were made that extremist preachers in Tahrir Square were encouraging the youth to engage in terror, adding in the same intervention that gay sex orgies were taking place there (El Shimi 2011).

The importance assigned to the media was demonstrated by the desperate measures used to assert media control, which ranged from the drastic to the highly sophisticated. On Friday, 28 January, Egypt became the first country in history to completely shut down the Internet. Mobile networks were also brought down, while the regime used its control of Nilesat to block some TV channels. The Cairo offices of Aljazeera were also ordered to close. Libya and Syria used sophisticated technologies to disrupt satellite transmissions of Arabic-language TV stations, but the disruption affected many other networks as well. Outright violence, including kidnapping and murder (often through snipers), was also used to silence or obstruct media reporting. More than twenty-one journalists were killed covering the early months of the Arab revolutions.

In addition, some rather sophisticated campaigns of misinformation and co-optation were used. The Syrian regime, for example, relied on sympathetic media personnel and artists to spread its message. This included attempts to sell the narrative that the protests were the work of extremists and foreign agents intent on destabilising the country and diverting it from its 'enlightened' path. This arrangement covered not only news reports and opinion programmes, but drama as well (Ratta 2012).

However, it was the front-line troops used to quell the protests that revealed the true nature of the regimes. As the quintessential 'police state', Egypt deployed the police under the watchful eye of the state security apparatus. The situation was similar in Tunisia, another typical police state. In Libya, it was the 'Qaddafi Brigades', troops under the direct command of Qaddafi's sons and close confidantes, supported by the ultra-loyalist Revolutionary Committees, an assortment of quasi-tribal militias and loyalists (including some foreign mercenaries). In Yemen, it was also troops under President Salih's own sons and close relatives that took on the protesters. In Syria, it was the *shibbiha*, militias made up of hard-line Ba'ath loyalists, orchestrated by the ubiquitous and competing organs of the *mukhabarat*, in particular the feared Air Force Intelligence. The whole affair took on a blatant sectarian tinge, since the core of the army (dominated by the thoroughly sectarian Fourth Brigade, commanded by the president's own brother, Maher Asad) and the *mukhabarat* were under the uncompromising dominance of the minority Alawite sect of the Asads. In Bahrain, it was the army that was deployed, soon to be backed by Saudi troops. Here also, the sectarian alignment was clear to see: many Sunnis demonstrated in support of the regime and the Sunni-dominated army and welcomed the Saudi troops.

Significantly, most of these regimes largely mistrusted the military. It was usually heavily penetrated by the *mukhabarat*, and under a tight leash, as coups had always been the greatest fear of incumbent regimes. Armies were kept very small in countries like Tunisia and Bahrain (together with most monarchies), while a variety of techniques of neutralisation and control was used in countries with large armies. In Egypt, senior officers were carefully selected and given strong economic incentives to remain loyal. In Syria and Yemen, tribal-sectarian loyalties were the tools used, while multiple armies and formations were pitted against each other. Here, Eva Bellin's distinction between institutionalised and patrimonial security apparatuses, and her prediction that the former could make the transition to post-authoritarian regimes easier, are relevant.

An institutionalized coercive apparatus is one that is rule-governed, predictable, and meritocratic . . . there is a clear delineation between the public and private that forbids predatory behavior vis-à-vis society. . . . In contrast, in a coercive apparatus organized along patrimonial lines staffing decisions are ruled by cronyism; the distinction between public and private mission is blurred, leading to widespread corruption and abuse of power; and discipline is maintained through the exploitation of primordial cleavage, often relying on balanced rivalry between different ethnic/sectarian groups. (Bellin 2004)

The revolutions have partly borne out some of Bellin's predictions about more institutionalised forces finding it easier to accept the inevitability of change. Instead of fearing ruin by reform, their worry would be that lack of reform would destroy these institutions. Patrimonial systems, by contrast, would resist reform and could successfully delay it by cultivating and exploiting divisions within society (Bellin 2004).

Some caution is in order, though, when applying this analysis, since 'institutionalisation' within authoritarian regimes is always partial and often only apparent. All institutions are heavily penetrated by intelligence organs, party elites and other loyalists. Corruption is often used as a tool of control, with officers permitted to enrich themselves as a reward for loyalty, but this 'corruption' can be used as a weapon against those who waver. On the other hand, even predominantly patrimonial coercive institutions, such as those in Yemen and Libya, have behaved in unpredictable ways during the uprisings. It is mainly in Syria and Bahrain that patrimonialism appeared to function in ways that made it impossible to unite the people around democratic reforms.

The revolutionary process itself played an important role in transforming the scene and shaping the new realities. As mentioned earlier, the general scene had been set for broad-based collective action, facilitated by the increasing isolation of regimes and the emerging consensus among the opposition. However, neither the opposition nor the regimes had anticipated the spectacular success of the protests. The very revolutionary process forged a new shared identity of citizens, and successfully 'restored the meaning of politics . . . [and] revalued the people, revealing them in all their complexity – neither heroes nor saints, but citizens' (El-Ghobashi 2011).

It is this process of transformation that made these revolutions unique. The Arab region, contrary to frequently made claims, was not one that acquiesced to authoritarianism meekly. Quite the contrary: revolts against despotism were frequent and very violent. Numerous uprisings and revolts had erupted from the 'Urabi revolution of 1882 and the Mahdist uprising in Sudan around the same time (1881), through the Arab Revolt of 1916, and the various revolutions and uprisings in Libya (1911–31), Egypt (1919), Iraq (1920), Sudan (1924), Syria (1925) and, of course, the repeated Palestinian uprisings which started in 1929, not to mention the numerous struggles for independence, of which the Algerian revolution was the most noteworthy. The post-independence era also had its fair share of uprisings, even though most were often either limited or localised in their objectives (food riots, local grievances, etc.) or restricted to an isolated constituency (the revolt of Egyptian army conscripts in 1986).

With a few exceptions (the Egyptian uprising of 1919, the Algerian revolution, the Sudanese revolutions of 1964 and 1985 and Lebanon's Cedar Revolution of 2005), most of the revolts that took place in the region were mainly ethnic (the civil wars in Sudan, the Kurdish uprisings in Iraq and the Somali conflicts), religious/sectarian (Shi'a and *salafi* revolts in Saudi Arabia from the late 1970s, Shi'a protests in Iraq and Bahrain, localised uprisings in Yemen, Islamist insurgencies in Syria (1980s) and in Egypt and Algeria in the 1990s) or separatist (Iraq, Sudan, Yemen during various periods). By their very nature, such events did not help mobilise a united people against incumbent regimes; quite the reverse, in fact: they were used to consolidate authoritarianism by exploiting the mutual fear and mistrust between sections of the population. Even in countries like Lebanon, where consociational democracy was accepted as the only game in town, the unique combination of sectarian polarisation and foreign intervention repeatedly contributed to the subversion of democracy and handing the country over to foreign-backed (mostly Syrian-imposed, but occasionally Israeli-backed or Gulf-supported) autocrats.

This is why the regimes were as surprised as anybody by the size and extent of the protests, especially since their 'experts' (and even many independent academics) continued to discount any serious threats posed by what they saw as the fragmented and localised character of protests (El-Ghobashi 2011). Of no less significance was the way ruling elites deliberately tried to maintain and even induce the fragmentation of the political community through what I would like to call 'induced insecurity'. In this instance, insecurity becomes a direct product of the regime's own mode of operation, or of the choices of various political actors. For example, the insistence on maintaining narrowly based sectarian regimes or personal rule, with the inevitable escalation of repressive and exclusionary measures, made it possible to transform protests that started with democratic and inclusive objectives into inter-group confrontations. Even in partially democratic countries, such as Lebanon and Iraq, conscious choices key political actors made to 'play the sectarian card' have made these democracies look increasingly authoritarian. Sudan, which occupies a position in between, also suffers from an intense sectarian–ethnic polarisation that has made the mobilisation of broad-based mass protests very difficult (El-Affendi 2012).

The dividing line between revolutions which have succeeded and those which have not can be thus drawn where socio-political cleavages, such as Islamist–liberal (Egypt, Tunisia) or tribal–regional (Yemen), which appeared intractable and threatening, have been overcome. Where mutual reassurance and trust managed to overcome the 'induced inse-curity', various groups joined together to topple dictators. But where the idea that threatened groups could find protection only under a 'good dictator' persisted, a sizeable section of the population rallied to the side of incumbent (Syria, Bahrain and – to a lesser extent – Sudan) or would-be dictators (Iraq).

In cases where the divisions persisted, whether political (Libya), sectar-ian (Bahrain) or political–sectarian (Syria), the uprisings degenerated into a civil conflict in which one side or both asked for foreign interven-tion. The NATO intervention in Libya (March–October 2011) helped resolve the conflict, while the Saudi intervention in Bahrain helped shore up the regime. However, Syria remains a battleground for Iran and Russia on one hand and the West, Turkey and most Arab countries on the other. This is a reminder that the Arab regimes are firmly embedded within the regional and international systems, and their survival does not depend on internal dynamics alone.

The counter-revolution, which culminated in Egypt's military crack-down from 3 July 2013, and the emergence of an 'authoritarian coalition', has learned these lessons. The need to contain what some see as an Islamist threat has been invoked to rally anti-Islamist forces to the side of dictators. The media was first used to stoke fear and mistrust and divide the revolutionary coalition. As happened in Syria, many 'liberals' and some of the left supported an authoritarian 'solution'. Ruthless tactics were then used to ban and break up demonstrations, control the media and forbid political and civic activism. There is a determination to avoid 'repeating the mistakes' of Mubarak or Ben Ali by ensuring that people remain divided and public spaces closed.

Since then, the creeping counter-revolution has infected Libya and Yemen. Tunisia appears to be the only Arab Spring country to have escaped this trend, but not completely, since it has practically re-elected Ben Ali's party. The newly elected president, Beji Caid Essebsi, has criticised his rival in the presidential contest for alienating Egypt and

Syria and has promised to mend relations with these countries if elected. It is no secret that Essebsi has enjoyed strong support from conservative regimes in the region, which means Tunisia is now firmly back in the counter-revolutionary camp. A majority of Tunisians feel safer with their own version of the 'just despot'.

2.6   Oil, Conflict and Mutual Insecurity

The idea of a benevolent dictator or a 'just despot' (*mustabid 'adil*) has deep roots in modern Arab political thought, and was initially advocated by modern reformers like Muhammad Abduh (Afifi 2008). However, in more recent times, it has constituted one aspect of the crisis of modern ideologies, in particular liberalism. For example, in the Syrian case, it has been argued that many liberal intellectuals were motivated by 'a belief in the backwardness of Syrian society, which ostensibly can progress only through an enlightening (*tanwiri*) process led by benevolent minority rulers' (Ratta 2012). Similar sentiments were behind the rallying of many leading intellectuals to the side of regimes from Morocco to Jordan. The rise of Islamism from the 1970s has led many liberal intellectuals to seek the protection of 'enlightened' despots in Egypt, Tunisia, Kuwait and even Saudi Arabia, before disillusionment finally set in. Even now, intellectuals fearful of an Islamist takeover in Egypt or a Shi'i coup in Bahrain seek safety with the military or royal house.

No more paradoxical has such an alignment been than in Saudi Arabia, where liberals emboldened by the American presence in the region from 1990 openly petitioned the royal family for political reform and women's rights. However, when it became clear that opening the system up would benefit hard-line Islamists who could mobilise much more support than liberals could, most liberals either fell silent or threw their lot in with the monarchy. In recent years, a rather intriguing liberal–royal alliance began to take shape, where the monarchy grants 'liberals' the freedom to criticise Islamists and the religious establishment and offers them 'protection' from the wrath of the conservatives in return for loyalty to the monarchy (Doran 2004). Moreover, the Gulf monarchies, often wrongly accused of promoting militant Islamism, are in fact actively promoting liberalism: through media outlets directed to the youth (such as MBC and Rotana networks), modernised education or encouraging modern lifestyles as in Dubai and Bahrain. However, democracy is not at all on their agenda.

This interesting alignment partly explains the remarkable fact that most monarchies have not only largely escaped the recent tidal wave of popular revolutions, but were considerably strengthened by it, emerging as powerful regional actors and transition facilitators. The pan-Arab media, largely controlled by Gulf countries, played a prominent role in facilitating and sustaining the revolutions. Some explanations for this bucking of the trend pointed to the fact that the monarchies enjoyed 'an extraordinary degree of legitimacy in the eyes of their people', while most took pre-emptive or speedy remedial action, either to forestall or respond to protests. Thus the monarchies in Morocco, Jordan, Oman and Kuwait took steps to respond to demands for change and reform, with varying degrees of reluctance. In Saudi Arabia and UAE, where protests were minimal or non-existent, the rulers took pre-emptive action that was mainly economic in nature (more handouts, improved services, etc.), as well as security-driven measures (Ottaway and Muasher 2011).

In their chapter in this book (Chapter 1), Elbadawi and Makdisi marshal significant evidence to emphasise two related points: first, that authoritarian regimes in high-resource, low-population countries (like the GCC countries) rely less on repression than on generous welfare expenditure to consolidate their hold on power; and, second, the much-discussed 'neighbourhood effect' is also significant here (Gates et al. 2012). This effect is most pronounced in the case of Kuwait, which had otherwise appeared to be making progress in democratic rights compared to most other Arab countries. However, pressure from neighbours who fear 'contagion' has always pushed Kuwait into anti-democratic measures, like the repeated dissolution of parliament. In response to its own 'spring', representing the most serious challenge the ruling family had faced, Kuwait has cracked down severely on dissent. These measures were taken in conjunction with economic inducements and divide-and-rule approaches in order to weaken the opposition.

In the case of the Gulf monarchies, the ability to manoeuvre was facilitated not only by being resource-rich states, but by their role as increasingly important global economic actors, even 'a decisive factor for the future trajectory of global capitalism' (Hanieh 2011). This in turn bestows additional international legitimacy, in the same way as China's global economic dominance has enhanced the legitimacy of an otherwise problematic political system.

This special status of the Gulf also sheds more light on the findings of recent studies which pointed to a positive correlation between two variables (oil wealth and the prevalence of conflict) and the durability of Arab authoritarian systems (Elbadawi, Makdisi and Milante 2011). Elbadawi and Makdisi (Chapter 1, this volume) argue that the oil effect works through provision of higher levels of employment, funding for tools of political repression and 'positive' and 'negative' externalities, respectively, associated with neighbourhood democracies and neighbourhood conflicts. And indeed oil does provide ample resources to both fund state largesse and underwrite the robustness of its security apparatus. It also tends to attract international allies, enhancing the geo-strategic importance of the region. In the case of the Arab region, oil wealth was also used to secure dominance of the pan-Arab media, and thus achieve cultural hegemony.

However, the complex interrelationship between oil and conflict is not easy to fathom. There is a sense in which oil can both generate conflict and remedy it, often at the same time. For example, the discovery of oil in South Sudan in the early 1980s was partially responsible for reigniting the civil war in 1983, as it heightened grievances over wealth sharing. At the same time, the start of oil export in 1999 helped the peace process, offering an incentive to the rebels to seek a share in this new wealth, coupled with the worry that otherwise the new resources would enable the regime to fight the war more effectively. Currently, disputes over oil are at the heart of the ongoing Sudanese North–South tensions (and within South Sudan). In a similar fashion, oil played an important role in the eruption of the Iraqi–Kuwaiti conflict of 1990, and in the Iran–Iraq conflict. Oil also invariably attracts powerful international actors, and thus contributes to instability, even as those actors profess keenness on stability.

Conflict also relates to democratisation in complex ways. To start with, most of the conflict in the region involves Israel, which has managed nevertheless to remain a (highly distorted) democratic system. Israel also faces problems of religious extremism and radicalism, which were also accommodated within its political system. Another regional power, Turkey, is also involved in conflict (internally and with Cyprus), and has had to deal with Islamist activism. But it has also managed to progress along democratic lines. Therefore, conflict remains also a prominent and complicated aspect of the 'neighbourhood effect'.

The connection between conflict and democratisation is also interactive, making it difficult to determine cause and effect. For while authoritarian regimes exploit conflict to roll back freedoms (as when a state of emergency is declared), any authoritarian system is by nature engaged in an open conflict with society, or sections of it. In this regard, the discourse about an 'authoritarian bargain' needs to be re-examined or even abandoned, since it is a 'bargain' concluded at gunpoint. By its very nature, an authoritarian system deploys a battery of repressive and surveillance measures designed to restrict people's freedoms and choices. If it decides to 'sweeten' these measures by providing welfare and other economic benefits, it would be a misnomer to call that a bargain. By definition, a 'bargain' is a deal of give and take. But if someone takes over my house at gunpoint, and then says you can stay in part of the house and have some food and warm clothing, that cannot be called a bargain. It is even worse when such regimes use 'welfare' and employment as a weapon, providing only for loyalists and punishing dissidents or minorities by further deprivation. In this regard, authoritarian regimes are inherently conflictual, even when that conflict does not involve open armed warfare.

In some cases, as we have seen in Algeria in the early 1990s, in today's Egypt, in Iraq during al-Maliki's premiership, in Yemen and (to a lesser degree) in Lebanon, conflict is being generated from within a presumably 'democratic' context by one or more parties refusing to play by the rules. In such cases, conflict is the consequence of attempts to subvert the democratic process. One can subsume under this most of the processes (coups, uprisings or civil wars) which cause the collapse of democracies in the earlier phase of Arab independent history. There is thus a need to dig deeper into the underlying causes of conflict, which should be seen as a dependent as well as an independent variable. For democratic systems are optimum conflict resolution mechanisms, but conflict can also destroy democracies if societies face deep divisions. This happened during the English, American and Spanish civil wars, and too often after that.

It can be argued that overt armed conflict is radically different from the latent conflict of repressive governance. This is true if both the repression and anti-regime protests remain limited. However, as mentioned earlier, the two could easily merge, as we have seen, for example, in the Syrian and Libyan protests, which turned quickly into civil wars. In Egypt after 3 July 2013, police action (and even the judicial process) has become a form of war against dissidents, as the August 2013 massacres and mass death sentences passed on political opponents (between 500 and 700 at a time!) show. If we look at all civil wars, whether in Lebanon, Sudan, Iraq and so forth, we find that all had started from protests against state policies that escalated into mass violence.

Similarly, interstate violence or extra-regional intervention differ in impact from civil conflicts. However, interstate wars are rare in the Arab region, as most of the conflicts are either internal or due to foreign intervention. Even the conflict with Israel ceased to involve interstate wars, and is conducted by proxy through non-state actors. By the same token, foreign interventions, such as the war in Iraq, tended to transform quickly into civil conflict. More important, all civil conflicts can be sustained only by some form of foreign support. Wars are very costly affairs, and unless the combatants can lay their hands on a resource (such as diamonds, timber or similar valuables), then such wars cannot be sustained without foreign support (Fearon 2004).

All levels of conflict are thus interlinked, as is their impact on democratisation. Authoritarian rule usually relies on foreign support or derives legitimacy from claims of standing up to foreign enemies, or both. Reaction against despotism can easily escalate into civil war, which in turn invites foreign intervention and support. As in the cases of Lebanon and Sudan, deep divisions that escalate into violence can undermine existing democratic systems. The way to arrest this vicious cycle is to restore consensus and resolve highly contentious issues.

If we go back to the Gulf (and more generally, the monarchic) 'exception', we can again see how the interaction of oil and conflict helped stabilise these systems. The conflicts and upheavals of the 1970s and 1980s, which included the October 1973 war with Israel, the Iranian revolution and the Afghan war, all helped the monarchies. They did so first by hiking the price of oil, second by enhancing solidarity among these countries (the Gulf Cooperation Council was set up in 1981 in response to the Iran–Iraq War) and third by increasing the geopolitical significance of the region and incentivising major powers to offer strong support. Developments from the 1990s, including the Second Gulf War, the 'war on terror' and the end of the Cold War, coupled with the weakening of radical states, enhanced this trend. The perceived 'Islamist threat' (starting with Iran) has also increased external interest in the region, bringing in more foreign support. Having enjoyed long stability and reasonably prudent economic and political stewardship, the political elites in these countries are acting with increased self-confidence – so much so that they are now actively encouraging revolutions in some Arab countries (Syria and Iraq) and leading counter-revolutions elsewhere.

This appearance of calm and stability could be deceptive, however. The wealth and prosperity of these countries, and the enthusiastic international support they are enjoying, have camouflaged the underlying conflicts and problems without resolving them. As we can see in Kuwait, Bahrain, Jordan and, to a lesser extent, Oman, sizeable sections of the population are far from satisfied with the status quo. More ominous, in both Saudi Arabia and Bahrain, the protests have taken on a disturbingly sectarian flavour. This is a two-edged weapon, since regimes could – and did – play the 'sectarian card' to isolate the protesters. Up to now, the success of Gulf regimes consisted of managing to keep the violence and repression to a minimum, even in hot spots like Bahrain. However, the tensions could then threaten to feed into a wider regional conflict. With the United States and Israel keen on enlisting the help of Gulf countries in containing Iran, and with the Shi'i–Sunni polarisation evident in conflicts in Iraq, Syria, Yemen and Lebanon, these localised conflicts threaten to become part of a region-wide confrontation, a renewed 'Cold War' that is getting hotter by the minute. Such developments could then bring turmoil to the whole region and set the democratisation process in many countries back years. We can see the spectacular rise of the Islamic State in Iraq and the Levant (ISIL) as just one symptom of the threatened disintegration.

2.7   Stabilising Democracies

The lessons from recent Arab history, as outlined in the foregoing analysis, point to specific problems facing the stabilisation of democracy in this region: what theoreticians came to call 'democratic consolidation'. The surprising durability and longevity of Arab despotic regimes had recently focused attention on how to overthrow such regimes, rather than on how to stabilise the democratic systems that emerge. In countries like Sudan, toppling military regimes has proved much easier than sustaining the successor democratic systems. In Lebanon, the Arab country with the longest experience with democracy, stabilising democracy has also remained elusive.

It is important to stress here that this is not exclusively an Arab problem. In France, it took five attempts before a workable 'Fifth Republic' proved reasonably stable. Belgium, the *locus classicus* for 'consociational democracy', is currently in the midst of one of its prolonged crises. It is only thanks to its long tradition of commitment to democracy, and the European 'neighbourhood effect', that the crisis did not escalate into conflict or lead to the breakup of the country. Germany (and many other European countries) began to experience stable democracy only after the last war, and then only under the watchful eye of American occupation, which is still ongoing. There is, therefore, a need to work overtime on evolving appropriate institutions, tailored to the specific social, cultural and political conditions of each country, before democracy can be consolidated.

The fragility of earlier Arab democratic experiments, and of Arab liberalism more generally, was partially due to the fragmentary nature of political society. This was, in turn, related to the fragility of the Arab states, the impatience of warring elites and the negative contribution of clashing utopias. The combination of this fragmentation, fragility and uncertainty about trajectories generated an intense insecurity among elites and various components of society. A chronic legitimacy deficit, due to popular mistrust of rulers seen as corrupt, ineffective or clients for foreign powers, further exacerbated this insecurity. The determined attempts to export revolutions during the Arab Cold War, and again after the Islamic revolution in Iran, increased regime insecurity and made democracy a low priority for most actors. Insecure leaders often resorted to exploiting or creating existing social cleavages, as we have seen in the reliance of 'revolutionary' leaders in Iraq and Syria (and even South Yemen) on sectarian and tribal loyalties to maintain their grip on power.

It is regrettable that, after a brief reprieve during the revolution, the forces of the counter-revolution are again reviving these destructive techniques. During the revolutions, the symbolism of the national flag was universally and spontaneously embraced and was meant to emphasise the idea of common citizenship and loyalty to the nation. The flag trumped every other identity and commitment. It affirmed that everyone who was in the Square or on the street was first and foremost a citizen and a democracy activist, whatever else he/she may be. And this is the fundamental foundation of every democratic order.

However, the mutual trust the common revolutionary struggle generated remained fragile, and was quickly undermined as the revolutionary coalition in Egypt, for example, passed through a number of crises as various groups adopted mutually incompatible strategies. Supporters of the old regime (and even some 'liberals') were motivated by mistrust of the Islamists to attempt to subvert the democratic process, as shown by their enthusiastic support for the July 2013 military takeover and the brutal crackdown that followed. In Libya and Yemen, rival factions have deliberately cultivated tribal, regional or sectarian cleavages to obstruct the democratic process, and civil wars have erupted as a result.

The way these divisions were constructed and manipulated is a reminder that such cleavages, whether ethnic, sectarian or tribal, are not written in stone and need not always have a negative political role. Such identities also remain fluid, as can be seen from shifting alliances in Lebanon, Sudan, Iraq and elsewhere. In many cases, the cleavages are the outcome of political conflict and not its causes. Such identities could also be easily accommodated by devising appropriate democratic bargains, including consociational democracies or federal systems, which guarantee citizenship equality but permit multicultural and multi-ethnic self-expression.

The clearest indication of this is the way a new 'sectarian' divide is being engineered by exaggerating the Islamist–secular divide in Egypt and other countries. Responsibility in this falls on all sides. As the Tunisian example shows, the readiness of the Islamists to show flexibility (even in the face of unfair demands by their opponents), in contrast to the inflexibility of the Egyptian Islamists, can make the whole difference. Similarly, the decision to remove the inflexible and sectarian-inclined Prime Minister Nouri Maliki has indicated the way forward in Iraq.

The revolutions were not just a struggle for freedom from tyranny, but also an enactment of a conflict of visions. In Tahrir Square and elsewhere, two impulses confronted each other. On one side, insecure regimes (and groups, for the regimes had constituencies as well) peddled fear and mistrust, tried out various divide-and-rule strategies, used the media to mislead, defame and frighten, and deployed state institutions to subvert, corrupt and terrorise citizens. On the other, democracy protesters emphasised unity, mutual trust, tolerance and acceptance of each other, commitment to freedom for all and determination to fight tyranny at whatever cost. The protesters also used the media to inform, enlighten, unite and mobilise. The dominant narratives will determine the trajectory. If the prevalent narratives describe opponents as 'terrorists', 'unbelievers' or 'tyrants', then it is war. You cannot have democracy where one party is 'evil' and untrustworthy, since democracy entails the possibility that this party could accede to power. Narratives of insecurity and mutual demonisation are not the route to democracy, but to mass atrocities and genocidal violence (El-Affendi 2015).

The sustainability of democracy will depend on maintaining the 'Spirit of the Square' and its narratives of unity and mutual tolerance of democratic citizens. Additionally, mutual trust needs to be safeguarded by strong institutional guarantees: clear constitutional safeguards of rights, in particular minority rights, the integrity of state institutions, the independence of the judiciary and a credible electoral process. The power of institutional safeguards can be seen in the way group behaviour is shaped by institutional settings. For example, Indian Muslims, who share a cultural identity and long history with their brethren in Pakistan and Bangladesh, have not manifested any of the political pathologies infecting those neighbouring countries, and have remained active and constructive participants in the democratic process, often in adverse circumstances. Similarly, ethnic groups engaged in conflict in their home countries in Africa or the Arab regions do not engage in similar hostility as immigrants in the United States or Europe, but often join hands and cooperate within various associations seeking to promote the interests of immigrants. Recent studies of transition in Eastern Europe have also confirmed the efficacy of the institutional setup in shaping political expectations and conduct (Mishler and Rose 2001).

However, in addition to institutional safeguards, dominant political or national groups must also go out of their way to reassure others against possible abuse of power, especially in this formative phase where the rules of the game are still being formulated. As the experiments in Egypt indicate, it may be important not to privilege the 'formal' procedures of democracy (elections, etc.) over the substantive processes. The fact that the Islamists received a majority vote cannot obviate the need to safeguard equal citizenship rights for Christians, or allay the fears of the liberal and secular constituencies. While Islamists continue to affirm their commitment to inclusiveness and consensus, more needs to be done to ensure that these pledges are honoured. It was failure to do this that made the military takeover and the retreat from the path of democracy feasible.

In this regard, the role of the judiciary could be crucial. One of the most important steps to dismantle the architecture of the 'Black Hole State', with its deliberate subversion of state institutions and abuse of other state resources, is to re-establish institutional propriety. Under the old regimes, institutions were subservient to the whim of the ruler, and controlled through the terror mechanisms of the *mukhabarat*. In the new order, all state institutions, including the military and security apparatus, must be subject to the rule of law. In this regard, the combination of a properly functioning judiciary, assisted by a well-drafted constitution and free and vibrant media, is indispensable. Hannah Arendt has famously argued that the stability the post-revolutionary American political system enjoyed (in contrast to the French and Soviet revolutions) was due largely to the pivotal role the Supreme Court played as a guardian of the constitution, and as a check on all other institutions: it is a body that has authority, but no power (Arendt 1963). One of the main reasons behind the collapse of Egypt's democratic experiment is the failure of the excessively politicised judiciary to play its proper role as an impartial guardian of democratic rights.

The role of the intellectuals is also crucial. Our account has ascribed the speedy collapse of post-independence proto-democracies to their own self-contradictions and failure to live up to their own 'liberal' rhetoric. The regimes were only liberal in name, but in practice they were auto-cratic systems that were a projection of the colonial order which they inherited, with the added vice of corruption. However, at a deeper level, they had engaged in an early version of the 'guardianship of the liberal', seeing themselves as presiding largely over backward or 'Bedouin' socie-ties in need of 'modernisation'. This narrative had also been promoted by many leading Arab intellectuals, who continued to peddle the argument of underdeveloped societies not yet ready for democracy (Salamé 1994). Intellectuals were also responsible, ironically, for producing the radical nationalist narratives underpinning the military regimes that replaced the early liberal experiments. In both cases, the 'people' were not deemed fit to govern themselves, because they were not liberal enough or not pro-gressive enough or not Islamic enough. Intellectuals, including Islamist intellectuals, have also contributed to the current crisis together with the media and some civil society and 'liberal' political actors. The fledgling post-Arab Spring democracies were undermined by divisive narratives of fear and hate which destroyed the solidarity needed to sustain democracy, and are currently threatening to destroy whole societies. They have already done so in Syria. Failure to develop inclusive narratives of democratic citizenship is still the central problem obstructing democratic progress.

2.8   Conclusion

The central question confronting us here is how to sustain the revolutionary momentum that has briefly managed to overcome the 'Black Hole State', but has not yet dismantled it in favour of a democratic and democratising state. As we have seen, the political-social structure surrounding this state has grown out of the insecurity of the political elite in charge of a precarious and legitimacy-challenged state. As the 'liberal' project of the heirs of the colonial state undermined itself by duplicity and incompetence, its even more insecure successors dedicated themselves to state-building at the expense of nation-building. Resources, ample for some and scarce for most, were inordinately diverted towards building a robust security establishment, which in turn sought to perpetuate itself by multiple interventions that subverted social institutions. Civil society was stifled, and social forces fragmented and pitted against each other. In a sense, the state was at war with society, and dedicated most of its energies to undermine its vitality worse than the most vicious colonial project.

In fact, the mistakes of past regimes are being repeated, in some cases, as in Egypt and Tunisia, by the same personnel. The ruling elites, from Farouk and Nasser to Mubarak and Sissi (and their equivalents elsewhere), blame the people for their failure to win legitimacy and popular support. When the opposition becomes more popular, they do not ask themselves why people preferred the Brotherhood or this or that group, but they turn violently on the people, seeking to 'educate' them. These tactics have been used by almost every Arab regime, and have consistently failed. The regimes remain as unpopular and incompetent as ever, and these tactics actually make things worse.

The miracle of the Arab Spring was to prove that Arab civil society was alive and well, and full of vitality, in spite of decades of subversion and wilful destruction. In the ensuing battles, civil society pitted its ethical vitality and practical resourcefulness against the vicious state apparatus of repression and won. This is one reason to be optimistic about the *ultimate* irreversibility of the processes the Arab Spring generated. 'Whatever ups and downs may follow, we are witnessing the beginning of a process by which democratization is becoming rooted in Arab societies' (Roy 2012). But the emphasis here is on *ultimate*. As was the case in the wake of the French Revolution, setbacks can and do occur, but the overall momentum is unstoppable. Any political group desiring to take power must take heed of this, and operate within its parameters. Indeed, even the anti-democratic forces claim to be operating in the name of democracy. The Arab revolutions have not only finally demonstrated conclusively the futility and unsustainability of autocracy, but have also shown the way towards more inclusive systems. The arguments that Arabs are not fit for democracy or do not want it were conclusively refuted. In the past, the common adage was that it is either authoritarianism or chaos. In the current context, the alternatives are either democracy or chaos, either Tunisia or Somalia; nothing in between.

However, there is also no ignoring that the 'Black Hole State' has transformed society and is a hydra that cannot be defeated and dismantled overnight. In entrenching itself in society, it has built vast networks of beneficiaries, literally multiple 'armies' (military, security, party, business, etc.) of supporters. It was a mistake that most revolutionaries did not want to compromise with these armies, insisting on a clean sweep, with purges, trials and so forth. Pushed to the corner, constituencies of the *anciens régimes* were forced to fight back, including in Tunisia. They have used their ample resources and strategic position within the state to overcome the fragmented and disoriented revolutionary coalitions and institute the old order in a more vicious and vengeful form.

When we embarked on this project, there was plenty of optimism in the air about the future of Arab democracy. Today, however, the forecast is darker than it has ever been in the whole of Arab history. The counterrevolution is now in full swing, while the proponents of democracy are in despair and in retreat. Stabilising democracy presupposes the existence of ruling elites struggling to promote and establish democracy, not ones who see democracy as a threat because the people could not be trusted. The idea of a 'liberal' dictatorship (or 'guardianship') is as old as colonialism (for a detailed discussion, see El-Affendi 2011: 'Political Culture'). Are we back then to our early problematic of 'democratic deficit' mode rather than a consolidation challenge?

It is certainly the case that the current regime in Egypt is not a democratising one, and anti-democratic trends have been strengthened almost everywhere else. The promising alternative approaches adopted in Tunisia (and more recently in Iraq with the forced resignation of al-Maliki), may be more promising and indicate a better way forward than the carnage in Syria and elsewhere. But even here there are challenges. More dangerous is the apparent regional anti-democratic backlash, with powerful countries not satisfied with cracking down on their own people, but supporting anti-democratic forces in other nations. Unluckily for our region, we do not have one, but two anti-democratic coalitions (at least) – one led by Iran, the other by Saudi Arabia. Both are busy working to support friendly despotic regimes and extinguish any hope for democracy.

It is more likely than not that these efforts will fail. But the great tragedy is that the resources of the region are again being wasted on a losing battle, a course that is not without its consequences. For as we have seen in Somalia and as we are seeing in Syria and Iraq today, insisting on fighting this unwinnable war does not just waste millions of lives and precious resources that will need a lifetime to restore. It will most certainly destroy the countries involved. Dictators may fail, and they will fail, but states will also fail. I have elsewhere called the sectarian conflagration in the region the 'Other Samson Option' (borrowing the term from Seymour Hersh's characterisation of Israel's nuclear programme) (El-Affendi 2014). The parties in the Arab region have launched a nuclear holocaust by unleashing sectarian animosities that will have a much worse impact on the region than many nuclear weapons.

This is the opposite of what is needed for restoring or consolidating democracy, that is, the unity of the people. For the people (the *demos*) to rule, the *demos* has to exist as an entity. Like suicidal terrorists, the enemies of democracy have decided to do away with the people in order to save the 'state'. The suicide vehicle (the state) is not likely to survive the explosion. And without a state, democracy is impossible.

Part II

Case Studies: Successful, Protracted and Painful Transitions

3 Tunisia: The Prospects for Democratic Consolidation

Mongi Boughzala and Saoussen Ben Romdhane

Introduction

During the past two decades, and up to the uprising of December 2010, repression was growing at all levels of Tunisian society, elections were tightly controlled and political freedoms were suppressed. In parallel, open corruption, mainly at the highest level of government, became part of daily life and constituted a threat for a large part of the population, including the private entrepreneurial class, the natural ally of the regime. At the same time, social and regional disparities were increasing, and unemployment, especially among the youth, was persistent, averaging about 30 per cent in the period 2007–10. All these factors combined to create mounting tensions and widespread discontent culminating in a general uprising, which forced the president, Ben Ali, to leave the country on 14 January 2011. It was a sudden and rapid end to his regime and the beginning of a long and uncertain period of transition. After three years of profound uncertainty, the adoption of a new constitution and the appointment of a new technocratic government in January 2014 marked a major breakthrough and was a historic moment. The transition process culminated in the successful free election of a parliament and of a new president in the last quarter of 2014, in accordance with the rules set down in the new constitution. These elections consolidated the foundations of the political transition, but the transition process is still in its beginnings.

The risk of a setback is less than it used to between 2011 and 2013, but cannot be dismissed because the revolution was not led by a unified leadership with a well-defined social and political project, and the political leadership that emerged after the removal of Ben Ali was and remains fragmented. Many dormant splits and conflicts emerged. Consequently, the building of institutions has proved time-consuming, complex and proceeding in a very uncertain environment according to only vaguely specified rules. It is therefore not surprising that a consensus on institution building was hard to attain. The political parties which emerged after the first elections in December 2011 and formed a government coalition were unable to meet the expectations of the youth and the rest of the population.

However, the adoption of the January 2014 constitution and the democratic election of the current government has already proved a major first step in the right direction. It has become clear that an autocratic regime dominated by a single party could no longer be sustained in Tunisia, for it would only lead to more political and social instability and to renewed unrest, which Tunisian society could not support for very long. Thus, as we will argue in this chapter, the only potentially stable state in Tunisia is a democratic regime; the issue that needs to be addressed is the convergence towards this stable state. The purpose of this chapter is to analyse the prospects for a successful and consolidating transition to democracy, given the fundamentals and the factors underlying the Tunisian uprising. It is organised in two sections. In the first section, we study the process and the main explanatory factors underlying the uprising and the overthrow of the Ben Ali regime. In this context, we examine the probable factors that have combined to halt the democratisation process, during the period from Tunisia's independence (in 1956) up to the end of 2010, and those that explain the overthrow of the autocratic regime. In the second section, we analyse the path of the transition to democratisation and describe how the country went from chaos to successful free elections but not yet to a fully successful transition. The remaining and decisive phase is the social and economic transition. Democracy will not be sustainable if the serious social and economic issues are not resolved.

3.1   Factors Underlying the Overthrow of the Authoritarian Regime

3.1.1   The Analytical Framework

Several waves of democratisation involving tens of countries have recently occurred across the world, mainly in the 1980s and 1990s, but not all of them were successful. For instance, Brazil, Chile, Spain, several Central and Eastern European countries and Indonesia experienced rather successful transitions to democracy. Russia evolved towards an intermediate quasi-democratic state, while Pakistan has strayed off the path towards democracy. A number of studies and competing theories have proposed explanations for the determinants in the overthrow of authoritarian regimes and the eventual success of the transition to democracy. In this section of our chapter, the focus is on the factors underlying the overthrow and the beginning of the transition phase in the case of Tunisia.

The main question is: what led to the uprising and the collapse of the old regime?

Gleditsch and Choung (2004) argue that unequal economic growth influences the stability of autocracies and increases the likelihood of crises in general. Freund (World Bank 2011) shows that a set of economic and social factors, such as the lack of natural resources, increasing income levels, urbanisation and gender equality, increase the likelihood of transition incidence. According to the traditional 'modernity' theory advanced by Lipset (1959), democracy is 'secreted out of dictatorship by economic development'. Acemoglu, Johnson, Robinson and Yared (2008; 2009) argue that although income and democracy are positively correlated (in the long run), no evidence exists of a causal relationship between them, which may be seen as a critique of the Lipsetian theory. Elbadawi and Makdisi (Chapter 1, this volume) argue that economic development variables remain important determinants of the transition to democracy in the long run. They also show that the level of unemployment is particularly relevant for explaining recent Arab revolutions (in Tunisia, Egypt and Yemen), but for the Arab region as a whole they fail to explain the Arab democracy deficit relative to other comparable regions (or to the Arab exception). Rather, 'oil and conflicts and their interactions appear to explain this persistent deficit' (Elbadawi and Makdisi 2011).

Raj M. Desai and colleagues (2009) postulate that Arab rulers have for the past decades regarded their people as their subjects, and, in order to secure their loyalty and make them accept all political restrictions, they have provided them with government jobs and a generous welfare state (education, health care and subsidised foodstuffs and transportation). It would appear that in Tunisia and in many Arab countries, for nearly half a century this trade-off between political rights and welfare, the so-called authoritarian bargain, was popularly 'accepted' or at least not rejected, but, more recently and especially in the first decade of the new millennium (2001–10), it has become much harder to sustain. In particular, the rapid growth of the labour force and of the number of university graduates meant that the state could no longer secure government jobs for these groups. As a result, youth unemployment and anger reached uncontrollable levels, leading to widespread popular demands for change.

In fact, in the case of Tunisia, both the authoritarian bargain hypothesis and the Lipsetian modernisation theory provide useful insights, but neither of them gives a full understanding of the mechanisms behind the overthrow of the former authoritarian regime. Acemoglu and Robinson (2012) present a different framework and a new perspective, but this is still insufficient for understanding the transition process.

However, it is possible to adapt and integrate these three points of view within a more comprehensive framework.

Acemoglu and Robinson (A and R) argue that inclusive political institutions are the key factor, giving rise to inclusive economic institutions and consequently to inclusive growth and prosperity, and they claim that, in the long run, inclusive economic institutions are inconsistent with extractive (non-inclusive) political institutions. In their attempt to understand 'why [certain] nations fail' and others succeed, A and R contend that, historically, the key factor for growth and development has been the presence of inclusive political institutions. This means that, in the long run, no country can sustain inclusive economic institutions and widely distributed prosperity if its political institutions are not inclusive. Our main point is that inclusiveness is often incomplete, and partly inclusive economic institutions combined with inequality may generate a change to more inclusive political institutions; which will give rise to more growth and shared prosperity. The conceptual link between political and economic institutions and growth is insightful, and the A and R book is a major contribution to the understanding of the patterns of economic development. However, the A and R theory is not, by itself, fully consistent with the democratisation and growth processes that have taken place in various emerging countries. Political institutions matter – this is widely agreed – the issue, as in Barro (2013), is which institutions and how. A and R leave too many questions unanswered. In particular, they do not say how inclusive political institutions emerge and develop. They seem to assume that this happens exogenously since they focus on various cases of the transplantation of modern institutions by European settlers in various parts of the world. In fact, in the long run, political institutions are also endogenous.

Recent history, including in Tunisia, shows that extractive political institutions do not always give rise to extractive economic institutions and economic failure. Many countries achieved fairly inclusive economic institutions and rapid growth for decades under autocratic regimes. Should a change in political institutions occur, economic development and education will more likely give rise to more inclusive political institutions. Democratic and inclusive political institutions may indeed be secreted out of development and inclusive economic institutions, and, of course, once inclusive political institutions are consolidated the way will be broadly open to more economic development. This is how the Lipsetian modernisation theory may be reconciled with the A and R hypothesis. They may even be just two pieces in a general dynamic theory. In other words, they are complementary and feed into each other.

Moreover, inclusiveness is not a static state; it is a highly complex process and is never completed. Political institutions evolve constantly. This was true in particular in the eighteenth and nineteenth centuries and remains true even in the twentieth and twenty-first centuries in Western countries (Europe and North America), where inclusive political institutions are the most developed.

For countries that have, at least in part, inclusive economic institutions and political institutions that tend to the extractive, the transition towards more inclusive political institutions, and hence to democracy, will be powered by development. Education and openness to the rest of the world, and also social and regional inequalities, may accelerate the process, while factors underlying the 'authoritarian bargain', mainly rents from natural resources, may slow it down or even halt it. Tight fiscal constraints and a high level of public debt, which reduce the opportunities for establishing any kind of authoritarian bargain, are likely to force autocratic governments to make compromises and ultimately to step down. Evidently, a successful transition to inclusive political institutions and democracy should give rise to more inclusive economic institutions and opportunities, less inequality and more prosperity and so on.

We argue that this general framework is a good fit in the case of Tunisia. In spite of the regional disparities and the lack of opportunities for the younger generation that characterise this country, Tunisian economic institutions were sufficiently inclusive. The development efforts made during the 1960–2010 period benefited most of the Tunisian people in all Tunisia's regions, at least in part. However, regional disparities, concomitant with the performance of development and education, were major additional underlying factors in the rebellion and accelerating factors in the overthrow of the previous regime.

Rising levels of unemployment and growing regional disparities, alongside a large informal sector offering mainly low-quality jobs, generated growing pressures for reform. The population became increasingly politically restive, with growing popular aspirations for political and economic change. However, this rebellion would not have been so effective if development and progress in terms of education had not included the disadvantaged regions. The presence of a large pool of educated youth facing limited economic opportunities and an increasingly repressive political regime and asking for structural change is the centrepiece of the argument. The transition to a more coherent and more inclusive system would not be conceivable without the educated youth and middle class, who are the outcome of the development achieved over the past half-century. Repression and lack of freedom could no longer be held consistent with the changing structure of Tunisian society, and the uprising was a clear manifestation of the urgent need for new, more inclusive and more appropriate political institutions. Indeed, Economic openness became increasingly incompatible with the auto-cratic regime and restrictive political institutions, and this incompat-ibility aggravated the instability of the autocratic political system and led to its overthrow.

The next subsection (3.1.2.) explains in what sense Tunisian political institutions were not inclusive and how corruption has become a source of discontent, especially among the middle class and the educated youth, and a source of weakness for the regime. The focus in the third subsection is on economic performance; the purpose is to show the partial inclusive-ness of economic institutions and their interactions with the political institutions.

3.1.2   The Political Context

After independence in 1956, the Neo-Destour party, the main party that fought for independence, was the predominant political force in the country, and it easily managed to seize power and to impose a de facto one-party regime.

In March 1959, the Constituent Assembly elected in 1957 voted in a constitution making Tunisia a republic and abolishing the ruling, albeit very weak monarchy. Bourguiba was then elected as Tunisia's first president. However, it was the beginning of an increasingly auto-cratic regime and not of a nascent democracy. Bourguiba's term of office was regularly renewed formally, according to a non-open and a non-transparent mode of election, dominated by his sole, ruling party and under the control of the subdued Ministry of the Interior. He was president of the republic for thirty-one years (1957–87), and president of the Destour Party (PSD) since its foundation in 1934 (later, in 1964, the party was renamed the Socialist Destour Party or PSD).

In 1963, all the opposition parties, notably the Communist Party, were outlawed. In 1975, Bourguiba was voted president for life. The major trades union organisation (UGTT), which had played an important role, not only in organising and protecting workers, but also in the fight for independence, had to fit into the one-party system, as did all the other national and civil society organisations.

Nevertheless, it is undeniable that the Bourguiba regime, while highly autocratic, performed well in some fundamental areas, particularly in building the basis of a modern state and the institutions managing basic public utilities and promoting mass education and female emancipation. There was also a holistic view of development, even though this regime performed poorly in certain aspects of its economic policy, leading to several economic crises. In 1964–65, the country went through a severe balance of payment crisis followed by what was the first rebellion on the part of the UGTT. In 1978, the UGTT challenged the government again and led an uprising which was crushed, and the trades union leaders were jailed. This was an initial expression of the aspirations to freedom and social justice. As a response to this movement, in 1981, the Bourguiba government conceded what was a short-lived initial opening up to democratisation. The Communist Party was reinstated and the creation of other new parties allowed. This was also the year of tentative pluralistic legislative elections (held in September 1981), but the process rapidly failed and the government demonstrated that it was not willing to share power. It preferred to keep relying on repressive forces: the party machine, the police and, occasionally, the armed services. In retrospect, it was a missed, aborted opportunity to embark on a transition to more inclusive political institutions.

All in all, it can be said that the Bourguiba regime promoted social progress through fairly inclusive economic institutions and economic development. Programs. It also built modern but extractive political institutions; and it was politically harsh and repressive.

By the mid-1980s, Bourguiba was growing increasingly senile and unable to govern the country; his power was obviously weakening and there was a *fin de règne*, which opened the way for Zine El-Abidine Ben Ali to assume political power. On 7 November 1987, a few months after his appointment by Bourguiba as prime minister, Ben Ali organised a coup and took power. He did not need to use any military force to be accepted, as the situation was ripe for change. At the beginning, Ben Ali's government implemented several institutional reforms and even attempted to democratise the system. In fact, everything quickly returned to the one-party regime dominated by the same old Socialist Destour Party (PSD), renamed the Constitutional Democratic Party (RCD). Moreover, all political power gradually became more than ever highly concentrated at the level of the presidency.

Later, in 2001, 2004 and 2009, by means of constitutional amendments, Ben Ali ran for additional terms. These abuses were accompanied by increasing political restrictions on human rights activists, the political opposition, journalists and the media, and by the further weakening of the existing institutions of state, including the judiciary. As for the legislature, it had always lacked sufficient strength to assert itself. Presidential and parliamentary elections were held formally, but the members of parliament

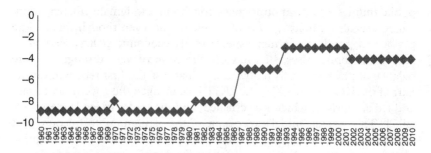

Figure 3.1: Evolution of the Polity Index
Source: Authors based on Polity IV Project Database: Political Regime
Characteristics and Transitions, 1960–2010.

were actually selected and appointed by the party and the president prior
to the elections. In the process, Ben Ali's extended family and entourage
amassed power and privileges. The Ben Ali regime was plagued by corruption and, in practice, was far more authoritarian than some indicators of
the level of democracy (or autocracy), such as Polity, showed it to be.

The widely used Polity IV database[1] shows that, during the Ben Ali era,
Tunisia moved from a very low −9 score, corresponding to a complete
autocracy, to an anocracy or a milder autocracy with scores in the −4 to −3
range. It is true that Tunisia went through attempts at partial democratisation in 1981 and 1993, as already mentioned, but these were both short-
lived and failed to fulfil their promise. The opposition parties were in fact
completely powerless, being either banned and repressed, or entirely submissive to government control. To this extent, the Tunisia Polity IV scores
did not accurately reflect the Tunisian reality; this confirms the cautions
certain researchers expressed concerning the limitations of the methodology followed in estimating these scores (e.g. Munck and Verkuilen 2002).

A closer analysis of the Polity IV database components relating to the
Tunisian case shows that the improvement recorded is mainly the result of
the political competition sub-indicator, which substantially improved
(from 3 to 6) in 1993 (see Figure 3.2), and not of the other governance
indicators. This score (Figure 3.2) was influenced by a seeming opening up
of the political scene to opposition parties in 1981 and 1993, the attempts
to 'pluralise' the composition of the chamber of deputies in 1993 and the
presidential elections in 1994. In reality, these measures of pluralisation
were cosmetic at best and intended to deceive national and international
opinion, and the political competition was actually fictitious.

---

[1] The polity score is composed of six measures that record the main qualities of executive
recruitment, constraints on executive authority and political competition.

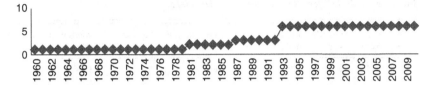

Figure 3.2: Evolution of the Political Competition Indicator
(POLCOMP) of the Polity Index
Source: Authors, based on Polity IV Project Database: Political Regime
Characteristics and Transitions, 1960–2010.

When they took place, the elections were far from genuinely contested,
clean, free or fair. The development of civil society was stalled, and the
freedoms of expression and press were suppressed. In reality, the system
of power relationships and the constitutional and legal arrangements that
organised political life in Tunisia remained essentially authoritarian with
hardly any room allowed for opposing opinions.

Other available indicators of democracy confirm this view. For example,
according to the Economist Intelligence Unit's measure of democracy,[2] in
2010, the Tunisian regime was rated as authoritarian, with a democracy
index of 2.79 (the score ranges between 0 and 10; a score of 10 implying
complete democracy), and the country ranked 144 out of 167 nations.
Compared to 2008, the score had actually declined and the country had
gone down two places in the overall ranking. It is also important to note
that a score of zero is assigned to the subcomponent related to the electoral
process and pluralism. Nevertheless, a year after the revolution the ranking
extensively improved, and in 2011 Tunisia experienced the greatest
increase in a democracy score for any country. Consequently, the regime
moved from an authoritarian to a hybrid one. The democracy index
continued its growth path in 2012 and 2013, thanks to the progress of
the electoral process subcomponent (see Table 3.1). However, the civil
liberties subcomponent is still considered relatively low (less than 5).

The Bertelsmann Transformation Index (BTI), which analyses and
evaluates the quality of democracy, also confirms the country's weak
democracy performance before the revolution. In 2010, Tunisia ranked
102 out of 128 countries, with a low score of 3.78.[3] While the situation
improved after the 2011 uprising, the BTI score remained low in 2012

[2] The Economist Intelligence Unit's Index of Democracy is based on five categories:
electoral process and pluralism; civil liberties; the functioning of government; political
participation; and political culture. Countries are placed under one of four types of regime:
full democracy, flawed democracy, hybrid regime or authoritarian regime.
[3] Scale 1 (lowest) to 10 (highest).

Table 3.1: *EIU Democracy Index, 2010–2013*

Tunisia	Rank*	Overall score	Electoral process and pluralism	Functioning of government	Political participation	Political culture	Civil liberties
2010	144	2.79	0.00	2.86	2.22	5.63	3.24
2011	92	5.53	5.33	5.00	6.67	6.25	4.41
2012	90	5.67	5.75	5.00	6.67	6.25	4.71
2013	90	5.76	6.17	5.00	6.67	6.25	4.71

* out of 167 countries
Sources: Democracy Index. The Economist Intelligence Unit.

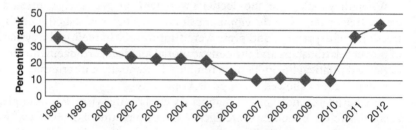

Figure 3.3: Voice and Accountability, 1996–2012
Source: Worldwide Governance Indicators 2012.

and did not exceed the value of 4 (i.e. partial democracy status). But it reached 5.8 as a result of the constitution adopted in January 2014.

Voice and accountability improved in 2011 and 2012, following the first elections to the National Constituent Assembly on 23 October 2011.

For two decades, the multibillionaire clan of President Ben Ali (mainly on the part of the ruler's wife, family and in-laws), which increasingly led to the alienation of the government from the people, controlled both the polity and key segments of the economy. The Ben Ali clan and its cronies abused all types of institution at all levels. They managed to control the distribution of wealth and jobs, to accumulate assets illegally and in the process to strengthen their hold on power.

Again, while the 'control of corruption' indicator appears to have underestimated the level of corruption (see Figure 3.4), the report published by the national commission in charge of investigating corruption cases (November 2011) offers solid information and ample evidence for the extent and depth of corruption. This national commission, established in the weeks after Ben Ali's overthrow, included government accountants, lawyers and experts in administration and property.

Table 3.2: *CPI Score Relates to Perceptions of the Degree of Corruption, 2000–2014*

Year	Rank	CPI score
2000	32	5.2
2001	31	5.3
2002	36	4.8
2003	39	4.9
2004	39	5.0
2005	43	4.9
2006	51	5.0
2007	61	4.9
2008	62	4.6
2009	65	4.2
2010	59	4.3
2011	73	3.8
2012	75	4.1
2013	77	4.1
2014	79	4.0

* CPI Score relates to perceptions of the degree of corruption as seen by business people and country analysts and ranges between 10 (highly clean) and 0 (highly corrupt).
Source: Transparency International.

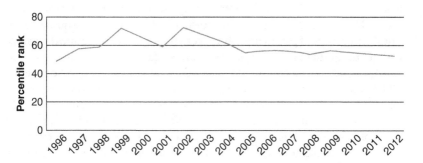

Figure 3.4: Control of Corruption, 1996–2012
Source: Worldwide Governance Indicators 20102012. Percentile rank among all countries ranges from 0 (lowest) to 100 (highest).

The report's findings, based on some 5,000 complaints, reveal a vast system of structured corruption by which Ben Ali, his in-laws and their cronies enriched themselves. Some major examples of this are the stakes they acquired in the most lucrative businesses, exemptions from customs dues and appropriation of public land. Government institutions such as the tax authorities and the judiciary, and even private and state-owned banks, were under their control. Private entrepreneurs who refused to participate in their schemes were subject to harassment which took various forms, otherwise their business would come under threat.

Deeply rooted corruption and bad government led to the alienation of all social classes from the regime and to the loss of most of the domestic support it had initially enjoyed. It became increasingly isolated, rejected and despised even by its main supporters, private entrepreneurs and the police.

No doubt, these factors constituted major factors to the undermining of the hegemony of the regime and its eventual downfall. However, the need for political change was primarily powered by economic factors.

3.1.3   The Economic and Social Context

3.1.3.1   The Authoritarian Bargain and the Lipsetian Hypotheses

Let us say from the outset that not everything about the economy was bleak before 2011. Actually, during the past five decades, Tunisia has achieved a relatively good economic performance, compared to its neighbours and other Arab countries. It maintained a relative degree of macroeconomic stability combined with rapid economic growth and rising levels of per capita income. The average economic growth rate was around 5 per cent, which is higher than the MENA countries' average (excluding resource-rich countries). With the exception of a few episodes, the economy also maintained a healthy balance of payments. Moreover, the economy was quite diversified, with a substantial growing role for the manufacturing and service sectors; which respectively accounted for more than 20 per cent and 60 per cent of GDP. The development of the agricultural sector was slower, and, consequently, its relative contribution to the economy, as a share of GDP, decreased to about 10 per cent. Exports also diversified with an important share of manufacturing, about 70 per cent. Table 3.3 shows that even after the world financial crisis the pre-2011 Tunisian economy was quite resilient.

Starting in the early 1970s, a series of policies designed to promote investments and attract foreign investors was adopted. Tunisia succeeded in promoting its export sector while concomitantly witnessing a growing internal market driven by domestic demand. The outcome was a rapid development of both the private sector and export markets. The proximity to Europe, a low-paid labour force and a serviceable infrastructure, as well as political and social stability, contributed to this progress.

This progress also covered various social fields, leading to a generalised access to education for both boys and girls, and, for a large part of the

Table 3.3: *Macroeconomic Indicators (2008–2011)*

	2008	2009	2010	2011
GDP (US$ billions)	44.878	43.523	44.290	46.623
GDP per capita (US$)	4,354	4,170	4,200	4,375
GDP growth rate (%)	4.5	3.2	3.7	−1.9*
Population growth rate (%)	1.03	1.03	1.06	1.14
Government debt (% GDP)	43.3	42.9	40.4	42.8
Population (million)	10.314	10.420	10.531	10.650
Urban population (%)	65.8	65.9	66.1	66.2

Source: Compiled by the authors from IMF (2013)*, WDI (2011) and INS (2012).

population, to health care and housing facilities mainly via subsidised housing and loans. Furthermore, the water and electricity infrastructure and social services were developed to serve the population at large while food and transport subsidies were extended.

The rising level of education in the country was particularly impressive. In 2010, the proportion of the labour force which had access to, at the least, a secondary education, reached on average 55 per cent for both men and women, compared to around 8 per cent in 1966. Similarly, 17 per cent had a tertiary education, compared to a little more than 1 per cent in 1966. Access to schools at all levels was equally available to both sexes. Actually, female student enrolment eventually outstripped male student enrolment; more than 60 per cent of university graduates are women.

The number of health care facilities and doctors has also grown remarkably.

The positive socio-economic performance strengthened the government's legitimacy and secured the loyalty of a large majority of the people; thus they validated the authoritarian bargain hypothesis, at least until 2000/2001. The Bourguiba regime, in particular, enjoyed widespread popularity and legitimacy for more than two decades, extending into the early period of the Ben Ali regime (1987–2000). With the revenues generated by growth, and in spite of the drying up of oil revenues (a limited surplus was available in the 1970s), the government could still afford to suppress or silence most dissidents.

Altogether, Tunisian development provided opportunities for large sections of the population and was, overall, pro-poor. It also resulted in a growing middle class, which, according to the Brookings database, comprised more than 40 per cent of the population in 2010. To that extent, economic institutions and growth over the past decades have been increasingly, though not fully, inclusive.

Table 3.4: *The Structure of the Labour Force by Education Level, 1966–2011 (percentage of labour force)*

	1966	1975	1984	1994	2001	2006	2011
Higher	1.2	1.4	3.3	7	10	15	17
Intermediate (Secondary & Vocational)	7.1	128	20	29	30	31	38
Low (Primary or None)	91.7	85.7	76.8	64	60	54	45
Total	100	100	100	100	100	100	100

Source: INS Labour survey 2001 to 2011 and population census 1966, 1975, 1984, 1994.

Table 3.5: *Provision of Public Health*

Year	2006	2007	2008	2009	2010
Percentage of public spending on health care as a share of total government spending	7.1	6.8	6.5	6.8	
Number of individuals per medical doctor	994.3	968	865	839	812
Number of individuals per dentist	5450.0	5447	4490		3370
Number of inhabitants per pharmacist	4490.5	5020	3386	3341	3260

Source: Ministry of Public Health.

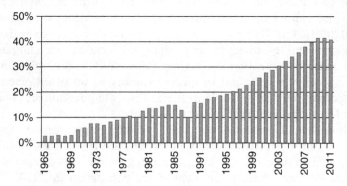

Figure 3.5: The Tunisian Middle Class (1965–2011)
Source: Brookings database, 2012.

This also meant that, as Tunisia developed economically and opened to trade, its social structure became more complex, with salaried labour becoming the predominant social category, comprising close to 70 per cent of the labour force (INS Labour Survey 2012b), more and more educated. These developments carried with them the seeds of change as per the Lipsetian modernisation hypothesis, that is, as the country developed the need for democracy and more participative institutions grew.

3.1.3.2 The Weakening of the Authoritarian Bargain and the Economic Imbalance and Social Disparities

As time passed, the cost of maintaining the authoritarian bargain was increasing, while its positive impact was gradually decreasing. In particular, the government budget was increasingly unable to satisfy growing social demand, especially in terms of employment for the tertiary-educated youth.

Investments and Employment More generally, the limits of the development policies and strategy pursued gradually became apparent, starting in the mid-1980s. The import substitution strategy led to several crises, including a severe balance of payment crisis in the mid-1980s. In 1986, (the year before Ben Ali took over), Tunisia had to go through a stabilisation and structural adjustment programme (SAP) supervised by the World Bank and the IMF. This programme included the standard SAP package: liberalisation of foreign trade, privatisation of state-owned enterprises, devaluation of the national currency and a restrictive budget policy. Although stabilisation was achieved with an adequate degree of success, the structural adjustment measures and the first wave of reforms brought the usual mixed socio-economic consequences. More unemployment and less investment were among the negative effects. Even though economic stability was quite quickly restored, the rates of growth and private investment remained below the 1970s level. The investment code under Law 120–93 and its several amendments failed to stimulate a substantial flow of foreign investment despite its high cost, estimated at the equivalent of 2.2 per cent of GDP, or 11 per cent of fiscal revenue per year (Ghazouani 2011). The privatisation of state-owned enterprises undertaken between 1987 and 2008 (217 enterprises were privatised, yielding nearly $4 billion USD) was permeated with corrupt methods, thereby contributing to the degradation of the business environment.

Furthermore, the majority of private sector enterprises remained in the low productivity, low skills, low wages category. In particular, the key manufacturing sectors (mainly the textile and garment, electrical and mechanical industries), as well as the tourism sector, are based mainly on low-skilled labour and provide limited job opportunities for better-educated workers. Hence, the demand for skilled labour has been limited and unemployment, especially among the youth and the educated, has been widespread.

The negative effects of the stabilisation and adjustment programme were exacerbated by the growing level of unemployment. According to government (INS) data, the overall average unemployment rate stood at 13 per cent in 2010, corresponding in actual numbers to approximately 500,000 unemployed (this number jumped to more than 700,000 in 2011, most of these individuals being young).

Graduate youth queued up for formal jobs, mainly government jobs. Only when they despaired of finding formal employment would they try to find other work or to start their own businesses in the private sector, often in the informal sector, which usually did not provide the type of decent work (in the ILO sense) they were seeking. Such low-quality jobs (e.g. construction work, vending) do not allow for a move out of poverty and do not attract the better educated. Unemployment rates for young university graduates (15 to 29 years old), were above 30 per cent and reached 44 per cent in the poorer regions. They were higher for girls. Elbadawi and Makdisi (Chapter 1, this volume) identify high unemployment, that is, above 10 per cent, as one of the major factors in the Arab uprisings.

Table 3.6 shows that the majority of the unemployed, more than 70 per cent, had completed secondary education at least, if not higher education.

While most of the focus has been on university graduates, not enough attention has been paid to the hundreds of thousands (about 200,000 in 2010 and 280,000 in 2012) of angry young people with a secondary education but limited skills. They have been ignored, are the least integrated and feel the least hopeful about their condition, even when employed, because they often work in the informal sector. It is important

Table 3.6: *Unemployed by Level of Education (all ages in percentages)*

Illiterate	6.2	6.6	4.2	3.6	4.8	4.5
Primary	42.0	38.3	33.8	30.3	27.0	24.1
Secondary	37.4	36.1	39.8	40.1	39.7	39.4
Higher	14.4	19.0	22.2	26.0	28.5	32.0
Total	100	100	100	100	100	100

Source: Survey on employment, INS 2012.

to keep in mind that this category of young people contributed the most to the uprising and is likely to continue to foment unrest and violence if its problems are not urgently addressed.

In short, limited economic opportunities, social exclusion and bad governance, engendered by cronyism and anti-competitive practices, allowed a privileged minority to capture the lion's share of the benefits of growth and led to a general sense of frustration in the population.

Poverty and Regional Disparities Following the revolution, in September 2011, the National Statistics Institute published revised poverty estimates showing that the national average poverty rate in 2005 stood at 11.8 per cent. Moreover, the breakdown by region showed that these national averages hid wide variations, with poverty rates as high as 29 per cent in the centre-west of the country and as low as 5–7 per cent in the centre-east and Greater Tunis regions. The north-west and centre-west (NW, CW), also the more rural regions, remain the poorest in the country (Table 3.7). Although country-wide inequality has decreased, the poor rural regions remain the most important contributors to overall inequality.

Regional disparities have largely been the outcome of the unequal distribution of public funds and investments. The centre-west and north-west regions were clearly disadvantaged during the period 1962–2010, receiving less investment than the Greater Tunis region and other eastern regions. This disparity is not surprising because most of the members of the ruling class came from these favoured regions.

Table 3.7: *Poverty and Extreme Poverty Rates by Regions (2000, 2005 and 2010)*

	Poverty			Extreme Poverty		
	2000	2005	2010	2000	2005	2010
Greater Tunis	21.0	14.6	9.1	4.3	2.3	1.3
North-East	32.1	21.6	10.3	10.5	5.4	1.8
North-West	35.3	26.9	25.7	12.1	8.9	8.8
Centre-East	21.4	12.6	8.0	6.4	2.6	1.6
Centre-West	49.3	46.5	32.3	25.5	23.2	14.3
South-East	44.3	29.0	17.9	17.5	9.6	4.9
South-West	48.7	33.2	21.5	21.7	21.1	6.4
Total	32.4	23.3	15.5	12.0	7.6	4.6

Source: INS, 2012. Premiers résultats de l'enquête nationale sur le budget, la consommation et le niveau de vie des ménages en 2010. Tunis.

Many social indicators corroborate the persistence of large disparities between regions in terms of basic infrastructure, health care and education. Despite the progress in the national health indicators, notable regional disparities in health care are evident. Whereas the life expectancy rate was estimated to be seventy-seven years in the governorates of Tunis and Sfax, it stands at seventy years for Kasserine (in the middle-west) and Tataouine in the south of the country (the population section of the Labour Survey for 2010). Similarly, infant mortality rates in the south-east (21 per mille) and the middle-west (23.6 per mille) were higher than the national level (17.8 per mille) in 2009.

Illiteracy is higher in the poorer western regions. Thus in 2010, rates exceeded 30 per cent in Jandouba (33.9 per cent), Kasserine (32.8 per cent), Siliana (32.3 per cent), Kairouan (32 per cent), Beja (31.3 per cent) and Sidi Bouzid (30.2 per cent), all in the west of the country. In contrast, it was less than 10 per cent in Greater Tunis, 14.6 per cent in Sousse and 12.5 per cent in Monastir in the eastern coastal districts.

Although the youth in the poorer regions benefited from free access to education, the quality of their training was poorer and their dropout rates were higher. Consequently, they had diminished access to good, formal jobs. This was a determining factor in the uprising: their access to education made them more aware of their social rights and of the social and regional unbalance and so provoked their anger, and sustained their aspirations for a new political and economic order.

In conclusion, relatively rapid economic development accompanied by rising levels of education and the gradual opening up of economic institutions became increasingly incompatible with persistent regional disparities, the lack of opportunity for the youth and the highly restrictive political regime. The friction caused by the disparity between relative economic openness and highly repressive and extractive political institutions was a determining factor in the rebellion and the overthrow of the autocratic regime in Tunisia. The anger the youth expressed ignited the process. The end of the authoritarian bargain was another accelerating factor.

3.2   The Path to Democratisation

The ability to abolish many of the symbols of the old regime in a peaceful manner after the 14 January rebellion and the successful election in October 2011 of the National Constituent Assembly (NCA), in spite of the absence of a legitimate government and the prevailing chaos, were early important milestones in the transition to democracy in Tunisia. The adoption of the new constitution in January 2014 and then the establishment of a new technocratic government constituted both a culminating point and a crucial step forward. The free election of a parliament and of the president in the last quarter of 2014, according to the rules laid down by the constitution and under the supervision of an independent national election commission, confirmed Tunisia's transition to political democracy. It was a very hard and uncertain road, but so also will be the way ahead. Much more remains to be done in order to consolidate this initial victory. The first challenge is to ensure the move from chaos to democracy and to generalise the rule of law. The next major step is the implementation of social and economic reforms and the achievement of a more inclusive and rapid form of economic growth.

3.2.1   *From Chaos to Democracy*

The outcome of the NCA election in October 2011 was the emergence of Ennahdha, the Islamic party, which was the winning party with 89 out of 217 seats. The remaining seats were divided between 10 parties and a large number of independent candidates. Since Ennahdha did not have a clear majority to govern by itself, it joined forces with two other parties, the CPR and Ettakatol, to form a government supported by a 138-seat majority coalition. Thus, the so-called Troika government was born, but it did not have a real political platform and many fundamental disagreements occurred between the three parties.

The main commitment of the NCA and of the government was to write the new constitution before October 2012. In fact, rather than one, it took three years to write it. The management of the transition during this period proved an extremely difficult and uncertain process. The transition has lasted much longer than originally anticipated partly because the Troika lacked vision and cohesion. Social unrest and tensions aggravated by growing unemployment and a serious economic slowdown characterised this period. Widespread chaos in all aspects of the society, including within the NCA, reflected the difficulty of reaching a national consensus. Tunisia was formerly seen as a homogeneous society with hardly any significant conflict, but the troubles and events of the revolution have shown that this impression is incorrect. Important disagreements have emerged: regional disparities, north vs. south, east vs. west, urban vs. rural, formal sector vs. informal sector. More recently, an important cleavage concerning attitudes towards religion has emerged and developed. For the Islamists, Islamic laws (that is to say the Shari'a) ought to be the fundamental pillar of social and political life, and a major reference for legislation and regulations governing society; while the rest of the population, that is, the majority, hold more modern and rather secular views; a controversy that Tunisia could have done without.

Table 3.8: *Selected Economic Indicators, 2010–2016*

	2010	2011	2012	2013	2014	2015	2016 (Estimate)
Real GDP growth (per cent)	2.6	−1.9	3.7	2.3	2.3	0.8	2.0
CPI inflation (period average, per cent)	4.4	3.5	5.9	5.7	4.8		
Current account balance (per cent of GDP)	−4.8	−7.4	−8.3	−8.4	−9.1	−8.9	−7.7
Gross official reserves (US $ billions, eop)	9.5	7.5	8.7	7.7	7.7	7.6	8.3
Gross official reserves (in months of next year's imports)	4.4	3.4	3.9	3.4	3.44.2	4.3	4.6

Source: IMF, 2016.

Moreover, the political uncertainty, the worsening of the state of security and the social unrest negatively affected the functioning of the economy since 2011, more severely in certain branches, namely tourism and the phosphate industry, than in others. National and foreign investment and economic growth slowed dramatically from around 5 per cent per year to negative growth and then to a sluggish level between 1 and 3 per cent (see Table 3.8). Concomitantly, domestic and foreign deficits increased to levels that were a matter for concern. The budget deficit increased to around 6 per cent of GDP, compared with less than 3 per cent in 2010, the trade deficit reached unprecedented levels (around 15 per cent of GDP) and inflation accelerated to close to 6 per cent in 2012 and 2013). In short, the macroeconomic situation deteriorated considerably, leading to even more discontent. As a result of this poor performance, international credit rating agencies (such as Fitch and Standard and Poor's) downgraded Tunisia's debt and financial institutions, and the Tunisian currency, the dinar, kept depreciating (Table 3.8).

The assassinations of two opposition leaders in February and July 2013 marked the emergence and then the proliferation of terrorist threats and attacks.

During the four years following the revolution, the Troika government did not really deal with the social inequalities and unemployment which were at the root of the popular uprisings. The focus was on ideological and political debate, which might have been relevant for the debate over the constitution but did not reflect any of the initial concerns of the revolution, in terms of employment, justice, dignity and the fight against corruption.

In this context, by the end of 2013, after months of confrontation, the majority of the parties and key partners reached a breakthrough. In the midst of widespread discontent and anger, and of the deep disagreements in the NCA between the Islamists and their opponents, a strong movement emerged in favour of a modern and secular constitution. The secular parties in the opposition and civil society organisations led this movement. It reached its peak in the protests against Ennahdha and the Troika government in the summer of 2013. Building on this movement, four major national organisations (trade unions, business, human rights organisations and the lawyers' national council, L'Ordre National des Avocats Tunisiens), the so-called quartet, initiated a more open and constructive national dialogue. Its purpose was to achieve what seemed impossible within the NCA, a consensus over the constitution and the main national institutions. One of the main conditions was to agree on a road map according to which the Troika government would step down. Ennahdha participated in the dialogue and indeed agreed to step down from power, and the outcome was the end of the acute political crisis, the adoption of a modern constitution and the transfer of power to an independent technocratic government. The purpose of this government is to guarantee that the preconditions for free and fair elections under the supervision of the independent national election commission[4] and according to the terms fixed by the constitution are met, as well as to run the country in the meantime.

It was a real struggle between forces pushing towards social segmentation, religious sectarianism and chaos, and those forces attached to national unity, to building modern and democratic institutions and to social and economic progress. The successful legislative and presidential elections during October–December 2014 gave victory to the latter. The main result is a successful transition towards democracy and in a sense from chaos to consensus. However, in spite of this big leap forward, the situation remains fragile and it is not a final victory because little has been achieved on the economic front.

3.2.2   The Way Forward

Can political transition towards democracy be consolidated in the context of a weak economy, and is democracy a sufficient condition for the enhancement of the economy?

---

[4] www.isie.tn

The debate over the influence of democracy on economic development is still open. However, strong arguments support both the idea that economic development variables are key determinants of a transition to democracy in the long run (Elbadawi and Makdisi, Chapter 1, this volume) and the view that democracy has a positive impact on economic development and on globalisation (Eichengreen and Leblang 2008; Quinn 2000). Other studies, based on robust theoretical and empirical evidence, show that reforms needed for inclusive economic growth are closely correlated with democracy (Amin and Djankov 2009; Giavazzi and Tabellini 2005; Giuliano, Prachi and Spilimbergo 2010). Their influence could run in both directions with a far greater effect being felt from democracy on reform, since democratic regimes undertake economic reform in order to enhance the welfare of the population and improve the quality of institutions. Autocratic regimes are less likely to carry out reforms because they seek to preserve rents and protect their elite.

In the case of Tunisia, as of late 2016, this debate is more specific and is focused on the factors that will influence the next phase in the consolidation of the transition process, which mainly concerns the economic sphere. The complete stabilisation of the country and the strengthening of the democratic process depend on the ability of the current and next governments to design and implement a coherent economic strategy that responds to key economic and social demands, mainly of the youth that led the revolt (jobs first and foremost). Otherwise, if key economic and social expectations are not dealt with adequately (given that they cannot be fully met in the short run), the transition process will remain under threat. Unrest and social division may increase. A genuine dynamic and dialectical relationship exists between economic factors, institution building and the transition to democracy, but at this stage it is economic factors that are the determining ones, far more so than any of the others.

Implementing a comprehensive strategy with a focus on creating employment opportunities for the youth and inclusive growth should be the current policy priority and also for the coming years. Employment should target young men and young women equally, given that female participation in the labour market remains very weak (persistently around 25 per cent) and their unemployment rate is twice that of men (23.3 per cent for women, 13.9 per cent for men in the first quarter of 2013). But this will not occur without the empowerment of the youth and their participation in national policy and decision making.

Obviously, neither government nor the public sector can provide jobs for all the unemployed immediately or meet the employment needs of the ever-increasing numbers of young people. The main role for the government in the long run is building the right environment for the creation of increasing numbers of good, formal, private sector jobs. Nevertheless, during the transition phase, the rapid formulation by the government of a credible employment programme is a crucial condition for the consolidation of the nascent democracy. This programme, in addition to immediately boosting private sector growth and job creation, should include, within the limits of the national budget, a package of government-supported jobs.

Despite a currently uncertain landscape, Tunisia has a unique opportunity to free its economy from the bottlenecks and red tape that previously impeded its development and to implement the institutional reforms necessary for creating a climate conducive to rapid and inclusive economic growth.

So far, little has been achieved in this direction. Growth and job creation are still way below expectations. Thus, although it is still unlikely that the country will fall back to chaos, the outcome of the next phase is still uncertain.

Hope may come from the youth, who will continue to be highly dynamic and the main driving force for reform until their demands are satisfied. More than half a million young unemployed, most of them with university or at least secondary school education, have overcome their fears and apprehensions which were created by the repression of the past regime and might, in the future, demonstrate again should their demands for jobs and dignity continue to be ignored. The emergence of a vibrant civil society is also an important source of support for forces in favour of completing the transition. This means that the youth and civil society could, paradoxically, generate more instability and, at the same time, push the government and all the other political partners to take actions that favour inclusive growth.

The final outcome will depend on a number of factors which determine the number of possible transition paths. Is there a single path (or a single equilibrium) or multiple identifiable divergent paths? In other words, is democracy a state of steady equilibrium and the only equilibrium to which the transition may lead? If not, what is described as multiple equilibrium, are there several alternative possible regimes that could materialise and hence the country might then find itself switching from one equilibrium to another? The multiple alternative paths may include the emergence of a new dictatorship or a move to a fully fledged democracy or to an intermediate form. These regimes may be more or less stable. A single stable equilibrium would mean that, logically, were there to be any shock or deviation from the equilibrium, the existing powers and mechanisms could ensure a return to the initial stable situation.

This question was relevant in the early days of the Arab Spring and it remains relevant now, after the successful political transition phase in Tunisia. Our view is that democracy is the only possible steady state for Tunisia and more generally for the Arab Spring countries as a whole, but the mechanisms leading to such a steady state are uncertain and may even be too weak or not effective. The transition to this steady state may be slow and, if not countered, often not linear. Instability and even chaos may persist for quite a while, maybe even for a long time as in Libya, Syria and Yemen. However, a return to autocracy would not be a stable alternative; it may not last.

In the Tunisian case, the initial threat has been due to the existence of only one strong political formation, the Ennahdha Party, which seeks to build an Islamic state and to dominate. The corollary is that, if it succeeds, the opposing political forces would be reduced to mere followers of events (if not banned) and the country would head towards an Islamist autocracy. Our point is that this is not sustainable. Equally unsustainable would be a path that seeks to suppress the Islamist movement, as in the past two decades in Tunisia (and currently in Egypt). Ennahdha (like Islamists in general) is here to stay but it lacks sufficient resources to respond to key and urgent social demands and needs, and it does not have enough support to achieve and sustain a total predominance. It is a strong party but does not have the requisite complete support of the security forces (the army and/or the police), and it cannot rely on any enduring source of rent income to establish a new authoritarian bargain (Tunisia is not a resource-rich country).

Given that the secularist forces have gained a certain degree of strength, the question is: will they be able to efficiently address the economic and social issues and aspirations in order to complete the transition process and to ensure its consolidation? Our main point again is that the only alternative to the democratic transition is simply chaos and instability. A stable democratic path is contingent on the design and implementation of an appropriate economic and social strategy involving a number of important reforms in the coming years. The main political partners seem aware of this crucial condition, and Tunisia has the key ingredients for successfully completing the process. The first few years, and then the first decade, will be crucial ones and will determine the viability and the stability of the ongoing transition. The most serious threat comes from the persistent divergent forces that are pushing towards division and social fragmentation. Some conflicts based on regional, tribal, religious and ideological divides are still there. The potential losers from the necessary political and economic reforms are also quite powerful. There are, however, also forces for cohesion and cooperation. The key question is which of these forces will prevail, and whether the channels of cohesion and dialogue are strong enough to keep the country together. In most of the Arab Spring countries, the forces of conflict and division have been so far stronger than the forces of cohesion and social progress. In Tunisia, based on the trends observed, it is reasonable to expect that it is the forces of cohesion that will prevail.

3.3   Conclusion

The Tunisians have proved that they can disagree and can argue very strongly about political and collective issues, but at the end of the day they can manage to reach an agreement in spite of the deep cracks that have appeared in the social body of the nation. Tunisian society has proved its ability to develop consensus out of a diversity of views about social choices. The 2014 elections show that not only are the Islamists not the majority in Tunisia, but the secularists (not opposed to Islam but to Islamism), who form the majority, are less fragmented than in 2011. The outcome of the 2014 elections shows that the initially fragmented secularist majority was able, after many failed attempts, to form a broad coalition. Nida Tounes was the party that won against Ennahdha in the October 2014 legislative and presidential elections. Ennahdha accepted its second place in the results. This is a major step and a necessary condition for the consolidation of democracy. The remaining challenge is to build on this successful, but fragile phase and to achieve the necessary consensus on economic and social strategy.

For the time being (2016), uncertainty remains a key word and chaos, of various possible degrees, is not to be totally excluded. However, there is a greater reason for hope in the case of Tunisia. Popular movements guided by political parties and civil society organisations expressed in many ways, in particular through protest and participation in the 2011 and 2014 elections, their awareness of the need to save the country and to make the revolution a genuine opportunity for its betterment. Great challenges remain but, logically, the fundamental conditions for complete transition to a stable pluralistic democratic regime have been fulfilled.

Convergence on this steady state requires effective leadership and greater cohesion and, above all, a form of innovative, participative and inclusive economic strategy, one focusing on society's expectations and the aspirations of the youth. This is, to a certain extent, in the making, but it remains in part hypothetical. The youth, especially the angry and unemployed, those who have been ignored and the least integrated, remain the main driving force for change and a source of hope for the success of Tunisian democracy.

It is not enough to have pluralistic and fair elections. The development of solid institutions driven by the desire to achieve social objectives is also crucial. Inclusive political and economic institutions should go hand in hand. Inclusive growth, decent jobs for the youth, the challenge of confronting regional disparities and poverty should be top priorities for political leaders and should be taken into account when designing political and economic institutions.

The situation has not stabilised, but the only conceivable steady state is through a successful democratic and pluralistic transition; the alternative would be instability but not autocracy. However, there is no method by which one can rigorously estimate the probability that this will be soon achieved or not achieved.

4   Egypt: The Protracted Transition from Authoritarianism to Democracy and Social Justice

Noha El Mikawy, Mohamed Mohieddin and Sarah El Ashmaouy

4.1   Introduction

It is important to state at the outset that Egypt's revolutions of 25 January 2011 and 30 June 2013 are the latest in a series of waves that constitute a protracted attempt to establish inclusive and liberal democratic development in the country. The first wave extended from 1923 to 1952 and was known as the liberal era of modern Egypt. It was characterised by political liberalisation under occupation and no social programme of equity. The second wave, from 1952 to 1954, was characterised by political struggle between the military, the Muslim Brotherhood and the pre-1952 aristocratic elite. The winner was the military elite; it consolidated its power and initiated the Nasserist regime which introduced social programmes and one-party rule. The third wave of protest demanding democracy in 1968 was meant to correct the military and political failures of the Nasserist era. The fourth wave spanned the period 1976 to 1987, during which Egypt had four rounds of multi-party parliamentary elections and witnessed the dismantling of the Nasserist social programme in favour of a liberal economic programme that then gave way to crony capitalism.[1] By the mid-1980s, the political regime had adopted structural adjustment and stabilisation policies which signified the beginning of a flagrant abandonment of the social contract that had been in place.

The state was now no longer committed to fulfil its constitutional obligation of employment for all. A series of liberalisation policies, along with structural adjustment and stabilisation and, finally, privatisation, ended any commitment to maintain equitable social and economic rights.

---

[1] Earlier attempts to retreat from these obligations by lifting subsidies on basic food items and other goods had resulted in massive riots in January 1977, thus exposing the fragility of political liberalisation under economic stress.

This signalled the beginning of the story of socio-economic exclusion, police brutality and shrinking political liberties.

In what follows we detail the major elements of this story, relying on empirical data. Three categories of increasing exclusion are examined. The first is economic and pertains to unemployment, informalisation and poverty, as well as the rent economy. The second is social and relates to health, education, gender, and food and fuel subsidies. The third is institutional whereby we examine the politics of exclusion.

In so doing, this chapter aims to examine the structural factors (economic, social, cultural and political) that explain the waves of democratisation that have taken place since 2011. Furthermore, this chapter looks at the prospects for transition through the lens of four potential trajectories.

The protracted transition in Egypt, as explained here, takes up the Elbadawi and Makdisi approach, namely a long-term view of transitions as they unfold reflecting alternating periods of upturn and downturn. Given that Egypt is a populous non-oil country, we focus on the unemployment story, the patchy modernisation process and the partial openness of the political system in the thirty years preceding the 2011 transition.

The literature on transitions to democracy acknowledges the neighbourhood effect. In the case of Egypt, the neighbourhood effect has been largely unfavourable. Supporters of the Muslim Brotherhood's rise to power (Turkey, Qatar and Iran, each for its own reasons) and opponents of progressive liberal change in Egypt (Saudi Arabia, UAE and Kuwait) have been conservative illiberal forces. The outcome of the situation in Syria is likely to affect Egypt, though it is difficult to assess in which direction. The situation in Libya and Sudan, two immediate neighbours of Egypt, accentuates the adverse neighbourhood effect. In the Western world, the United States and the Europeans adopted a hesitant position, maintaining their concern for stability in the Middle East. Western policy towards Egypt tended to adjust to unfolding events on the ground without exerting a markedly favourable impact on liberal democratic prospects. The authors of this chapter are well aware that regional and international forces could influence the path Egypt will take in the years to come. In this chapter, however, the authors focus on domestic dynamics that highlight the political, social and economic forces at play within Egypt.

4.2   The Drivers of the Transition

The Egyptian case offers several drivers that have, in combination, produced an explosive context which promised to initiate a transition to a more liberal democratic regime and to restore a more progressive discourse on social justice to Egypt's development agenda. We take up the structural drivers first, followed by the institutional and socio-political ones.

4.2.1 Structural Drivers of Economic and Social Exclusion

Elbadawi and Makdisi's analysis (Chapter 1, this volume) pertaining to factors influencing democratic transitions arrives at the conclusion that: (a) natural resources impede democratic transitions when managed by less than fully democratic regimes and (b) high unemployment, beyond a certain threshold (above 10 per cent), *promotes* democratic transitions.[2] In this section we discuss the rentier economy and unemployment, adding other structural drivers of exclusion.

4.2.1.1 The Rentier Economy in Egypt

While Egypt cannot be described as a full rentier economy (like the small oil-rich economies), it is still true that rent has systematically played an important role in its economy, politics and social life for the past half century. Economically, rentier economies lack incentives to create jobs because they neglect work-intensive production sectors. In this respect, before 2011 Egypt was no exception. With population growth, the weakness of the productive sectors led to poor job creation and thus to severe social marginalisation. Politically, rents allowed the state to have access to revenues independent of the production process, thus freeing the state from the need to raise revenue domestically from taxation. This relative independence of government from the taxpayers alleviated the pressure on the regime for political accountability.

Rent and foreign sources of income never exceeded 15 per cent during the 1990s except during 1993–94 and 1994–95 and declined to about 12.5 per cent at the turn of the millennium (El Beblawi 2008). Since then, as Table 4.1 shows, the relative share of rent and foreign sources in the Egyptian economy has been rising systematically, accounting for about one third of the GDP between 2005 and 2007.

Workers' remittances in Egypt have represented a substantial, stable flow of rent. Along with India, Mexico, the Philippines and Turkey, Egypt is one of the five largest recipients of remittances in the world. Until the late 1990s, their relative weight and absolute sum was the equivalent of the revenues from tourism and the Suez Canal combined. They represented the single largest source of foreign exchange revenue.

---

[2] http://siteresources.worldbank.org/INTLM/Resources/390041-1141141801867/227536
4-1278449864397/8InformalityENG.pdf

Table 4.1: *Rent and Foreign Sources in the Egyptian Economy 2005–2010 US$ Billion*

Year	Oil Exports*	Tourism**	Suez Canal	Workers' Remittances***	Foreign Aid	Total Rent	GDP	Rent as % of GDP
2001	2.6	4.3	1.8	2.7	0.7	12.1	97.3	12.5
2002	2.4	3.3	1.8	4.3	0.4	12.2	91.5	13.3
2003	3.2	3.4	2.2	3.6	0.9	13.3	83.4	15.8
2004	3.9	3.8	2.8	3.9	0.4	14.9	80.1	18.6
2005	5.0	6.8	3.3	5.0	6.8	26.9	89.8	29.9
2006	7.4	7.9	3.5	5.3	9.9	33.1	107.4	30.8
2007	7.4	10.3	4.1	7.7	12.6	42.1	130.3	32.3
2008	11.2	12.1	5.2	8.7	7.2	44.4	162.4	27.3
2009	7.9	11.7	4.8	7.1	3.1	34.6	188.6	18.3
2010	8.0	13.6	4.5	7.7	4.2	38.0	218.5	17.4

Sources: For the years 2001–10, see www.economywatch.com/economic-statistics/Egypt/ GDP. For 2005–10 data on oil revenues and GDP, see IMF, *World Economic Outlook*, 2011 and 2012. For tourism, the Suez Canal, workers' remittances and foreign aid, see The World Bank, WDI and GDF, 2010. Cols 7 and 9 are calculated by the author from data in the table.

*Oil and gas represented another rentier revenue, besides the Suez Canal and proceeds from public sector exports. Egypt possesses modest reserves of oil, but the situation is brighter with respect to natural gas reserves. Egypt imports petroleum products, but remains a net exporter in energy products.

**The only sources of foreign exchange available to the banks were the sovereign sources of tourism, which average about 12.5 per cent of GDP for 2008–10 (Table 4.1).

***Note that workers' remittances are a special form of rent. From a worker's point of view, he/she is earning his/her income against expended effort or work. However, from a recipient country's point of view, remittances are more akin to aid or non-requited money transfers (El Beblawi 2008, p. 21–22).

Remittances to Egypt constitute an important part of family economics. In fact, migration to the Gulf regenerated the middle class, allowing it to maintain its pattern of consumption and enabling its members to marry their children off and embark on a limited level of investment. Remittances also ensured the continued survival of the poorer classes of migrants. They allowed migrant workers to secure necessary social services such as education and health care for their relatives as state expenditure on basic services declined. Increasing private expenditure on basic services, thus, put less pressure on the state and held it less accountable for its mismanagement of the limited resources available.

The Egyptian government's attitude towards the export of natural gas is an example of the rentier mentality. In late April 2006, headlines in major governmental newspapers announced the inauguration of the largest plant for liquefied gas in Egypt and that Egypt would, therefore, be the sixth largest exporter of natural gas in the world. Less than four months later, the government announced its intention to acquire nuclear reactors because of expected future shortages in energy resources. It is generally known that the oil and gas reserves in Egypt will be depleted within two or three decades. Under the circumstances, one would question the wisdom of expanding Egypt's gas exports. However, within the framework of the rentier mentality, gas exports are the easiest way to generate foreign exchange (El Beblawi 2008: 25).

The decline in the amount of rent in 2009 and 2010 to levels comparable to those which prevailed in the mid-1990s should not be taken as an indication of an improved economic performance. The GDP data for 2006 and 2007 in Table 4.1 indicate an annual economic growth rate of 7.1 and 7.2 per cent per annum respectively, compared to about 5 per cent between 2004 and 2005. In 2006, the government decided to transfer the control and supervision of private retirement funds (\$28 billion)[3] to the Ministry of Finance, which included these funds as part of the national economic account, thus showing seeming economic growth. Given that these funds were the equivalent of about 3 per cent of the GDP in 2006–07, this means the real growth rate for 2006 and 2007 was around 4 per cent, that is, the real growth rate declined.

4.2.1.2 *Unemployment and Informalisation*

Unemployment and informalisation mean a lack of social protection and job security, and uncertainty about the future. The latter also means excessive exploitation of the workforce, with limited opportunities for workers to protect their rights through legal measures. All of this accentuated a sense of social injustice in Egypt which manifested prior to January 2011 in successive demonstrations temporary workers organised in public and private sector companies who were demanding that their jobs be made permanent.

Recent available evidence from labour market surveys shows considerable improvement in conditions over the past decade and half, as expressed by the declining unemployment rate (Assaad and Roushdy 2007). However, this improvement was accompanied by increasing informalisation of the economy. We define informalisation as labour that is deprived of any formal contractual agreement, which implies that the

---

[3] In Egypt, employees in both government and private sector companies resorted to the creation of private funds to supplement their meagre state retirement benefits. These private funds were subject to legal control and supervision by the Ministry of Social Affairs. As such, these funds did not show in the national economic accounts in previous years. Over the years, the accumulated sums of these funds reached L.E. 200 billion (US\$ 28 billion).

worker is not socially protected. According to the World Bank, in Egypt informality rose between 1998 and 2008. The percentage of those not contributing to social security rose also during this period, from 49 per cent to 58 per cent, and the percentage of those working without formal contracts rose from 56 per cent to 62 per cent.[4]

While accurate statistics on the informal sector are not available, one can largely discern the state of affairs from the growth in the number of SMEs, a good portion of which tends to be informal. As shown in table 4.2, the number of small and micro enterprises (SME) – defined as those enterprises that employ up to 50 workers – was estimated in 1998 to be around 3.3 million economic units, compared to 2.9 million in 1988. As to total employment in the SME sector, by 1998 this had grown to around 7.3 million, equivalent to a 2.8 per cent average annual growth rate or around 38 per cent of total employment. Given the same rate of growth, it is estimated that the number of workers in the sector grew to 8.3 million by 2004. The Institute of National Planning (INP) and United Nations Development Program (UNDP) expected that the number of employed workers in SMEs would reach almost 12 million by 2015 (UNDP/INP, 2005, pp. 107–09).[5]

Informal employment can also be measured using Workforce Sample Survey (LFSS) data, which define informality by the number of private sector workers employed outside establishments (including agriculture). Under this definition, informal employment reached 10.8 million in 2008, representing 48.1 per cent of total employment. Female workers constituted approximately 20 per cent of informal employment, representing 48 per cent of total female employment. The data show that almost 23.7 per cent work in the government and 3.4 per cent in the public sector, while the formal private sector employs 22.9 per cent and the informal private sector employs 48.1 per cent.[6] The International Labour Organization (ILO), for example, argues that the increase in informality in Egypt is due to the shrinking of the public sector (a composition effect). Yet other observers have demonstrated an augmentation in informality, even in the supposedly formal segment of the private sector, whereby it increasingly tends to adopt informal employment strategies that have

[4] According to the World Bank study that produced preliminary results a few weeks before the Egyptian uprising in January 2011, those who were informally self-employed made up 28 per cent of total employment; informal enterprises, which by definition do not contribute to social security benefits, took up 44.5 per cent of the workforce (World Bank Quick Notes Series #49, December 2011).

[5] According to the census of 2006, Egypt has 2.4 million SMEs with fewer than ten workers, which employ 5.2 million workers in total, and another 39,000 SMEs with between ten and fifty workers. SMEs account for more than 80 per cent of employment in Egypt's non-agricultural private sector, including both formal and informal (www.mof.gov.eg/mofgal lerysource/english/overview.pdf).

[6] Heba Nassar, Growth, Employment Policies and Economic Linkages: Egypt. Employment Sector. Employment Working Paper No. 85 (Geneva: ILO, 2011).

resulted in the rise of the relative share of informality from 60.8 per cent to 67.3 per cent and in the public sector from 2.5 per cent to 4.3 per cent between 1998 and 2006.[7] This shift has taken place despite very limited mobility between the public , formal and informal sectors as indicated by data available for the two years 2008 and 2009 (Table 4.3).

Over the past three decades, more and more new entrants to the labour market have started their careers in the informal sector; those who moved to formality were likely to be the better-educated males. J. Wahba (2000) found that in the early 1970s, 20 per cent of workers began their working lives in informal jobs, but by 1998, 69 per cent of new workers started in informal employment. The available data show an increase in the proportion of first jobs without contracts between 1975 and 2005. Informal workers in 1998, who had become formal by 2006, that is, movers, were predominantly male. Another important dimension of the transition to formality was education. Those with university degrees who were employed in 1998 without a contract had a 16 per cent probability of having a contract in 2006 compared to around 3 per cent among the illiterate (Assaad 2007; Wahba 2009).

4.2.1.3 Impoverishing the Middle Class

One of the aims of Egypt's First Republic of 1952 was the expansion of the middle class. Thus, the gradual impoverishment of the middle class announced the dwindling legitimacy of the First Republic. Furthermore, the impoverishment of the middle class announced the failure of social justice policies, as a small and economically weak middle class indicates poor upward social mobility. The progressive impoverishment of the middle class after the rising expectations of the brief socialist era from 1956 to 1971 is documented by recent research undertaken by the Egyptian Centre for Economic Studies and in a regional paper published by the UN University World Institute for Development Economics Research.[8]

Several factors lay behind this impoverishment. The state's relinquishment of its responsibility for creating jobs in the public sector and the civil bureaucracy, as well as reduced public expenditure on job-creating industries and basic social services, are among the main causes of this impoverishment. Because a considerable percentage of the middle class depends largely on the government for employment, low wages and salaries, especially in the public sector, contributed to the impoverishment of the

---

[7] ILO-World Bank, The Challenge of Informality in MENA. Promoting Job Quality and Productive Employment in the Middle East and North Africa: What Works? (Turin: October 2010). siteresources.worldbank.org/INTLM/Resources/390041-1141141801.

[8] ECES Policy Brief #29, April 2012, pp. 2–3 and K. Abu-Ismail and N. Sarangi. Rethinking the Measurement of the Middle Class. WIDER Working Paper 2015/023, February 2015, wider.unu.edu.

middle class. Starting salaries remained below the minimum wage and could be increased only through bonuses and other privileges, which normally constituted 80 per cent of the monthly wage/salary.[9] Though salaries in the private sector were higher, social protection coverage remained deficient because many private sector workers had temporary contracts with insecure social protection coverage in a country where universal social protection is not available.

The informalisation of the economy is a corollary of the impoverishment of the middle class. The informal sector is not only a sponge that soaks up entrants to the job market from among the poor, illiterate and unskilled; it also acts as a magnet for those members of the middle class whose salaries are not sufficient to allow them to make ends meet and for university graduates seeking a job. According to the World Bank, in Egypt the percentage of those in the informal sector with tertiary education almost doubled in the period 1998–2008 from 11 per cent to 20.5 per cent.[10] According to Safwat El-Nahas, head of the Central Agency for Organisation and Administration (CAOA), around 500,000 Egyptian civil servants were hired on temporary contracts and some continued working under these conditions for ten years.[11] According to the World Bank, sectors of the economy known for quality jobs (such as public enterprises, construction, wholesale and retail trade, transportation and communication, manufacturing and financial services) were increasingly offering informal jobs. As a result, the informal economy of the self-employed and unregistered, or the employed in unregistered micro and small enterprises, comprised 36 per cent of the Egyptian GDP.[12]

4.2.1.4 *Pronounced Poverty and Spatial Inequality*

In the results of four successive official Household Income and Expenditure Surveys conducted by the Central Agency for Public Mobilisation and Statistics (CAPMAS) during the past decade and a half, one notices the large regional variance that characterises poverty in Egypt. Poverty is worst in Upper Egypt, where in 2000 more than 20 per cent of the population was designated poor in seven of the nine governorates. A decade later, the same

[9] In a recent study of public hospital physicians, the basic salary of a physician was said to be less than 300 Egyptian pounds a month ($49); with bonuses, it goes up a little, but remains below the minimum wage.
[10] http://siteresources.worldbank.org/INTLM/Resources/390041-1141141801867/22753 64-1278449864397/8InformalityENG.pdf
[11] http://english.ahram.org.eg/NewsContent/3/12/36314/Business/Economy/Half-a-mil lion-public-servants-will-get-minimum-wa.aspx
[12] http://siteresources.worldbank.org/INTLM/Resources/390041-1141141801867/22753 64-1278449864397/8InformalityENG.pdf

region showed an alarming rise in the proportion of the poor, who repre-sented 51 per cent and 29 per cent of the rural and urban population respectively. By contrast, poverty was the lowest in the metropolitan region, where only 5.1 per cent of households were poor, that is, living below the poverty line, thus constituting only 4 per cent of the country's total number of poor. Between 1995 and 2000, the incidences of poverty declined by about one third in the metropolitan region. Since then, for most of the metropolitan region governorates, income poverty has continued to decline, reaching a low of 6.9 per cent in 2008–09, yet by the advent of 2010–11 it rose to 10 per cent, although this was still lower than its level of 13.1 percent in 1995. More noticeable is the significant increase in the Upper Egypt region. Rural Upper Egypt, where 25 per cent of the total population lives, has continued to have the highest rates of income poverty, accounting for 51 per cent of the population in 2010–11 (twice the national rate). In Lower Egypt, urban poverty declined considerably between 1999 and 2000 and 2004 and 2005, yet it almost doubled by the advent of 2008–09 and has stagnated since. As for the border regions, urban poverty has declined since the 1990s, whereas rural poverty has increased threefold since then.

Hence, social policies of the successive regimes of Nasser, Sadat and Mubarak have failed to redress a systematic bias against the rural areas in general and rural Upper Egypt in particular, leading to a geographic concentration of poverty and hence to the exclusion of large segments of the Egyptian population from sharing in the benefits of growth. To be sure, the rural populations took part in the revolution. They were notice-ably present in Tahrir Square between 28 January and 11 February 2011, and in other regional capitals, and they continued to demonstrate against the government in the form of road and railway blockades and marches. The formation of numerous independent trade unions and farmers' and fishermen's associations was another indication of their discontent.

Data on income and human poverty as measured according to the UNDP human poverty index provide a different picture of poverty in Egypt. Table 4.4 gives the overall rates of both income and human poverty in the period 1995–2011. The data show that while improvement in human poverty standards was on the rise, income poverty was going up. In other words, while people in Egypt were becoming better educated, they were at the same time getting poorer. With more education Egyptians expected more from life, yet they were getting less under Mubarak, which led to a mounting sense of frustration which, in turn, helped feed the increasing popular demands for change. As such, educa-tion became a mechanism of exclusion rather than of inclusion. While this is not restricted to the Mubarak era but dates back to Sadat's time, it reached a peak in the time of Mubarak.

Table 4.2: *Number of Small Economic Units According to Formality/Informality*

Year	Formal	Informal	Total
1988	502,325(17.1)	2,432,522(82.9)	2,934,847(100.0)
1998	546,445(16.4)	2,776,031(83.6)	3,322,476(100.0)
% Change	8.7	14.1	13.2
Annual % of Increase	0.9	1.4	1.3

Source: Calculated by the authors from ELMS98 data files.

Table 4.3: *Inter-sectoral Mobility in Egypt, 2008/2009 (Figures in hundreds)*

	Public 2009	Formal Private 2009	Informal Private 2009	Total
Public 2008	95%	3%	2%	100%
	1,113	30	27	1,170
Fr.Private 2008	20%	45%	35%	100%
	103	229	173	505
Inf.Private 2008	4%	8%	88%	100%
	75	155	1,681	1,911
	1,291	414	1,881	3,586

Source: ILO data base.
Note: the figures indicate the actual number of people that have shifted during 2008/2009 from one sector to another.

4.2.1.5 Growing Social Exclusion

Public expenditure on social services, food subsidies, education and health has been either mismanaged or cut. Public spending on education declined, from 16.5 per cent in 2002 to 11.5 per cent in 2006, as a percentage of total expenditure, and from 5.2 per cent to 4.0 per cent, as a percentage of GDP (UNDP 2008). Meanwhile spending on health has remained very low, not exceeding 4 per cent of government expenditure. Such a decline is not without ramifications for equity, equality and social exclusion.

4.2.1.5.1 Bad Targeting of Subsidies   Subsidies are major mechanisms that are theoretically intended to combat poverty and inequality in Egypt. The structure of subsidies in Egypt covers agriculture, transport, student health insurance, medical and milk subsidies for children (amounting to 4 per cent of all subsidised items), housing (1 per cent), loan subsidies (1 per cent), export promotion (5 per cent) food (22 per cent) and energy (67 per cent).[13] Together they account for about 10.8 per cent of GDP.[14] Despite the high level of spending on the safety-net and subsidy system, subsidies did not benefit those at the bottom of society. Not only did public policies fail to address income and human poverty issues, but deteriorating economic conditions forced the middle classes to partake of the resources the state allocated for the poor.

Looking into the various components of subsidisation, that is, food, electricity, energy and safety net transfers, the data show clearly that the policies of the state were entirely biased towards the richer upper 20 per cent of income groups. In 2004, the top income quintile had 24 per cent of subsidised food allocations compared to 17 per cent for the lowest income quintile, while the shares of the three middle-income groups from the bottom up stood at 18, 19 and 22 per cent respectively. By the advent of 2008–09, as shown in Table 4.4, very little had changed in this state of affairs.

With regard to the energy subsidy, the richest 20 per cent of the population amassed 34 per cent of electricity and energy as opposed to only 13 per cent given to the poorest quintile. Only in safety-net cash transfers did the poorest 20 per cent of the Egyptian population outdo their richest counterparts since they accessed 24 per cent and 17 per cent, respectively.

In sum, rich households benefited to a disproportionately greater degree than poor households from the energy subsidies. Figure 4.1 shows the direct benefits to households from four subsidised petroleum products. Individuals in the richest quintile received two and a half times more of the energy subsidy than the poor.

[13] Magda Kandil, Reforms of Public Finance in Egypt: Energy Subsidies in Egypt. Meeting on Price Subsidies in Egypt: Alternatives for Reform (Cairo: ECES, 2012). PowerPoint presentation. Available on the Internet.
[14] The government projected that it would pay almost $16 billion to subsidise energy in 2012 (www.cfr.org/egypt/reforming-egypts-untenable-subsidies/p27885). The fiscal cost of food subsidies reached about 2 per cent of gross domestic product (GDP) in 2008–09 (LE 21.1 billion, or US$ 3.8 billion) after stabilising at around 0.9 per cent of GDP between the fiscal years 1996–97 and 2000–01 (The World Bank 2010). The rising cost of food subsidies can be explained by increased international commodity prices, exchange rate depreciation, increased number and/or quantities of subsidised food items and expanding coverage of ration cards.

Table 4.4: *Poverty Incidence in Egypt by Region (headcount index), 1995/1996–2010/2011 The definition of poverty is that of the World Bank (US$ 1.25 per person/day).*

Year	1995/1996		1999/2000		2004/2005		2008/2009		2010/2011	
Region	Urban	Rural	Urban	Rural	Urban	Rural	Urban	Rural	Urban	Rural
Urban Governorates	13.1	N.A.	9.01	N.A.	8.5	N.A.	6.9	N.A.	10.0	N.A.
Lower Egypt Governorates	8.34	21.53	17.93	11.26	8.9	20.8	7.2	16.7	10.0	17.0
Upper Egypt Governorates	10.82	29.32	36.33	34.68	26.1	43.6	21.3	44.0	29.0	51.0
Frontier Governorates	5.63	13.82	10.38	11.33	N.A.	N.A.	5.0	23.0	4.0	33.0
Total	11.02	24.80	9.21	22.07	N.A.	N.A.	N.A.	N.A.	N.A.	N.A.

Source: For 1995–96, as cited in El-Laithy et al. Poverty and Economic Growth in Egypt, 1995–2000. World Bank Policy Research Working Paper 3068 (June 2003), p. 23. For 2004–05, quoted after The World Bank, Arab Republic of Egypt, Upper Egypt: Pathways to Shared Growth. (Washington, DC, Oct. 2009), p. 1. For 2008–09 and 2010–11, see www.capmas.gov.eg.

Notes: N.A. Not Applicable or data not available. In 1995–96, north Sinai includes poverty incidence estimates for south Sinai.

Source: For 2004/2005 see The World Bank, 2005; For 2008/2009 see S. Aboulenein, H. El-Laithy, O. Helmy, H. Kheir-El-Din and D. Mandour (2010).

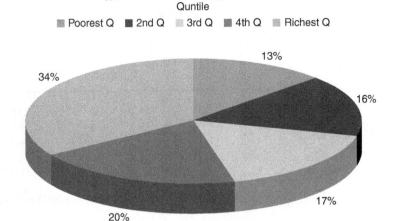

Figure 4.1: Egypt: Distribution of Energy Subsidies by Quintile in 2004
Source: Deutsche Bank AG DB Research, 2013.

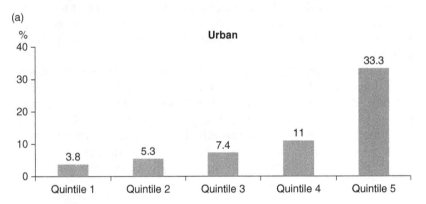

Figure 4.2a: Egypt: Distribution of Energy Subsidies by Quintile in 2004

There are also considerable rural/urban disparities as far as subsidies are concerned that cut across income quintiles. Unfortunately, the only available information on subsidised expenditure on energy dates back to 2004. As shown in Figures 4.2a and 4.2b, while the poorest urban quintile accessed 3.8 per cent of these allocations, their rural counterparts enjoyed an edge, accessing 5.6 per cent. In contrast, the wealthiest quintile of the urban population received 33.3 per cent, whereas the rural quintile consumed

(b)

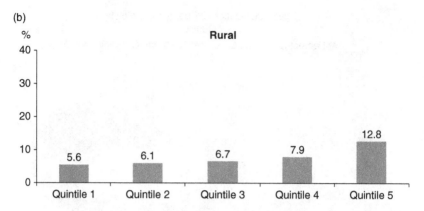

Figure 4.2b: Egypt: Distribution of Energy Subsidies by Quintile in 2004
Source: 2a and b quoted after Kandil (2012).

only 12.8 per cent. If the fourth quintile of urban population is added to the wealthiest one (the 40 per cent wealthiest in the population), then its proportional share rises to 44.3 per cent, in contrast to 20.7 per cent for the wealthiest rural 40 per cent. Overall, Egypt's urban population consumes 60.9 per cent while its rural population claims 39.9 per cent of subsidised petroleum.

Not only are the Egyptian poor the ones who rely heavily on subsidised goods and services; the middle classes also rely on subsidies because of the deterioration in their living standards and economic condition. As shown in Figure 4.3, in 2004 the richest 20 per cent consumed 28 per cent of all subsidised goods and services compared to the poorest quintile's 16 per cent. Further, the pattern of food subsidy allocation by population share or by poverty share still favours urban Egypt, especially Cairo.

4.2.1.5.2 Education   The statistics for education show considerable improvement in access to schooling over the years. For example, between 1992 and 1996, the number of classrooms across Egypt increased by 53 per cent, and by 1997, nearly all Egyptian villages had primary schools. Gross enrolment rates improved at all levels of education, exceeding the enrolment rates in lower-middle-income countries for secondary and tertiary education. Notwithstanding improvements in access, social expenditure did not always reach the intended groups. In education, all students, irrespective of family income, are entitled to free state-run education.

Table 4.5: *Percentage of Income and Human Poverty in Egypt by Governorates, 1995–2011*

Year	Income Poverty	Human Poverty
1995/1996	19.4	N.A.
1999/2000	16.7	24.8
2004/2005	19.6	22.5
2008/2009	21.6	22.1
2010/2011	25.2	N.A.

Source: The figures for 1995 are from Table 4.3, and the rest is calculated from Household Income and Expenditure Surveys for the corresponding years.
Source: See Galal (2003).

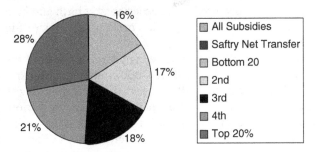

Figure 4.3: Distribution of All Subsidies and Safety Net Value by Quintile FY 2004
Source: World Bank (2005).

Speaking in terms of quintile income distribution, this was further reinforced by a biased allocation of public expenditure in the education sector in favour of the non-poor, that is, the middle, fourth and highest income quintiles. The most recently available data date back to 1997. They show that the lowest quintile of the population had access to only 3 per cent of higher education expenditure, while for the richest quintile it was exactly fifteen times higher (Table 4.5). Similarly, the richest quintile received 24 per cent of the government's expenditure on education compared to 15 per cent for the poorest one.

Exacerbating this problem is the low quality of education. It produced graduates who lacked the necessary skills the labour market required, making graduates unemployable and thus contributing to rising unemployment. In 1998, unemployment among the educated was 9.6 per cent, compared to only 1.8 per cent among illiterates. The potential for being unemployed and unemployable as an educated person further discouraged the poor from partaking in any degree of education. The diminishing financial returns of education contributed to the decline of the value of education itself. As a result, illiteracy remained high in Egypt when compared to other countries at the same level of socio-economic development.[15]

Hence, education in Egypt appears to have acted as a mechanism of social exclusion and not social inclusion, on one hand, and as a major contributor to the desertification of the Egyptian mind and a sluggish mass culture, on the other.

4.2.1.5.3 Health   Health status and conditions improved in Egypt over the past decades. The poorest quintile did better than other income groups in terms of health insurance coverage, with almost 80 per cent of its members covered in 2002. Furthermore, between 1992 and 2001, a notable improvement occurred in life expectancy at birth and in mortality rates in both urban and rural areas, with a more notable pace of improvement in poorer regions.

Despite this improvement, an increasingly large amount of the health care budget was privately financed. In 2000, public health expenditure represented 1.75 per cent of GDP, whereas the corresponding share for private health expenditure was 2.05 per cent. It is worth noting that private sector spending on health care rose from 50 per cent of total spending on health care in 1996 to 60 per in 2004. Today, there is a growing private sector that is largely unregulated and unorganised, providing health care of a questionable quality.

Furthermore, corruption in the health care sector became rampant. In 2010, the scandal of the National Assembly members' involvement in corrupt practices relating to treatment at the expense of the state received wide coverage in the media, where it was revealed that, in one year, about 160 members of the parliament had access to health care worth more than L.E. 4 billion.

In addition, regional disparities appeared in the distribution of health care services and inequities in access to and utilisation of health care services. In principle, Ministry of Health and Population (MOHP) facilities should provide free care for the poor, but Figure 4.4 suggests that the MOHP health care services may not have been adequately serving the needs of the poor in all the governorates. Urban governorates, especially Cairo and

---

[15] In Tunisia, enrolment in education stood at about 98 per cent and 96 per cent for males and females, respectively, aged fifteen to twenty-four years, while the comparable rates for Egypt for the same age group were 88 per cent and 82 per cent, respectively (UNICEF Statistics). www.childinfo.org/files/MENA_Tunisia.pdf.

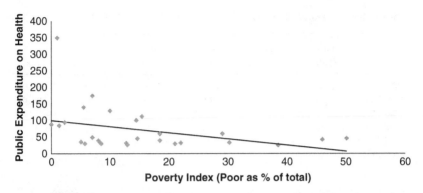

Figure 4.4: Correlation between Poverty and Government Expenditure on Health (by governorates) 2003
Source: Based on government budget data, 2003

Alexandria, had the lion's share, while rural governorates suffered from a pronounced shortage in the standard of service, in the qualifications of the service providers or in infrastructure and allocation of resources.

Speaking of gender, health outcomes and public spending are markedly biased towards males. This is due, in large part, to the high rate of expenditure for male workers covered by health insurance funds.

4.2.2 Institutional Drivers: Political Exclusion

Things could have been less explosive had the matter been confined to socio-economic exclusion, bad as that is. What added insult to injury was political and cultural exclusion.

4.2.2.1 Corruption, Lack of Information and Impunity

A concentration of non-accountable control over economic resources and assets to which only a privileged elite enjoyed unfettered access took place in a context of increasing impunity, protected by an opaque regime of information. This culminated in rampant corruption. Although these trends started in the 1970s, they gained momentum in the early 2000s.

Though comparable to the situation in the surrounding region, corruption trends in Egypt were massive in extent and type. A U4 report[16] suggested that corruption encompassed money laundering, kickback payments to obtain government tenders and political corruption. The U4 survey of corruption in Egypt in 2010 revealed that '47 per cent of business

[16] U4 is a Web-based resource centre for development practitioners who wish to effectively address corruption challenges in their work. www.u4.no.

Table 4.6: *Distribution of Food Subsidies by Quintile 2004/2005–2008/2009*

	1st Quintile	2nd Quintile	3rd Quintile	4th Quintile	5th Quintile	Total
2004/2005	17.0	18.0	19.0	22.0	24.0	100.0
2008/2009	18.6	19.3	19.9	21.2	21.0	100.0

Source: For 2004–05, see The World Bank (2005). For 2008 –09, see S. Aboulenein, H. El-Laithy, O. Helmy, H. Kheir-El-Din and D. Mandour (2010).
Source: Global Integrity.

Table 4.7: *Distribution of Education Expenditure by Income Group, 1997*

	Quintiles				
Educational Level	Poorest	Second	Middle	Fourth	Richest
Basic-Secondary Education	20.0	23.0	20.0	20.0	16.0
Higher Education	3.0	13.0	16.0	23.0	45.0
Total	15.0	19.0	20.0	21.0	24.0

Source: See Galal (2003).
Source: Transparency International.

owners who took part in the survey reported paying bribes to receive government tenders'. Although widespread, these corruption trends were mostly found in the domains of health care, education and policing.

This occurred at a time when public information about government dealings was restricted by laws 135/1950 and 121/1975. These laws prohibited the publication and use of government information and records, allowing for a concentration of power to go unchecked despite Egypt signing the UN Convention Against Corruption in 2002 and its ratification in 2005.[17]

The first result of this unchecked concentration of power was an increasing gap between the intended objectives of the anti-corruption regulations and de facto practice of corruption. This trend was reflected in the data of Global Integrity and corroborated by the Arab Reform Initiative in its 2012 State of Reform in the Arab World report.[18]

[17] U4, Anti-corruption Resource Center.
[18] Arab Reform Initiative (2012). The State of Reform in the Arab World: Arab Democracy Index, 2011: 9–10. Available on the Internet at: www.arab-reform.net/sites/default/files/ari-rep11%20ang%20final%20.pdf.

Table 4.8: *Global Integrity Indicators for the Years 2007, 2008 and 2010*

Year	Legal Framework Score	Actual Implementation[19]	Gap	Overall Score
2010	70%	34%	36%	54%
2008	67%	38%	30%	54%
2007	66%	36%	30%	53%

Source: Global Integrity.
Source: For the years 1987/1990 to 2000/2005, compiled by the authors from data published in Kienle (2001), passim. For 2005/2010, see Rabie (2012).

Table 4.9: *Egypt Corruption Index over the Past Ten Years*

Year	Indicator	Year	Indicator
2002	3.4	2007	2.9
2003	3.3	2008	2.8
2004	3.2	2009	2.8
2005	3.4	2010	3.1
2006	2.9	2011	2.9

Source: Transparency International.
Source: For 1979–84 to 1995–2000, see Hashem and El Mikway (2002), p. 55; for 2000–05 to 2011, see Rabie (2012).

4.2.2.2 Rigging Elections

The concentration of power and control resulted in the deterioration of government accountability, as reflected in Global Integrity and Transparency International indicators (Tables 4.8 and 4.9), which showed a deterioration in the index for Egypt from 3.4 in 2002 to 2.9 in 2011 (with 10 indicating no corruption and 0 total corruption). The concentration of non-accountable power was bound to result in the rigging of parliamentary elections as manifested in Transparency International and other national and international human rights organisations' reports on the 2005, 2007, 2008 and 2010 elections. In addition, the World Bank worldwide governance indicators came to affirm the picture by reporting growing political instability.

[19] An integrity indicators scorecard assesses the existence of, effectiveness of and citizen access to key governance and anti-corruption mechanisms through more than 300 actionable indicators. Scorecards take into account both the existing legal measures and the de facto realities of their practical implementation. They are scored by lead in-country researchers and blind reviewed by a panel of peer reviewers. www.globalintegrity.org.

Table 4.10: *Opposition Seats in the National Assembly, 1987–2010*

Year	No. of Opposition Seats	%
1987–90	94	21.0
1990–95	29	7.0
1995–2000	27	5.9
2000–05	66	13.0
2005–10	110*	19.8
2010	1	00.2

Source: For the years 1987–90 to 2000–05, compiled by the authors from data published in Kienle (2001), different pages. For 2005–10, see Rabie (2012).
Source: Compiled by the authors from data published in Kienle (2001) passim and Rabie (2012).

Corruption in parliamentary elections took the form of bribing voters, coercion to scare those who could have voted against Mubarak and the ruling party and the outright rigging of election results. The turnout never exceeded 20 per cent during Mubarak's regime because of a lack of trust in electoral procedures and the system of representation.

4.2.2.3 *The Political Exclusion of the Opposition*

Constrained mechanisms of accountability and of freedom of expression and organisation were increasingly provoking protests and strikes, reflecting a growing lack of trust between the government and the people. Small but significant civil liberty groups resorted to bringing strategic cases for litigation designed to uncover the abuse of power and the squandering of public assets and resources. With the lack of trust came an institutional impediment to development, as Hazem El Beblawi argued in 2012.[20]

Any ruling regime in any given nation gains its legitimacy in part from the presence of an opposition in the political system in general and the parliament in particular. However, over time the Mubarak regime systematically excluded opposition groups from the political scene, although it could not entirely prevent them from winning election to the National Assembly. Table 4.10 shows both the absolute and relative share of the opposition in the National Assembly over the period 1987 to 2010. This declined from a high of 21 per cent in the 1987–90 assembly to a low of

[20] Hazem El Beblawi, *Four Months in the Government's Cage* (Cairo: Dar Al Shorouq, 2012).

Table 4.11: *Businessmen in the National Assembly*

Year	Total Elected Seats	No. of Elected Businessmen	% of Total Elected Members
1979–84	382	7	1.8
1984–87	448	N.A.	—
1987–90	448	14	3.1
1990–95	444	31	7.0
1995–2000	444	71	16.0
2000–05	444	77	17.3
2005–10	444	83	18.7
2010	444	97	21.8
2011	508	69	13.6

Source: For 1979–84 to 1995–2000, see Hashem and El Mikway (2002), p. 55; for 2000–05 to 2011, see Rabie (2012).
Source: For 1987–2000, compiled by the authors from data published in Kienle (2001), ff. For 2005, see UNDP and League of Arab States (2010), p. 44. For 2011, see data collected by the Egyptian Center for Women's Rights.

about 6 per cent in the 1995–2000 assembly. It rose subsequently, reaching a high of 19.8 per cent in 2005–10. The strong showing of the opposition in 2005–10 threatened the plan of the ruling National Democratic Party (NDP) to pass the reins of power from Mubarak to his son.

The last parliamentary elections in 2010 were organised in three successive rounds. The Muslim Brotherhood performed well in the first round. The regime responded with blatant ballot rigging and a brutal use of force to prevent voters from reaching the polls. The response of opposition candidates of all political orientations was to boycott the elections in the second and third rounds. As a result, there was no opposition in the 2010 parliament. The opposition formed a shadow National Assembly. Mubarak mockingly commented: 'Let them entertain themselves.' This, however, proved the last nail in his era's coffin.

4.2.2.4 The Marriage between Capital and Politics

Between 2007 and 2011, an overlap of economic and political power took place. Individuals from the private sector elite became leading members of the policy committee of the ruling party and chairpersons of sectoral committees of the parliament. This was evident in the increasing presence of businessmen in the parliament and in government. Their number in the parliament rose from 7 out of 448 in 1981 to 107 in 2000, which made, as shown in Table 4.11, 1.8 per cent in the 1979–84 assembly, 8.3 per cent in 1995, 17.3 per cent in 2000 and 18.7 per cent in 2005.

When Prime Minister Ahmed Nazif formed his cabinet in 2004, business-men constituted about 24 per cent of it, whereas they had had almost no presence in the previous cabinet of Atef Ebied.[21] Not surprising, the collusion between business and political leaders and their control of both the government and the National Assembly led to growing popular resentment.

The rise of powerful businessmen in the National Democratic Party was exemplified by the case of Ahmed Ezz, who exploited this state of affairs to control the steel industry in Egypt, holding more than 60 per cent of market share. The famous case of the Monopoly Law demonstrates his influence. During voting on the law inside the parlia-ment, Ezz publicly ridiculed members who spoke in favour of imposing a very stiff penalty of L.E. 10 million ($1.64 million) on monopolistic practices. This led them to approve a very lenient anti-monopoly law that came to be known as the 'Ahmed Ezz Law'.

More important is the fact that in the last pre-revolution assembly, those businessmen dominated all the assembly's specialised committees. Ahmed Ezz became head of the Finance Committee; while other busi-nessmen chaired other important committees. With businessmen already controlling the cabinet, their control of the state was complete.

Even tourism, with its large-scale investments in hotels and resorts, ended up in the hands of a small elite with close contacts to state officials. While it might be expected that, generally speaking, tourism would ben-efit the private sector and large investments would tend to benefit small and medium-sized service enterprises in Egypt, in fact these investments benefited a small circle of politically connected businessmen, while those employed in tourism qualified primarily as low-income workers.

4.2.3 Socio-political Drivers: Cultural Exclusion

4.2.3.1 The Political Exclusion of Copts and Women

The political representation of the Coptic community was always consis-tently low. During the Mubarak era, it retreated yet further. As Table 4.12 shows, Coptic representation in the first elected National Assembly during the Sadat era (1979–84) was 3.7 per cent, which was well below Copts' relative share of the total population. In all successive elections, their representation in the assembly never exceeded 2.2 per cent, and in four of them it held constant at a mere 1.4 per cent. Mubarak did not make any

---

[21] Gouda Abdel Khalek and Mustafa K. Al Sayyid, 'Egypt: Development, Liberalization and the Persistence of Autocracy', in Elbadawi, I. and Makdisi, S. (ed.), *Democracy in the Arab World: Explaining the Deficit* (London: Routledge, 2011), pp. 256–81.

Table 4.12: *Copts in the National Assembly, 1979–2011*

Year	Elected	Hired	Total	Total Per Cent
1979–84	14	N.A.	14	3.7
1984–87	4	5	9	2.0
1987–90	6	N.A.	6	1.3
1990–95	1	5	6	1.4
1995–2000	—	6	6	1.4
2000–05	3	3	6	1.4
2005–10	1	5	6	1.4
2010	3	7	10	2.3
2011	6	5	11	2.2

Source: Compiled by the authors from data published in Kienle (2001), different pages, and Rabie (2012).
Source: Site of United Copts on the Web. www.coptsunited.com.

attempt to push for a policy that would give the Copts their fair share of political representation but used his presidential prerogative to co-opt – through direct presidential appointment – a number of them as members of the National Assembly. By contrast, their parliamentary representation in 1942 under the government of the Wafd party had been about 26 per cent.

Over the years, the regime claimed that it could not encourage an increase in Copts' political participation for fear of antagonising the increasingly growing phenomenon of fundamentalism. The Coptic Church appeared to adopt the same view, at least as far as Islamic fundamentalism was concerned. The official stance of the church under Pope Shenouda appeared supportive of the regime. When the revolutionary forces called for demonstrations on 25 January, the church instructed its constituency not to participate. On the other hand, secular Copts and Coptic political activists (e.g. George Isaac and Hanna Gebrail) took part in the uprisings from day one. These were the Egyptian Copts who helped found movements like Kefaya and challenged Mubarak's regime in the courts on legal and constitutional grounds.

Women too were socially and politically excluded. Although they make up half the population, women have never seen their representation in parliament exceed 4 per cent, as shown in Table 4.13, except in 2010 when Egypt applied an affirmative quota system. Before this, both their absolute and their relative share went down, though it was not only Mubarak who excluded women from political participation. Egypt was, and is still, a male-dominated society.

Needless to say, female exclusion in Egypt extends to all realms of life. Their unemployment rate is more than double that of men and

Table 4.13: *Total Number of National Assembly Elections Candidates and Number of Women Candidates and Women Elected and Hired, 1987–2011*

Year	Total No. of Candidates	Total No. of Women Candidates	% of Women Candidates	No. of Elected Women	No. of Hired Women by Presidential Decree	Total No. of Women in the National Assembly	% of Women in the National Assembly
1987	3,592	22	0.006	14	4	18	4.0
1990	2,676	45	1.68	7	3	10	2.2
1995	3,980	71	1.78	5	4	9	2.0
2000	N.A.	—	—	4	4	8	1.8
2005	N.A.	—	—	8	N.A.	8	1.8
2010	N.A.	—	—	56	—	56	12.6
2011	4064	638	15.7	5	5	10	2.0

Source: For 1987–2000, compiled by the authors from data published in Kienle (2001), ff. For 2005, see UNDP and League of Arab States (2010), p. 44. For 2011, see data collected by the Egyptian Center for Women's Rights.

Table 4.14: *Events of Religious Violence Against Copts, 1972–2012*

Period	Urban	Rural	Total
1972–80	3	6	9
1981–90	15	4	19
1991–2000	51	24	75
2001–12	30	29	59
Total	99	63	162

Source: Site of United Copts on the Web.

they are overrepresented in the informal sector.[22] On the social front, that is, education and health services, abundant evidence proves cultural and material discrimination against women. All this explains the massive and effective participation of women in the revolution of 25 January. However, it was this same society that, unchanged, turned its back on women at the first bend in the road, so to speak, after the revolution.

4.2.3.2 Religious Violence

Increasing religious violence strained the fabric of society. A recent report on Global Restrictions on Religion (Pew Forum 2009) rated Egypt high in terms of religious hostility and intolerance, and very high in terms of government restrictions on freedom of religion, with scores of 7.6 and 6.5 out of 10, respectively (10 indicating absolute hostility and 0 absolute tolerance). While reliable data on incidents of religious violence are limited, the data available indicate that religious violence in Egypt was on the rise between 1972 and 2011. Table 4.14 shows that the overwhelming majority of incidents occurred during the Mubarak era (94 per cent of all incidents). During his presidency, three times longer than Sadat's, the number of violent incidents multiplied sixteen fold. Almost 97 per cent of all religious violence took place in urban areas, with Upper Egypt and Cairo accounting for the majority of incidents.

---

[22] Jackline Wahba, The Impact of Labour Market Reforms on Informality in Egypt. Gender and Work in The MENA Region Working Paper Series, No. 3 (Cairo: The Population Council, 2009). Wahba (2009: 15) shows, although new entrants, whether male or female, to the labour market are more likely to find initial employment in the informal sector, the probability of moving to formal employment is much greater for men than for women.

4.2.4   Regional Marginalisation: The Declining Regional Role

Egypt's declining role in the region deepened popular dissatisfaction with the Mubarak regime and provoked a sense of national humiliation in the population.[23] The unsuccessful negotiations with the Nile basin countries meant Egypt could not play a leadership role concerning an issue of vital importance to the country. Many in the opposition in Egypt blamed the regime for neglecting its relationships with Nile countries upstream, as a result of which several such countries signed a water basin agreement without the consent of Egypt.[24] Similarly, the secession of South Sudan in 2012 dealt a blow to Egypt's strategic depth. This demonstrated Egypt's declining influence in regional politics and diplomacy.[25]

Similarly in 2010, the situation in Gaza underlined Egypt's inability to stand up to Israeli action even when that resulted in humanitarian crises for the Palestinians, as the opposition argued. The renewed Israeli blockade and the Freedom Flotilla case revealed a weakened regime in Egypt, one that had lost any influence concerning the region's most important conflict. The numerous demonstrations in Cairo and Arish in solidarity with the inhabitants of Gaza under siege, which had started at the end of 2009, continued to take place in 2010. This included a demonstration that took place in Tahrir Square in January 2010. Calling themselves the 'Freedom for Gaza March', the demonstrators condemned the Arab regimes' participation in the siege of Gaza.[26]

4.3   The Awakening

All of these drivers of exclusion were equally bringing Egyptians to the edge of rage. Certain factors helped to ignite this rage and to provoke an uprising that awakened revolutionary demands.

---

[23] Egyptians had no national victory to celebrate apart from winning the African Cup of Nations football championship, which the national team did three times in a row. Mubarak's oldest son appeared at all the African Cup of Nations matches, posing as the Godfather of the game. President Mubarak made sure he himself was given credit for all these football triumphs.

[24] www.egyptindependent.com/news/nile-basin-ministers-fail-reach-agreement; www .egyptindependent.com/news/environmental-voices-egyptian-soft-power-too-late-ups tream-nile-states

[25] www.egyptindependent.com/news/experts-warn-israeli-presence-nile-basin-states

[26] www.egyptindependent.com/node/9153; www.egyptindependent.com/node/8788; ww w.egyptindependent.com/node/11351

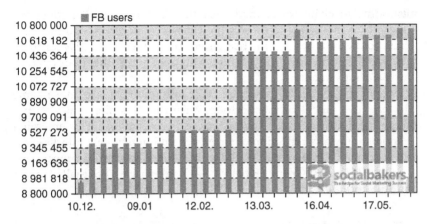

Figure 4.5: Facebook Users in Egypt between December 2011 and May 2012

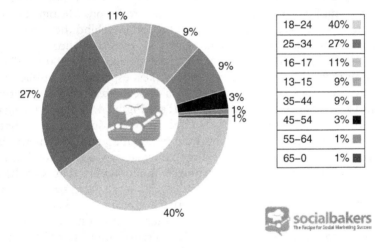

18–24	40%
25–34	27%
16–17	11%
13–15	9%
35–44	9%
45–54	3%
55–64	1%
65–0	1%

Figure 4.6: Facebook Age Distributions for Egyptian Users
Note: LAS: League of Arab States and Regional Powers in general;
SCAF: Supreme Council of the Armed Forces; EU: European Union

4.3.1   Social Media and Middle-Class Keyboard Activism

Egypt experienced an increase in civic engagement by the middle class which took the form of keyboard activism. As elsewhere in the world, Internet access and Facebook users (dominated by the younger generation) increased rapidly (Figures 4.5 and 4.6). However, it would be misleading to claim social media led the Egyptian uprising when the hundreds of thousands of those who went onto the streets did not have access to the Internet.[27] This being said, social media did play a role in mass mobilisation, especially of those who were not, at that point, part of any social movement.

Noteworthy in the Egyptian case is the formation of social movements with effective modes of mobilisation, reliant on less hierarchical structures and with more diverse and decentralised functions. This emerging phenomenon was a reflection of a new generation of young middle-class and Internet-savvy Egyptians. They all enrolled in various movements such as Kefaya, Kolena Khaled Said, alongside Football Ultrass and April 6th (see annex).

4.3.2   The Labour Movement

Both media and academic analyses of what has transpired in Egypt since 25 January 2011 have mostly focused on the role of youth, middle- and upper-middle-class youth alike, in the revolution. Despite the iconic symbolism of Tahrir Square, it was the forces behind the scene, namely the working class, that brought Mubarak's rule to an end.

Worker protests were rare in the 1990s and early 2000s. The year 2006 marked an increase in major strikes, especially in public, private and privatised companies, and to a lesser extent in the government sector,(Benin 2010; El-Mahdi 2011; see Figure 4.7). It was the struggle of the working class in Suez, that decidedly working-class city, that kept the flame of the revolution burning between 25 and 28 January. It was the three days preceding 11 February that saw a near total strike by industrial workers and government functionaries that signalled the demise of Mubarak's power. On 28 January, these struggles put an end to the state-corporatist approach towards worker unionisation which culminated in the announcement of the establishment of the Egyptian Federation of Independent Trade Unions (EFITU), the teachers following suit soon after. Since then, some 1,000 new unions independent of the state-sponsored Egyptian Trade Union Federation (ETUF) have been established (Benin 2013). According to Nadeem Amin al-Din of the Egyptian Centre for Economic and Social Rights (ECESR), the number of strikes escalated rapidly in the post-revolutionary period, reaching 1,377 in 2011, 1,969 in 2012 and more than 2,239 in 2013 (Aminal Din 2014).[28]

---

[27] Wael Ghoneim, *Revolution 2.0* (Cairo: Dar al-Shorouq, 2012).
[28] The centre further reports a total of 5,212 protests (labour and non-labour) in 2013, of which about 82 per cent took place before 30 June.

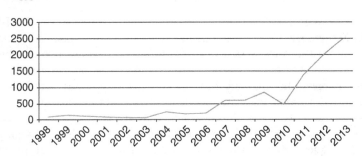

Figure 4.7: Number of Strikes by Egyptian Workers, 1998–2013
Source: Annual reports of the Land Centre for Human Rights.
Numbers for 2011–13 are from Amin al-Din (2013) and ECESR
(2014).

4.3.3   *Public Interest Court Cases*

After years of documenting and reporting on human rights violations, human rights lawyers were becoming more experienced and effective at public interest litigation. Beyond seeking justice for individual grievances (usually for individuals from socio-economically marginalised groups), they went on to litigate in public interest cases that uncovered the systemic exclusion of the poor. These were cases of the systemic violation of social and economic rights and a skewed use of public assets against the poor. Some of these cases highlighted how the state was squandering state-owned land. Other cases defended people's rights to health care, decent work or education by aiming to stop privatisation of basic social services and/or increases in the cost of privatised social care beyond the means of the poor.

There were demands for better wages and improved working conditions. Presented in 2008, the demand for a minimum wage was substantially revived by Nagi Rashad, a worker who decided to sue the government for its decision not to implement a minimum wage policy. Leading the case was Khalid Ali, attorney and director of the Egyptian Centre for Economic and Social Rights (ECESR). On 30 March, the court ruled in favour of Nagi Rashad and Khalid Ali obtained a ruling ordering the president, the prime minister and the National Council for Wages to implement a minimum wage policy that reflected the current cost of living.[29]

---

[29] http://mideast.foreignpolicy.com/posts/2010/05/12/egyptian_workers_demand_a_li
ving_wage; http://egypttoday.com/news/display/article/artId:699/Khaled-Ali/secId:34.

The year 2010 witnessed an important case won by the ECESR. In September, Cairo's Administrative Court issued a 'landmark decision' to annul the privatisation of three public companies, two of which had been sold to a Saudi investor. Following massive protests by workers in the companies, the ECESR brought the case to court on their behalf. The court found that 'the companies were sold at prices far below their true value'. Moreover, the court held that 'the ongoing review of privatisation and other economic transactions made during the Mubarak era had raised questions of corruption, conflict of interest and lack of transparency'. Nadim Mansour, an attorney at the ECESR, declared in 2010 that more cases would be brought to court; indeed, five cases were presented.[30]

The Egyptian Initiative for Personal Rights (EIPR) obtained an equally important ruling against the new pricing system the Ministry of Health had established in 2009. This system linked the prices for medicine to the global market instead of to production costs. Decree no. 373/2009, establishing a new pricing system, was passed. The case was filed in the names of three staff members in EIPR, on the basis that the 'new pricing system threatened the accessibility and affordability of medicines in Egypt, especially the price of generic drugs'. The court held that 'any system should seek to fulfil the "health security" of all Egyptians'. The case was the first to question the affordability and the accessibility of medicines in Egypt and it indicated a strong movement by Egyptian civil society in favour of the right to health care, neglected until then.[31]

4.3.4   The Tunisian Inspiration

The Tunisian revolution provided Egyptians with an unprecedented inspiration. Solidarity with the Tunisian uprising was publicly expressed days before 25 January at a basketball game in Alexandria when the Ultrass of the Itihad Club of Alexandria chanted, 'Tunis, Tunis'.[32] On 28 January, after a sudden crackdown by the police on demonstrations, social media pages started to refer to the Tunisian uprising. Three Facebook pages were initiated from Tunis in support of fellow revolutionaries in Cairo.

Social media linking the Tunisians and the Egyptians were particularly useful at key moments such as during the violent crackdowns on Mohamed Mahmoud Street and in the city of Port Said. Social media messages from Tunisia pointed to similar tactics by the Tunisian police

---

[30] www.lawsofrule.net/2011/10/15/illegitimate-privatization-in-egypt/
[31] www.bikyamasr.com/12701/egyptians-struggle-to-get-medicine/; www.escr-net.org/doc s/i/1312208
[32] Akram Khamees, *Thawret Jeel Ultrass* (Cairo: Arab Organization for Human Rights, 2012), p. 67.

and sought to boost the morale of the Egyptians during difficult episodes. And while the printed media was sceptical about the relevance of the Tunisian experience to Egypt, social media in Tunisia and Egypt helped to establish a strong sense of shared experience and aspiration.

4.4   The Aftermath of January 2011

The years following the January revolution revealed the difficulties involved in transforming a power structure that condoned autocracy and exclusion.

4.4.1   On the Political Front

After Mubarak's resignation on 11 February 2011, the Supreme Council of the Armed Forces (SCAF) came to power on 13 February by dissolving the parliament and suspending the constitution. The SCAF announced it would stay in power for six months (it turned out to be longer), after which elections could be held. On 19 March, the SCAF held a constitutional referendum on proposed amendments to the constitution. In a political scene torn between rejecting and approving the amendments, the vote resulted in a 78 per cent 'Yes' vote for the amendments, with many voting for an assumed Islamic future as insinuated by the Muslim Brotherhood (MB). On 30 March 2011, the SCAF re-affirmed some articles of the suspended constitution, determined the conditions required of candidates for presidential office and set the dates for the elections to both houses of parliament.[33] The SCAF temporarily lifted the state of emergency and set the standards of a constitutional committee to draft a new constitution.

The SCAF's position in the new political scene created fear among the groups and parties that had led the uprising. Its violent response to continuing demonstrations and protests, as well as the increased number of military trials of civilians, provoked concerns about a 'stolen revolution'. These fears were ignited again in 2013 after the deposition of the Brotherhood (more on that later). But it was the SCAF's second constitutional declaration that presented a serious potential obstruction to the establishment of a genuine civilian democratic state. Limiting the power of the coming president and his control over the armed forces, the second constitutional declaration confirmed the army as a powerful player in the political game.[34]

[33] www.sis.gov.eg/en/Story.aspx?sid=54554
[34] http://english.ahram.org.eg/News/45350.aspx

The first day of the parliamentary elections was 28 November 2011. For a month the parliament became the only venue where all political parties could participate in the new political process. But the mostly new, inexperienced and unstructured political movements could not agree on matters pertaining to laws for the regulation of parties' lists and quotas for women, Copts and independents. While some pushed for a 'democratic' system of elections with no quotas for any social group, others argued the need for positive discrimination. The inability of political movements and parties to agree on a desired electoral model caused a minor crisis.

The parliamentary elections had three stages, ending on 3 January 2012. The outcome of the vote revealed the dominance of the Muslim Brotherhood's Freedom and Justice Party (FJP) and the Islamic Salafist movement led by al-Nour's party,[35] with the Muslim Brotherhood winning 45 per cent of the seats, the Salafists 20 per cent and the liberal parties 35 per cent. At that point, the Egyptian state had completed one round of the transition, with a regime of co-existence between a pre-revolution judiciary, a military-dominated executive and an Islamist-dominated parliament. The political scene looked as shown in Figure 4.8.

A crisis erupted in this system between April and June 2012. In April 2012, the Administrative Court suspended the constitutional committee composed of 100 lawmakers on the basis that its overwhelming Islamist composition went against the rules of the first constitutional declaration. This came after the resignation of twenty-five members of the committee in protest against the FJP. The crisis continued until 14 June 2012, when a ruling by the Constitutional Court declared that the laws regulating the parliamentary elections were unconstitutional.[36] The direct result of the ruling was the immediate dissolution of the parliament by the SCAF. The SCAF resumed its full legislative powers immediately thereafter. The SCAF also announced that it had selected 100 people who would form the Constitutional Assembly should the political actors be unable to agree on a new Constitutional Assembly. The SCAF regularly affirmed that it would stand by its promise to hand over power in June 2012.

Presidential elections were organised and after two eventful rounds, the MB candidate, Muhammad Morsi, won. In the meantime, the Egyptian political scene had become clouded with uncertainty especially regarding the constitutionality of the new committee set up to draft the

---

[35] www.reuters.com/article/2011/11/28/us-egypt-election-idUSTRE7AR08V20111128
[36] Members of political parties had been allowed to contest the 30 per cent of seats saved for independents, which violates equal opportunity for independents.

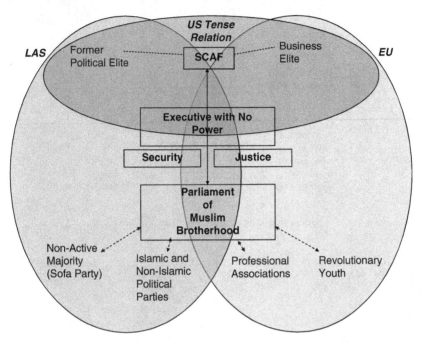

Figure 4.8: The Scene in 2011
Note: LAS: League of Arab States and Regional Powers in general;
SCAF: Supreme Council of the Armed Forces; EU: European Union

constitution.[37] With the Islamist parliament dissolved and an Islamist president sworn in, the new Egyptian political scene looked as shown in Figure 4.9.

While most of the discussion gravitated around who was to take over the executive branch of government and who was to dominate the legislature, important developments in the political transition were unravelling, notably in the relationship between the executive and the judiciary. The battle between these two branches of government revolved around two issues: (a) stopping or containing the consolidation of power by the MB and (b) protecting the independence of the judiciary from encroachment by the MB. Both issues fed on each other: the more the judiciary tried to contain the MB, the keener the MB and its presidency were on achieving a rapid conclusion to the encroachment project.

The judiciary's battle to stop or contain the MB's consolidation of power took its most obvious form in the standoff between the MB and the Supreme Constitutional Court (SCC). When the Islamists won

[37] http://edition.cnn.com/2012/06/30/world/africa/egypt-morsi/index.html

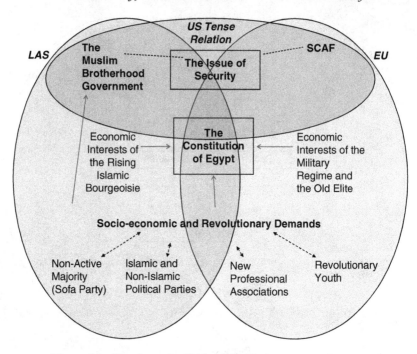

Figure 4.9: The Scene in 2012–2013

a clear majority in the parliamentary elections of 2012, the SCC issued a ruling declaring the election law unconstitutional. The SCAF used this ruling to dissolve the parliament. It remained dissolved well into 2013. The MB reacted with a presidential decree that put legislative power in the hands of the Islamist president. Furthermore, the Islamist president replaced the prosecutor general and reduced the number of judges on the SCC, thus eliminating activist figures inside the SCC.

The president then issued a constitutional declaration that made his decisions immune from legal contestation. The response was massive street mobilisation which was met with brutality on the part of the MB.[38] A rebel movement (Tamarud) was formed with the aim of deposing Morsi by the end of his first year in office (30 June) and calling for early presidential elections. This movement received increasing support from the people, who were suffering from a dearth of basic necessities such as bread, gasoline, propane gas and electricity.

[38] That is, attacks on sit-ins in front of the presidential palace and the shooting of demonstrators at Moqattam in front of the headquarters of the Muslim Brotherhood in March 2013.

MB rule was increasingly running into trouble. Economically, the MB regime failed to address the deficit, declining foreign reserves and unemployment, as well as workers' demands related to wages and contractual relations, and it accepted the conditions for an IMF loan. Politically, the Morsi regime adopted an exclusionary policy, favouring members of the Brotherhood when filling high-ranking positions in the state apparatus (which became known as the 'Brotherhoodisation' of the state).

By mid-June 2013, Tamarud had collected 22 million signatures. In late June 2013, Minister of Defence Abdel Fattah el-Sisi gave a one-week ultimatum to all political powers to resolve their differences and reach a consensus. On 30 June, millions took to the streets demanding that Morsi step down and calling for early elections. When Morsi did not respond, el-Sisi issued a forty-eight-hour ultimatum, asking Morsi to acknowledge the demands of the people. When by 3 July Morsi had still not answered, el-Sisi removed him from office, detained him and called upon the president of the Supreme Court to take over the office of the presidency. The president assembled a civilian interim government and the Minister of Defence announced a roadmap, including the suspension of the 2012 constitution, constitutional amendments and parliamentary and presidential elections, among other things.

The Brotherhood and its supporters staged sit-ins on a street intersection called Rabeaa Adaweya Square and in Nahda Square in front of Cairo University. They were calling for the reinstatement of Morsi and of the constitution of 2012. These sit-ins lasted for more than forty days. The state continued to threaten to disperse the sit-ins by force, while national and international forces continued to seek a reconciliatory solution to the stalemate. On 14 August 2013, police and military moved in to disperse the sit-ins. Brutal clashes ensued in different governorates between the MB and the security forces. A state of emergency was declared and a curfew imposed in fourteen governorates. The Egyptian government continued to confront demonstrations organised by the MB and its supporters, while most senior MB leaders were rounded up and detained, pending trials.

Towards the end of 2014, the number of MB-driven demonstrations declined and the interim government proceeded with a roadmap. A ten-member technical committee drafted constitutional amendments. A fifty-member committee representing all segments and political forces in society (except the MB) initiated a dialogue about the constitutional amendments.

A constitution was passed in early 2014, and presidential elections held in mid-2014 resulted in Field Marshall el-Sisi, minister of defence in the MB government, becoming the third president of Egypt since the uprising of 2011. The constitution gave the parliament new powers, though it did not regulate the method of parliamentary elections, leaving that to an electoral law to be drafted later. The constitution included important statements on liberties and freedom which were courageously negotiated by an activist professor who was a member of the university-based March 9th Movement, established during the Mubarak era. What the constitution did not do was reduce military privileges.

As of early 2015, the situation in Egypt had several defining features:

- Continued lack of a vision for social justice despite the piecemeal reforms that resulted from the issuance of an investment law, subsidy reduction policies, conditional cash transfers and an economic summit for international donors that took place in 2015;
- Continued reliance on economic support from Saudi Arabia, the UAE and Kuwait which repeats Mubarak-style investments for large projects and real estate initiatives;
- Continued trade union fragmentation and political party bickering;
- Continued dissipation of civil society by means of police crackdowns and ministerial control through a decree that required the registration of all NGOs and other entities engaged in civic work, even if they are registered either as not-for-profit, or commercial, consulting and/or legal firms. Several such NGOs adjusted their status to comply with the ministerial decree, while others closed down or suspended their work;
- Continued attacks on the 25 January uprising as a foreign-led conspiracy, though the 2014 constitution hailed it in its preamble as a fully fledged revolution;
- Continued closing off of public spaces in the face of political protest through a battery of laws that restrict demonstrations and others that declare many public areas and university campuses as military spaces and hence condemn anyone arrested in them to military trials;
- Continued deterioration of professional standards in the media; and
- Continued control of Internet-based discussions.

4.4.2   On the Economic Front

The Saudis, Kuwaitis and UAE welcomed the developments in 2013, donating US$12 billion to Egypt. The interim government announced an economic stimulus package and succumbed to popular pressures for social justice measures by adopting a minimum wage policy. With the ascent to power of Field Marshal el-Sisi, the newly appointed government announced a major national project, the digging of a second Suez Canal parallel to the old one. Egyptians were asked to contribute to the financing of the project, and within a few weeks, the government announced the collection of billions of dollars from Egyptians who bought shares in the new project with a promised 12 per cent dividend. The government managed to push through a courageous reduction of subsidies and an increase in fuel prices, coupled with ration cards for food and fuel and a conditional cash transfer programme for the poor. An economic summit was organised in early 2015, and an investment law was issued on the eve of the summit.

4.4.3   On the Social Front

The systemic rise in worker militancy as a key constituent of the revolutionary movement was a major concern for all the regimes in power after January 2011. The localised demands for better wages and living conditions by trade unions were, unsurprising, severely curtailed by the police. A court ruling in mid-2015 increased restrictions on the labour movement by making strikes a violation of Shari'a law; this ruling covered public sector workers.

The military and the MB were unlikely allies against the emergent trade union movement, casting something of a shadow over union organisers' hopes for more favourable conditions after the revolution.[39] The military took a harsh stand against trade unions, criminalising strikes and work sabotage, arresting protesters and union activists, using the military's own workforce to undermine strikes as the events of the bus drivers' strike demonstrated.[40] The SCAF shelved reforms Ahmed al-Bora'i had proposed when he was minister for manpower and an ally of the independent trade union movement.

The rise of workers' movements and demands were of concern to the MB. Historically, the working class was never one of the strongholds of the MB. Politically, the MB's alliance with the military after 11 February against the demands of the working class antagonised the union movement exemplified by the EFITU, the Egyptian Democratic Labour Congress (EDLC) and the Centre for Trade Unions and Workers

[39] The military has a unique place in the political economy of Egypt. Its vested military-industrial interest ranges from advanced weapons systems to consumer goods, stretching from bottled water to poor-quality home appliances. Its factories employ a mix of conscripts and civilians. Ian M. Hartshorn (2013). 'Worker's Revolutions and Worker's Constitutions: Egypt and Tunisia in Comparison'. www.sas.upenn.edu/dcc/sites/www.sas.upenn.edu.dcc/files/uploads/HartshornPennDCC.pdf.

[40] Sharif Abdel, 'Does Egypt's Resurgent Labour Unrest Pose a Threat to Sisi's Power?' (8 May 2014) www.europesolidaire.org/spip.php?page=article_impr&id_article=31837.

Services (CTUWS). The military, the MB and the Salafist Al-Nour party successfully derailed calls for unity between the Tahrir activists and the independent unions in February 2011. A call for a general strike in February 2012 was aborted by a combination of repression and the active intervention of the MB, which mobilised its activists in the workplace to argue in favour of giving the newly elected parliament a chance to deliver reforms.[41]

According to the Mahrousa Center for Socioeconomic Development, about 3,819 worker protests and strikes took place in 2012, of which 29 per cent happened under the SCAF and 71 per cent after the election of Muhammad Morsi.[42] In the first half of 2013, 1,972 protests and strikes took place; this was about 88 per cent of all the workers' protests that year, which totalled 2,239. All in all, this amounts to about 4,684 workers' protests and strikes between June 2012 and 30 June 2013, that is, under Morsi's rule.

This rise in worker activity during MB rule explains why the MB tried to infiltrate the trade unions. This was known as the Brotherhoodisation of the trade unions. Decree 97 of 25 November 2012 removed all members of the ETUF executive board who were more than sixty years old, replacing them with those candidates who had received the second-largest vote tallies in the 2006 national union elections. This measure could have wound up installing as many as 150 Muslim Brother appointees at the helm of ETUF's constituent unions.[43]

As the MB threatened the nature of both the state and society, it also antagonised wide segments of the Egyptian people, including the working class. In reaction, workers were eager to sign up to the Tamarud campaign. Workers collected hundreds of thousands of signatures, endorsing the call for early presidential elections. The Centre for Trade Union and Worker Services, a mainstay of the independent trade union movement since its establishment in 1990, used its six offices around the country to collect the Tamarud petitions.[44]

Morsi's removal signalled a truce between the state and the unions. The number of workers' protests dwindled considerably in the second

---

[41] Anne Alexander, 'Workers and the Arab Revolutions' (December 2013), http://socialis treview.org.uk/386/workers-and-arab-revolutions.

[42] Al Mahrousa Center for Socioeconomic Development, Egypt's Struggling Labour Movement. http://muftah.org/egypts-struggling-labour-movement/#.VMN2gGSUemE.

[43] Ibid.

[44] Heba F. Al Shazli, 'Where Were the Workers on the Days before and after 30 June 2013?' www.jadaliyya.com/pages/index/13125/where-were-the-egyptian-workers-in-the-june-2 013-p.

half of 2013.[45] Furthermore, although the 2012 constitution gave the trade unions the right to organise, the EFITU announced that its members were ready to work day and night for Egypt and to support its new interim government.[46] The appointment of Kamal Abu Aita as Minister for Manpower was also a sign of the reconciliation between the state and the workers.

Nonetheless, the interim government of Adly Mansour and that of President el-Sisi launched a sweeping crackdown on the workers' movement.[47] Labour leaders were arrested at their homes in dawn raids, worker sit-ins came under attack by riot police and union leaders were summoned by the military.[48] Workers, including bus drivers, postal workers, refuse collectors, dockworkers, doctors, pharmacists and steel and textile workers, staged walkouts, occupied factories and held sit-ins and other stoppages. According to the ECESR, trade union actions accounted for 70 per cent of all documented protests in the first quarter of 2014.[49] Prime Minister Mehleb appointed Nahed al-Ashry, a career civil servant who since the Mubarak era has been siding with businessmen and factory owners against workers, as Minister for Manpower. She opened her era as minister by proposing a controversial twelve-month ban on strike action, which independent unions denounced.[50]

The situation in the countryside is no better. It is where about one third of the Egyptian workforce is employed in agriculture, and it is where about 57 per cent of the population, the majority of whom is poor, lives. The Egyptian peasantry has seen the limited gains achieved during Nasser's era dwindle. Resistance to the return of landlords under Mubarak was brutally crushed. Since 2011, thousands of peasants have formed independent unions, including a women's agricultural union, and farmers have mounted protests against what they described as 'new feudalism'.[51]

[45] ECESR (2014) Egypt: Annual Protests Report 2013. http://ecesr.org/wp-content/uploads/2014/07/Protest-report-2013-Web.pdf.
[46] Al Shazli, Where Were the Workers?
[47] The government imprisoned at least 16,000 people, many of them rounded up in mass sweeps, and killed up to 2,500. A court in southern Egypt sentenced more than 1,100 alleged Brotherhood members to death, among the largest number of death-penalty sentences in modern history.
[48] www.thenation.com/article/179752/does-egypts-resurgent-labour-unrest-pose-threat-sisis-power#
[49] Ibid. [50] Ibid.
[51] Brian Slocum, 'The Left and the Workers Movement in Egypt's Democratic Revolutions'. www.thenorthstar.info/?p=7986.

4.5   The Future of Egypt's Protracted Transition: Scenarios

Principles of freedom, dignity and social justice were upheld by the diverse societal forces that came together in January 2011 to achieve in record time (eighteen days) the removal of a president. No well-organised social movement with alternative governing structures and corresponding policies guaranteed the fulfilment of these principles. Thus, the uprising did remove a president and his ruling party, although it did not have the revolutionary machinery either to take over power completely or to start radical progressive programmes to reverse political, social and economic exclusion.

Observers of the Egyptian transition to date see two features common to Egypt's modernisation process: (i) a division in the Egyptian elite between those who espouse the democratic principle of majority rule and those who want to defend liberal freedoms and liberties (Watani vs. Umma parties; Wafd vs. liberal constitutionalists),[52] with the latter always the weaker of the two; and (ii) an inability to attain minimum levels of consensus to safeguard a liberal democratic future through a historic compromise within the elite.[53]

The Egyptian demands for freedom, dignity and social justice seem unlikely to be realised simultaneously in the short run. The history of transitions worldwide tells that these demands are not automatically guaranteed by the holding of regular elections in a multi-party system. Transitions to democracy are often associated with a disappointing or inadequate progress towards social justice, and with a mixed record on protecting freedoms.[54] Furthermore, the literature on democratisation tells us that three variable conditions exist that affect the prospects of its consolidation: (a) variables related to the strategic choices of the political elite in charge during the transition; (b) structural variables related to economic and social developments which result in social movements pushing for democracy and justice; (c) a neighbourhood effect.[55]

[52] Amr al-Shalakany, *Izdihar wa Inhiyar al-Nukhba al-Qanuniyya fi-Misr 1805–2005 (Rise and Fall of the Legal Elite in Egypt 1805–2005)* (Cairo: Dar al-Shorouq, 2013), pp. 209–11.
[53] Noha El-Mikawy, *Consensus Building in Egypt's Transition Process* (Cairo: AUC Press, 1999).
[54] Philippe C. Schmitter, 'Twenty-Five Years, Fifteen Findings', *Journal of Democracy*, 21:1 (2010), pp. 17–28. Jose Antonio et al., 'What Makes Democracies Endure?', *Journal of Democracy*, 7:1 (1996), pp. 39–55. Adam Przeworski (ed.), *Sustainable Democracy* (Cambridge, 1995).
[55] For a good summary of this literature, see Adam Przeworski, 'Democracy and Economic Development'. http://politics.as.nyu.edu/docs/IO/2800/sisson.pdf and ESCWA Working Paper E/ESCWA/ECRI/2014/WP.1, November 2014. 'Beyond Governance and Conflict: Measuring the Impact of the Neighbourhood Effect in the Arab Region'. www.escwa.un.org/divisions/ecri_editor/Download.asp?table_name=ecri_documents&field_name=id&FileID=272.

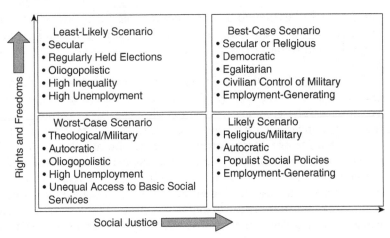

Figure 4.10: Strategic Choices of the Political Elite

4.5.1   Strategic Choices of the Political Elite

The future of Egypt's transition will depend on the choices the political elite makes along two spectrums: liberties and freedom, and social justice. These spectrums produce four scenarios (see Figure 4.10).

During the Mubarak years, Egypt experienced the worst-case scenario. It had a combination of religious and military opinion-makers, it was autocratic, its economy was oligopolistic and resulted in high unemployment and unequal access to social services. The uprising of 2011 promised to move Egypt out of that quadrant, though most of the relevant actors on the political scene failed to forge a consensus on the means of achieving the best-case scenario. In the early days of 2012, while preparing for Egypt's first open presidential elections, the political elite developed weak policies on liberties, freedoms and social justice. As our review of the policies of various presidential candidates shows, principles of freedom, liberties, dignity and social justice were not coined in language that clearly asked for the removal of all forms of discrimination and exclusion, reducing bias for the haves and empowering the have-nots. There was no truly distributive agenda.

Short of perpetual revolution, which a country as central to the regional balance of power as Egypt is cannot afford, the trajectory Egypt must take to move from the lower left-hand quadrant to the upper right-hand quadrant may have to be reformist, with waves of revolutionary explosion every time vocal segments of civil society realise that the reform policies and the intentions behind them are not moving Egypt enough out of the worst-case scenario quadrant. In other words, it may be that Egypt is set to go through rounds of 'refolutions', to borrow a term coined by Assef Bayat.[56]

Throughout this process, Egyptian civil society's liberals and democrats will have to keep checking Islamist as well as military aspirations to dominance. The combinations that could keep Egypt within either the lower left-hand quadrant or the upper left-hand quadrant revolve around either a secular or religious regime under strong military tutelage. This would mean continued socio-economic exclusion in the name of economic growth pursued at a rate from which only the few would benefit. This in turn could also mean continued political exclusion and violation of human rights in the name of national security. In other words, secularism alone or regularity of elections alone will not guarantee social justice.

These scenarios are, however, not static; they may evolve with the evolution of political Islam in Egypt. As Asef Bayat anticipated in the 1990s, political Islam could practically evolve from within into a phenomenon that combines religiosity and rights, Islam and modernity. This is what he called post-Islamism, a practicality, not a dogma. Non-MB leaders of thought, such as Ahmed Kamal Aboulmagd, Ibrahim El Hudaiby and Heba Raouf Ezzat, represent that desire for a post-Islamist evolution.[57] The strength and strategic engagement of the liberal secular forces that led the way in the first eighteen days of the Egyptian uprising with those practical groups of Islamists will partially determine how fast this post-Islamic reality develops. Until early 2013, this scenario was delayed by the fragmentation of the liberal non-religious forces on several fronts and blocs. By the advent of 2015, this trend was delayed by a confrontation between the military and extreme Islamist groups, leaving no room for compromise.

Moving out of the two left-hand quadrants (least-likely and worst-case scenario) also depends on the military. It may harbour some hopes of returning a secular neoliberal elite to power, one that does not call for distributive inclusive socio-economic rights, one that reinvigorates the economy with monopolistic investments and a relatively high growth rate that does not trickle down. This would be a return to a growth model driven by an oligopolistic elite at the expense of equal access to assets and services and decent jobs. The military might utilise the polarisation in

---

[56] Assef Bayat, 'Paradoxes of Arab Refolutions', in Jadaliya www.jadaliyya.com/pages/index/786/paradoxes-of-arab-refo-lutions.

[57] See Asef Bayat on the post Islamist alternative https://openaccess.leidenuniv.nl/bitstream/handle/1887/17030/ISIM_16_What_is_Post?sequence=1 and Tarek Ramadan, *The Arab Awakening* (London: Allen Lane, 2012).

society between Islamists and non-Islamists and also benefit from waves of popular anger harsh economic conditions induce. This would mean bringing Egypt back into the lower left-hand quadrant. Or the military might find a modus operandi with an Islamist group, supported by a constitution that protects the military's economic, administrative and professional interests.[58] One area of concern for the military has been its long-held entitlement to hold a number of governorships and public enterprise managerial posts upon retirement. This is geographical and sectorial. Geographically, the highest concentration of military men in civilian leadership posts is found in Cairo and the coastal cities. The sectors of production, of services (health care and education), of energy, of transportation and media and information, as well as environment and sport, also have military men in managerial positions.[59] Beyond administrative interests, one of the military's core interests is safeguarding its own institution, which was guaranteed in the constitution of 2014.[60]

4.5.2 Structural and Institutional Change

The ability of Egypt to move towards the best-case scenario (upper right-hand quadrant) will largely depend on the ability of the working class, the peasantry and the urban poor to build an effective unified front that seeks to overcome the profound socio-economic inequalities in the country. In other words, structural change towards social justice would require an ability by the forces that created the momentum of the first eighteen days of the 2011 uprising to sustain their impact and turn their calls for deep structural changes into programmes and policy options that achieve freedom, dignity and social justice. If that does not happen, these forces will be overwhelmed by either a religious or a security-driven agenda that will insinuate itself into all state institutions in order to consolidate power, but not to achieve dignity and social justice or expand freedoms.

[58] Through the 2014 constitution, the military has gained privileges not dissimilar to those of other military establishments, such as in Latin America or in Turkey. These include military budgets protected from civilian control, as well as control over security policies through a national security council that shares in presidential decisions related to strategic issues.

[59] Starting in December 2011, 'Askar Kazeboon' (the Military are Liars) has been an important movement for spreading awareness about the deeply ingrained nature of military rule in Egypt and the extent of the change needed to really and actually put an end to the militarisation of politics. Askar Kazeboon developed a map indicating all governmental and central positions that former military officers occupy. The list includes 349 posts.

[60] The constitution of 2014 protects military budgets and trials of civilians. The post of Minister of Defence has been protected from presidential caprice by a constitutional article that makes him an appointee of the Supreme Military Council, not the president; this is, however, a transitional article for two presidential terms as per article 234.

As we argued earlier, the impoverishment of the middle class makes it compete for state resources with the poor and, in many instances, crowd out the poor and succumb to calls for stability before anything else. This is likely to continue until the economic model picks up competitive and productive momentum to reduce the burdens of the middle class, allowing it to be an ally of the workers' movement and of the poor in their struggle for equity and justice.

Structural and institutional reform towards the best-case scenario in the upper right-hand quadrant will need to be backed by a constitution. The current 2014 constitution safeguards rights and freedoms by prohibiting any amendment of its articles that would reduce them. It also prohibits prolonging a presidency beyond two terms (article 226). The 2014 constitution has a chapter on 'rights, freedoms and responsibilities' which enshrines the right to dignity, privacy, physical integrity and equality before the law; it criminalises torture and discrimination; it respects the right to free movement, freedom of information, belief, expression, organisation, creativity and scientific research; it criminalises forced eviction, endorsing the right to housing; it enshrines freedom of the press and the independence of state-owned media; it respects the right of women, children and the disabled; and, most important, it declares all the international human rights conventions which Egypt ratified a part of national law.

The ability to claim rights under the constitution hinges upon the judiciary. The judiciary, however, was hit hard during the transition. It continues to have two schools, representing a divide between those who uphold the rule of the majority at any cost and those who defend liberties and freedoms without succumbing to majoritarian sentiments. It is also a profession that insulates itself under the guise of keeping independent of society, and thus it rarely sees the injustice of many socially, economically and politically conservative laws in Egypt (Brown 2014).

A move towards the best scenario in the upper right-hand quadrant will have to be negotiated in the context of much-needed and profound institutional changes. These institutional changes include a process of transitional justice (documenting violations, taking responsibility and apologising, receiving sentences for crimes and/or amnesty, maintaining a collective memory and institutionalising security sector reforms).[61] Furthermore, an enabling environment for the protection and fulfilment of freedoms and liberties will require access to information (enshrined in

[61] The constitution of 2014 commits the parliament to issue a law regulating a process of transitional justice in its first term (article 241).

the 2014 constitution, articles 57 and 68), and effective mechanisms for political, administrative and judicial accountability accompanied by social accountability mechanisms from the village-level upwards.

Nothing short of a profound institutional overhaul will bring about an inclusive, distributive political economy in Egypt. This will require a major restructuring of security forces, as well as higher research and education institutions and local governance institutions. It is this development project that stalled under Mubarak for thirty years.

4.5.3   The Neighbourhood Effect

It should not be forgotten that the neighbourhood of the Egyptian transition is a volatile one. Literature about the neighbourhood effect on democratic transitions speaks of effects related to emulation (or inspiration), diffusion of democratic values and practices, convergence towards democratic values and systems or disruption by oppression or conflict or both.[62] In the case of Egypt, the inspiration, as discussed earlier in this chapter, came from the Tunisian revolution in 2010, and particularly the ousting of Ben Ali in January 2011.

Beyond a brief moment of inspiration, the regional effect on Egypt goes in directions seemingly antagonistic to a transition towards greater liberty and social justice. The region is known to have the worst record for extremist/terrorist attacks, to have some of the highest levels of military expenditure and some of the largest numbers of refugees and internally displaced people. All observers of neighbourhood effects worldwide agree that such a neighbourhood can produce only drivers of oppression, not democracy and justice. Egypt is affected by all these features either directly or indirectly. It has seen violence and extremism; it has a high rate of military expenditures; it has suffered from an infiltration of armaments through the Libyan and Gazan borders. This regional context gives dominance to security arguments over genuine reform or social justice, at least in the short run.

In conclusion, in managing the unfolding situation it has to be recognised that little love is lost in relations between Egypt, North Sudan and South Sudan and Libya. The situation will be challenging for all.

In the wider regional context, Egypt has been mired in socially and economically conservative alliances. Under the MB government, Egypt was in alliance with Qatar and Turkey and neither supported social justice

---

[62] ESCWA Working Paper E/ESCWA/ECRI/2014/WP.1, November 2014 'Beyond Governance and Conflict: Measuring the Impact of the Neighbourhood Effect in the Arab Region'. www.escwa.un.org/divisions/ecri_editor/Download.asp?table_name= ecri_documents&field_name=id&FileID=272.

or freedoms and liberties. Under el-Sisi's government, Egypt has been in alliance with Saudi Arabia, UAE and Kuwait. These are the only countries that have shown an interest in supporting the government of Egypt, especially economically. None of the states that supported Egypt under the MB and el-Sisi are known to be staunch believers in or supporters of a vision of social justice and liberties.

The final neighbourhood effect, often cited in the literature, is that of proximity to democratic or welfare models (resulting in diffusion of or convergence towards democratic values and practices). In the case of Egypt, the closest such neighbour is the European Union, which has, in the past four years, shown very little appetite for concerning itself with Egypt. While the European Union and the Scandinavian embassies in Cairo have continued to refer to Egypt's weak record on human rights, the European Union's financial support for Egypt has been minimal. The European Union has continued to be consumed with its own internal Euro-zone problems, with its own issues of extremism and terrorism, and with refugees. This could entail a return to the security-driven EU–Egypt relationship, to the detriment of any effect by the European Union on liberties and freedoms or on a vision for social justice. What is more, the fact that the Egyptian government and official media have excelled in building a narrative that demonises European support for Egyptian civil society has meant that the possibility for a diffusion or convergence effect has been effectively dampened. The picture would not change much were the United States to be included in the neighbourhood effect.[63]

4.6   Conclusions

The profound socio-economic exclusion described at the beginning of this chapter may come to form the most binding of constraints on the transition. Establishing an agenda for inclusive and progressive social justice is quite a daunting prospect, given Egypt's constrained budget, one quarter of which goes to debt servicing and another 30–40 per cent of which goes to subsidies and salaries.[64]

In fact, given the history of social democracy during transitions, things do not bode well for the Egyptian situation. Social democrats often end up compromising to keep the bourgeoisie happy. Will Egypt develop social constituencies that can form a pact between the middle class and

---

[63] Thomas Carothers, 'Democracy Aid at 25: Time to Choose', *Journal of Democracy*, 26:1 (2015), pp. 60–76.
[64] Beblawi, *Four Months in the Government Cage*.

the working class? Will the generation of the young (up to thirty-five years old) manage to transform their successful street mobilisation into institutions for the expression and articulation of social policy options? Will Egypt's economic development model continue to take a liberal path that emphasises using rent revenues to sustain growth but not equity? Or will Egypt turn to a progressive model including the financing of social services and social policies (e.g. by progressive taxation) and encouraging job-creating industries to achieve more equity of access to assets, resources and income?

Strong centralisation is arguably one of the most persistent characteristics of Egyptian regimes. It has meant that areas outside the capital have been consistently marginalised, creating an urban–rural divide that is as much economic as it is social and political. Interestingly enough, the totality of the Egyptian political scene since 2011 has adopted a centrist approach. No one seems to consider local government a key ingredient to achieving revolutionary demands for social justice. Indeed, this is understandable because the implications of political decentralisation are as yet undetermined, given that local electoral laws and inter-governmental transfer of funds are not yet designed.

All waves of transition in Egypt have so far resulted in only partial success in building institutions for freedom and accountability. Five years of transition since 2011 manifest a continued tendency towards vulnerable and unstable coalition-building that has resulted in a non-optimal partial rupture with the past. The constitution passed in 2014 is a case in point. While it respects social and economic rights, it continues to give way to an authoritarian bargain in which security precedes freedoms. The installation of institutions as islands of autonomy (the military, judiciary and al-Azhar) has to play out in the coming years before one can judge whether its impact on liberal democracy is positive or negative. Whether such islands of institutional autonomy hamper or provoke political oppression remains to be seen.

Finally, the polarisation inside Egypt as a result of the rise and fall of the Brotherhood may result in conflict as articulated in Elbadawi and Makdisi (Chapter 1, this volume). It is already obvious that the political contest between the Brotherhood and the rest of the political forces in Egypt is creating the grounds for an oppressive bargain against various forms of opposition and dissent; a bargain that so far enjoys support from wide sections of the middle and lower classes that fear the threat of instability. This polarisation has its own regional and international neighbourhood effects, a subject that will require further examination beyond this study.

Over the past thirty years, Egypt has experienced a process of modernisation that has been patchy. Economic growth rates were among the highest in the region, but have not resulted in broadening the access to the living standards and sense of well-being of the middle class. On the contrary, this class became impoverished. Additionally, growth in Egypt up to 2010 was accompanied by high (more than 10 per cent) unemployment and a limited ability to create jobs. The latter was partially an effect of the semi-rentier nature of Egyptian growth. With unemployment reaching 14 per cent (the official rate) three years into the transition, a possible incentive for more democratisation now exists, according to Elbadawi and Makdisi (Chapter 1, this volume).

'Bread, Freedom, Human Dignity and Social Justice': this was the iconic slogan chanted by those who crammed into Tahrir Square from 25 January to 11 February 2011. In other words, democracy and social justice were and still are at the heart of revolutionary demands, thus reflecting the inseparable relationship between the social/economic and the political. If revolutions are measured by their structural outcomes as processes of social transformation, then there has been neither a revolution nor a 'refolution', to use a Bayat term, or even modest reform in Egypt so far. There has been an uprising that toppled a ruler, but no structural change; Egypt in fact runs the risk of reproducing Mubarak's regime. The only positive outcome to date is the politicisation of the Egyptian population, and that is an important step for a people in the long and protracted struggle for freedom, liberties and social justice.

ANNEX: EXAMPLES OF SOCIAL MOVEMENTS

4.6.1   Kefaya

In 2000, mass protests filled the streets of Cairo in support of the Second Intifada. In 2003, a group of protestors formed an anti-war movement in reaction to the American invasion of Iraq. It is in these protests that the seeds of the Kefaya movement lie. In 2004, the movement was officially created with a slogan 'la li'l-tawrith', against the possible succession of Gamal Mubarak. The movement was the first to intensively use the Internet and mobile phones to reach out and raise awareness of the political and social causes it espoused. Kefaya also established strong ties with the labour movement, recognising its weight in social mobilisation and its role as an actor in the opposition. Its eventual disintegration was led by its failure to unite all colours of the youth rainbow, after its leadership supported an anti-hijab statement. Beyond its own existence,

Kefaya had created an infrastructure of mobilisation. In fact, two-thirds of the founders of the 6 April Movement were members of Kefaya.[65]

4.6.2   April Movement

In 2008, an important social movement coordinated a generalised strike in Mahala. This national strike was believed to be the biggest civil disobedience movement against the Mubarak regime. The 6 April Movement demonstrated a capacity to mobilise and to actively oppose Mubarak. It was a critical force during the uprising. Its leaders split after the parliamentary elections of 2012.

4.6.3   March Movement

Created in 2004 by Professor Abu'l-Ghar in collaboration with other colleagues, the 9 March Movement for the Independence of Universities is an active stance against the profound interference of the state security apparatus and the government on university campuses. It aimed to change the corrupt system of faculty appointments, which was believed to be the reason behind the continuous decline in the level of higher education. The movement also endorsed a fight for better salaries and pensions, launching awareness campaigns to mobilise students and staff against decisions believed to have harmed the quality of higher education or that were impeding freedoms and liberties. It was only in 2005, after staff and students joined a Kefaya protest against the Mubarak regime, that the movement attracted media attention and came to be known to the general public. In 2010, members of the movement were prevented from running for the faculty club elections, which was the first instance of open and direct harassment. Among the movement's triumphs is a successful court case against police on campuses. In January 2011, the members of the movement were present in Tahrir Square, in their personal capacity, not on behalf of the movement. During the eighteen days of the revolution, the movement organised protests in many cities outside Cairo.

4.6.4   Kolena Khalid Said

The most notable and perhaps influential shift in Egyptian protest movements in the past decade has been 'Kolena Khalid Said'. Provoked by the death of an Egyptian blogger after his arrest and brutal torture at the

[65] 'Badau al-Tareek', *al-Ahram*, 8 August 2012, p. 13.

hands of the police, a Facebook page was launched to raise awareness about his case. Gaining huge momentum, the Facebook page became the symbol of the anti-Mubarak protests, joining in the call for action on 25 January. The influence of the page on the Egyptian scene was such that *Time* listed its founder and administrator, Wael Ghoneim, as one of the 100 most influential people in the world in 2011. NATO regarded the page itself as the biggest dissident Facebook pages, with more than 1 million users.

4.6.5   Ultrass

These are social football fan clubs that are not controlled by the football clubs. Thanks to the Ultrass, football became an occasion for people to gather in their thousands out on the streets throughout Egypt to sing, dance and mingle as football fans, regardless of gender or social status. Any such gathering in the thousands for any other reason would have been illegal under the pre-2011 emergency law. The Egyptian uprising was punctuated by the activities of this movement and by its relationship with the Egyptian police force. In fact, it was part of the infrastructure that contributed to the build-up of street mobilisation in 2011. The Ultrass started in Egypt during the height of football euphoria which the Mubarak family ironically had thought to use to legitimise Gamal Mubarak's succession to the presidency. In 2007, fans of the National Football Club (Ahli) in Alexandria established a fan club and called it the Ultrass Red Devils. The Ahli fan club in Cairo followed suit and founded the Ultrass Ahlawi. Other Ultrasses were concurrently or consequently established by the fans of Zamalek, Ismailia, al-Etihad and so forth. It is estimated that paying membership is around 11,000 for Ultrass al-Ahli and 9,000 for Ultrass Zamalek, the two biggest Ultrasses in Egypt. Ultrasses also have Facebook pages that attract a great number of non-member fans: Ultrass al-Ahli has a Facebook page with 330,000 subscribers and Ultrass Zamalek has 135,000 subscribers.

The Ultrasses depend on voluntary membership and membership fees in the range of 10 to 50 Egyptian pounds per month. The funds are controlled by the fan club and not the football club. The fan club has its own governance structure and hierarchy that extends from leaders to heads of neighbourhood sections to cheerleaders during football games. The code of ethics of the Ultrasses necessitates total loyalty to the team even when it loses a match. The Ultrasses became a thorn in the back of the Egyptian regime. This escalated to outright animosity at several matches where skirmishes with the police resulted in casualties. Animosity led the Ultrasses to adopt political slogans, for instance in support of the Palestinians in Gaza or for the Tunisian revolution. The 6 April and Kolena Khalid Said Facebook pages announced the participation of Ultrasses in the demonstrations on 25 January. Various accounts describe how the Ultrasses helped protect demonstrators in Tahrir Square during the camel episode and on other days of violence.[66]

[66] Khamees, *Thawret Jeel Ultrass*, pp. 21, 59–60, 67–9.

5   Syria: The Painful Transition towards Democracy

Raed Safadi and Simon Neaime[1]

5.1   Introduction

Greater Syria, located at the crossroads of three continents, has long been a battleground for the empires and dynasties that came to lay claim to its fertile fields and forests. Independence changed the locus of decisions, but even today Syria – the beating heart of Arab nationalism – continues to bleed. Much of what the Syrian people gained from throwing off foreign control was quickly lost to a home-grown absolute autocracy under the Assad regime.

From the time it gained its independence in 1946, until the ascendency of Hafez al-Assad to its presidency in 1971, Syria experienced tumultuous, strife-filled times as competing factions wrestled for control of the country's government, with coups, counter-coups and intermittent civilian rule. A short-lived, democratically elected government took over Syria in 1947 under the leadership of Shukri al-Kuwatli. This was also the year that saw the birth of the Ba'ath Party, which was established by a group of secular, socialist Arab nationalists under the motto 'Unity, Liberty, Socialism'. The Ba'ath Party espoused pan-Arabism, liberty from foreign control, self-determination and Arab socialism.

President al-Kuwatli was quickly overthrown in 1949 by a military coup led by Colonel Husni al-Za'im, who himself, within five months, was overthrown by another coup, led by Colonel Sami al-Hinnawi. The latter was quickly deposed by another colonel in the army, Adib al-Shishakli, all within the same year. The nine years that followed (1949–58) saw twelve different rulers assuming the reins of power in Syria.

In 1958, Syria and Egypt formed the United Arab Republic (UAR). This union lasted for three years and dissolved in the aftermath of a Syrian military coup led by Colonel Luwa'i al-Atassi, who, again, and within five months, was deposed by Colonel Amin al-Hafez. Both of these colonels were also members of the Ba'ath Party, and their reigns, albeit short-lived

[1] The authors are grateful to Samir Makdisi, Mohamed Mohieddin and Saoussen Ben Romdhane for their valuable comments and suggestions on an earlier draft.

(1963–66), marked the beginning of the long and decisive hold of the Ba'ath Party over Syria that continues to the present day. In 1966, Colonel Nur El Dine al-Atassi overthrew Colonel al-Hafez. For the first time during its recent history, Syria had a president who managed to remain in power for several years before he was deposed in November 1970 and replaced by an acting president, Ahmad al-Khatib. President al-Khatib stayed in power for three months (November 1970–February 1971), enough time to prepare for Minister of Defence Lieutenant-General Hafez al-Assad to assume, and for the next thirty years to exercise, absolute power over both party and country.

Upon being acclaimed as president by a popular referendum in March 1971, al-Assad quickly moved to establish an authoritarian state that muted any open discussions and dissenting voices that might present even the least threat to the regime. Following his death in 2000, his son Bashar assumed power and, like his father, proceeded to rule Syria with an iron fist. The Assad rule of Syria had become dynastic and would continue to shackle the country's economy, society and polity until our present times.

On 15 March 2011, and in the middle of what has come to be called the 'Arab Spring', the people of Damascus declared a 'Day of Dignity' and demanded the release of political prisoners. The reaction of the regime to reasonable demands for justice and free speech was swift and brutal: more people were arrested, triggering a 'Day of Rage' rally in the southern city of Deraa. There, security forces began their armed suppression of an unarmed civilian population. Five years have passed since peaceful demonstrations turned into a widespread, vicious armed conflict that eventually attracted armed fundamentalist groups, which managed to bring under their control large parts of northern Syria and western Iraq though as of mid-2016 had been losing ground to regime forces in both countries. According to UN sources, recent 2015 estimates put the death toll at close to 250,000 men, women and children (UNOCHA 2015).

All in all, tens of thousands of Syrians have gone missing, more than 200,000 are locked up, and more than 2 million are homeless inside Syria. A further 2 million have been living in squalor outside Syria in Turkey, Lebanon and Jordan.

While many of the groups calling for fundamental reform in Syria are non-confessional, if not secular, in their orientation, sectarian undertones have been ever present since the outbreak of the civil conflict. The regime has attempted to mobilise support from its own and other constituencies by describing all opposition parties as 'Jihadi' terrorists. Strictly fundamentalist groups that have joined the conflict have indeed openly declared their intention to establish their own Islamic state and as of late 2015 were in control of large parts of the country. In contrast, the various moderate opposition groups, some clearly non-confessional, have had no appreciable influence on developments in the Syrian conflict. They did manage to come together in late 2012 under the umbrella of the 'Syrian Opposition Coalition'. But in contrast to the fundamentalist groups, whose objectives they also oppose, parties supporting the Coalition have not succeeded in extending their control over significant parts of the country. Conflicting aims have led to armed confrontations between them, which in turn has tended to weaken their role in the conflict.

Note that the Islamic State (Daesh) invited itself into Syria's conflict under the pretext that foreign 'crusaders' were at war with Islam. In fact, the majority of Syrians consider Daesh itself a foreign (and brutal) force. Of course, as some writers point out, religion can be and has been employed as an instrument to promote authoritarian rule, with clerics beholden to the ruler (Aldashev, Platteau and Sekeris 2013). Indeed, Daesh and similar groups have advanced to brutal levels the instrumentalisation of religion in an attempt to achieve their own goals (cf. Makdisi 2015). While the rise of Daesh has cruelly disrupted Syria's potential road towards democratic governance, we hold to the view that the current conflict will yet pave the way for the demise of the fundamentalist groups: our premise is that both domestic and external interests will in due course converge to thwart the assumption of power by these groups. However, on its own, this development would not necessarily assure the emergence of a democratic order in Syria. For this to happen, other challenges would also need to be overcome, including in respect of the emerging sectarianism in the country and, perhaps more important, the influence of Syria's neighbours that continue to harbour non-democratic regimes. Indeed, this latter factor has played a major role in sustaining the Syrian and other Arab autocracies, as demonstrated in the works of Safadi (2011) and Elbadawi and Makdisi (2011). The prospects for a democratic order will depend on how the Syrian conflict will yet be resolved, the political coalition assuming the reins of power in the post-conflict period and its ability to steer the country towards democracy.

Our premise is that when attempting to establish the guidelines for a democratic transition, the required political and economic freedoms are inseparable. An economic awakening in Syria should go hand in hand with the political awakening under way for over five years now despite the emergence of fundamentalist groups. It is not too soon to start imagining and deliberating the nature of this awakening. As Syria regains peace and stability, joins the ranks of democratic societies and reclaims its rightful place in the international community, it needs to establish the foundations for a well-regulated market economy, and to enhance its integration in regional and eventually global markets for goods, services and ideas. A well-regulated, inclusive, private sector-led growth, on one hand, and a solid, accountable and democratic governance structure on the other, should be the new politico-economic model for Syria.

The remainder of this chapter is divided as follows. Section 5.2 discusses the underlying factors that have led to the current uprising. Section 5.3 discusses the required institutional and economic changes for a democratic build-up in the post conflict phase. Section 5.4 concludes this chapter.

5.2   The Uprising: Underlying Factors

Rapid population growth and a growing, increasingly literate and digitally connected youth living in non-inclusive political and economic environments underlie the ongoing upheavals across the Arab world. This is a region that, since gaining independence from its various colonial rulers, has been dominated by corrupt, authoritarian regimes, mostly operating in closed markets, and in which human rights are abused on a daily basis, and the rule of law and property rights are regularly violated under the guise of security and the preservation of unity. Over time, these practices have combined to create an urban–rural schism, a growing gender and income inequality and a weak private sector that has consequently failed to generate sufficient employment, especially for the youth (see Elbadawi and Makdisi, Chapter 1, this volume, for an analysis of the major factors underlying the transition process in the Arab world). Syria is no exception: despite many promises of reform, the Syrian regime has not only maintained a strict authoritarian rule, but has fostered rent-seeking activities and built corruption networks that have gradually replaced all state institutions. The successful uprisings in Tunisia and Egypt acted as the spark for the initial Syrian uprising. However, its underlying factors can be traced to growing popular resentment of the exclusionary political and economic systems associated with the harsh autocracy that has prevailed since 1971, reinforced by a conflictual regional environment, intermittent cosmetic political and economic reforms and limited economic opening notwithstanding (cf. Abba 2011; Diaz 2011; Hinnebusch 2012; Syrian Centre for Policy Research 2013). Not surprisingly, the uprising has encouraged the active intervention of external parties, some in support of the regime, and some against. Iran, Russia and Hezbullah, the Lebanese Shia party, have backed the regime, while the opposition's foreign backers have mainly been the Arab Gulf states, Turkey, France, the United Kingdom and the United States. The Syrian uprising has thus gone beyond its own internal dynamics to become an integral part of the region's major geopolitical conflicts.

5.2.1   Underpinnings of the Political Regime, 1971–2000

As noted earlier, the late President Hafez al-Assad assumed power in 1970 following a bloodless intra-Ba'ath Party coup, known as the Corrective Movement. His coup came after twenty-one other coups and counter-coups that were Syria's political leitmotif from independence in 1946 until Assad's assumption of power. The Assad regime did not completely consolidate its power until early 1982, when it violently suppressed a Muslim Brotherhood insurrection in the city of Hama.[2]

Knowing full well the fate of his predecessors, Hafez al-Assad concentrated power in the presidency, arrogating to himself all-important decisions regarding foreign policy, national security, internal politics and the economy. The executive, legislative and judiciary branches of government came under the control of key figures in the Ba'ath Party, whose dominance in state institutions the constitution mandated.

To ensure full political control, the president nominated all ministers and senior officials of the state, who, in practice, were assigned limited executive rights. The regional command of the Ba'ath Party, and other secondary circles of the power system, proposed candidates for government posts and key civil service positions, but the president always made the final selection. The government did not govern according to any specific programme, but rather took decisions according to the interests of the power system. All dissent was suppressed, the need for home 'security' to confront external hostile powers used as a pretext. Indeed, the state of emergency that one of Hafez al-Assad's predecessors had imposed in 1963 remained in force until Bashar al-Assad rescinded it in April 2011, apparently as a gesture of goodwill to the protestors. However, freedoms of association, expression and assembly were always strictly prohibited.

As Assad and many of his aides belonged to the Alawite community, his assumption of power gave rise to grievances on the part of the Sunni majority, which, however, remained subdued. They saw power, with all the privileges that go with it, resting exclusively in the hands of a minority sect. The fact that the ruling Ba'ath Party was secular did not materially alter these perceptions. The authorities also treated the Kurds, Syria's

---

[2] Thousands were killed and whole segments of the city were obliterated. This action followed a series of violent incidents and clashes between the Brotherhood and the regime dating back before Hafez al-Assad had assumed full power in 1970, and inevitably led to measures that strengthened the authoritarian hold of the regime.

largest non-Arab minority, as second-class citizens subject to systematic discrimination. However, the civil war has come to alter Kurdish status: any post-uprising political setup cannot but accord them the full rights of citizenship.

With time, the party's monopoly of power over all major public sector decisions has given rise to systematic corruption, with key decision-makers taking advantage of their positions to extract sums illegal. Suffering from low rates of pay, the army and the judiciary system have also fallen prey to corrupting influences (Lust-Okar 2006).

In his March 1999 inauguration speech, and prior to starting his fifth constitutional term, Hafez al-Assad signalled a limited relaxation of the authoritarian approach of the prior three decades. He emphasised the importance of responsibility in the context of 'the people's democratic system'. He also noted that the enlargement of the decision-making circle, as well as an increase in opportunities for open discussion and public participation, would facilitate the democratic process and strengthen the country. Furthermore, he called for various economic reforms and described the public sector as the basis of the national economy, instrumental in maintaining an economic and social balance.

During the 1998 parliamentary elections that preceded the 1999 presidential referendum, held to re-elect the president for a fifth term, public political debates were authorised, but within prescribed limits. This prompted a heated rivalry for the parliament's assigned independent seats (83 out of a total of 250) and gave rise to public calls for fighting corruption, modernising the administration and expediting reform of the public sector.

The motivation for this move, after three decades of strict authoritarian rule, was the president's wish to rearrange the political and security landscape in anticipation of his death and the assumption of power by his son. With a view to achieving this objective, he replaced a number of key security officials with personnel closer to his son.[3] Parallel preparations for the takeover by Bashar al-Assad included his undertaking official

---

[3] Between July 1998 and early 2000, the army's chief-of-staff, the director of the Department of General Intelligence and the chief of internal security at the department, the commander of the air force and the chief of military intelligence were all forced into retirement. As the majority of these 'security pillars' had reached the legal age for retirement, these moves could have been seen as part of a normal process of change. Historically, however, Hafez al-Assad had not changed his political, military, security or even his administrative staff when they reached the legal retirement age. Only when one of the staff committed a notable error would he be removed from the circle of power, but with due respect to his status and role in exchange for his political loyalty. The stability of Hafez's regime strongly depended on the loyalty of his security staff, and thus the release of numerous key security officials indicated an underlying motive to surround his son with key personnel deemed loyal to him once he assumed the reins of power.

and public tours with extensive media coverage. Though he had no formal status in the state, Bashar gave extended political interviews, in which he demonstrated a strong understanding of key international shifts and currents, especially of the important Lebanese portfolio at a time when Syrian troops were still deployed in Lebanon. The media began to focus more closely on Colonel Bashar al-Assad's campaign to modernise the state and reduce corruption through economic and administrative reform.

Soon after peace negotiations with Israel stalled in early 2000, Hafez al-Assad fell terminally ill. Given his strict control of the regime, legislative and executive institutions virtually collapsed during his illness (Maoz 1985; Seale 1988; Wedeen 1999). Only the security forces maintained their effectiveness. State paralysis ensued, bringing in its wake another wave of deep economic and social crises. Nonetheless, party and state apparatuses were mobilised to assure a smooth succession after his death.

5.2.2   Sustaining the Political Regime

When Hafez al-Assad died in June 2000, potential constitutional hurdles that would have prevented his son from being elected as president were overcome by popular referendum. Bashar al-Assad was elected to succeed his father exactly one month later. As earlier stated, Hafez had in fact meticulously prepared this succession, ensuring that potential contenders – including his brother, Rifa'at al-Assad, and trusted lieutenants loyal to him since the very beginning, including his long-serving though token vice-president, Abd al-Halim Khaddam, and the minister of defence, Mustapha Tlas – had no choice but to submit to this dynastic succession and embrace it.

More important, what these and other political and military 'barons' who had accompanied Assad to power, and reached high-level positions in his regime and amassed enormous wealth, feared most was that Bashar would either reform the system or, worse, would remove them from power individually. In the event, Bashar, rather than risk prompting a collective backlash by the 'old regime', targeted selected senior government and military personnel and replaced them with individuals loyal to him. As a result, many key figures of the old regime were arrested, exiled or fell prey to an 'anti-corruption' campaign. The latter move gave the impression that a new era was dawning and earned Bashar a considerable amount of popularity among Syrians.

Upon his accession to the presidency, Bashar consolidated his power by becoming General Commander of the Armed Forces, Secretary-General of the Party and leader of the Progressive National Front. Thus, and despite an outward appearance of youth and modernity, he followed his father in holding the monopoly of power in the state and the party: power in Syria had now made a full transition, from the state to the Ba'ath Party to, effectively, the House of Assad.

At the beginning of his reign, Bashar al-Assad enjoyed a certain measure of support both domestically and internationally especially since, in the aftermath of the events of 11 September 2001, Syria agreed to cooperate on counterterrorism initiatives. Leaving the United States to attend Hafez al-Assad's funeral, Secretary of State Madeleine Albright stated that she hoped Bashar al-Assad would 'take on the mantle' of his late father. She later described Bashar as a 'reformer' determined to modernise his country. Secretary Albright's optimism about a new era in US–Syrian relations appeared justified. The Europeans, too, were supportive of the new president and sought to move forward on the Syrian track of the EU–Mediterranean agreement.

This period of grace, however, was short-lived. In the aftermath of the 2003 Iraq War, Syria's bilateral relations with the United States rapidly deteriorated, and in December 2003, President George W. Bush signed the Syria Accountability and Lebanese Sovereignty Restoration Act passed by Congress. To be clear, the objective of foreign, principally US, pressure on Syria has been related to its role in the region and the Arab–Israeli conflict, Syria being a major actor in it, rather than to any push for democratic reform, foreign rhetoric in this regard notwithstanding.

The Act provided for the imposition of a series of sanctions against Syria unless it ended its support for Palestinian terrorist groups and its intervention in Lebanon, ceased its pursuit of weapons of mass destruction, and met its obligations under UN Security Council resolutions regarding the stabilisation and reconstruction of Iraq. In May 2004, the United States determined that Syria had not complied with these conditions and implemented a series of sanctions against it. Bilateral relations were soon to experience another low following the assassination of the former Lebanese prime minister, Rafiq Hariri, in February 2005. This assassination came in the wake of the UN Security Council Resolution 1559 co-sponsored by France and the United States in 2004, which called for 'all remaining foreign forces to withdraw from Lebanon'. Syrian units stationed in Lebanon since 1976 were consequently withdrawn in April 2005. The regime's reaction to its international isolation was to seek strengthened relations with Iran; importantly, the crackdown on dissidents accelerated.

However, the regime managed to develop a more positive relationship with the European Union (EU), but not one without emerging strains.

The EU and Syria had been engaged in discussions for a Euro–Syrian partnership under the Barcelona Agreement and the EU had launched several large assistance programmes for administrative and economic reforms over the previous decade. However, though the partnership agreement was initialled in 2004, the EU chose to postpone ratification as a means of pressuring Syria to modify its political course (i.e. to become more accommodating of Western interests in the region, including in terms of its stance on the ongoing crises in Lebanon and in Iraq and an eventual reconciliation with Israel). While human rights issues were also raised, in practice, they did not have a high priority for the Western agenda.

The Syrian regime has proved steadfast in the face of Western pressure, no matter what objectives were being sought. Its hold on power remained strong all the while, and as will be described in the next section, it has pursued additional measures to liberalise the economy and open it up to direct investment (Carnegie Papers 2006). Syrian political activists advocating political reform have generally distanced themselves from close contact with Western governments, in particular the United States. One reason is their fear of persecution by domestic authority on the grounds of complicity with foreign powers. Another reason is that many Syrian activists do not believe that the real aim of foreign pressure is to foster a change in Syria's political climate that would allow for the initiation of a democratic process, but that, as noted earlier, it is otherwise. In practice, economic or political sanctions imposed on Syria have produced a negative effect. Even pro-reform Syrians have considered them unjust, aimed not at promoting domestic reform but at extracting concessions from the Syrian regime on the Iraqi, Lebanese or Palestinian fronts, where Syrian and Western interests have diverged. The Iraq War, for example, by ending favourable Syria–Iraq economic relations, generated discontent among the Syrian people and promoted further support for the regime (Carnegie Papers 2006).

Noteworthy is the reluctance of Western powers to engage with the Ba'ath Party itself or to employ systematic pressure to encourage democratic practices. Even the Euro–Syrian partnership, which deepened Syria's involvement with the West, did not establish any practical modality for fostering democracy in the country. Possibly, Western pressure could have been more effective if instead it had relied 'on conditional aid and diplomatic pressure to convince the Syrian government to improve human rights' (Carnegie Papers 2006, no. 69, July).

Less surprising was the internal recognition of Bashar's unlimited authority over Syrian state and party institutions. The official epigraph which the incoming leader coined was 'change through continuity'. It conveyed a very powerful message to the population: the desire for greater political participation can best be served not through violent protests against the regime, but rather through a gradual process of political and economic reform under his leadership. Beneath Bashar al-Assad's ubiquitous portrait on the streets of Damascus a banner read: 'The leader is to unveil a new era.'

Indeed, in his inaugural speech, Bashar al-Assad waved the banner of reform and instructed the authorities to respect 'the other opinion'. He declared that there could be no democracy without the development of institutions and administrative reforms, adding, 'We should face ourselves and our society bravely, and conduct a courageous dialogue in which we reveal our points of weakness'. The speech sounded to intellectuals, dissidents and Western powers like a call for change and they began calling publicly for economic and political reform.

Syria enjoyed then a brief political opening up and a Damascus Spring of sorts blossomed. Buoyed by Assad's actions and proclamations, which later turned out to be illusionary, Syrians began to rediscover political activity and several human rights organisations, yearning for a political voice and debate, re-emerged or were established to support the new president in what they saw as cautious steps towards reform.

In September 2000, ninety-nine writers and artists signed a charter demanding the lifting of the 1963 state of emergency, the release of political prisoners, the return of political exiles, freedom of the press and the right to hold public meetings. They called it the Statement of 99. It signalled the start of what came to be known as the Damascus Spring. For close to a year dissidents met unimpeded, and on occasion the official press even gave them a voice. Civil servants wrote petitions to the president calling for reform and appealing for an end to the emergency law. The movement never called for regime change or challenged the legitimacy of Bashar al-Assad's succession to the presidency.

In November 2000, on the occasion of the thirtieth anniversary of the revolution that brought Assad's father to power, the Mazza prison was shut down and 600 political prisoners were amnestied. Assad also allowed the six constituent parties of the governing National Progressive Front to open provincial offices and to produce their own newspapers. This prompted Abdul Kader Kaddoura, the parliamentary speaker, to declare, 'Syria is telling its citizens that a new phase has begun, one that is characterised by forgiveness and love'.

It was a only matter of time before the attendance at more than sixty dialogue forums (*muntadayat*), which had blossomed during the

Damascus Spring, began to alarm the security apparatus of the regime. In August 2001, the Damascus Spring came to an abrupt end when Mamun al-Homsi, an independent legislator representing Damascus, was arrested after he launched a hunger strike to protest against the widespread corruption found in state institutions. The regime then labelled the reformists agents of the West who sought to undermine Syria's stability. All the forums were disbanded and the Damascus Spring quickly turned into a Damascus Nightmare and the most prominent activists and leaders, such as Michel Kilo, Riad Seif, Riad al-Turk and Aref Dalila, joined Mamun al-Homsi in prison, charged with 'attempting to change the constitution by illegal means'.

In 2005, another flurry of debate took place, as well-known dissidents were freed. At the height of international pressure on Syria during that year, spurred by Syria's involvement in Lebanon and its conflict with the United States over Iraq and Palestine, a group of Syrian intellectuals, including Islamists, Kurds and young campaigners who had recently emerged in cities all over Syria, released the Damascus Declaration, which called for Syria's transformation through peaceful means from a 'security state to a political state' based on free and regular elections, a democratic constitution, the rule of law, pluralism and individual rights.[4] However, President Assad chose to follow the 'old guard' approach, rather than ride on the success of and enthusiasm for the forums and attempt to forge a new power base. When, in March 2011, people demonstrated across the country calling for change, the regime responded brutally, fearful of losing its power.

In brief, isolated and ineffective attempts at reform notwithstanding, the Syrian political regime has been fearful of moving forward politically lest it lose control, choosing instead to maintain strict authoritarian rule. This, as discussed later, has been accompanied by a national economic management that, to a large extent, served the interests of the business class allied with those in power, though admittedly the Syrian economy has, on the whole, progressed notably in the past decades (see later in this chapter). Nonetheless, growth has been accompanied by persisting inequities and corruption and, in recent decades, rising levels of unemployment, especially of the youth, averaging about 18 per cent in 2009–10 (Table 5.1).

---

[4] The Declaration, written by prominent dissident Michel Kilo, labelled the Syrian government as 'authoritarian, totalitarian and cliquish'. Once again, the domestic debate around the Damascus Declaration was short-lived; however, the majority of the signatories remained active and later participated in the Antalya and Istanbul conferences that led to the formation of the Syrian National Council in October 2011.

Table 5.1: *Syria: Socio-economic Indicators, 2006–2013*

	2006	2007	2008	2009	2010	2011	2012	2013
Unemployment, total (% of total labour force)	8.20	8.40	10.90	8.10	8.40	8.5	25	35
Unemployment, youth total (% of total labour force)	18.30	19.10	22.40	16.70	19.20	–	–	–
Human Development Index (HDI)	–	0.636	0.642	0.643	0.649	0.651	0.654	0.67
FDI (inflows in millions of US dollars)	–	1,242	1,467	2,570	1,469	–	–	–

Sources: World Development Indicators, UNCTAD, HDI report 2012.

5.2.3   Cosmetic Economic Reforms, a Modicum of Growth

The economic landscape the Assad regime created is a mirror image of its political reality: highly centralised and dirigiste. The two Assad regimes have followed a state-led economic development model anchored in a strong interventionist-redistributive mentality that includes heavy reliance on state planning, import substitution policies, initial nationalisation of private and foreign assets (later limited measures of liberalisation were introduced; see later in this chapter) and a social contract whereby the state provided education, housing, health care and food subsidies.

As already noted, over time, the party's monopoly of power has given rise to systematic corruption, with key decision-makers taking advantage of their position to extract illegal profits. Suffering from low salaries, the army as well as the judiciary system has fallen prey to corrupting influences. Unsurprisingly, and despite early, relatively high rates of economic growth and living standards, the national economy has been marred with significant inefficiencies and periods of stagnation, occasional cosmetic attempts at economic reforms notwithstanding.

Under Bashar al-Assad, minor touches of reform, including some measures of economic liberalisation, did not change the fundamental aspects of the Syrian economy: heavy dependence on volatile oil markets, limited private sector activity despite some opening up, limited job creation and declining integration into the world economy. This is perhaps not surprising in view of the influence of entrenched interests and the regime's power base, which have combined to resist substantive economic reforms.

Table 5.2: *Syria: Macroeconomic Indicators, 2009–2015*

	2009	2010	2011	2012	2013	2014a	2015a
Nominal GDP (USD million)	53,967	60,185	54,479	44,727	38,068	29,866	36,530
Real GDP growth (annual %)	6.00	3.20	–3.40	–18.80	–15.00	4.20	6.20
Exports of goods and services (USD million)	10,884	12,273	10,288	3,876	2,675	3,899	6,019
Exports of goods and services (% GDP)	20.17	20.39	18.88	8.67	7.03	13.05	16.48
Imports of goods and services (USD million)	13,948	15,936	17,598	10,777	8,917	9,824	11,109
Imports of goods and services (% GDP)	25.85	26.48	32.30	24.10	23.42	32.89	30.41%
Services balance (USD million)	2,079	3,860	429	32	(456)	(377)	(213)
Services balance (% GDP)	3.85	6.41	0.79	0.07	–1.20	–1.26	–0.58
Trade balance (USD Million)	(3,064)	(3,663)	(7,310)	(6,901)	(6,242)	(5,925)	(5,090)
Trade balance (% GDP)	–5.68	–6.09	–13.42	–15.43	–16.40	–19.84	–13.93
Inflation (Consumer prices: Av. % change)	2.6	4.4	4.8	36.9	46.4	17.8	14.2
Population growth (annual %)	2.67	1.47	1.92	–1.96	–4.08	1.51	1.97
Population (million)	20.1	20.4	20.8	20.4	19.6	19.9	20.3

Source: Economist Intelligence Unit – Country Report. a: EIU forecasts.

Syria's economy was relatively developed when the country gained its independence in 1946. From then on, through the mid-1970s, it enjoyed unprecedented levels of economic growth: the average annual GDP growth rate during that period was a little more than 6.0 per cent at constant 1963 prices. Rising oil prices, intra-regional flow of capital and workers' remittances from abroad helped to fund social development and public investments in infrastructure, health care and education, as well as state-owned enterprises operating behind impregnable walls. By the end of the 1970s, the Syrian economy had shifted from its traditional agrarian base to relying on commercial, service and industrial activities. The main sources of Syria's national income were oil and tourism. Nevertheless, the economy continued to rely heavily on foreign aid and grants to finance both its budget and its trade deficits; Arab aid transfers and Soviet assistance also supported mounting defence expenditure.

By the mid-1980s, Syria's interventionist-redistributive model ran out of steam as the prosperity of the past all but disappeared, and even went into negative territory (−2 per cent GDP growth rate in 1982–83) in the wake of a rapid decline in oil prices, lower export revenues, drought that affected agricultural production and a decline in workers' remittances. This prompted the government to rethink its economic management approach and to adopt policies that might achieve macroeconomic stability, a greater participation by the private sector in economic activity and a higher degree of integration in global markets. The government reduced its spending, cut down on imports and launched anti-corruption campaigns against black market currency dealers.

By the end of the 1990s, however, the pace of economic liberalisation had slowed, favouring members of the powerful elite: during the period 1997–99, Syria's economy grew by an annual average of 1.5 per cent (Figure 5.1), and in 1999 the economy actually shrank and unemployment rocketed to an estimated 20 per cent.

Bashar al-Assad inherited an economy that had been facing grave economic challenges, including restoring economic growth, addressing a rising population, alleviating poverty, providing jobs, attracting investment and tackling a large external debt. The government initiated modest economic reforms, starting with a rethink of the regulatory environment in the financial sector, including cutting lending interest rates, licensing private banks and consolidating the numerous rates of exchange. It also began to reform its state-led economy, with initiatives such as liberalising the agriculture sector and privatising several state monopolies. Other reforms included a reduction in subsidies on certain items, most notably gasoline and cement, and the re-opening of the Damascus Stock Exchange, which had been closed for forty years. In addition, legislative

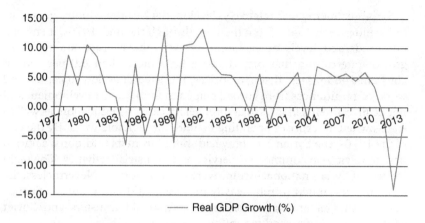

Figure 5.1: Real GDP Growth (%), 1977–2013
Source: Euromonitor from National Statistics/Eurostat/OECD/UN/
International Monetary Fund (IMF), World Economic
Outlook (WEO).

decrees to encourage corporate ownership, and to allow the Central Bank
to issue treasury bills and bonds for the government debt, were adopted.
Other structural reforms included the simplification of investment procedures, modernisation of accounting standards and the streamlining of
the tax system.

Partly as a result of these and other reforms, the economy made
a remarkable turnaround and registered impressive performance in
2004 when GDP grew by 6.9 per cent, and onwards with growth rates
averaging 4.7 per cent during the period 2005–10 (Figure 5.1). Indeed,
up to the outbreak of the uprising the country's macroeconomic performance, in contrast to its socio-economic record (see later in this chapter),
was relatively robust. Not only were GDP rates of growth relatively high,
but inflation rates were under control, declining to 4.4 per cent in
2010 (Figure 5.2). Further, financial reforms allowed private banks to
operate in Syria for the first time, and they managed to attract expatriate
savings. In addition, the inflow of direct foreign investment, particularly
from the Gulf States, increased from $111 million in 2001 to $1.47 billion
in 2010. Unemployment rates were not excessively high (less than
10 per cent though youth unemployment rates were higher). But one
should keep in mind the point that Syria's traditionally bloated public
sector, employing roughly one quarter of the total workforce, has acted as
a cover for actual unemployment. Money-losing state-run companies

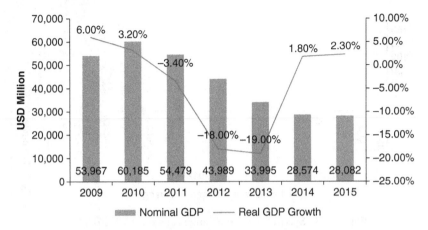

Figure 5.2: Nominal GDP & Real GDP Growth, 2009–2015
Source: Economic Intelligence Units, Syria Country Reports.

have been kept afloat, the government justification being that their privatisation would generate considerable social disruption.

Since 2009, growth performance has greatly deteriorated, primarily as a result of the ongoing conflict, but also due to the negative impact of the global financial crisis and prolonged droughts, the rate of growth deteriorating to an average of about −15 per cent in 2011–13 (Figure 5.2). This deterioration has been accompanied by continued high youth unemployment, though this has been tempered by the huge exodus of Syrian refugees and the recruitment of young men by the militias.

Real GDP growth rates bottomed in 2013 at −19 per cent. This was coupled with a steep devaluation (a fourfold deprecation) of the Syrian pound (SYP) from SYP 40 to 1 US dollar in January 2011 to SYP 140 to 1 US dollar in December 2013 (Figure 5.3), accompanied by a significant depletion in foreign exchange reserves at the Central Bank from USD 19.5 billion at the end of 2010 to USD 1.8 billion at the end of 2014 (Figure 5.4). Moreover, both the trade and current account balances continued to register a deficit for the aforementioned reasons during the period from 2009 to 2014 (Figure 5.5). The deteriorating economic situation, however, is yet to assist in producing a political settlement acceptable to both the authorities and the various opposition groups.

Prior to the uprising, deep and comprehensive economic reforms were always hindered by the business community's allegiance to the regime. Involved with influential members of the regime in rent-seeking activities

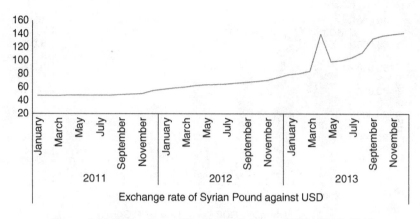

Figure 5.3: Syrian Pound Exchange Rate per USD, 2011–2013
Source: Economic Intelligence Units, Syria Country Reports.

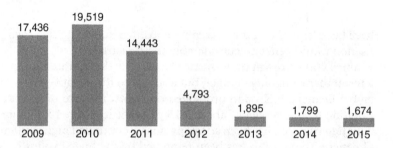

Figure 5.4: End of Year International Reserves, 2009–2015
(USD Million)
Source: Economic Intelligence Units, Syria Country Reports.

(oil, foreign trade, mobile phones, etc.), the Syrian business community gave its support to the regime, indicating little interest in fostering democratic development. Foreign companies across all sectors have operated in Syria for decades through middlemen (sponsors) within the power system, weakening the strength of Western pressure to liberalise. Western oil companies, in particular, have invested heavily and have begun operations in cooperation with the Syrian authorities, which is the only way to gain access to the Syrian market. This state of affairs is not unique to Syria but begs the question whether market liberalisation and reform on their own could promote the formation of a business community interested in a genuine democracy, or would simply give rise to crony capitalism.

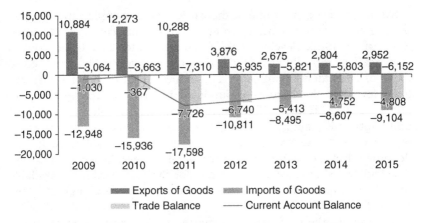

Figure 5.5: Trade and Current Account Balances, 2009–2015
(USD Million)
Source: Economic Intelligence Units, Syria Country Reports.

Despite measures taken to liberalise the economy, competition in Syria remains limited and substantial barriers to entry continue to plague many economic sectors. Some productive sectors remain firmly in the hands of the government, while for others foreign entry remains subject to certain types of restriction. Public sector monopolies control cement production, sugar refining, fertilisers, oil refining, port operation, alcohol, cotton, some cereal products, tobacco, pharmaceutical products, salt, fish, fruit, olive oil, animal feedstock, water distribution, aviation, electricity, telecommunications and insurance. Inefficient state-owned enterprises and public authorities play key roles in many value chains through, for example, exclusive control of the procurement and sale of cotton and wheat, exclusive control of yarn-making and provision of infrastructure.

It is also the case that the Syrian economy remains relatively isolated from the global markets for goods, services and ideas. International trade is highly restricted by both tariff and non-tariff barriers, and all the efforts at liberalisation, including the shortening of the import negative list (list containing prohibited products and/or products subject to strict import regulations), have been countered by a web of protection that distorts economic incentives and discourages competition. This negative list consists of agricultural and industrial products, such as flowers, animal products, forestry products, vegetable oils, sugar-based products, quarrying products, plastic and rubber products, leather, wood, craft products and so forth.

Syria's tariff regime is one of the world's most complex and opaque, both in absolute terms and in comparison to other countries at similar levels of economic development. While tariff rates have been reduced from their historically high levels, they are still very high compared to those of other developing countries. Before 2002, different tariffs and taxes levied at the border accumulated to produce a duty of up to 255 per cent (IMF 2006). The customs reforms that followed sought to unify duty rates, and have gradually reduced the rate to a maximum of 65 per cent. However, the tariff schedule is not consolidated in one document but rather dispersed over several decrees; hence it is not easy to calculate a simple average tariff rate for Syria. According to available data, Syria's effective tariff protection rate is one of the highest in the region.[5]

In addition, the tariff regime is marred by a complex web of exceptions and special rates determined according to the origin of the import and the entity importing it. Around 200 state-owned companies enjoy different levels of subsidy and protection; many also have the exclusive right either to import certain goods or to grant licenses for key imports. Syria bans the import of certain final goods that compete with Syrian enterprises. There are also goods which it is prohibited to import. One may argue that quite legitimate public policy objectives (security, health care or protection of the environment) may lie behind these prohibitions, but in Syria the list is extensive and the criteria are not publicly known. Not only have these practices injected further distortions into the economy, but also they have given rise to a culture of rent-seeking. According to a World Bank study, quantitative restrictions add up to the equivalent of a 19 per cent across-the-board tariff on all imports (Chemingui and Dessus 2003). Unsurprisingly, the World Bank's ease of doing business rankings for 2011 placed Syria at 134 out of 183 countries.

In addition, economic growth in Syria has not been inclusive. It has not led to a significant amount of job creation or poverty reduction. Low firm turnover (firm entry and exit) translated into a narrow pool of young firms that grow and create jobs. High unemployment (35 per cent in 2013, Figure 5.6), coupled with a low labour participation rate of 50 per cent in Syria, has resulted in a very low ratio of employment in the working-age population. Notably, the unemployment problem in Syria, and across the region, is largely a youth phenomenon. Young people between fifteen and

---

[5] According to the IMF, in 2004, the effective tariff protection rate in Syria was equivalent to 9.3 per cent of total imports, an average that then was only exceeded by Algeria and Morocco (IMF, Syria 2006). This average also ignores the high level of 'leakage' from the official receipts on account of widespread corruption.

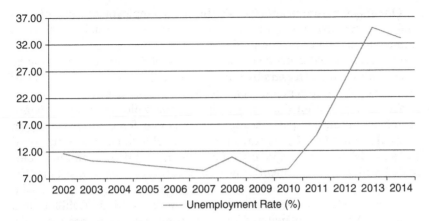

Figure 5.6: Unemployment Rate (%), 2002–2014
Source: EIU, Euromonitor from National statistics/Eurostat/OECD/
UN/International Monetary Fund (IMF), World Economic
Outlook (WEO).

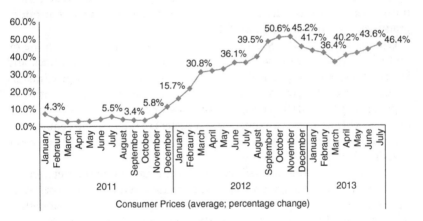

Figure 5.7: Monthly Inflation Rates (%), 2011–2013
Source: Economic Intelligence Units, Syria Country Reports.

twenty-nine years old account for 80 per cent of the unemployed in Syria
(Kabbani and Kamel 2009).

High unemployment rates were coupled with significant increases in
the rate of inflation, increasing from 4 per cent in January 2011 to about
46 per cent in December 2013 (Figure 5.7).

One major reason behind Syria's chronic unemployment is the bloated public sector that employs roughly one quarter of the total workforce in money-losing, state-run companies kept afloat under the pretext that their privatisation would generate considerable social disruption. Syria's public sector attracted job seekers by offering greater job security, higher wages and generally more generous benefits than those of the private sector.

Another reason for the persistently high unemployment rate is demographics: during the past decade, Syria's labour force has grown by an annual average of 2.7 per cent, a rate comparable to neighbouring countries but far higher than in any other region. And these high rates coincided with the government's dwindling resources that constrained its ability to provide new employment opportunities for the youth who have been characterised as a 'generation in waiting' (Dhillon and Yousef 2009). The paucity of job opportunities at home has led many Syrians to leave the country. However, since the 1980s, their opportunities for finding jobs in foreign countries have been on a declining trend on account of low growth in Europe, and the GCC plans to nationalise its labour force. The unemployment problem in Syria is further accentuated by a serious mismatch between the skills young people possess and those business seeks, suggesting Syria's education system has failed to produce graduates with marketable job skills.

On the demand side, Syria's GDP has remained dependent on the oil and agriculture sectors, which are subject to fluctuating oil prices and levels of rainfall, respectively. The oil sector provided approximately 20 per cent of the government's revenues and about 35 per cent of its export receipts in 2010. The agriculture sector contributed to 20 per cent of GDP. Oil and services exports and transfers of income and remittances from abroad were the main sources of foreign earnings, but since the uprising these have declined substantially.

In summary, economic failures, including in labour markets, credit availability and housing, alongside bureaucratic red tape, weaknesses in the mode of governing, lack of corporate transparency and the operation of political institutions in Syria, have denied young Syrians the job opportunities and the social support their fathers enjoyed before them. These factors have deeply affected the 'generation in waiting' and combined to trigger calls for change.

5.3   Moving Forward: Institutions for Economic Development and the Democratic Build-Up

Whatever the eventual outcome of the continuing military conflict, the Syrian uprising is expected to lead to a fundamental change in the country's political landscape. Were the fundamentalist groups to emerge triumphant and consolidate their power base, then diagnosing the prerequisites for a successful democratic transition in Syria would be difficult to visualise. As already noted, we shall therefore assume that the rise to power of the fundamentalist groups is a temporary phase, hopefully very short-lived, and that the post-uprising political scene will witness substantive moves towards democratic governance. As Syria, hopefully, moves in this direction we should keep in mind the experiences of transitions in other regions of the world which teach us that poor economic performance, especially during the transitional period, can cause serious setbacks in the unfolding of the democratic process (cf. Amin et al. 2012). We offer next what we believe are the cornerstones of the economic reforms that would need to be implemented in support of the country's move to democracy.

Lessons from the experience of transition economies argue against any 'shock therapy' and in favour of a gradual approach to reform. Syria needs to abandon, in a gradual manner, its state-led, dirigiste economic model in favour of a market-based one. The country needs to unleash the traditional entrepreneurial spirit of Syrian industrialists and merchants; open and fair competition should replace the system of privileges that has besieged the economy for more than four decades now. The key objective here will be to enhance the productivity and competitiveness of the Syrian economy, and put it on a path where growth and employment generation are led by a well-regulated private sector.

Experience shows that reforms should be pursued across different areas of policy in a complementary way, in order to promote an acceptance of change by helping to ensure that those disadvantaged by one reform benefit from another, and to foster synergies between policies. The key to successful transition lies less in individual policies themselves than in the way policies interact; the benefits of an open trade and investment regime, for example, will only be fully realised if a proper form of economic governance (discussed later) is in place, which can translate into appropriate macroeconomic policies; efficient labour markets and a regulatory environment that encourages the entry and exit of businesses and protects and safeguards public interests; and an education system that enables skills to match evolving needs. While this will mean pursuing policy reforms in parallel, the precise sequence may need to be flexible.

Thus, while an open economy is an essential component of sustainable and inclusive economic growth, complementary policies are also needed in order to realise fully all its benefits. In other words, the positive results from an open economy are not automatic; other policy choices matter as well.

One of the most fundamental of the complementary policies needed is the establishment of an adequate system of economic governance that is built on strong institutions and protected by the rule of law, these two being crucial for ensuring property rights and for lowering transaction costs. We believe that supporting the establishment and the strengthening of domestic economic institutions in Syria is the starting point for achieving sustainable growth and political freedom. The questions are, what institutions and how to build them?

Early contributions on these issues came from Douglass North and Mancur Olsen among others, but in our current context the main protagonist has been Rodrik, who addresses the question of which institutions matter and how to establish them (see Safadi et al. 2011). On the former issue, he identifies five critical areas:

- Property rights, strictly speaking, control over property rather than legal rights per se;
- Regulatory institutions to correct externalities, information failure and market power, such as anti-trust bodies, banking supervision and, more controversially, coordination of major investment decisions, as Rodrik argues was provided by Korean and Taiwanese economic intervention;
- Institutions for macroeconomic stabilisation, for example a lender of last resort;
- Social insurance, this often means transfer programmes, but Rodrik argues that other institutions such as jobs-for-life can also play the same role; and
- Institutions to manage social conflict.

On the issue of how to establish institutions, Rodrik makes two observations:

- There is no single optimal set of institutions – there are many ways of achieving the same objectives.
- Moreover, the interactions between institutions mean that the package needs to be considered as a whole (or at most in a few broad parts) rather than piece by piece.

Institutions can be adopted from abroad or evolved by trial and error locally. Rodrik prefers the latter, although he recognises that it often provides political cover for an unwillingness to reform, and that it takes time and can involve being drawn down blind alleys. The critical issue here is the legitimacy of the institutions. Adopting foreign institutions can often be an efficient way of shortening the learning process and, indeed, good policy-making will always seek to learn from the experience of others. The requirement, however, is that the institutions are sought as solutions to locally identified problems and are adapted to local needs and conditions in quite subtle ways. There is a world of difference between a society facing a problem and looking abroad for something it can adapt to its own needs, and an external force declaring that a certain institution will be good for it.

At the external level, emphasis should be placed first and foremost on fostering economic justice by providing direct support for social, human and economic development programmes that help the population. That would include opening up to international markets and promoting Syria's engagement in international economic organisations including the World Trade Organization. The basic objective of such moves would be to complement domestic efforts to build strong and credible economic institutions and maintain sound economic policies.

5.4   Concluding Remarks

Gross economic mismanagement and a harsh authoritarian political system have combined to thwart Syria moving towards freedom, equality and prosperity. The uprising-turned-civil-war (now five years old) is taking an increasing toll on the population, the infrastructure and the economy. The final outcome is yet uncertain; however, what is expected is that, despite the attempts of fundamentalist groups to control the country, the uprising will eventually bring about a profound political change and lead to a pluralistic, democratic Syria. 'The Day After' requires a fundamental rethink of the political and economic role of government, how to rebuild state institutions and reformulate economic policies in a credible, inclusive and non-sectarian way.

As hopefully democracy is restored, a new model of economic development in Syria should emerge, one that would help sustain democratic reform by responding to the aspirations of the Syrian people. This would include inclusive socio-economic policies and the promotion of good governance, which would go hand in hand with building democratic institutions to create a political environment more conducive to growth, equitable distribution of the fruits of growth and, following the settlement of the crisis, the daunting task of reconstruction. The hope, in other words, is that the seeds of reforms will grow into an accountable and equitable political and economic system, formed by a freely elected and accountable parliament and a constitution that guarantees equal rights and obligations for all its citizens in accordance, we should add, with the UN Universal Declaration of Human Rights. This is the daunting challenge that lies ahead of Syria and its people.

Building democratic institutions in Syria means providing the opportunity for the most disadvantaged groups to participate in politics, institutionalising their rights to make choices and/or challenge public policies and to hold future governments accountable. This is not to say that democratisation is a magic recipe that would address immediately the many political and economic problems Syria faces emanating from its present crisis, but it undoubtedly constitutes a major means of putting the country back on a sustainable path to democracy, prosperity and development. In the foreseeable future, to build such capacities and institutions it will be necessary to overcome two major challenges. The first is the challenge to break rent-seeking corruption networks that have managed over the past decades to reproduce themselves, influence the ruling Ba'ath regime and policy-making in Syria, weaken the state apparatus and mainly serve the interests of a privileged few. The second is to overcome any religious and/or ethnic animosities the current uprising may leave in its wake. If it is possible to surmount these major obstacles, then the consolidation of democracy in Syria will be greatly strengthened.

The uprisings in the Arab region and the economic crises they have faced have exposed the weaknesses of their adopted development models and have raised questions about how to reshape political regimes and economic policies and create the space needed to address the needs of all citizens in society, including those of the most deprived. The neoliberal economic model, centred on fiscal and monetary stabilisation and economic liberalisation implemented in most Arab countries, has yielded a relatively acceptable level of economic growth and managed generally to meet the goals of economic and financial stability. Fiscal deficits have been contained. Monetary and inflationary pressures have been, over all, smoothed. Oil booms have kept the region upbeat with oil-abundant countries delivering far more than the less developed ones. However, the impact of such economic choices has not led to the desired outcomes in terms of socio-economic equality, human development, human rights and political reforms. Indeed, in some cases, economic liberalisation has aggravated existing disparities in society, with an accentuated economic and political marginalisation for the majority of the people. It is for this reason that we place an emphasis on a holistic developmental approach that should be adopted in a post-crisis Syria, one that integrates the economic and social spheres with strong and accountable democratic institutions.

We are basically advocating a move away from the old Syrian policies of the 'minimalist' welfare state to a model that aims to achieve at once three major objectives: stability, broad-based inclusive growth and social equity. Social policy needs to provide social security and basic services to the Syrian population and to ensure basic human rights are secured in place. A genuinely democratic and accountable governance in Syria, we submit, will be able to implement such a model.

6   Kuwaiti Democracy: Elusive or Resilient?

Ibrahim Elbadawi and Atif Kubursi

6.1   Introduction

Among the monarchies of the Gulf, Kuwait stands alone as a shining example of a unique, albeit partial, democracy with an elected parliament, regular elections (and often irregular ones), a constitution that guarantees basic human rights and the powers of the parliament and a long tradition of power struggles between the legislature and the executive dominated by the royal family and the emir. Judged against the democracies of Latin America, Africa and Asia, Kuwait's democracy loses its uniqueness, and its deficiencies become more glaring and troubling. For example, the widely used Polity IV Index shows Kuwait to be in the authoritarian category, only a minor nudge better than the neighbouring Gulf states (Figure 6.1).[1] However, we hasten to note that though the Polity Index is credited as being a product of the 'objective' assessment of the capacity of political institutions to promote political competition, as well as enforce constraints on the executive branch of the government, nevertheless it was found (Munk and Verkuilen 2002) wanting in terms of reflecting the vitality of democratic traditions at the societal level.

As we will document in the subsequent analytic narrative of the evolution of Kuwaiti society and political institutions, it is probably correct to suggest that the Polity score does not fully reflect the state of democracy in the country, though it appropriately embodies the lack of democratic transition. For example, in 1993, following the First Gulf War,

The authors would like to acknowledge the research support Dhuha Fadhel provided. They are grateful, without implications, to Samir Makdisi and Ali Abdel Qadir Ali for their helpful comments on an earlier draft.
[1] The Polity IV Index is based on two concepts: 'institutionalised democracy' (DEM) and 'institutionalised autocracy' (AUT). The DEM score is coded according to four measures of regime characteristics: competitiveness of executive recruitment; openness of executive recruitment; constraints on the chief executive; and competitiveness of political participation. These measures, along with regulation of participation, form the basis for calculating the AUT score. The Polity score (POL) is computed by subtracting the AUT score from the DEM score, resulting in a score from −10 (strongly autocratic) to 10 (strongly democratic).

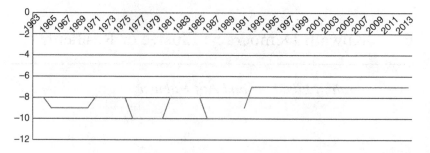

Figure 6.1: The Story of Democracy in Kuwait (Polity Index),
1963–2013
Source: Marshall, Gurr and Jaggers (2014).

a significant jump occurred in the Polity score, but it has remained
stationary ever since. This story actually coheres with other country-
specific evidence from Kuwait regarding the lack of democratic consolidation in this country.

The societal aspects of democracy are generally thought to be better
reflected by the twin Freedom House (FH) indices of civil liberty and
political freedom. These two measures are derived from the Freedom of
the World survey produced by Freedom House. Scores between 1 (free) and
7 (not free) are assigned to the categories of political rights and civil liberties.
The political rights category measures the extent to which a government is
chosen by means of the free and fair elections of candidates. The civil
liberties score essentially measures freedom from government oppression,
encompassing the strength and objectivity of the rule of law as well as
personal freedoms, such as those of expression and religion. Unlike the
Polity score, the FH indices are subjective measures, and this is regarded
as their main weakness; however, their most desirable feature is that they
more accurately reflect the strength of the democratic tradition in a society.[2]

---

[2] The political rights index, based on a checklist of eight questions relating to standard norms
of political freedom, informs the scoring of this category. In addition, two questions are
added to account for the special circumstances of traditional monarchies and to account for
safeguards for ethnic minorities. Thus, for example, for countries with a score of 7, 'political
rights are absent or virtually non-existent due to the extremely oppressive nature of the
regime or severe oppression in combination with civil war'. A checklist of fourteen questions
relating to standard norms of civil liberties informs the scoring of this category. These
questions are classified into four broad categories of 'freedom of expression and belief',
'association and organisation rights', 'rule of law and human rights' and 'personal autonomy
and economic rights'. In rating countries on the basis of the checklist on civil liberties, it is
those rights enjoyed in practice that are used instead of the constitutional guarantees of such
rights. Thus, countries rated 7 have virtually no freedom and an overwhelming and justified
fear of repression characterises their societies.

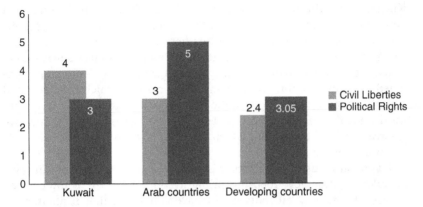

Figure 6.2: Civil Liberties and Political Rights inside and outside Kuwait, 2002–2013

Figure 6.2 compares the average measures for Kuwait in the 2000 decade to the median values for the Arab and developing countries. The evidence suggests that Kuwaiti society enjoys a far better degree of civil liberty than the median Arab country and that it is similar to the rest of the developing world on this score. On the other hand, though political rights are better than in the rest of the Arab world, they have not yet matched the standard for the developing world.

A democracy designation that changes with the comparator group against which it is judged is not, perhaps, a comforting status, but this has become the most defining characteristic of Kuwaiti partial and relative democracy. It is not an absolute designation; it is contingent on the neighbourhood within which it is located. It is anchored on historical and geographic factors and structural characteristics that have long been determining considerations. They do not augur well for the future, but democracy in Kuwait, regardless of its difficulties and setbacks, has taken root; full democracy is still elusive, but what has been achieved remains resilient and enduring.

Democracy in Kuwait goes by many names, from part-time democracy, to truncated democracy, to interruptible democracy, and even to 'bedouincracy',[3] but the fact remains that, regardless of terminology, Kuwaitis have forged a special system in the Gulf, significantly different from what were and remain the organising polity principles of their neighbourhood. Its origins extend to the early days of the formation of

---

[3] This designation draws from 'Bedou' [*badw*], the Arabic term for 'nomads', and is meant to emphasise the influence of the traditional nomadic culture on the societies of Arabia, including their political institutions.

Kuwait under the leadership of the Al Sabah family, which originated outside Kuwait and managed to build a formidable alliance and partnership with coastal trading and pearl-gathering families outside the direct zones of influence and control of the British empire and its trade routes to India. Geography, history and the political astuteness of the emir combined to define the formative tenets of the system, which have endured with the many ups and downs, the many forward steps and a few backward ones that have shaped its development, setbacks and distinctive features up until today, and which other Gulf states have not been able to emulate or develop.

The main focus of this chapter is to develop a case study of Kuwait's turbulent democracy, focusing primarily on a number of interrelated aspects: First, how oil rents might have acted as either facilitators or impediments to democratic transition in Kuwait. What role did external factors play in delaying the full transition into democracy? Does the stability of these factors and instruments explain the persistence of forces thwarting the full transition to a fully fledged democracy in Kuwait?

Second, how strong is the authoritarian bargain in Kuwait and how is it connected to the country's transition to democracy? What role did international and regional wars, lack of meaningful diversification, high unemployment, a weak private sector and the rise of political Islam, the conflict between Iraq and Iran, foreign military bases and inequality, play in increasing or diminishing the probability of transition to democracy in Kuwait?

Finally, in what ways can economic and social policies (at both the macro and micro levels) best support and cement the democratic processes in Kuwait and protect them from serious relapses?

Kuwait's democratic development and uniqueness are rooted in certain historical processes and the circumstances that defined and shaped these processes over two centuries. A historical perspective is indispensable and also instructive in highlighting the forces that have conditioned the birth and development of the Kuwaiti polity. History alone is, however, not sufficient for a full understanding of the current situation and all the tribulations that have been experienced and will most likely be experienced in Kuwait; geography and a host of other critical factors intersect and work within a common framework to shape Kuwait's future and its potential democratic transition.

Section 6.2 provides an historical overview of the evolution of the Kuwaiti political process, while Section 6.3 highlights the role of oil rents in shaping this process through a discussion of the political economy of resources that curses the country. Section 6.4 focuses on the consequences of the Iraqi invasion in 1991 for the political discourse in the post-liberation era. Section 6.5 attempts to articulate the insight gained from the received literature to assess the prospects for deeper democratisation in Kuwait. Section 6.6 concludes the discussion.

6.2 Kuwait's Illusive Transition to Democracy: A Historical Perspective

Kuwait's political system is markedly different from those of other Gulf states on account of its particular historical roots and of its geographic location in the northern quarter of the Gulf, distant from the Indian Ocean and the maritime routes that Britain guarded zealously to protect its exclusive control of India in the nineteenth century. The southern Gulf states were not as fortunate. They fell directly under Britain's protection and control as they lay closer to India, directly on the maritime routes connecting India and Britain.

Britain subsidised the rulers of the southern states in its quest to control and neutralise them, and therefore they were economically independent of their people. Britain often intervened with force of arms to keep these compliant rulers in power when its rule was challenged (Said 1998). As a consequence, the rulers of these states felt little pressure or need to bargain with indigenous opposition groups. They had no need of them in economic terms, and they could count on British support to suppress any challenge to their rule.

Kuwait, away from the direct trading and maritime routes to India, received less attention, focus and help from Britain. On the contrary, from the very early days when the Bani Utub settled in Kuwait, the polity they ruled was based on consensus and agreement between the tribes and dominant trading families, be it those monopolising the caravan trade with Basra and Aleppo or the pearl trade (Salem 2007), because the rulers depended on these families for their financial support. The most distinguishing feature of the rise of the Al Sabah to power in Kuwait was the fact that it was not accomplished by force or with the backing of Britain (Atallah 2011).

There is more than one version of how the Al Sabah came to power (Crystal 1995), but all suggest that they had to depend on their diplomatic skills, their capacity to rally other tribes and their knack for forging a consensus to establish and maintain their rule. When other rulers depended on force and religion (Saudi Arabia) or British power (Muscat and Sharjah), the Al Sabah relied on negotiations and the coalescing of disparate interests.

In the absence of any major source of wealth, such as the pilgrimage to the holiest Islamic shrines in Mecca and Medina, which provided the

Al Saud with fiscal revenues, or the British subsidies that Muscat and other Gulf rulers relied on, the Al Sabah depended on the merchant class who controlled the caravan trade and the pearling industry. Dependence on this diversified source of income proved crucial in sustaining Al Sabah rule when the pearl trade crashed after the First World War. This was in contrast to what happened in Qatar; when the pearl trade collapsed, the Qatari rulers had no other source of revenue. This diversified economic structure allowed the Al Sabah to sustain their rule during difficult economic times. The lessons learnt from this episode remain valuable for the future of their rule and the staying power of democratic processes in the state of Kuwait.

The balance of power between the merchants and the emir shifted with the state of the economy and the capacity of the merchant class to barter its wealth for power and representation. Britain had often interfered in the southern Gulf states and purposely tipped the balance of power in favour of compliant rulers; it did not do so in Kuwait. The balance of power between the emir and the merchant class in Kuwait was more fluid. The dependence of the emir on the merchant class and its sources of wealth, either stable or footloose, implied that the Al Sabah could not rule without being accountable to those who supported them financially and would have been compelled to stand alone in any conflict that might have arisen between the two sides. In turn, this meant that the power of the emir was constrained by the wealth and solidarity of the merchant class. This goes a long way in explaining why the history of the relationship between the merchants and the emir was a mixture of conflict and accommodation.

At one point in the mid-nineteenth century, the merchant class threatened to leave Kuwait unless the emir, Mubarak, rescinded a tax he had imposed to finance his military adventures (Crystal 1995). Actually, pearl-collecting families left for Bahrain and merchants loaded boats with their movable wealth and threatened to sail away, and so the emir had to rescind the tax. The transferability and fluidity of the wealth of the merchants did not escape the emir. The crucial factor here is not only wealth, but also its fluidity.

This episode underscored the anxiety and flexibility of the merchant class and culminated in 1921 in its demand for the formation of a council to protect its interests. This marked the beginning of the institutionalisation of the power of the merchant class, which comprised a homogeneous group cemented by intermarriage, common class interests and its willingness and ability to leave Kuwait. The merchants' success was, however, limited. Emir Jaber promised to consult the council, but did not. It was not until the merchant class was able to organise politically in the wake of a number of economic setbacks that took a heavy toll on its affairs that the emir had to concede power.

Any one of the economic reversals that befell Kuwait in the early 1930s would have been enough to crystallise the interest of the merchant class in political organisation. In combination they proved very effective in finally wresting the concessions that depreciated the power of the emir and limited his authority. These reversals included the Saudi economic blockade of Kuwait, the collapse of the pearl industry as a consequence of Japanese competition, the global economic depression of the 1930s and the emir's escalating taxes. When these were taken together, the development of a political structure designed to protect the dwindling wealth of the merchant class could not be resisted.

Economic difficulties and concerns about shrinking wealth finally brought the merchant class together to form a joint programme that would permit merchants to share power with the emir by forcing him to accept the creation of the first political representative body, the National Assembly of 1938, with specified legislative powers. The merchants had petitioned the emir asking for an elected assembly and had drawn up a list of the 150 notables who would constitute the electorate and would elect an assembly of fourteen representatives. This consolidation of power and influence by the merchant class could not have succeeded had the divisions and conflicts within the royal family reinforced it. These conflicts provided the backdrop for the acquiescence of the emir in sharing power with the assembly, which at first he had refused to accommodate. Dissention within the royal family and cohesiveness in the merchant class increased the effectiveness of the latter in wresting concessions from the emir and in strengthening merchants' ability to bargain for a greater accommodation. Despite the short life of the assembly (six months), it managed to cancel the pearl tax, the export duties, the import taxes on fruit and vegetables and other monopolies (Atallah 2011). Perhaps equally if not more important was the merchants' success in establishing the fact that people and their representatives were the basic source of authority, and their success in increasing their responsibility to extend further over the budget, justice, public security and the raising and distribution of state revenues. When they attempted to extend their authority to oil revenues, the emir dissolved the National Assembly, but not before they had succeeded in creating the crucial precedent of basing authority on representatives and extending their authority to new areas and issues, including requiring the emir to call for new elections.

In 1939, a new electoral list of 400 names was drawn up and an assembly of twenty members, which the emir hoped would bolster his authority and powers, was elected. When the new assembly refused to accommodate the emir, it too was dissolved and its members arrested (Atallah 2011).

It took years of struggle and contest to give birth to the assembly of 1938, and before it Kuwait saw the growth of many municipal councils, as well as trade and professional associations, that were vibrant and, probably, British inspired and nurtured. These councils survived the many dissolutions of the assembly and became constituent parts of Kuwaiti civil society. Scholars have frequently argued that the solidification of a representative political structure served the interests of the emir and the royal family; it provided them with an instrument to use in the face of internal and external threats to the emir's powers (Crystal 1995), but the royal family and the emir had made, or were forced to make, many concessions that, in the absence of the cohesiveness of the merchant class and the growth of civil society, would have been unimaginable.

This brief historical note serves to underscore the tenuous and contested nature of the relationship that governed the struggle for power between the emir and the merchant class, the apparent lack of interest on the part of Britain in interfering in order to tip the balance of power in favour of either group unless trade or security issues were involved, the importance of the relative cohesiveness of the two parties in the confrontations, the role of wealth and its foot-loose nature in determining the balance of power, and the relative influence of the parties over the emerging outcomes in the push for at least partial democratic representation.

Had oil not been discovered, it is reasonable to suggest that democratic processes would have continued to solidify and take root in Kuwait. Indeed, there would have been ups and downs, relative successes and many failures, but the trend to wider representation and broader powers given to the people would have been more meaningful, more significant and more evident. The discovery of oil, and the large rents that flowed from its exploitation and the nature of the oil property rights that directed these rents to the rulers, created a new dynamic and unleashed new forces that on the whole were anti-democratic and troublesome and worked to delay democratic trends and processes and a transition towards a full democracy.

6.3   Oil and Democracy: The Political Economy of the Resource Curse

The discovery of oil in the Gulf in the 1930s catapulted the region onto the centre of the stage of world events. The region is now established as the site of two thirds of the world's known oil resources, and 20 per cent of the world's oil output and more than 37 per cent of seaborne oil exports pass on a daily basis through the narrow straits of the Gulf. It is difficult to exaggerate the role of oil and oil revenues in shaping events and the course of history in the Arab region, and of Kuwait being the second, albeit distant second, oil producer and exporter after Saudi Arabia in the Gulf.[4]

From the Suez crisis in 1956 to the invasion and occupation of Iraq in 2003, oil has been and continues to be a major determining factor in the life and destiny of the region. Its abundance, low cost of recovery and the wide difference between the marginal cost of its production and the international price have combined to make the region not only the source of any new incremental supplies of oil, but also a region with a large surplus of capital and finance, and a major market for industrial products and services.

Oil rents replaced other sources of income (zakat,[5] British subsidies and commercial taxes and tariffs) for the rulers and their states. The emir now had an independent source of finance, and he no longer depended on the merchant class for his sustenance and initiatives. He felt powerful enough to break the tacit agreement he had worked out with the merchant class for sharing power; awash with cash, he even went so far as to pay the merchants the sums he owed them. In many respects, oil reversed the normal historical relationship between the rulers and ruled, making the latter dependent on the ruler instead of the typical opposite relationship (Luciani 1987; Tilly 1975).

In addition, oil rents allowed the rulers to buy the loyalty and acquiescence of the population in what has become commonly known as the 'authoritarian bargain', where rulers trade off citizens' political rights for services, public jobs, grants and cash lump sums, all financed by the oil rents (Lam and Wantchekon 1999; Ross 2009). The Kuwaiti welfare state, built on oil revenues, provides free education and health care; grants rent, electricity, water and telephone subsidies; and guarantees public service jobs, income subsidies, disability assistance and many other generous programmes such as no other country in the world provides (Tetreault and Al-Mughni 1995).

In an indirect fashion, oil stunted the emergence of the private sector. It was dwarfed by a well-greased public sector and it derailed

---

[4] Kuwait, with large oil reserves, was producing in 2012 an average of more than 2.6 million barrels of oil per day. In comparison, Saudi Arabia was producing close to 10 million barrels of oil per day and consequently commands far greater regional political clout than Kuwait.

[5] In Islam, zakat is an obligatory act of charitable taxation ordained by God to be performed by every Muslim whose net wealth has reached a certain threshold every year. Zakat is levied at 2.5 per cent of all 'zakat-able' assets after deducting specific liabilities for the year. Items like jewellery and gold are 'zakat-able' items and their worth should be factored in when calculating totals.

diversification initiatives that could have created alternative sources of income and rent outside the public sector. In addition to this, therefore, oil increased the power of the state and its security apparatus, and the formidable resources and advances oil rents made available to them. The state used its powers to prevent and to delegitimise the formation of political and social groups that might have demanded an increased voice and participation in political decision-making (Putnam 1993).

Moreover, the control of substantial oil resources and the accumulation of huge petro dollar surpluses availed the state the protection and support of powerful external allies, most notably the major Western powers and particularly the United States. Though more recently it has become increasingly difficult for these Western countries and their oil companies to ignore egregious violations of human and political rights in the Gulf states, they have in the past actively intervened to prevent democratisation when it was seen as unfavourable to their oil-related economic and geopolitical interests (the literature on oil and global power interventions is vast; for a few scholarly writings, see Alnasrawi 1991; Ghalioun and Costopoulos 2004; Ibrahim 1982; Pickering and Kisangani 2006).

Perhaps less appreciated is the fact that the Dutch Disease which oil has engendered in the region has severed a number of relationships that are the keys to any democratic and advancing society. These include the decoupling of effort and reward, of meritocracy and resourcefulness and job allocation and of consumption and production. Income and wealth are distributed on the basis of proximity to the ruler rather than effort or skill, rampant consumerism creates false demands whose satisfaction depends on docility and compliance. It is difficult to conceive an authoritarian bargain being sustained in a society that clings to traditional values and habits. The Dutch Disease raised the exchange value of the Kuwaiti dinar, which made it difficult for Kuwait to export other products and flooded the local market with cheap imports, diminishing the chances of local production competing effectively. Potential diversification of the economy was thwarted, and so was the development of a healthy private sector wedded to the interests of domestic capital.

Non-oil exports in Kuwait accounted for only 6 per cent of Kuwait's total exports of goods in 2007 as compared to 8.4 per cent in 2002. The oil sector share of total government revenue has increased over time, rising from 68 per cent for 2006 to 81.5 per cent for 2010. Moreover, the second source of revenue for the government is derived from the oil revenues of previous years invested abroad by the Kuwaiti Investment Authority. In 2010, investment income represented 13.3 per cent of total government revenue. This situation has enabled the government to reduce the rate of taxation on individuals and businesses, with some kept down almost to zero. The Kuwaiti government thus became essentially economically independent of its citizens. This, in turn, led to a reduction in the powers of the elected assembly and tipped the balance of power in favour of the emir.

Generally, upholding democratic values necessitates protecting and guaranteeing citizens' independence, security and freedom from coercion and fear. Oil wealth in societies that are essentially non-democratic has diluted and distorted these values, and may have even robbed the citizens of the necessary behavioural norms conducive to democratic development and transition. The case of Kuwait fits the predictions of the recent theoretical literature on democracy and resource rents. For example, in a game theoretic model, Ali and Elbadawi (2012) demonstrate that authoritarian regimes in societies endowed with very high levels of rent per capita, that is, immense reserves of natural resources and a low level of population, have a comparative advantage over other authoritarian governments to which these are unavailable. These governments have control over sufficiently large amounts of resources which they can redistribute to their respective populations, through public employment and other direct and indirect outlays, in order to effectively remove any incentive to revolt. The prediction of this model is premised on the presence of autocratic, or at least not fully democratic, incumbent elites; and that the optimality of the rent-sharing strategy requires that the elite in a given state has control over sufficiently high levels of rent per citizen. Both conditions, which the case of Kuwait fully accounts for, were corroborated empirically by Elbadawi and Makdisi (2012), hereafter EM.[6]

Furthermore, following the received literature, EM also argue that incumbent elites in resource-rich societies are not likely to adopt a purely public sector employment strategy, as they might also find it necessary to use their resource rents to build an apparatus of political repression designed to preempt or quell any incipient or unfolding revolt. However, a direct measuring of political repression reveals that there is no evidence that Kuwait has relied on this instrument. This is done through a measure called Physical Integrity Rights, which is an annual index that ranges from 0 (repression free) to 1 (worst level of repression), and accounts for the incidences of torture,

---

[6] In February 2011, the authorities in Kuwait announced that every citizen would receive US $3,500 and that basic foodstuffs would be free for one year. Moreover, the government approved a record budget of US $70 billion, a large share of which would finance fuel subsidies and salary increases for public sector employees. This package was linked to the commemoration of the twentieth anniversary of the country's liberation from the Iraqi occupation and the fiftieth anniversary of independence (Barany 2012). However, it is also interesting to note that, as commendable as they may be, these substantial transfers in an already highly generous social welfare system came just a few months after the outbreak of the 'Arab Spring'.

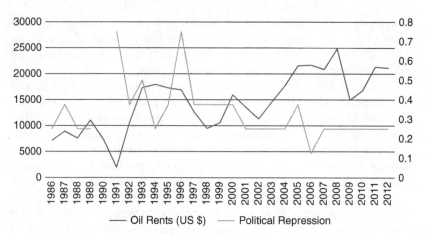

Figure 6.3: Oil Rents Per Capita and Political Repression in Kuwait

extrajudicial killing, political imprisonment and disappearances that are attributable to the government (Cingranelli-Richards dataset 2008).[7] According to this index, except for a couple of years during and after the Iraqi invasion (1991 and 1996), political repression in Kuwait was comparatively speaking very limited and had declined precipitously by the turn of the 2000 decade, which also witnessed a steep growth in resource rents per capita (Figure 6.3). This is consistent with the evidence for the median GCC country, which had a score of only 0.29 during the second half of the 2000 decade; second to only the developed country score of 0.18. On the other hand, the median populous oil-dependent Arab country scored 0.69, thus constituting the closest region to the scale of 1 (worst level of repression).

The relatively limited reliance on explicit political repression by the ruling families in Kuwait, and some other GCC countries for that matter, as a means of fending off revolts and maintaining their hold on power, also coheres with EM's formal findings. They find that a medium to high degree of political repression impedes democratic transitions; however, the former does not fully account for the effect of rents in societies endowed with high levels of resources (i.e. the inclusion of political repression does not render the rent effect insignificant). They interpret this finding to suggest that the incumbent elites relied on political repression only as a supplementary means of forestalling democratic transition.

---

[7] The original index decreases with the degree of repression, the most repressive cases being coded as 0 while the repression-free cases receive a code of 8. For ease of exposition, we inverted and rescaled the variables so that it increases with the degree of repression and is contained in the [0,1] interval.

However, political repression is likely to be a less efficient strategy for fending off democratic transition than policies promoting public employment. This may help explain why the populous Arab oil group has been susceptible to democratic regime change, especially in the context of the ongoing Arab Spring, while so far the GCC countries seem relatively unaffected by it.

As a premier source of rent, oil wealth in these societies has reversed the normal relationship between the rulers and ruled, tipped the balance of power in favour of the rulers and financed the authoritarian bargain that has allowed the state to purchase political accommodation as well as to cultivate the support of foreign powers.

While it is hard to exaggerate the importance of oil in diluting democratic processes and values in the Gulf in general and Kuwait in particular, it is still important to recognise that other variables and determinants are also significant in explaining the obstacles to and forces and trends towards democracy in Kuwait and the region.

Lipset (1959) argued that high incomes and rapid economic growth rates are necessary ingredients for the democratisation process; they are typically associated with higher levels of education, effective and efficient institutions, and good governance structures. There is no doubt that high incomes and high growth rates based on large amounts of oil rent have made a positive contribution to the social development of Kuwait through education and improved health, but these are negated by the many countervailing factors associated with oil wealth. We have alluded to some of them and will highlight several others later in this chapter.

Oil rents did not smooth over all contentions and politically contested issues. Actually, oil created some grievances of its own and heightened social tensions between groups and classes. Those disenfranchised and denied citizenship (bedouins and others) became more active and vocal. The stakes for these groups in remaining submissive and accepting marginalisation became quite high. It is also difficult to conceive that oil could purchase a permanent and deep loyalty for the regime from the people. Nationalists, intellectuals, Islamists and Nasserites did not succumb fully to the authoritarian bargain, and showed their dissatisfaction with the regime at several junctures, but particularly during crises such the 1956 Suez campaign, the 1967 Arab–Israeli war, the 1979 Islamic Revolution in Iran, the 1982 Israeli invasion of Lebanon, the 1980s Iran–Iraq War, the 1990 Iraqi invasion and the 1991 liberation of Kuwait and so forth. These events radicalised large groups who vented their frustrations and aspirations through demonstrations and violent clashes with the security forces of the state. The radicalisation of the political discourse can

Table 6.1: *The Evolution of Political Polarisation in the Kuwaiti Parliament*

	2000		2012	
Political Movements	No of deputies	%	No of deputies	%
1. The Sunnite Islamic group	15	30	21	42
2. The coalition of the deputies of the 1982 Maglis	13	26	–	–
3. The democratic coalition	3	6	–	–
4. The constitutional coalition	3	6	–	–
5. The Shiite group	6	12	7	14
6. The government supporters	10	20	–	–
7. The popular coalition	–	–	5	10
8. The independents	–	–	14	28
9. The national coalition	–	–	3	6
Total	50	100	50	100
The polarisation index[1]	–	0.66	–	0.75

Source: This table is a translation from Arabic of Table 1 of Ali (2012).

Notes: 1. *The polarisation index (PI) is calculated as follows:*

$$PI = 1 - 4 \sum_{i=1}^{n}(0.5 - \pi_i)/\pi_i,$$ *where π is given by the share of the political group to the total number of parliamentary deputies and n is the number of political groups in the Maglis. Note that the maximum degree of polarisation is achieved when there are only two groups with equal shares of representation (i.e. $\pi = 0.5$ and PI = 1).*

perhaps be seen in the increasing political polarisation among the representatives in the legislature (*majlis al-umma*). According to an index of political polarisation (Ali 2012), the *majlis* (parliament) experienced a significant transformation between 2000 and 2012, as the divide between the Sunni Islamists, who account for 42 per cent of the seats, on one hand, and the Shia and the ruling family supporters, on the other, became gradually sharper. The traditional secular and Arab nationalist forces had all but lost any meaningful representation in the *majlis* by 2012 (Table 6.1).[8]

The political polarisation discourse in Kuwait is primarily a product of the underside of the oil rents-based authoritarian bargain, where the attempt to buy acquiescence and compliance through payouts and, to a lesser extent, political repression has inadvertently sharpened tribal

---

[8] Though the parliament was dissolved in January 2013 by a court order and a new, more pro-government parliament was elected, the shift in the political preferences does not seem to have changed much.

loyalties and sectarian politics, and has invigorated political Islam. The emergence of the transnational sectarian militias, and most notably the Islamic State in Iraq and Syria (ISIS), is another threat that could tip the balance and upset the traditional accommodation between Sunnis and Shi'is and between the royal family and the people. Moreover, the rising sectarian tensions in the region associated with the struggle for regional supremacy between Iran and certain Arab countries has further fanned the flames of sectarian tension in diverse Arab societies from Lebanon to the Gulf, and Kuwait is no exception. The closer ISIS gets to the borders of Kuwait or the more intense the region-wide sectarian divide becomes, especially in Iraq and Yemen, the greater the actual threat to political equilibrium in Kuwait. These challenges are unique in the Gulf, in the sense that significant segments of its population tend to identify themselves in sharp sectarian terms, and this has the potential to torpedo Gulf exceptionalism and immunity from conflict. Again, assuming that regional wars are an extreme instance of overall regional tension, this perverse development at the Kuwait level would corroborate EM's findings regarding the negative consequences of a conflictive and unstable neighbourhood for democratic transition.

In addition to the lingering corrosive consequences of the Arab–Israeli conflict, which has been shown to have generally impeded Arab demo-cratisation, the prospects for Kuwaiti democracy have been severely damaged by the two Gulf Wars and their aftermath. Indeed, when the political space narrowed and was delegitimised, other spaces opened up, particularly religious and social. Kuwaiti Shi'is organised politically at *husayniyyas*, Sunnis at mosques and secularists and nationalists at *dewa-niyyas* (Ghabra 1991).

Other relevant factors to consider are the potential repercussions of the impressive economic development of neighbouring Gulf countries, which has been based on huge oil rents that have permitted them to undertake massive public projects and investments. Both Qatar and Dubai, whether through direct or indirect exploitation of oil rents, have surpassed the economic performance and centrality of Kuwait in the Gulf. The challenge of Dubai is particularly meaningful as it underscores the power and relevance of diversification and the role of the private sector. When, a few years ago, it led the Gulf in economic and cultural advance-ment, Kuwait failed to match Dubai's performance and achievements on both these counts. The Dubai challenge is, indirectly, also a challenge to democracy in Kuwait. A comparison between Kuwait and the UAE in terms of ranking in the global index of 'doing business' makes clear that the former lags significantly behind in all but two indicators (Table 6.2). A few observers have argued that Kuwait's economic performance is hamstrung

Table 6.2: *Doing Business Rankings: Kuwait vs. UAE, 2012*

	2012	
	Kuwait	UAE
Ease of doing business	67	33
Starting a business	142	42
Dealing with construction permits	121	12
Getting electricity	57	10
Registering property	88	6
Getting credit	98	78
Protecting investors	29	122
Paying taxes	15	7
Trading across borders	112	5
Enforcing contracts	117	134
Resolving insolvency	48	151

Source: www.doingbusiness.org/data/exploreeconomies/kuwait/.

by political wrangling and democratic shenanigans and, therefore, it could do better with less democracy rather than with more.[9] While it is true that lately the parliament has approved few projects, it is a fact that democracies are noted for increasing the transaction costs of decision-making but reducing the chances of making mistakes and allowing unchecked corruption.

Oil may have moderated political demands for more democracy, but it has not eliminated them. The struggle for representation and accountability continues unabated in Kuwait. The next section takes up the subject of political developments and the struggle for greater democracy despite the accumulation of oil wealth.

6.4   Democracy and Democrats in Post-liberation Kuwait

The Economist (30 June 2012, p. 39), commenting on the dissolution of the parliament on 20 June 2012, highlighted what has become a defining characteristic of the Kuwaiti parliamentary system that 'among all the monarchies of the Gulf, Kuwait has easily the most powerful parliament – up to the point where it collides directly with the interests of the Al Sabah family'. This collision has occurred on a number of occasions and has led with increasing frequency to the summary dissolution of the parliament, the most recent dissolution taking place on 16 June 2013, when it

[9] See for example *The Financial Times*, 22 April 2012; and *The Economist*, 30 June 2012, p. 39.

happened for the sixth time in seven years and for the twentieth time since the parliament's inception. The twentieth parliament was elected on 27 July 2013 with the opposition boycotting the election.

The Kuwaiti electorate has become dismayed by voting for candidates who will not stay long enough in office to accomplish anything. The fate of the June 2012 parliament was no different to previous ones in recent times (*The Economist*, 30 June 2012, p. 39). While parliamentarians have indeed had the power to question (grill) not merely the ministers but the prime minister, who is typically a high-ranking member of the Al Sabah, this power has resulted in parliaments being hamstrung by diminishing life expectancy. They are often blamed for forestalling and blocking economic projects, progress and reform. The increased political fragmentation and divisiveness so flagrantly displayed in the conduct of the parliament mirrors the rampant polarisation in the society itself, with shifting alliances among nationalists, tribal representatives, Islamists and sectarian politicians. This polarisation has not permitted agreement on the implementation of many economic projects proposed by the government, the last of which is the Kuwaiti metro system. In contrast to the relative stability of other Gulf countries, Kuwait has been witnessing protests in public places with increasing frequency, and the opposition has called openly for constitutional monarchy and full democracy.

A number of hypotheses can be tendered here to explain why the transition to full democracy in Kuwait is difficult and, perhaps, unlikely. These hypotheses will be examined against the existing theoretical literature on transition to democracy and will be tested empirically in the subsequent sections.

Among the most crucial obstacles to transitioning to full democracy in Kuwait is the **inhospitable neighbourhood** that surrounds it. Among the six countries comprising the GCC, Kuwait is the only state with any degree of democratic institutions and practices. All the others are confirmed authoritarian states with Polity scores that rank them among the most authoritarian regimes in the world. They have made little or no progress towards democracy over the past five decades. More important is that most of these regimes feel threatened by the counter example of Kuwait.[10]

The **emasculated private sector** and the limited success of diversification in Kuwait have both eliminated any alternative to the public sector as an economic venue for the working population.

---

[10] For example, some Kuwaitis believe that the emir has dissolved the parliament on numerable occasions under pressure from their influential neighbour, Saudi Arabia (*The Economist*, June 2012, p. 39).

The prominence of the public sector has contributed to the weakening of the private sector and all civil society institutions. As the literature points out, a direct relationship obtains between civil society institutions and political participation and democratic institutions and processes (Besley et al. 2005; Camacho et al. 2011; Casey et al. 2011). This relationship being weak in Kuwait, it is not surprising that democratisation has suffered as a consequence and will continue to suffer until such time as the private sector and civil society are invigorated and can play their rightful and appropriate roles.

Over the whole period from 1981 to 2010, real GDP in Kuwait grew at an annual rate of about 3.4 per cent (World Bank 2011). Despite the significant increase in non-oil GDP over the period from 2001 to 2007, its share in total GDP declined to 45.4 per cent in 2007 as compared to 57.1 per cent in 2001 and 60.5 per cent in 1997. The Kuwaiti manufacturing sector, which held the promise of leading the diversification initiative, has proved a disappointment. GDP in the manufacturing sector grew at only 2.9 per cent over this period, while total GDP maintained a slightly higher rate of growth with an average of 4.2 per cent between 1990 and 2010. The manufacturing sector's contribution to the country's GDP dropped from 8.7 per cent in 1990 to only 6.7 per cent in 2010. Productivity in most sectors has been at best static, and in many instances it has declined over the past two decades (Estrin 2005).

The private sector in Kuwait contributes a relatively small share of the GDP, accounting for only about 25 per cent in recent years (World Bank 2011). This share has not changed since the 1990s. This stands in marked contrast to the share of the private sector in other Middle East and North African (MENA) countries where it is much larger and exhibits a continued tendency to rise. More than 90 per cent of the Kuwaiti labour force works for the government.

Kuwait has attracted very small sums of foreign direct investment (FDI) in recent years (both in absolute terms and in relation to GDP), despite enjoying very favourable conditions for such investment according to UNCTAD (UNCTAD 2011). For example, in 2007, Kuwait attracted $123 million in FDI according to the United Nations' 2008 World Investment Report. This is the lowest amount in all the MENA countries, with the exception of the Palestinian territories. Even Yemen attracted almost four times as much investment. Qatar, the second least popular destination for foreign capital in the six states of the petroleum-rich Gulf Co-operation Council, received ten times more in FDI than Kuwait. The relative paucity of FDI has, in turn, contributed to constrained private sector development.

Kuwait is particularly sensitive to political events in the Gulf region but less so to political events and developments in the Arab world as a whole. Relations with Iran are strained and little progress has been achieved in stabilising and normalising relationships with the Iraqis. Political tensions tend to empower the government and shield it from political demands. The government has become adept at capitalising on political issues in the region in order to postpone political reforms and accommodate calls for a greater political voice and greater participation for its citizens.

Wealth and income growth in Kuwait have not been associated with higher and better employment opportunities, either for Kuwaitis in general or for the educated subset in the labour force. But it is also true that unemployment rates in Kuwait are not particularly high. This fact has militated against any possible widespread sense of frustration or violent calls for change, reform and accommodation. The unemployment factor has thus not been a significant element in triggering demands for greater accommodation and the opening up of the system.

6.5   The Theoretical and Empirical Literature: The Search for Clues

Two important questions will guide the discussion that follows as to the probability that Kuwait can initiate and sustain a substantive democratisation trend, and what policy measures are relevant and effective in the transitional period to sustain the march towards more democratic forms of governance.

The received literature, most notably the seminal work of Przeworski and his research associates (2000), suggests that the probability of transition from an authoritarian to a democratic regime is characterised by a certain set of empirical regularities that survived extensive empirical testing, including two pivotal ones that we regard as highly relevant in the case of Kuwait.

First, authoritarian regimes that assume power in relatively rich societies are likely to experience a higher frequency of demise (i.e. higher probability of transition to democracy: P_{AD}). However, though the link between democracy and income has been the hallmark of the so-called modernity theory of democracy, it has been met with some scepticism in the literature. For example, a certain strand of the literature is focused on the non-determining role of income in the probability of a transition to a democracy. Ulfelder and Lustik (2005) point out that, for such a transition, previous experience of democracy is of value in both resource-rich and other countries, while economic recession increases its likelihood; also, in countries where they prevail, higher levels of civil liberty and non-violent collective action will help to initiate the transition. Moreover, taking a long historical view, Acemoglu, Johnson, Robinson and Yared (2008; 2009) focus on the relationship between economic, political and historical factors. They argue that although income and democracy are positively correlated (over long periods of time) no evidence appears of a causal effect. Instead, certain omitted, most probably historical, factors seem to have shaped the divergent political and economic development paths of various societies, leading to the positive association between democracy and economic performance. They thus call for a re-evaluation of the modernisation hypothesis with a much greater emphasis on the underlying factors affecting both variables, as well as the political and economic development path of societies.

Second, perhaps at least partially ameliorating these doubts about a direct 'linear' interpretation of the link between the democracy and income voiced in this literature, in a subsequent paper Przeworski (2004) showed that the income effect is conditional and only obtains because high income is usually associated with past regime instability, as measured by the frequency of the collapse of democracies followed by transition to an authoritarian form of regime prior to the establishment of the incumbent authoritarian regime. He finds that the income effect becomes insignificant in a transition model that also accounts for the frequency of instability in any previous democratic regimes. EM further corroborate this finding.

At this juncture, it is pertinent to ask whether these two fundamental cross-country findings (i.e. the modernisation effect and the frequency of attempts at establishing democracy) are relevant to Kuwait. We think not, for two reasons at least. First of all, the ruling Al Sabah family came to power long before the country became wealthy as a major oil exporter. Second, the high degree of oil-dominated wealth in Kuwait and other GCC countries has been associated with a very high degree of regime stability.

To the extent that Kuwait is endowed with a very considerable amount of oil rent that allows the incumbent ruler to increase social welfare and hence maintain some measure of an authoritarian bargain, these modernity factors are not likely to be critical in accounting for the country's experience of democracy, or its prospects in the near term. Similarly, the hypothesis concerning attempts at establishing democracy does not apply to Kuwait.

Instead, resource rents and regional externalities are likely to be the decisive factors, to which we will turn next, mainly drawing on the implications for Kuwait of EM's empirical results.

6.5.1 The Resource Effect

Ross (2009) tested the impact of gross oil income per capita on demo-cratic transition in a Przeworski 'benchmark' model. Furthermore, Ulfelder and Lustik (2005) tested the impact of resource rents in a variant of a similar model, though it focused to a greater degree on political and human development controls rather than, as in the Przeworski model, on overall income per capita and growth. Both authors found that natural resource rents (specifically oil wealth in the case of Ross) were robustly and negatively associated with the probability of democratic transition. This again would mean that Kuwait is not likely to make a smooth transition to democracy as long as revenue from oil rents remains massive and dominant.

Ross (2009) argues that, as a measure of natural resource rent, the oil income share of the GDP is flawed because it does not account for the share of resource rent spent in the domestic economy. Moreover, GDP is not the appropriate scale variable because the democracy impact of rent/GDP is subject to multiple sources of bias, as third factors (such as history, geography, corruption, etc.) are likely at work, affecting both democracy and growth, and hence the rent/GDP ratio. Instead, he proxies oil rent with the total value of the resource income divided by population. He argues that his oil income per capita can be used to 'test the starkest version of the "oil hinders democracy" claim: does the value of a country's geological endowment – regardless of how well it is man-aged, and how it influences the rest of the economy – affect the account-ability of government?' However, EM argue that the gross natural resource income measure tends to overstate the extent of resource rents because it does not account for the cost of the product. Fortunately, thanks to new global data on natural resource rents, EM can avoid this problem.[11] Whatever transformation is allowed, the oil rents in Kuwait are huge and the per capita value remains very high on account of a large numerator and a low denominator.

Moreover, using the new data on resource rents in an extended demo-cratic transition model, EM extended the benchmark in Ross and other literature in two important ways. First, they find that the curse effect of resources on democratic transition is conditional on the initial state of democracy. In particular, they find that natural resource rents do not constitute a hindrance to democratic transitions in societies that have

[11] The new resource rents variables are based on the World Bank's 'genuine' saving database which adjusts oil and other mineral incomes to the cost of production and transfers to non-government investors, such as the oil and mining companies (see Hamilton 2008).

P(regime change)

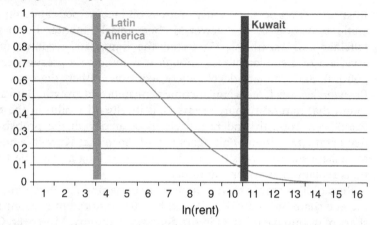

Figure 6.4: Resource Rents and the Probability of Democratic Transitions

already achieved a minimum standard of an advanced partial democracy (i.e. initial Polity score equal to 6 or more). The second critical finding is that the resource curse on democracy is subject to an effect of scale, in which only the top quartile range of the per capita resource rent appears to have a robust corrosive impact on the transition to democracy. This includes Kuwait and most other Arab oil economies.

As the analytic narrative of the preceding sections suggests, on both accounts oil rent is likely to constitute a major impediment to democracy in Kuwait. To underscore the critical role of oil as an impediment to democracy in Kuwait, we use simple simulations based on EM's regressions (Figure 6.4). The regression results in Figure 6.4 are based on the regression results # 1 of the Appendix Table 6.A.1. These regression results account for the traditional modernity variables, the threshold effects of the resource rents, the democratic legacy, initial democracy, home wars and the average regional Polity score. The simulation shown in the figure is derived by changing the values of the rents per capita from the lowest value (zero resource rent) to the maximum per capita rent in the sample. All other variables are held constant at their mean value for Kuwait (during 2005–09), the last period in the EM regressions.

The simulation confirms that resource dependency is a very powerful challenge for the consolidation of democracy in Kuwait. Given the prevailing average country characteristics of Kuwait, including its estimated oil rent per capita of more than $28,000 in 2012, the probability of

Table 6.A.1: *Probability of Democratic Transition*

Variable	Random Effect Probit [1]		Random Effect Probit [2]		Random Effect Probit [3]	
	Coefficient	Z	Coefficient	Z	Coefficient	Z
Real GDP pc Growth	-9.89***	-3.15	-9.3	-2.16	-8.93***	-3.16
Log Rent per capita	-0.47***	-4.49	—	—	—	—
Dum_25–75*Log Rentpc	—	—	—	—	-0.23***	-2.85
Dum_75*Log Rentpc	—	—	-0.06	-0.93	-0.31***	-4.17
STRA	1.96***	5.26	1.73	3.73	1.55***	4.54
Other Oil-Dependent Arab	-3.74**	-2.41	—	—	—	—
SSA	-1.35**	-2.25	—	—	-3.01***	-3.97
LAC	—	—	-1.28	-1.73	-2.30***	-2.88
SCA	-1.97**	-2.05	—	—	-3.39***	-3.55
EA	—	—	—	—	-1.98**	-2.39
Partial_Democracy	—	—	1.09	2.27	0.62**	2.21
Home war	—	—	-0.68	-1.34	—	—
Average Regional Polity	—	—	0.19	3.17	—	—
Ln MajArabWars_bddist-1	—	—	—	-3.00	-1.20***	-3.59
Constant	0.98	1.41	-1.4		1.97	2.62
Observations	449	—	323	—	449	—
LR statistic	69.62	—	28.69	—	30.57	—
Value	0.000	—	0.000	—	0.000	—
Log Likelihood	-154.44	—	-101.35	—	-141.91	—

Source: Based on Elbadawi and Makdisi (2012) regressions.

Notes: 1. *: for 0.05 < p-value ≤ 0.10;

**: for 0.01 < p-value ≤ 0.05;

***: for p-value ≤ 0.01

2. Definition of Regressors:

- Real GDP_pc Growth Rate: Real GDP pc growth rate in each period
- Ln Rentpc: Natural logarithm of resource rents per capita
- Dum_25–75*Log Rentpc: Interaction between Rentpc and a dummy variable for the two middle quartiles of the same variable
- Dum_75*Log Rentpc: Interaction between Rentpc and a dummy variable for the top quartile of the same variable
- STRA: Sum of transitions from democratic to authoritarian regimes during the period
- Other Oil-dependent Arab: Dummy variable = 1 for non-GCC oil-producing Arab countries, 0 otherwise
- SSA: Dummy variable = 1 if country is in Sub-Saharan Africa, 0 otherwise
- LAC: Dummy variable = 1 if country is in Latin America and the Caribbean, 0 otherwise
- SCA: Dummy variable = 1 if country is in Southern and Central Asia, 0 otherwise
- EA: Dummy variable = 1 if country is in East Asia, 0 otherwise
- Partial Democracy: Polity score multiplied by a dummy for Partial Democracy, where the latter = 1 if Polity score falls in the closed interval [1,8]
- Home war: Dummy that equals 1 if a country experiences civil or external wars during the period; 0 elsewhere
- Average Regional Polity: Average polity in the immediate neighbouring countries for the country in question
- Ln MajArabWars_bddist_−1 = lagged log of battle deaths from all major Arab wars in (1960–2009), weighted by distance from the Arab countries directly involved in the conflicts

a meaningful democratic transition (i.e. a significant and irreversible jump of three points in the Polity scale) is a minuscule 0.1. On the other hand, a comparator country with the same characteristics as Kuwait, but with average resource endowment at the Latin American level of only $20 per capita, is expected to have a probability of experiencing a democratic transition of more than 0.8, suggesting that the immense resource rents of Kuwait reduce the probability of deeper democratisation in this country eightfold. Therefore, economic diversification does not only make good economic sense, but it is also a vital catalyst in Kuwait breaking free from the orbit of the oil-driven authoritarian bargain that has essentially defined the country's political discourse.

6.5.2   The Regional Externalities

Gleditsch and Choung (2004) argue that economic factors influence the stability of autocracies and the likelihood of crises in general, but do not make transitions to democracy more likely. Past democratic experience and the neighbourhood characteristics matter more. Democracies are likely to emerge after the fall of a dictatorship in those countries that have had some prior experience of democracy, and in instances where there is a tendency for transitions to democracy to cluster regionally. These two factors appear to work in the opposite direction in Kuwait. On one hand, the historical record of Kuwait is rife with forays into democracy. Despite setbacks along the way, its past experience constitutes one of the factors favouring its future transition to a full democracy. On the other hand, the country is located in a decidedly authoritarian neighbourhood, which sometimes tends to militate against a stable democratic transition. The analytical narrative of the country's history suggests that, though Kuwait has had some legacy of spells of democracy, they have tended to be limited in scope and took place quite some time in the past. It is, therefore, highly likely that the neighbourhood effect has trumped any positive impact that might be associated with past democratic legacy.

Figures 6.5 and 6.6 clearly show how regional externalities can also substantially influence democratic transition. As before, the two figures are based on regressions 2 and 3 of Table 6.A.1. The simulation results in Figure 6.5 were drawn by varying the values of the regional Polity score from −10: extreme autocracy to +10: a healthy, functioning democracy, while holding all other variables constant at their mean value for Kuwait. Similarly, the simulation results in Figure 6.6 were drawn by varying the number of battle deaths in major Arab wars (including the civil, regional and Arab–Israeli wars) from the lowest to the highest values.

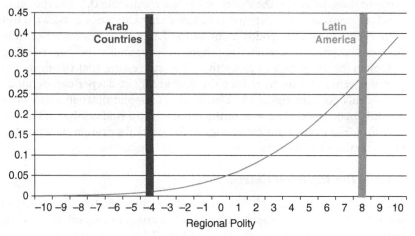

Figure 6.5: Resource Rents and the Probability of Democratic Transitions

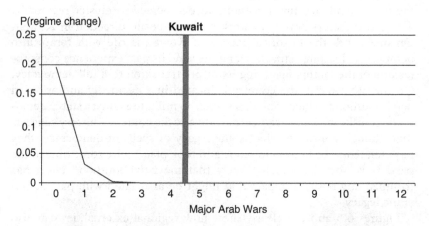

Figure 6.6: Major Arab Wars and the Probability of Democratic Transitions

According to the regional Polity simulation results in Figure 6.5, the probability of democratic consolidation in Kuwait would be literally zero (at 0.01), given the prevailing highly autocratic regional Polity score of −4.0. Instead, were Kuwait situated in Latin America with its high regional democratic standard (at an average regional Polity score of 8), further democratic transition and consolidation would be about thirty times more likely (at a probability of 0.3). The profound influence of the regional factor can be appreciated by noting that these simulation results obtain even given the presence of a massive amount of oil resource rent. In the same vein, the simulation results for the regional conflict scenario in Figure 6.6 suggest that, should the level of violence that has affected the neighbourhood recur in the future, there would be no prospects for future democratic consolidation in Kuwait.

These simulations seem to confirm that the cause of democracy in Kuwait will be substantially helped if the ongoing Arab Spring can lead to consolidation of regional Arab democracy and reduce regional instability and conflicts; the likelihood of this remains uncertain. This is further complicated by the rise of ISIS, the transnational sectarian militias and the widening regional sectarian divide on one hand, and falling oil prices on the other.

6.6   Conclusions: Prospects for Democratic Transition

The analytic narrative of the state of democracy in Kuwait in the preceding sections has highlighted oil dependency as the most critical factor impeding the progress of democracy in Kuwait, which has so far failed to consolidate and take root, despite the fact that it was a pioneering democratic experiment in the Arab region. Indeed, if anything, it has actually regressed over the years. Although resource dependency is a major challenge for Kuwaiti democracy, it is by no means destined. As the simulation results suggest, economic diversification and expansion of the non-oil economy is likely to have positive implications for democracy in the country, as it would also weaken the oil-driven authoritarian bargain. Moreover, as EM suggest, the resource curse operates through several channels that are subject to change. For example, regional externalities were found to have a robust influence on the effectiveness of the resource-driven authoritarian bargain. While regional conflicts and instability reinforce its corrosive effect, regional democracy tends to weaken it. In this context, our simulations suggest that, should the ongoing Arab Spring lead to broader regional stability and widening regional democratic polity, it could be a considerable boon to greater Kuwaiti democracy. The recent worsening sectarian divide in Syria, Iraq and Yemen, and most notably the ISIS challenge, can all be seen as reversing these likely positive effects of the Arab Spring phenomenon as the divide contributes to a sense of the system's vulnerability to regional and local challenges. However, perhaps it will be that the democratic legacy of Kuwait will eventually exert a more positive influence on a more Arab region-wide democratic neighbourhood.

In assessing the future of democracy in Kuwait, it is necessary to examine the broad influences, discussed earlier, in the light of the likely evolution of domestic institutions of political and economic governance and the ways in which they might be influenced by the shifting regional political and economic landscape, among other challenges. In the next section we discuss these issues, mostly by raising more questions, hopefully relevant ones, rather than by providing concrete answers.

6.6.1   Wither the 'Authoritarian Bargain'?: Domestic Factors

The first and perhaps the most important of the factors EM posit is the diminishing in the past twenty years or so of the overall dominance of the state, especially in its direct economic role, in the expansion of government-guaranteed employment and the provision of public services, such as free education and health. A major outcome of this development has been increased levels of unemployment. Privatisation has led to a reduction in state employment and social benefits that the private economy cannot compensate for. Instead, the high level of corruption and crony capitalism associated with the experience of privatisation in most of the Arab world has led to low and inequitable growth that has compromised the consequent downsizing of the economic role of the state. The Egyptian and Tunisian uprisings demonstrate that this could be a potent element in mobilising opposition in other autocratic Arab regimes (Altayib 2011).

A key question to ask at this juncture is if unemployment is likely to be a factor in weakening the oil-driven authoritarian bargain in Kuwait. We think not. The EM benchmark finding suggests that unemployment tends to weaken the authoritarian bargain and, hence, promotes democratic transition only when it exceeds a threshold of 10 per cent. Such a relatively high threshold was only exceeded by non-oil or populous oil countries, such as Egypt, Tunisia, Algeria, Yemen and Sudan. Unemployment in Kuwait and other GCC countries has been much lower. Moreover, the incumbent authorities in the GCC can and have consolidated the authoritarian bargain through various direct and indirect transfers to the public. For example, though the private sector contracted and lost a good part of its historic share of the economy, this did not lead to higher unemployment because a well-endowed public sector stood ready to increase the level of employment as needed.

A more likely means of weakening the authoritarian bargain in Kuwait is successful economic diversification. The experiences of those resource-rich countries which have managed to use their resource rents to develop dynamic diversified economies suggest that the adoption of a successful economic diversification strategy requires the presence of strong social groups favouring such policies, such as the exporting and farming communities in Norway and Chile. While Kuwait has no such constituency, the country nevertheless has a strong parliament and an aspiring educated class. It seems that the Kuwaiti parliament is focused rather on a traditional political agenda, which has probably weakened its potential for pushing the executive branch to adopt an aggressive plan for diversifying and modernising the economy. In fact, the supporters of the emir and the government argue that it is an aggressive parliamentary opposition that has held up economic reforms and investment, including a 30 billion dinar (US $108 billion) development plan aimed at diversifying the economy and attracting foreign investment. This has been the main argument used to justify the recent parliamentary elections, held in early December 2012 under a new election law that replaced the four votes per voter with just one per voter. This new system is widely believed to have been designed to minimise the influence of the opposition and to produce a parliament that cooperates more readily with the government. And, indeed it has, but at the expense of a broad boycott by the vast majority of the political forces in the country. In view of the very low turnout for the election,[12] the legitimacy of the new parliament, and hence its long-term survival and effectiveness, remains in serious doubt.

In addition to this, the recent emergence of ISIS and the other transnational militias and the widening sectarian conflicts in Syria, Iraq and now Yemen will not only halt any prospects for speeding up the democratic transition, but could as well be used to throttle the transition in the name of security.

A reading of the political discourse in Kuwait from a long-term perspective would suggest that there are two contrasting, though not entirely incompatible, strategies. On one hand, the ruling family and the bureaucratic elites in the public sector, and perhaps the majority of the business community, would like to see Kuwait moving along a path towards a modern diversified, though oil- and government-centric, economy that can sustain a properly functioning social contract, akin to the strategies already adopted or in the making in the rest of the GCC. However, unlike the other GCC countries, this 'economistic' approach must also allow for some measure of parliamentary oversight and control as well as preserve the other, albeit 'managed' whenever possible, historical political rights and civil liberties the Kuwaitis enjoy. On the other hand, the

---

[12] According to government estimates, the turnout was 40 per cent, while the opposition claims that it did not exceed 27 per cent. In both accounts, this turnout is much lower than the historical average of 60 per cent registered for previous elections.

parliamentary opposition and civil rights' activists seem substantially focused on a 'politicist' agenda, with some going so far as to demand the transition of Kuwait to a 'constitutional monarchy' with an elected government.

In our view, both strategies are likely to lead to a confrontational and acrimonious discourse, with neither objective easily achieved. However, a common ground that might position Kuwait on a gradual but steady path to a more profound degree of democratic transition and a more diversified economy is not impossible to achieve. However, this would require the opposition to embrace a 'politicist-plus' agenda that espouses gradualism and cooperation with the executive branch of government in order to achieve the diversified and dynamic economy desired; and also require the ruling family and its allies to accept an 'economistic-plus' agenda that would ultimately entail greater democratisation.

6.6.2   Whither the 'Authoritarian Bargain'?: the Regional Externalities

The Arab Spring should, inherently, have had a profound effect on Kuwait and other Gulf countries. Kuwait has a long history of engagement in the Arab nationalistic agenda, though this drive was somewhat weakened following the Iraqi invasion in the early 1990s. As the uprisings elsewhere have demonstrated, the driving force was the deep-seated ambitions of the people, not only for socio-economic advancement, but also for greater freedom and political participation. Naturally, political freedom without sustainable and equitable economic development will not be enough to ensure the legitimacy, much less the stability, of the nascent Arab democracies.

While these sentiments are inherently powerful and can transcend boundaries across the Arab world, especially among the Arab youth, the actual ramifications for a society like Kuwait will depend on how the situation in the regional environment develops. If the Arab Spring movement promotes democracy, following the Tunisian example, and develops into a participatory democracy that also achieves economic success, and if the Libyan and Syrian regimes manage to steer clear of sectarianism and narrow-minded fundamentalism, the impact on Kuwait would likely be positive and effective. To the extent that the Arab Spring can generate a regional policy that promotes strategic economic cooperation and regional peace, democracy in Kuwait will benefit greatly.

The nature of Kuwaiti society and its surrounding political geography suggests that it is likely to gain immensely if the regional scene were to evolve into a state of cooperation or, at least, enjoy reduced sectarian tensions and more regional economic cooperation in the Arab world and between the Arabs and their regional non-Arab neighbours, most notably Iran and Turkey. However, this is a very tall order.

Among other things, such an ideal regional environment requires the resolving of some thorny and lingering regional conflicts, above all the Palestinian question. Indeed as the EM evidence suggests, there are good reasons to believe that, without a just and comprehensive resolution of the Arab–Israeli conflict, it is probable that the process of democratisation in the Arab region will remain precarious. Furthermore, the open disagreement between Iran and most of the Arab world, especially over Syria, not only generates regional tensions, but also has marked sectarian consequences in several societies in the Arab world, including Kuwait. The destabilising effects of ISIS and the other regional sectarian conflicts have put further, new stresses on the political system of the area and have reintroduced the involvement of foreign military powers to regional conflicts. These new developments are likely to complicate and worsen the existing conflicts, and are bound to shake the recent political foundations of democracy in the region. They could easily shatter the Arab Gulf exceptionalism that has, so far, sheltered them from political upheavals and internal conflicts.

The question as to whether the Arab Spring will lead to regional stability and cooperation is still open. If it does, then the Arab Spring could potentially produce powerful externalities for democracy in Kuwait. But this, to say the least, is a very uncertain outcome, given the enormity of both the historical and the new challenges arising from the Arab Spring itself.

7   Lebanon: Sectarian Consociationalism and the Transition to a Fully Fledged Democracy

Samir Makdisi and Youssef El Khalil

7.1   Introductory Overview: the Underpinnings of Lebanon's Consociational Model and Its Practical Implications

Since independence in 1943, Lebanon's political system has been based on an arrangement for power-sharing between its religious communities. Referred to as a consociational democracy, it was embedded in an unwritten national pact by the leaders of the independence movement which specified the division of parliamentary seats between the Christian and Muslim communities on the basis of a six to five ratio in favour of the Christian community.[1] And while it also specified equal representation in cabinet posts and in appointments to major positions in the public sector (with equal shares assigned to the three major religious groups), the pact gave the Maronite community specific political privileges.[2] In practice, a power of veto by either community concerning approval of decisions on fundamental questions (e.g. declaration of war, international agreements, the electoral law, citizenship and, added later, administrative decentralisation laws) was provided for by the requirement that such approval was subject to a two-thirds majority in a vote.

The authors are grateful to Mohamed Mohieddin and Saoussen Ben Romdhane for very helpful comments on an earlier draft, and wish to express their gratitude to Layal Wehbe for her excellent research assistance.

[1] The constitution of the newly independent state guaranteed equal rights for all citizens. However, the national pact was based on Article 95, which specified that for a temporary but unspecified period, religious communities would be equitably represented in public employment and cabinet posts, though the principle of equity was not defined.

[2] Under the pact, it was agreed that the president of the republic would be a Maronite, the speaker of the house a Shi'i and the prime minister a Sunni. The office of the president carried with it substantial executive powers. For example, the president chaired the council of ministers and appointed the prime minister and cabinet members, albeit after due consultation with major political actors whose views could not be ignored. And the need to preserve the delicate sectarian balance, particularly between the three major religious groups, acted as a check on the powers of the presidency. Major amendments to both the electoral law and prerogatives of the president were introduced in 1989 (see later in this chapter). Throughout, however, a finely tuned formula of cabinet representation for Lebanon's various religious denominations (with equal representation for the three major ones) has been applied.

240

On the eve of independence, the declared rationale for agreeing on this form of political consociational governance was that in heterogeneous societies such as Lebanon's (and heterogeneity could be religious, linguistic, ethnic or a combination thereof), it tended to promote stability and democracy.[3] In practice, Lebanon's post-independence history attests to only a partial realisation of the intended objectives of its political model. On one hand, Lebanon's consociationalism did allow for a relatively high level of freedom of expression, the trappings of a modern democracy (parliamentary elections, multiple political parties) and the fact that no single group achieved dominance in running the affairs of the country, in contrast to elsewhere in the Arab world, at least until the Arab uprisings began to unfold in 2011. On the other hand, it did not ensure the envisioned political stability, nor did it lead to the establishment of a mature democracy: the Lebanese sectarian consociational model emerged as a form of constrained democracy in that it did not provide for equal political rights for all Lebanese religious communities and in consequence for all Lebanese citizens. If one of the major objectives of political institutions in democratic countries is to permit peaceful national dialogue and a peaceful resolution of political questions, then Lebanon's record in this regard is greatly wanting.

The structure of the Lebanese polity did not prevent the emergence of a long-lasting and devastating civil war (1975–90), or the occurrence of several episodes of major political unrest and conflicts preceding the war or subsequently in the post-civil war period (see later in this chapter). Admittedly, the causes of the civil war cannot be attributed solely to the country's political governance. A combination of domestic and external factors caused its outbreak (for an analysis, see Makdisi and Sadaka 2005). Briefly, the domestic factor was directly related to the prevailing sectarian system of power-sharing, principally among the three leading religious communities (the Maronites, the Sunnis and the Shia), which suffered from increasing domestic strains.

---

[3] In the literature, *consociationalism* refers to elite cooperation to prevent deep social divisions from destabilising democracy and provoking conflict. The elites seek to accommodate political conflicts through compromise or amicable agreement (mainly through defining the issue as a technical or economic problem rather than an ideological conflict). Characteristics of such democracies include grand coalitions and proportionality in the electoral system and in the distribution of public office and scarce resources. Further, the elite of each social segment may have a sphere of influence, either territorially or in the form of policy areas. The literature on consociationalism was launched by Lijphart (1969); for a review and critique, see Andeweg (2000), and for an empirical investigation of its relationship to conflict, see Binningsbo (2005). Andeweg notes that the main line of division in society is no longer between semi-permanent segments at the mass level but between elites and masses, and democracy may be served better by a relative emphasis on competition.

Foremost, in the period before 1975, were calls by domestic Muslim political leaders for a more equal form of power-sharing between the Christian and Muslim communities (with implicit economic benefits for the latter), which the Maronites tended to circumvent, fearing the political implications of even a limited loss of constitutional power. Additional domestic strains emanated from the uneven development of the various regions and wide disparities in income distribution (El Khalil 1996), which led to migration from rural to urban centres and to the unchecked and rapid growth of poor suburbs around the major cities, Beirut in particular (see Section 7.3).

In turn, external factors also placed increasing strains on the Lebanese political system. Principal among these factors was the rising military power of resident Palestinian organisations, particularly after the 1967 Arab–Israeli war, and direct and indirect external interventions, principally by Israel. While the activity of Palestinian organisations was ostensibly directed at keeping the Palestinian cause alive and continuing the struggle to reclaim Palestine, the Palestinian presence in Lebanon became intricately linked to Lebanese domestic political affairs. The domestic and regional political agendas could hardly be separated. The prevailing weaknesses of the political system allowed the Palestinian organisations to enhance their political and military positions by forging alliances with disenchanted Lebanese sectarian (Muslim) and non-sectarian political parties, as well as with groups that regarded such an alliance as a means to pressurise the Maronite establishment to accept political reform.[4]

On the other side, apart from frequent air raids and land incursions, Israel formed undeclared alliances mainly with Lebanese Maronite parties fearful of the growing Palestinian influence. Israeli interventions were intended to destabilise the domestic situation, shift the focus of the Palestine conflict away from Israel, and bring Lebanon within its orbit of political influence. It is this combination of domestic and external factors which eventually led to the inevitable outbreak of a civil conflict on 13 April 1975, despite the robust economic growth, rising real per capita income and the relative financial stability Lebanon had experienced in the period before 1975. Whatever the national socio-economic failings (see Section 7.III), they did not constitute an important trigger for

[4] The nature of the desired reforms differed from one Lebanese political group to another. Leftist and other non-establishment groups wished to introduce fundamental changes to render the system less confessional. Traditional Muslim groups aimed at readjusting the sectarian formula to ensure a distribution of power more favourable to the Muslim community. For both groups, political reform would offer greater economic opportunities.

the conflict, which pitted multiple national, but also foreign, actors against one another.[5]

Under external pressure, the war was finally settled in accordance with the Taif Accord (1979), named after the Saudi city of Taif, where, at the invitation of Saudi Arabia, members of the Lebanese parliament met and agreed on amendments to the constitution that were subsequently approved in a special parliamentary meeting in Beirut (November 1990).[6] The Accord reaffirmed the principle of sectarian power-sharing. However, recognising the shift in domestic sectarian balances, it envisaged, in principle, a more collegial form of political governance, divided between the major religious communities, and hence in principle a firmer basis for domestic political stability. One major manifestation of this anticipated collegiality are the notably diminished prerogatives of the president of the republic and the enhanced powers of the council of ministers, which is supposed to act as a collective governing body.[7] Pending future de-confessionalism of the political system, there has been a tacit understanding among the major political actors that the sharing of power between the country's religious groups will be maintained irrespective of any change in the population's religious composition, a matter we take up in Section 6.VI.

Significantly, the Taif Accord also allowed for the temporary presence of Syrian troops in Lebanon to help the Lebanese authorities establish law and order; the eventual withdrawal of these forces was to be subject to the mutual agreement of the Syrian and Lebanese governments.

---

[5] On the domestic front, the main protagonists were traditional Christian (Maronite-oriented) political parties (the so-called Lebanese Front) against an opposing alliance comprising the PLO and several Lebanese political parties and groups, notably 'Amal' (Shia-oriented) and the Progressive Socialist Party (Druze-oriented). The most notable direct foreign interventions were the entry of Syrian troops in 1976, albeit at the invitation of the then Lebanese government, and the Israeli invasion of Lebanon in 1982, which greatly intensified the civil conflict (for details and analyses of the war, see Corm 1994; Hamdan 1997; and Makdisi and Sadaka 2005).

[6] The Iraqi invasion of Kuwait in July 1990 encouraged outside powers (both Arab and Western) involved or concerned with the Lebanese conflict to help to resolve it as a prelude to the launching of the allied campaign led by the United States to liberate Kuwait at the beginning of 1991. Syria, a main actor in Lebanon's civil conflict, was one of the Arab countries that supported this campaign. The ratification of the Taif Accord did not lead to the cessation of hostilities in Lebanon until the removal of General Aoun in October 1990 through direct Syrian military action undertaken with tacit US approval.

[7] The council was henceforth to be chaired by the prime minister, unless the president decided to attend, but without the right to vote. In contrast to parliamentary decisions which are arrived at through a majority of the vote, the new constitution specifies that decisions of the council of ministers are to be arrived at by consensus and only failing that by majority vote. For 'fundamental' questions facing the country such as the declaration of war; international agreements; the electoral, citizenship, and administrative decentralisation laws; failing consensus, a majority of two thirds is required, subject to parliamentary approval.

Whatever the merits of the Taif Accord, in the post-war period Lebanon continued to face major political/sectarian tensions and underlying political instability, which were fed by direct or indirect foreign intervention. Israel continued to occupy a southern zone until forced to withdraw in 2000 under the pressure of constant attacks by Hezbullah.

On 14 February 2005, former Prime Minister Rafiq Hariri, an influential Sunni political figure, was assassinated. This murder triggered popular protests against Syria which, along with mounting Western pressure, forced the withdrawal of Syrian troops from Lebanon. With this withdrawal, the role of Syria as the influential arbiter of domestic political disputes ended. On 12 July 2006, Israel launched a full-scale war against Hezbullah (ostensibly triggered by a cross-border raid and the kidnapping of two Israeli soldiers), but could not defeat it. However, this led to UN Security Resolution 1701 of August 2006, which mandated a ceasefire and a substantial enhancement of UN peacekeeping forces in South Lebanon. While the immediate outcome of this war was that Israel failed to achieve its declared objectives, domestically it managed to intensify existing political divisions over specific national issues and to draw external parties into intervening even more deeply in the affairs of the country. The following two years witnessed serious political confrontations, including failure to agree on the election of a successor to the president of the republic, whose term ended in November 2007. It took intensive Arab mediation (the so-called Doha Agreement of 15 May 2008) to avert a civil conflict and bring about a political settlement. This resulted in the election of the commander of the army as the new president (25 May 2008), followed by the scheduled parliamentary elections in June 2009 and the formation of a government of national unity, as called for in the Agreement (see Makdisi, Kiwan and Marktanner 2011). Nonetheless, the political situation has since remained precarious: two major political groupings (dividing the Muslim community in large measure along sectarian lines, each allied with a group of Christian-dominated parties) have been competing politically, but are unable, so far, to agree on major questions facing the country. Indeed, when the president's term of office ended in May 2014, the major political parties in parliament could not agree on a successor and, as of mid-2016, the office of president remains vacant, with its functions assumed collectively by the council of ministers.

What can one surmise from this analysis?

It is true that the sectarian consociational model adopted on the eve of independence allowed for a significant degree of freedom and plural political activity which, until the recent Arab uprisings, set Lebanon's political system apart from the autocratic regimes that characterised the rest of the Arab world.

On the other hand, it also led to a weak central authority and weak political institutions which, in turn, gave rise to the emergence of the twin issues of unstable political equilibrium and poor governance (reinforced by a non-democratic regional environment, the persistence of the unresolved Arab–Israeli conflict and a frequent state of instability in the region. Generally, the prevailing domestic political environment tended to foster corruption, nepotism, clientelism and laxity in the upholding of the public interest, especially when it came into conflict with powerful private interests.

The great challenge Lebanon has been facing for a long time is how to transcend its sectarian-consociational system to achieve a fully fledged democracy that would at once lessen its great vulnerability to any outside influence and ensure a greater degree of political stability as well as accountability. Achieving this goal implies, in our view, resolving the sectarian question by moving towards a secular form of governance, that is, separating the religious and the political spheres. A more democratic and accountable political system, we would add, is expected to go hand in hand with improved institutional performance, from the lack of which Lebanon has been suffering, and hence a better quality of development.

The unfolding developments in the Arab world will test the resiliency of Lebanese consociationalism, presenting clear threats to it as well as opportunities for the country's democratic advance. A major aim of this chapter is to analyse post-independence politico-economic developments and, in the light of this analysis, to evaluate whether and how Lebanon can move forward to a more mature democracy and a more equitable form of socio-economic development.

Section 7.II briefly reviews the historical politico-economic roots of independent Lebanon; Section 7.III traces the politico-economic record up to 1975 under the post-independence consociational order; Section 7.IV takes up the war period from 1975 to 1990; Section 7.V analyses the post-1990 politico-economic developments under the adjusted consociational system; and, finally, Section 7.VI takes up the prospects and conditions for transiting to a fully fledged democracy.

7.2   Historical Politico-economic Roots of Independent Lebanon: Preparing the Ground for Consociationalism: A Brief Review

The politico-economic features of today's Lebanon (external political interventions, economic openness, weak central authority, sectarian politics, migration and growth that largely neglected rural areas) can be traced back to the second half of the nineteenth century that witnessed the emergence of modern Lebanese sectarianism (Makdisi 2000).

The civil war between Maronites and Druze in 1860 and the resulting massacres at a time of a weakening Ottoman empire intensified the political intervention of European powers. The Constantinople Conference in June 1861[8] defined the organisation of an autonomous state in Mount Lebanon, with a Christian majority and militarily isolated from the rest of the districts of Lebanon, which had Muslim majorities. Mount Lebanon was exempted from Ottoman taxes, and starting in 1864 was managing its own fiscal affairs and electing its own 'Congress' or 'Majlis' through voting by the local dignitaries or shaykhs. Access by the Ottoman army to the new entity was forbidden while its administrative supervision by the empire was located in neighbouring Beirut. The local governors of the seven districts constituting the Mount Lebanon state were nominated on a confessional basis by a consensus between the major European powers that had participated in the conference, with Italy later added to the group,[9] as were the judicial, security diplomatic posts, mainly benefiting Maronite appointees. The administration of this state in Mount Lebanon, its protection, and the local will to lead it into autonomy depended directly on the political, military and diplomatic support of the great powers of nineteenth-century Europe (Boustany 2008).

Beirut, which was the administrative link between the Ottoman empire and Mount Lebanon between 1862 and 1920, enjoyed an important accumulation of physical and human capital. The Beirut–Damascus road was constructed in 1875 and the port of Beirut in 1894 (Kassir 2003). Six foreign banks were established in Beirut and Damascus, and they relied essentially on the intervention of local money lenders. At the same time, this period witnessed the beginnings of development in the areas of education and health care spearheaded by foreign missionaries: the establishment of the Syrian Protestant College in 1866 (later named the American University of Beirut), and the French University of St Joseph in 1875, as well as the establishment of dispensaries and hospitals, were keystones in the subsequent development of the country (El Khalil 1996). The end of World War I in Lebanon also witnessed an important

---

[8] This conference was convened by major European powers (Austria, France, Great Britain, Prussia and Russia) and the Ottoman authorities to discuss the political fate of Mount Lebanon following the massacre of Christians in the civil war, which had prompted French military intervention.

[9] The districts were Batrun, Kesrwan, Metn, Jezzin, Koura, Zahleh and the Chouf. The confessional distribution of the local administrators (known as *Qa'im Maqam*s) was as follows: a Maronite for each of the first four districts, a Greek Orthodox for Koura, a Greek Catholic for Zahleh and a Druze for the Chouf.

inflow of migrants: the Armenian refugees fleeing from Turkey further enhanced the country's human capital.

Taken together, these developments created an important impetus for economic prosperity upon the creation of greater Lebanon in 1920, which also benefited from the doubling of its land area, the inclusion of the port of Beirut, an enhanced financial and physical infrastructure, as well as the addition of the fertile Beqa'a valley, which made for the previous lack of agricultural land from which Mount Lebanon had suffered. The young, bigger country benefited from the effects of economies of scale, as economic activity expanded over a wider area. Migration decreased due to the surge in local activity, but also to the recession from which the allied countries had suffered in the period after World War I. Commerce boomed and manufacturing expanded, covering cotton milling, cement manufacturing and oil refining during the 1930s: the national economy was, to a large degree, open. New technologies were introduced in both the agriculture and manufacturing sectors and labour became increasingly salaried. The period was also marked by the introduction of the official registry of landownership, which notably enriched money lenders as well as the clergy (El Khalil 1996).

It should be noted that these developments, which could be perceived as indicators of modernisation, were also linked to the country's sectarian setup, characterised by the relative dominance of the Christian community which, at the time, controlled major aspects of the national economy. Indeed, the formation of greater Lebanon by the French mandate was in close coordination with the Maronite patriarch, who was fervent in his support of this project, his position endorsed by a broad segment of the Lebanese people. One major reason behind the patriarch's support was that the new state included more Maronite villages; while it would also include Greek Orthodox communities, it would nonetheless continue the dominance of the Maronite community.

The central authority's political power, however, was weak, dominated by the French high commissioner. Taxation was limited, and missionaries and charitable institutions continued to provide education and health care services, though with increased provision for public sector education. Indeed, a relatively weak central authority was to become a constant feature of Lebanon's subsequent political governance, with a consequent weakness in its ability to maintain domestic stability in a sectarian-based political system.

At the internal level, the annexed, mainly Muslim regions, especially on the eastern and northern borders, had adamantly opposed their annexation. They felt as though they were being uprooted from their natural socio-political environment with all the economic disadvantages that might result from this. Unfortunately, their fears turned out to be not without basis. They barely benefited from the economic success Lebanon enjoyed in this and subsequent periods. Indeed, a little less than a century after the creation of greater Lebanon in 1920, the annexed regions continued to be marginalised while remaining the least successful in eradicating poverty.

It was against this historical background that Lebanon's independence leaders, representing the country's two main religious communities, agreed to embark on the sectarian consociational model described in Section 7.I.

7.3   Post-independence Consociationalism: The Politico-economic Record up to 1975

After independence, Lebanon enjoyed an impressive economic expansion which, in part, was rooted in the massive spending of the allied troops during World War II. Faced by a maritime embargo and military operations, the allied troops had to purchase locally, thereby boosting aggregate demand and stimulating national industrial and agricultural production.[10] This spending was accompanied by balance of payments surpluses and an impressive growth in bank deposits.

The end of the war brought about a decline in economic activity which was expected but which, as noted later, saw a degree of reversal following the partition of Palestine and the creation of the State of Israel by the United Nations in 1948, an event which the Arab countries and the Palestinians failed to successfully oppose both politically and militarily. The creation of Israel was accompanied by turmoil in the region; uprisings against the French and British mandates and against local governments in neighbouring Arab countries met with violent suppression. With the forced influx of Palestinian refugees in neighbouring countries, especially Lebanon, as a result of the actions of Zionist militias in Palestine, a long period of instability and war was to ensue.

On the economic front, the partition of Palestine had mixed effects. It led to the loss of an important destination for Lebanese agricultural exports. On the other hand, it isolated Haifa, which had been a major Arab centre for services and transit and a close competitor of the port of Beirut. As with the Armenians before them, the Palestinians provided Lebanon with further skills. In addition to agricultural labour, the Palestinians brought know-how in commerce, finance, medicine and

---

[10] In contrast to the 1920s, the number of factories doubled to reach 1,000 establishments in 1945.

engineering, as well as important inflows of financial capital. However, as noted in Section 7.I, the presence of the Palestinian refugees had important political implications. The growth of armed Palestinian resistance in the southern regions of the country with the declared objective of reclaiming Palestine eventually contributed to the civil war that was to break out in 1975 (see Section 7.IV).

Lebanon had already withstood a smaller conflict a few years after the US-sponsored Baghdad Pact, designed to confront Soviet influence in the region, was established in 1955. The Arab world had become polarised into pro- and anti-Western camps. This division was bound to have its impact on the Lebanese domestic political scene where a similar division quickly emerged, leading to short-lived civil strife in 1958.[11] The end of the strife in the same year was partly due to an agreement by the external powers involved in the Lebanese domestic scene which brought the chief of the army, General Chehab, to the presidency.[12] Historically, domestic military conflicts in Lebanon (as with other small countries) have often been settled by foreign intervention, keeping in mind, of course, that at times the outbreak of conflict itself was in no small measure due to such intervention.

The Chehabi period, from 1958 to 1964, presented itself as a challenge to traditional sectarian politics embodied in the consociational model. Chehab bet on social development and the modernisation of the state apparatus to establish domestic peace. His era witnessed the creation of the Central Bank, the Bureau of Statistics, the Social Security Fund, the Green Plan and several other institutions modelled on Western administrative institutions of the era. Important as they were, the reforms he introduced could not, in the final analysis, dislodge the entrenched traditional politico-sectarian interests and so pave the way for substantive political transformation at the institutional level. The question of substantive reform at the institutional level and in the practice of the political body has remained elusive up to the present time.

Political developments notwithstanding, Lebanon was able to achieve impressive economic expansion. Beirut became the major commercial hub in the region, assisted by the elimination of the port of Haifa from Arab trade routes. Lebanon's private sector oriented the economy and

---

[11] In the midst of the Cold War, Lebanon was politically divided between a pro-Western and a pro-Soviet camp. The former comprised mainly Christian parties backed by the West and Saudi Arabia. The latter included Muslim and leftist groupings backed by the United Arab Republic (Egypt) and the Soviet Union. Notably, Nasserism strongly fuelled political sentiments and constituted a major political stream within the Lebanese left from the early 1950s to the late 1970s.

[12] The main external powers were the United States, the UAE, the Soviet Union and France.

openness supported by a liberal, noninterventionist economic policy[13] helped the country's enterprising private sector forge ahead, especially in the areas of trade and finance, at a time when the neighbouring countries, especially Syria, chose to follow the command economy model.

The closing of the Suez Canal in 1967 and the major oil boom that began in 1973 were both favourable to Lebanon's open economy. Even before this boom, Lebanese expatriates in the Arab countries were involved in managing a large portion of the oil surplus accruing to the Gulf countries, which were short on domestic skills. The inflow of remittances from the Gulf and other regions of the world not only contributed to an increase in bank deposits, but also helped counter the traditional deficit in the trade balance. At the same time, relatively substantial capital inflows permitted the Lebanese balance of payments to generate almost continuous surpluses. Given the floating exchange rate policy which the monetary authorities had adopted and their desire to stem the appreciation of the national currency as a consequence of these surpluses, the Central Bank frequently intervened on the foreign exchange market in support, mainly, of the dollar. As a result the Central Bank managed to accumulate sizable foreign exchange reserves which it turned into gold reserves at a time when the price of gold was fixed in terms of the US dollar.[14] Further coups, revolts, wars and nationalisation schemes in other Arab countries promoted the country's role as a safe haven and shelter for Arab human and financial capital fleeing troubled countries.

The annual rates of growth from 1950 to 1975 ranged between 5 and 7 per cent in general, which was higher than that of most developing countries outside the Middle East (Chaib 1979). Significantly, these annual growth rates were accompanied by structural changes in the national economy. During the same period, the share of agriculture in the GDP declined from 20 to 9 per cent, while the share of the manufacturing sector, becoming increasingly export-oriented, rose from 9 to 14 per cent. Trade and services, however, continued to account for the largest share of the GDP, estimated at 67 per cent in 1974. The tourism sector increased fourfold between 1968 and 1974, to account for 10 per cent of the GDP. However limited, Lebanon's pre-1975 development manifested a diversification trend which the civil war brought to an end.

---

[13] Capital controls were abolished in 1948, and a banking secrecy law was passed in 1956. Furthermore, the customs union with Syria ended in 1950. These and similar measures promoted a liberal economic environment and attracted capital inflows from neighbouring countries which had exchange controls.

[14] As of the end of December 1974, the Central Bank's gold reserves were equivalent to 386 million US dollars, while gold and foreign reserves stood at 1.654 billion US dollars, accounting for more than 100 per cent of the year's import bill.

However, the rosy picture Lebanon's economic expansion portrayed hid important gaps and shortcomings at the socio-economic level. As noted earlier, the benefits of this expansion were largely confined to certain segments and regions in the country to the neglect of others. In contrast to the governmental focus on trade, finance and services reflecting an urban bias; rural developments, mainly in the northern, central and southern regions of the country (where there was a majority-Muslim community) were neglected.[15] Lebanon's development was lopsided in that its qualitative aspects or socio-economic content did not significantly improve. Available data indicate that the percentage of the groups with very limited income (poor and very poor) in the total population declined from the early 1950s to the early 1960s but, thereafter, remained the same until the early 1970s, at roughly one half of the population. The richest class (4 per cent of the population) continued to account for a sizable portion of the national income, about one third (Makdisi 2004). Similarly, while the levels of education improved, by 1970 the rate of illiteracy in Lebanon was still relatively high: an overall average of 32 per cent reflecting a 22.5 per cent rate for the group between six and twenty-four years old and 36.4 per cent for the group over fifteen years old (Republic of Lebanon, Central Administration of Statistics 1972).

At the regional level, Beirut and Mount Lebanon benefited the most from the national economic development and attracted the bulk of government spending. Mount Lebanon, which contained 18 per cent of the Lebanese people, had 45 per cent of the hospital beds (Owen 1988). The inequality indicators were also reflected in the banking sector: For the period 1970 to 1974, 3 to 4 per cent of depositors enjoyed 84 per cent of banking deposits, while about 45 per cent of private sector lending went to approximately 1 per cent of borrowers (Banque du Liban, *Quarterly Bulletin*: various issues).

It is therefore not surprising that the country witnessed massive internal migration: between 1960 and 1965, 20 per cent of the rural population (120,000 people) migrated to Beirut, mainly to its suburbs, which were poorly equipped to host such a large number of impoverished newcomers. A belt of poverty gradually surrounded the capital, in a demographically

---

[15] Indeed, in 1974, the religious leader of the Shi'i community, Imam Musa al-Sadr, launched a political movement, 'Amal', as a political and economic endeavour intended to enhance the position of the Shi'i community in the Lebanese sectarian system, as well as to act as a countervailing force to the growing influence of Palestinian organisations in southern Lebanon. Amal presented itself as a 'movement of the dispossessed', and its appeal was to a large extent based on the socio-economic conditions of the Shia community, which lagged behind other communities in Lebanon. It was to develop, especially after 1982, into one of the major warring factions in the Lebanese civil war.

polarised Lebanon where 52 per cent of the population lived in cities with more than 100,000 inhabitants and 39 per cent in villages with fewer than 5,000 inhabitants (Republic of Lebanon, Central Administration of Statistics 1972).[16]

One aspect of the ongoing modernisation process in Lebanon, which took place in an atmosphere of rapid social change and increased tension, was the increase in the power and organisation of its syndicates. The period 1970 to 1975, in particular, witnessed growing demonstrations and strikes by workers and students.[17] Worker activism was met with increasing brutality on the part of government forces: there were many martyrs, notably among the tobacco growers, industrial workers and fishermen.

In a sense, the consociational model which was adopted at independence to accommodate the religious pluralism of Lebanese society, to bring out its virtues and to stress the special niche Lebanon occupies in the Arab world, was put to the test. With the outbreak of the civil war it failed to hold together, despite the achievements of the Lebanese economy before 1975. However, as earlier pointed out and as will be touched on again, other major external factors also pushed Lebanon in the direction of failure. It has been argued that had it not been for the extremely stressful regional military and political conditions Lebanon had to face in the pre-1975 period, a major civil war could have been averted and peaceful political reform could have been achieved, despite internal regional and economic polarisation. We will return to this point in Section 7.IV.

7.4   The Fall into the Abyss: The Civil War Period, 1975–1990

As discussed in Section 7.I, in the end it was a combination of domestic and external factors that opened the door to a sectarian-oriented, sixteen-year civil war on 13 April 1975.[18] What further inflamed the domestic scene in the early 1970s, and indirectly also helped prepare the ground for civil conflict, was the intensifying social strife manifested in demonstrations and strikes by worker and student groups agitating for various social and civic rights.

---

[16] On a scale of zero to seven measuring development in Lebanon in the early 1960s, the country was given an average of approximately two, while the rural sector scored below one (IRFED 1962).

[17] The student body was generally united with respect to their demands pertaining to national education, labour and economic issues, but sharply divided regarding support of the PLO and its military status in Lebanon.

[18] The war witnessed three distinct phases: 1975–77, 1978–82 and 1983–90. For a review, see Makdisi and Sadaka (2005).

The war had a devastating impact on the human, political, economic and social levels. On the human level, the casualties of the war are put at 150,000 deaths, 200,000 seriously wounded, 50,000 with lesser injuries and 15,000 disappeared, out of a total population estimated at around 3 million people in 1990 (UNDP 1998). Further, it led to the forced internal displacement of 500,000 people (ibid.), mostly along sectarian lines. In consequence, the country's religious contours, both politically and geographically, came to be further accentuated, reversing an earlier trend that had seen a geographic integration of social groups belonging to different religions motivated by industrial and economic considerations. Population displacement, it should be emphasised, was not the result of internal conflict only. The Israeli invasion in 1978, but, more important, that of 1982, under the pretext of fighting armed Palestinian groups, also led to a massive population exodus (mainly of Shi'i Muslims), from the southern regions of the country largely towards Beirut and its suburbs, and stimulated a wave of migration particularly to the United States, Europe and Africa.[19]

Governmental authority now greatly weakened, the militias sought to enhance their economic and financial position by various means: looting, confiscation of private property, imposing taxes in the regions under their control, confiscating customs duties via seizing control of the ports of entry, the cultivation and trade of drugs, trading in contraband, outright thievery (including from 1975 to 1976, the pillaging of the port of Beirut and the downtown district), bank robberies and fraudulent banking practices, all flourished (Makdisi and Sadaka 2005). While public institutions continued to function nominally, in practice, the government largely lost control over them to the various warring militias, and, indeed, in September 1998, two competing governments emerged which were not unified until October 2000.[20]

---

[19] Emigrant remittances contributed more to the development of South Lebanon in the post-war period than to other regions of the country.

[20] When the six-year term of President Amin Gemayel was about to end in September 1988 without agreement on a successor, he unilaterally appointed the commander of the army, General Michel Aoun, as president of a council of ministers composed of the six members of the army command. The three Muslim members of the appointed council refused to serve. The government, at the time Gemayel's term ended, refused to acknowledge the legitimacy of the council he had set up, and considered itself the sole legitimate government of the country. Hence, two competing governments emerged. The government of General Aoun refused to acknowledge the Taif Accord, which the Lebanese parliament ratified in October 1989, followed by the election of Elias Hrawi as president of the republic. After a series of military engagements, Aoun was forced to leave the country in October 1990, and his departure paved the way for the unification of the Lebanese government and government administration.

The national economy experienced two distinct phases during the sixteen-year war which ravaged the country. After having witnessed a sharp depreciation of the currency in 1976, the Lebanese pound tended to remain stable up to 1982 at around LL4.60 per US dollar, compared to an average of LL2.75 per US dollar in 1975. In support of the pound came remittances and aid from the Gulf countries, as well as foreign financing of and local spending by the various military factions. The PLO, in particular, undertook a massive expansion of its military and administrative apparatus during the first six years of the war. Nonetheless, thanks to a resilient and entrepreneurial private sector, the national economy, though greatly battered, managed to survive, albeit at a tremendous social and economic cost. In the early 1980s, however, the economic and financial picture began to deteriorate drastically. The Gulf countries' economic recession, the vast destruction and heavy death toll resulting from the 1982 Israeli invasion and the consequent pulling out of the PLO from Lebanon, all led to a substantial decline in economic activity and a markedly worsening social situation. The government's financial and budgetary situation greatly worsened due to loss of revenue and increasing, mainly military, spending – with heavier borrowing requirements and rising public debt, its servicing began to surge. Whereas at the end of 1975, public debt was negligible, by the end of 1990, it had approached 100 per cent of GDP and debt servicing had reached 11 per cent. At the same time, monetisation of debt led to a substantial increase in broad money supply (385 fold), which, along with a declining Lebanese pound in nominal and real terms, fed inflationary pressures at a time of declining economic activity. The pound fell to an average of about LL700 for 1990 (and later to an average of LL1,713 in 1992, after which it began to improve, stabilising at around LL1,500 in early 1998. The resulting inflation, in turn, stimulated speculative activities, and, given the high concentration of banking credit where 200 bank accounts generally accounted for more than 50 per cent of total extended loans, struck one of the most devastating blows to Lebanese society by redistributing wealth in favour of a small minority, including warlords, to the detriment of the middle and poorer classes. At the end of 1990, real GDP stood at around 50 per cent of its 1975 level, with the share of government to GDP doubling to about 30 per cent. On the other hand, the potential rise in unemployment was partly tempered by emigration and recruitment by the growing militias.

Politically, the war brought a halt to the practice of consociationalism in Lebanon. The parliament elected in 1973 continued in place, but with only nominal powers, renewing its own mandate every four years on the grounds that the ongoing conflict did not permit the holding of national elections. However, the parliament did manage to keep the constitutional exercise of presidential elections going.[21] But, in practice, real power was in the hands of the militias. In the areas with Christian dominance, one faction, namely the so-called Lebanese Forces, had unequivocal control over political and military affairs. In the areas with Muslim dominance, up to 1982 an alliance between the PLO and so-called Lebanese patriotic parties held political and military sway, but subsequently with the forced withdrawal of the PLO, the Lebanese parties played a greater role.[22]

The period following the Israeli invasion of 1982 witnessed escalating inter-militia fighting rising to a climax with the attempt by the Amin Gemayel government to reach an agreement with Israel on 17 February 1983. The attempted agreement not only provoked intensified domestic fighting, but also intensified external interventions in support of one side or another and the entry of a new player, namely the Islamic Republic of Iran. As a result, human losses mounted and instances of social dislocation increased, resulting in yet further human tragedy and social dislocation, while the warlords consolidated their hold over the fragmented territory.[23] The civil war, which started between two more or less distinct groups, decayed into an insane saga of violence involving numerous armed organisations.

One major consequence, already discussed, of the civil war was the forced internal migration which accentuated the country's division along sectarian lines; another was the expanding size of the government, which further served the interests of confessional leaders in the decision-making process. Along with a diminishing middle class, these developments tended to reinforce the sectarian nature of Lebanon's consociational system and to weaken the incentives for reform that had been growing in the pre-war period and that normally accompany an expanding economy led by a growing middle class.

---

[21] During the civil war, presidential elections in Lebanon were preceded by intense security events: Elias Sarkis was elected in 1976 after the entry of Syrian troops within the framework of an Arab League Force, and Beshir Gemayel during the Israeli invasion of 1982. Less than a month after his assassination, his brother Amin Gemayel was elected president.

[22] After reaching Beirut in 1982, Israeli forces redeployed to settle in the security zone which Israel had established in southern Lebanon and occupied since 1978, until forced to withdraw in 2000. The Syrian forces, as noted earlier, entered Lebanon in 1975 and were forced to withdraw in 2005.

[23] For eight years, between 1983 and 1990, intermittent but heavy fighting broke out between the various militias, either to defend regions under their control or to expand into other regions.

7.5   The Post-1990 Adjusted Consociational System: Flawed Governance and Development

Like other major conflicts in the history of Lebanon, it took outside intervention by regional and international powers to settle the civil war. The United States was the major international player, while the two main regional players were Syria and Saudi Arabia, which had a history of competing regional ambitions which were reflected in the Lebanese political scene. Syria threw its support behind mainly Shia-dominated parties while Saudi Arabia allied itself with Sunni-dominated parties. However, from the end of the civil war in 1990 to 2005 when it was forced to withdraw, Syria was the major regional player on the Lebanese domestic scene by virtue of the sanctioned presence of its troops in Lebanon.[24]

Both phases have been characterised by highly flawed political governance when measured against the intended objectives of the Taif Accord itself, let alone measures of mature democratic behaviour (Makdisi, Kiwan and Marktanner 2011). Some observers would argue that the flaws of the pre-2005 period could be ascribed directly to the dominating Syrian political and military presence. We maintain that this assessment is, to a considerable extent, correct. However, the matter does not rest here. With the resumption of the traditional roles of the domestic political players in the period following the withdrawal of Syrian troops, Lebanon's political-institutional performance did not significantly improve, and, in some domains, tended to deteriorate Hence, intrinsic domestic factors must underlie the flaws in the forms of political behaviour seen in Lebanon, which we note later.

At the economic level, in both phases, and when quantitative measures such as the rate of growth are considered, it can be said that the country's economic record did not fare badly. But after the socio-economic quality of development, including severe environmental degradation and lack of proper urban and rural planning, is accounted for, substantial flaws remain.

In what follows we briefly take up the post-war political and economic developments, respectively.

7.5.1   *Political Developments*

One of the main objectives of the Taif Accord was to engender political stability by readjusting the form of power-sharing between the three main

[24] Following the end of the Cold War, Syria continued to have an influential regional role. By joining the allies in the first Gulf War against Iraq, it managed to acquire tacit US approval for the continued presence of its troops in Lebanon in the wake of the Taif Accord and the settlement of the civil war. The US stance was to change drastically after 2005.

religious communities as represented respectively by the president of the republic (Maronite), the speaker of the house (Shia Muslim) and the prime minister (Sunni Muslim). In effect, contrary to what was intended, the new distribution of power led to political jockeying among the holders of the three highest political offices. More significant, disagreements between them (basically more on account of their own vested interests rather than those of their communities) were not necessarily resolved within the council of ministers or the parliament, but outside these institutions within the framework of what came to be called the 'Troika', a set-up comprising the holders of these three political offices. And when unable to settle political disagreements among themselves, the ultimate arbiter and enforcer was the Syrian authorities. With a few exceptions, the emerging post-1990 confessional political leadership, which included major actors in the civil war, was increasingly more concerned with holding on to power and sharing the benefits of authority rather than with laying the foundations for proper governance. They assured the perpetuation of their political dominance through tailored electoral laws (prior to 2005 with Syrian tacit approval if not connivance), massive recruitment of personnel in the military and the administration drawn from the ranks of former militias and the appointment in key administrative positions of loyal followers, though few might have had the required credentials. Generally, the applied sectarian system of appointments permitted a high degree of non-accountability across the sectarian divide: corruption did not have a sectarian colour. In this vein, the ambitious reconstruction projects the late Prime Minister Hariri had initiated in the early 1990s (often criticised as grandiose and leading to an unsustainable burden of national debt) provided new profit opportunities for the governing class via lucrative projects which came their way for political and other reasons.[25]

The integration of the warlords into the government after the settlement of the civil war might have seemed a worthwhile price to pay in order to assure future peace and stability. Instead, the post-Taif period has been characterised by major flaws of governance, the general reinforcement of sectarian polarisation (along with an increased potential for reigniting confessional strife) to the benefit of the ruling political class and mounting obstacles to calls by non-confessional civil society groups for major changes in political and institutional behaviour.

---

[25] Infrastructural spending, during and after the reconstruction period, is considered by many experts to have been over-costly and inefficiently administered. More than twenty-five years after the end of the war and despite massive government expenditure, Lebanon still lags behind many developing countries in the domain of infrastructure, especially in the electricity and telecommunication sectors.

Even private professional lobbying groups came to be tainted with sectarian influences, one exception being the banking sector, which managed to consolidate its position in the national economy as a major mainly non-sectarian economic player.[26] It was able to enhance its position as an efficient lobbying group, distinct from the confessional political players, who form a club. This role stands in contrast to the increasing sectarian colouring of the trade unions that positioned themselves along confessional party lines. Instead of developing as defenders of the economic interest of workers across the sectarian divide, they fell prey to sectarian divisions and the influences of sectarian leaders, which in turn tended to weaken their bargaining position vis-à-vis employers as well as the government.

It was noted in Section 7.1 that, during the period following the assassination of Prime Minister Hariri in February 2005, dramatic political, security and military developments occurred: the immediate withdrawal of Syrian troops,[27] a series of political assassinations through 2008 and the war waged by Israel starting on 12 July 2006, with its subsequent adverse domestic political consequences. The Doha Agreement, which reset the political trajectory in May 2008, only temporarily succeeded in restoring relative political stability. The government of national unity called for under this agreement lasted until February 2011, when a one-sided new government was formed (comprising mostly the so-called March 8 grouping), excluding major political groups on the opposite side of the political aisle (the so-called March 14 grouping). In February 2014, it was replaced by a new government that included most of the major parties. While the new government was able to survive the non-election of a president and function with a modicum of cooperation between its principal supporters, it has not had a mandate to tackle the major political and economic issues facing the

---

[26] The monetary authorities encouraged the banks to reinvest their profits from 1993, which led to an increase in their capitalisation. This helped to position the banking sector to accommodate a growing inflow of remittances and foreign capital, mainly from the Lebanese diaspora, allowing for an important financial deepening of the national banking system. The ratio of commercial bank deposits to GDP increased from 190 per cent for 1990 to 307 per cent for 2012, though loans to the private sector had absorbed 28.6 per cent of total banking assets as of the end of December 2012, compared to 34.2 per cent at the end of 1990 due to the faster growth rate of assets. The private sector had received loans equivalent to 101.5 per cent of GDP as of the end of December 2012 compared to 71.2 per cent at the end of 1990. Noteworthy, the number of borrowers increased twenty fold from 1990 to cover more than 400,000 borrowers by the end of 2011.

[27] UN Security Council Resolution 1559 of 2 September 2004 had already called for this withdrawal. Following the assassination of Hariri, the Security Council passed Resolution 1595 (7 April 2005) establishing an independent commission to investigate the assassination; and on 30 March 2006, the council adopted Resolution 1664, which called on the secretary-general to negotiate an agreement with the Lebanese government on the creation of a tribunal of an international character to try those found responsible for this and subsequent political assassinations.

country, being subject to sensitive domestic political balances of power as well as traditional external political influences.

In parallel, in Syria, popular protests that initially broke out in March 2011 against the country's regime later tuned into a traumatic civil war involving multiple fundamentalist and other groups as well as foreign powers. As of mid-2016, it was yet to be settled and its eventual outcome determined. In the meantime, the Syrian conflict has led to a heightened level of political and security instability in Lebanon. In the summer of 2014, fundamentalist groups fighting the Syrian regime engaged in military attacks against the Lebanese army on Lebanon's north-eastern borders abducting, in the process, personnel from the security forces. Hezbullah in turn joined the fight, on the side of the Syrian regime, against armed fundamentalist opposition groups, especially in areas close to Lebanon's north-east borders. As a result, the security situation has since become increasingly precarious though, as of mid-2016, under control, due in large measure to the awareness of the major political parties of the potential negative implications, in national terms, of non-cooperation in facing the emerging security threat.

As practised, Lebanese post-Taif consociationalism has been incapable of resolving internal conflicts without resorting to outside intervention, which, indeed, has been a constant factor in Lebanon's political history since independence.[28] A lasting national reconciliation in Lebanon (whose contours we take up in Section 7.VI) is yet to be achieved.

7.5.2   Growth Trends and Socio-economic Developments

Since the end of the civil war, six phases of alternating growth trends in Lebanon can be discerned.[29] The first, stretching from 1992 to 1994, witnessed an accelerating growth rate averaging 6.3 per cent and reaching 8 per cent in the latter year;[30] it was induced by increasing public sector expenditure and private sector investments, led by the construction

---

[28] To cite some major examples: the resolution of the 1958 conflict needed the intervention of both the United States and Egypt; the Cairo Agreement of 1969, which settled the conflict between the Lebanese army and Palestinian armed groups, was brokered by Egypt; the settlement of the Lebanese civil war in 1989 (the Taif Accord) was arranged by Saudi Arabia with the support of the US and French governments; and, until its withdrawal in 2005, Syria, as noted, imposed a settlement (in accordance with its own interests) on any domestic political or sectarian conflict. In May 2008, it took the Doha Agreement to avert the renewal of civil conflict.

[29] The growth-rate data we cite later are based on Lebanon's published national income accounts and IMF estimates.

[30] We are excluding 1991, since the estimated growth rate for that year was exceptionally high, reflecting a rebound from the dramatic fall in the levels of GDP during the previous two years in consequence of continuing military clashes, mainly in the eastern suburbs of Beirut (Makdisi 2004).

industry. This increased expenditure took up the existing slack in the post-war economy, while expectations in the private sector were initially positive regarding future prospects. At the same time, a policy of anchoring the pound to the US dollar, implemented in late 1992, helped to gradually reduce the rate of inflation, but the increase in government spending led, in the absence of a concomitant increase in revenues, to a gradual deterioration of the budgetary and current account deficits and continued increase in public debt, as discussed later.

The second phase, from 1995 to 2000, saw a gradually declining growth rate with an average of 3 per cent, becoming slightly negative in 2000. This declining rate may be partly attributable to continued borrowing by the government at relatively high (though, over time, declining) real interest rates in order to finance persistent budgetary deficits, with a consequent dramatic rise in public debt (climbing from about 48 per cent of the GDP for 1992 to a little over 150 per cent for 2000). This led, in turn, to a 'crowding out' of private sector investments, and the persistence of generally relatively high borrowing costs for private enterprises. A policy of relatively high real interest rates, especially in the 1990s, was implemented in support of the exchange rate policy referred to earlier.

Other factors that contributed to the declining rate of growth in this period were prevailing regional political uncertainties and clashes with Israeli forces occupying a southern part of the country, all of which tended to limit the flow of private investment. Furthermore, the decline in oil revenues in the Gulf between 1990 and 1999 negatively affected regional investments and remittances from the Gulf region. In addition, while the rehabilitation of the infrastructure had a positive impact on the investment climate, lack of progress in administrative and political reform, not to mention increasing corruption, influenced this climate negatively.

The third phase, from 2001 to 2004, saw a recovery of the growth rate, which averaged 4.25 per cent, reaching an estimated 7.5 per cent in 2004. This improvement is related mainly to post-9/11 developments causing a reflow of Arab capital towards Lebanon and other Arab countries. The real estate sector and the tourism industry benefited the most from this development, and also contributed to the expansion of bank deposits, easing the pressure on banks in accommodating budgetary deficits.

The fourth phase, from 2005 to 2006, witnessed, as noted earlier, waves of political and security instability and a major military confrontation with Israel that caused a vast amount of economic destruction (of infrastructure, dwellings, factories and other enterprises) which led to a decline in the growth rate to an average of less than 1 per cent during these two years.

The fifth phase, 2007 to 2010, saw a period of impressive economic growth, with an average growth rate of 8 per cent despite an unstable political situation and limited progress in advancing structural reforms. This growth was partly spurred on by large capital inflows and increased investments, which permitted Lebanon to weather the global financial crisis.

The sixth and most recent phase, from 2011 to 2015, was marked by a decline in the average rate of growth to about 2.0 per cent. The underlying factors of this decline include an increased political polarisation leading to an impasse over the election of a new president which was supposed to take place in May 2014 (and by mid-2016 had yet to take place); increased regional uncertainties in the wake of the Arab uprisings; and, importantly, the spill-over from the Syrian crisis, all of which tended to depress direct domestic investments bearing in mind that the influx of a large number of Syrian refugees and the disrupted trade relationship between the two countries added to Lebanon's national economic burdens.

For the entire period of 1992 to 2015, the growth rate averaged about 4.4 per cent but admittedly, as noted earlier, exhibited wide annual oscillations, in part on account of the changing domestic and/or regional political scenes. Lebanon's per capita income (at constant prices, base year 2000) rose during the same period from $4,157 for 1992 to $8,092 for 2015 which places it in the upper-middle-income group of countries (WEO, IMF 2015).[31]

But whatever the growth and macroeconomic record, overall the quality of national development suffered. Consistent time series of various socio-economic indicators are, for the most part, unavailable. Still, existing research and surveys reveal that in a few areas such as health care and education, progress was achieved, but in other areas, little if any improvement was accomplished or else there was noticeable deterioration, as in the case of environmental degradation, unemployment, increased corruption and social inequity, accompanied by increasing concentration of

---

[31] In parallel the government's inability to contain or reduce budgetary deficits led to a rising public debt which at the end of 2015 stood at about 84.5 per cent of national income. Fortunately, the larger portion of this debt (61.5% at end 2015) is denominated in national currency and held by residents, a matter that over the years has helped the authorities to pursue debt renewal policies, and eased the pressure on their implementing fiscal policies to reduce the budgetary deficits. In addition, the Central Bank's anchoring of the Lebanese pound to the dollar since 1992 has helped promote stability in the foreign exchange market despite intermittent negative political developments. In the process the Bank has come to accumulate relatively large foreign exchange reserves which as of end 2015 stood at $37 billion in addition to the equivalent of $9.85 billion in gold reserves. Together they accounted for 260 per cent of the 2015 import bill.

political and economic power in the hands of the few (Leenders 2012; Makdisi 2004). And while, generally, developmental disparities between the regions have narrowed, certain districts, particularly in north and north-east Lebanon (Akkar, Minieh-Dannieh, Baalbek and Hermel), still lag far behind the rest of the Lebanese regions from a developmental perspective.

Available recent data indicate they have the lowest rates of employment (an inactivity rate of 56 per cent compared to less than 50 per cent in Beirut), have attracted the least participation on the part of the private sector (approximately 76 per cent compared to a national ratio of 87 per cent) and have severely lagged behind in health care services and infrastructure (18 per cent of households in the districts of Akkar and Minieh-Dannieh still have no access to sewers or use open sewers, compared to 5 per cent at the national level) (Central Administration of Statistics 2007 and 2009). Urban poverty was significant in Tripoli, with 57 per cent of households deprived with about 26 per cent being extremely deprived (Nehme 2010). An earlier study (UNDP 2008) points to the relatively wide disparity in per capita consumption between various regions of the country, as well as the geographic concentration of measured poverty levels and, as a correlate, the disproportionately higher rates of unemployment among the poor.[32] Unfortunately, reliable data on income distribution (e.g. the Gini coefficient) are not available.

Nonetheless, taken altogether, this picture reveals serious exclusionary aspects to Lebanese development that in certain respects have taken on a confessional colouring. This matter is directly attributable to very poor institutional performance,[33] in which, to say the least, the distinction between public and private interest became increasingly blurred, or was not recognised by the governing class.

7.5.3   Lebanon's Dilemma

It may be correctly argued that, despite repeated politico-religious tensions, Lebanon's consociationalism has had its positive dimension. It generally tended to promote moderate politics, safeguard freedom of expression and religious beliefs and protect the pluralism of Lebanese

---

[32] Using data from expenditure surveys for the year 2004/2005, the study finds that the bottom 20 per cent of the population accounts for only 7 per cent of all consumption in Lebanon, while the richest 20 per cent accounts for 43 per cent (more than six times higher). The north of the country has 20.7 per cent of the population, but 46 per cent of the most impoverished and 38 per cent of the poor as a whole.

[33] According to the World Bank Worldwide Governance Indicators, the Government Effectiveness' estimate for Lebanon decreased from –0.1 in 1996 to –0.3 in 2012 with a constant standard error of 0.2.

society. On the other hand, while agreed to nationally, the sectarian power-sharing system has amounted to a disparity between citizens in respect of political rights by virtue of belonging to different religious groups. In practice, it has tended to promote sectarianism and reinforce familialism and clientelism, and by extension corruption, as the mainstay of Lebanese political behaviour. Sectarian consociationalism could not prevent the outbreak of the civil war, even if the role of external intervention in its onset is given due recognition.[34] Indeed, as pointed out, sectarian divisions have facilitated these interventions, which more often than not have been of a destabilising nature.

It could be conjectured, as argued elsewhere (Makdisi et al. 2011), that in line with the modernisation hypothesis, Lebanon's relatively high per capita income, open society and partially democratic political system should have had a more positive impact on its political governance than that which has actually come to prevail. This review clearly demonstrates that the reason this has not been the case is related to inherent negative domestic elements, noted earlier, as well as to external factors that have tended to reinforce their negative influence and prevent Lebanon from moving forward towards a fully fledged democracy. These external factors include regional conflicts, in particular the pervasive influence of the Arab–Israeli conflict, the more recent but still raging civil war in Syria, the surrounding non-democratic regional environment and the effects of regional oil wealth.

We maintain that in some respects, sectarianism in Lebanon has acted as a substitute for the effects of resource rents in the case of oil-rich countries. For the latter, the rentier thesis implies a trade-off between political rights and economic welfare. In the case of Lebanon's strongly sectarian system, an implicit trade-off has occurred between entrenched politico-economic sectarian interests imbued with unaccountable low-level governance, on one hand, and the greater accountability/higher-level governance that a liberal consociational democratic system should have promoted, on the other. In practice, the tilt has been towards weak institutions, corruption, frequent social tension and the country not attaining, among other things, its developmental potential.

The civil war in Syria that broke out in 2011, and in which Hezbullah subsequently became an active party in support of the regime, the consequent inflow of large numbers of Syrian refugees into Lebanon and the emergence of armed fundamentalist groups along Lebanon's eastern borders have not only added to the country's economic and social burdens, but have also reinforced its sectarian strains and its vulnerability to

---

[34] For an analysis of the causes of the civil war, see Makdisi and Sadaka (2005).

external shocks. Nonetheless, the country has managed to hold together. A leading reason for this is that, despite contradictory political attitudes towards the entry of Hezbullah in the Syrian conflict, a broad national consensus has emerged that confronting the newly emerging fundamentalist threats should be given national priority.

7.6   Transiting to a Fully Fledged Democracy?

For all its failings, the Lebanese system has so far proved resilient in resisting substantial change through its ability to diffuse internal stress via the 'safety valves' of civic and religious freedom, scheduled parliamentary and presidential elections (no matter their shortcomings and blemishes)[35] and migration. Additional factors include both an open and a private-sector-oriented national economy which, the civil war period apart, has generally witnessed robust growth, as well as regional and international intervention in support of the system when it appeared to veer towards collapse under the weight of domestic conflict.

But if, in the past, various domestic and external factors converged to maintain Lebanon's sectarian consociationalism, albeit adjusted by the Taif Accord, are the present conditions, both domestically and regionally (taking account of the Arab uprisings and the recent emergence of armed fundamentalist groups in neighbouring Syria) now more favourable to a move towards a more substantive democracy? We submit that this question cannot be readily answered. On one hand, the factors favouring the preservation of the existing sectarian system appear robust. On the other, there are elements pushing in the direction of a more substantive democracy. In what follows, we attempt to discern the likely long-term outcome of these opposing trends.

At the regional level, the influences that have affected Lebanon's governance negatively, mainly intra-regional conflicts and regional oil wealth, remain in place with the recently emerging threat of fundamentalist groups acting as an overhang. On the other hand, should the demand for democratic change in the region initiated by the uprisings be sustained despite the recent growing influence of fundamentalist groups, it would potentially open the way for a more democratic region

---

[35] As noted above, not for the first time, when the term of office of the president ended on 24 May 2014, the parliament failed to elect a successor. As of mid-2016, a new president was yet to be elected. Earlier, on 31 May 2013, the parliament had taken the extraordinary step of extending its mandate for seventeen months, ostensibly on account of a deadlock over a new electoral law. And on 5 November 2014, under the pretext that the position of the presidency was vacant, it enacted another extension, thus keeping its mandate for an additional two years and seven months, until 20 June 2017.

as a whole. In turn, this development could be expected to have a positive effect on the Lebanese polity, the more so as the regional democratic space expands. The unsettled Arab–Israeli conflict, with all its negative ramifications, need not prove an insurmountable hindrance to political reform, to the extent that Lebanon can manage to overcome its sectarian divide by moving to a system that is basically secular.

This brings us to the internal and perhaps more important prospects for political change. We would like to postulate that for all the domestic political and/or politico-sectarian conflicts that have afflicted Lebanon since independence and continue to plague it, the factors pushing for political advancement are growing, admittedly, so far, at a relatively slow pace, despite what appear to be growing sectarian divisions.

We offer two major reasons for this postulate:

The first is the growing frustration with mounting socio-economic burdens in the post-civil war period that are ascribed to low-level political governance which is, in turn, linked to the sectarian system with its imbued politico-sectarian patronage. It is true that emigration has tempered the rise in the level of domestic unemployment, while substantial emigrant remittances have tended to support the national economy. Nevertheless, they could not counter the negative developmental impact of a highly flawed sectarian-oriented governance: non-inclusive development, increasing corruption, worsening income distribution and an increasingly skewed concentration of wealth, alongside other social inequities the adverse developmental impact of which has been reinforced by poor rural and urban planning. To all this should be added an increasingly failing public administration and below par judicial performance. Whatever the rate of economic growth and irrespective of rising per capita income levels in the post-civil war period, the aforementioned socio-economic developmental outcomes have been adding to the strains on the system.[36]

The second is the increasingly unacceptable discriminatory features of a political system which legislates unequal political and civil rights for the

[36] The anti-government civil protests that broke out in Beirut in September and October 2015 are telling. They were led by a few civil groups that managed to cast aside the sectarian fold and organise a united popular outcry against governmental corruption and inefficiency. The trigger was the accumulating bags of garbage on the streets of Beirut and elsewhere due to the inability of those in power to agree on the terms of contract renewal for the company responsible for garbage collection, run by people close to some of Lebanon's leading politicians.

The Corruption Perception Index (CPI) for 2014 ranked Lebanon 136 out of 174 countries, i.e. very close to the bottom 20 per cent of the ranked countries. The data show that corruption has generally been increasing since 1996, when Lebanon was ranked close to the upper 40 per cent of the ranked countries. Data for earlier years, as the CPI authors note, are not strictly comparable with the subsequent series.

citizens of the Lebanese state: as noted, parliamentary representation and cabinet appointments are based on sectarian quotas; the three highest political offices are earmarked for the three major religious groups, while matters relating to personal status (e.g. marriage, divorce, inheritance) are placed under the sole jurisdiction of the religious authorities of the community concerned. True, the system has so far managed to survive for the various economic and political reasons mentioned earlier. But because of its record of poor governance and of poor delivery of public goods, it has been increasingly viewed as obsolete, in need of fundamental reform that would take it away from confessionalism. In this context, an opinion poll on social and personal identity in Lebanon that Information International carried out in 2006 indicated that the majority of the participants identified themselves with family, followed by Lebanese identity, and only third by a religious identity.

Some writers point to the influence of the sectarian-linked educational institutions that abound in Lebanon, significantly more so at the pre-rather than at the university level, as one of the factors standing in the way of substantive democratic political reform (e.g. Bashshur 2003). While this may be true, we believe that on its own, this phenomenon is not likely to be an indefinite obstruction to a move towards a non-confessional or secular political system. Generally, Lebanon's relatively liberal multi-religious society has tended to promote not only mutual religious tolerance, but a continued recognition that religious freedom is a key element for the survival of the country's liberal traditions. To the extent that freedom is a shared value, we believe that bridging the gap between religion and a modern secular system is an achievable national task, despite the rise in recent years of fundamentalist groups who oppose this view. Other developing countries, whether with Muslim or Christian religious dominance, have attempted this reconciliation with a degree of success, and their experience should be instructive. Indeed, an official attempt was made in Lebanon in 1998 in this direction, though it did not come to fruition (see later).

Taken together, these factors, we believe, will increasingly impose a national preference for the choice of substantive political-administrative reform in the direction of secularism. We hasten to add that if choosing the secular road eliminates sectarian discrimination, it does not, on its own, address the failings of the Lebanese system noted earlier. Examples of non-democratic and corrupt secular countries abound. Rather, we submit, the move to secularism should be accompanied by other reforms that promote political accountability and governance, and generally raise the level of institutional performance. Otherwise, the country's political weaknesses will remain in place; its ability to address various socio-economic failings will continue to suffer from the negative influences of politico-business vested interests.

Given Lebanon's sectarian legacies, the transition to a fully fledged democracy may have to be undertaken in phases but with the ultimate aim of reaching a fully secular system that remains reconciled to the religious values of Lebanese society. Elsewhere (Makdisi et al. 2011), it has been argued that Lebanon's democratic reform should be undertaken with three interconnected objectives in mind: (1) a more embracing democracy that would include a uniform civil code for the status of the individual (e.g. concerning civil marriage, divorce, inheritance, etc.), that initially might possibly be optional; (2) the promotion of a more equitable society at the economic and social levels; and (3) ensuring, in the transition phase, a more effective and equitable political participation via a new electoral law that would lead to a fairer representation of the country's various political components, groups or parties, but with a long-term view to establishing the desired secular system (for further details, see preceding reference).

If implemented, whatever the sequence or phases of implementation, these legislative reforms are expected to facilitate parallel reforms in Lebanese public administration and the judiciary. In turn, greater legitimacy of political institutions, with their enhanced accountability, will establish the means for rendering the public sector more efficient and accountable. This reform would also help to lead to the creation of a new social contract that would promote the principles of socioeconomic equity and alleviate concerns associated with the eventual removal of the confessional system at the parliamentary level.

Concluding remarks: a caveat

Given its historical legacies, there is no doubt that Lebanon's transition to a fully fledged democracy faces major political obstacles, not least of which are the entrenched sectarian feelings that have been building up, in particular since the outbreak of the civil war in 1975.

Nonetheless, we believe that, if it does materialise, the wave of regional democratisation that may follow in the wake of the uprisings will tend to reinforce underlying Lebanese domestic factors pushing in this direction. At the same time, we are cognizant of the possibility that the important political changes the region has witnessed since late 2010 will not, in the immediate future, necessarily have this desired effect. The concern here is that, in the foreseeable future, the political trajectory unleashed by the uprisings can lead to the emergence of new forms of autocracy. Or, alternatively, it can lead only to partial democracies tending to retain a significant confessional dimension in the political system, rather than to fully fledged democracies that guarantee full citizen equality in political as well as civil rights. Such developments, we submit, will negatively affect attempts in Lebanon to overcome its sectarian stranglehold.

Whether justified or not, Lebanon's historic hesitancy to break out of the sectarian consociational model has been linked to fears, mainly on the part of Christian, politico-religious interest groups, but also of other civilian groups, that unless such a move is linked to adopting a secular democratic system, it would lead instead to the dominance of a particular religious group over the affairs of society with all the implications in terms of shifting politico-economic power and privilege in favour of the said group. Whatever the case, the gradual move to a secular, albeit democratic system, as proposed earlier, is precisely intended to assuage such fears, build confidence and promote the culture of a truly all-embracing democratic society with equal rights for all citizens across the board. While the time frame for such a transformation cannot be predicted, and indeed may not even materialise in the near future, as we see it, to opt or not for this national choice is tantamount to a choice between a more advanced and forward-looking Lebanon and a politically stagnant Lebanon.

8 Sudan: Transition to Democracy after 2011, a Dismembered State Navigating Uncertainties

Atta Elbattahani

> A country does not have to be deemed fit for democracy; rather, it has to become fit through democracy.   (A. K. Sen)

8.1 Introduction

8.1.1 Sudan's Current Predicament

The origins of Sudan's recent history lie in the early nineteenth century, and its current problems stem from the unsettled history of its formation both as a nation and as a state (Sorbo and Ahemd 2013).[1] Covering more than 1 million square miles (before the secession of its southern region) and containing diverse ethnic, tribal, religious and cultural groupings, in the late nineteenth century and for much of the twentieth century, the country was under colonial rule, first Turko-Egyptian (1882–85) and then British (1898–1956), the latter adopting various policies to control the population: South Sudan was ruled separately until the 1940s, Darfur was annexed in 1916,[2] and the rest of the country was administered by indirect rule. When the country obtained political independence in the early 1950s, the nationalists who took over the government were confronted with the colossal task of nurturing a common sense of national identity in various ethnic-national groups while at the same time opening up state institutions to a system of equal representation and accountability. In reality, however, the performance of the nationalist elites has never measured up to these historic tasks.

Benefiting from the colonial economy, the Northern (Arab-Muslim) elites had gained privileged access to strategic resources ahead of other ethnic-national and regional groupings. Though not united and often engaged in in-fighting, these elites managed – more or less – to keep

---

[1] An extensive and rich literature exits; see relevant references in the bibliography.
[2] No wonder, then, that both regions have been in conflict with the central government, with one seceding in 2011 and the other, Darfur, still negotiating an end to violence in the region.

politics as a domain exclusive to themselves and thereby have maintained their privileged access[3] to state power for most of the post-independence period (Karsani and Kameer 1986; Umbadda 1990). In response to exclusion by the Northern 'oligarchic monopoly' (Khalid 1990), marginalised regions, first the South and then others, took up arms in rebellion as early as the mid-1950s.

However, despite the rebel movements operating in South Sudan, and the unrest in other parts of the country, the country witnessed short-lived, multi-party democracies (1954–58, 1964–69, 1985–89) that were a result of transitions from military rule. But neither the transitions nor the regimes that followed (multi-party, civilian or one-party military) managed to resolve the country's on-going challenges: (i) to forge a unified national identity; (ii) to establish democratic, inclusive governance by breaking the Northern elite's hold on power; (iii) to transform the economy and deliver basic social services and the benefits of development. Although the periods of transition opened up a political space for competing political actors, a series of military regimes which dominated Sudan to varying degrees did little to build effective state institutions, let alone ensure any form of democratic government. With the end of each cycle, the country was left mired in identity conflicts and with diminished 'institutional democratic assets', that is, the rule of law, citizens' rights, process of government formation and so forth, as demonstrated by the Worldwide Governance Indicators.

Sudan has experienced periods of transition in the past: 1953–56; 1964–65; 1985–86; 2005–11 (Woodward, 1987 and 2008 and El-Battahani, 2003)[4] and this chapter has special interest in the 2005–11 failed transition. It was, to a large extent, this failure that led to the dismemberment of the state and the secession of South Sudan. Subsequent events and developments are analysed using a broad theoretical framework that attempts to distinguish between two patterns of transition (post-autocracy and post-conflict), and to identify the distinct dynamics of each transition process and how each shapes and is shaped by the variables identified by the Elbadawi-Makdisi model (2011, now referred to as E/M); and, more important, which transition route agents of change might opt for in the future and the implications of this for both state dismemberment and democratic reform.

---

[3] Drawing on Hazem Beblawi and Giacomo Luciani (1987) and Bob Pease (2010), I refer to this unearned, privileged entitlement arising from access to state power as a form of soft rent.

[4] These references relate to past transitions; I stress reference is made to past transitions because the legacy of failed transitions is not only in the mind of the political elites negotiating possible scenarios for political change, but this legacy has shaped the post-secession context, as will be dealt with later in this chapter.

In the aftermath of the Arab uprisings which coincided with the secession of South Sudan and mounting internal pressures for change, the ruling Islamic regime in Khartoum faced a stark challenge: to hold together what remained of the country and avoid further dismemberment of the state, they would have to make concessions to accommodate the Northern opposition and rebel groups in inclusive governance institutions; but this option would threaten the Islamists' interests in what is called *tamkin* (the monopoly of the instruments of power) and the control of state power.[5] This chapter attempts to explore the extent to which the expected transition would deal with the intricate question of national identity and democratic governance, that is, would these transitional arrangements keep the country united, avoid further state dismemberment and at the same time establish accountable, democratic government?

8.1.2   *Why has the Sudanese Transition been Delayed?*

The secession of South Sudan in 2011 coincided with the events that toppled Bin Ali in Tunisia, Mubarak in Egypt, Ali Salih in Yemen and Qaddafi in Libya, and set in motion a process of change in North Africa and the Middle East. In view of Sudan's previous successful uprisings against military regimes in 1964 and 1985 (Khalid 1990; Taisier 1989), it is only natural to ask not *if* Sudan would be affected by these recent Arab uprisings, but *when* and *how*?

This chapter poses several central questions: Why has any significant movement for change, akin to those which have appeared in neighbouring Arab countries (Tunisia, Egypt, Libya and Yemen), failed to materialise so far? How long can al-Bashir's autocracy hold out despite the pressing political and economic conditions? What explains the durability of the Sudanese autocracy? What are the interlocking factors that have apparently delayed a 'Sudanese Spring'? Do the agents of change have a policy based on democratising existing state institutions or on building a new regime in order to accommodate ethno-regional centrifugal forces and stave-off further state dismemberment?

8.1.3   *Prospects for Transition*

A marked feature of Sudan's recurrent failed democratic governance is not only the fact that it has been dominated by the autocratic Northern elites (the Northern power bloc, in the words of Taisier 1989), but that its modus operandi has been to rule through a shaky coalition of Northern

---

[5] Islamists both inside and outside Sudan regard the Khartoum regime as a bastion for radical Islamic movements in North Africa and the Middle East.

factions and actors in a fragile alliance with regional elites. These ruling coalitions have been shaped by an unstable equilibrium of compromises between the contending politicians, families and factions of the Northern ruling elites that are constantly in competition with each other for soft and hard rent resources (Awad 1967; Beblawi and Luciani 1987; Khalid 1990; Umbadda 1990). The military regimes that took over from the democratic regimes had to forge coalitions with these groups in order to sustain their rule. Thus, in order to protect their 'inherited' rent privileges, the Northern ruling elites presided over regimes that alternated between weak, multi-party governments and military, authoritarian rule, in what has frequently been described as a vicious cycle. To support their 'inherited' interests, the rent-seeking Northern elites opposed both building a multicultural, multi-ethnic nation and supporting democratic state institutions.

The radical Islamic elites of Inqaz[6] sought to break this cycle by restructuring the rent-based economy (and emerging as a hegemonic faction of the Northern ruling class) when, in alliance with army officers, they took power in June 1989. Through their strategy of *tamkin*, the Islamists emerged in complete effective control of all rent resources (both soft rents, i.e. employment and contracts, and hard rent appropriation of oil revenues). However, presiding over extractive economic institutions, the ruling Islamists of Sudan have failed to rehabilitate and expand the productive sectors of the economy.

Witnessing almost constant internal wars and anti-Western posturing on the international stage, the secession of South Sudan then left the country still under the leadership of radical Islamists. Thus it remained a victim of its own old autocratic politics and consequently faced the concomitant challenges of dwindling resource rents and deepening conflicts both within the ruling elites and between the Northern elites and the rebels in the marginalised regions, all of which threatens the state with further dismemberment and adds further challenges to the process of democratic change.

The Islamists' relatively long reign in Sudan has been sustained by (i) effective disposal of rents to impede democratic transitions; (ii) a co-opted and/or disorganised opposition; (iii) the use of repression; and (iv) the use of regional (Qatar, Turkey and Iran) and international links (China and Russia) to counter the effects of boycotts by Western countries. However, in the aftermath of the Arab uprisings, overreliance on state-patronage, repressive measures and skilful navigation through

---

[6] The Arabic word *inqaz* means salvation (i.e. to save or rescue); in the political context in which radical Islamic army officers use it, it means to rescue the country from immanent total collapse.

a disordered geopolitical environment are no longer sufficient to keep the regime afloat. Sudan's autocracy is facing major challenges stemming from the adverse effects of a failing economy and the loss of rents: these include long-established, built-in fissures in the body politic and deep-seated rivalries in the ruling class (both inside and outside government), the people's growing discontent and the military threat of rebel groups.

Indeed, there are signs that, with further splits in the ruling political class and an increasingly substantial sense of popular discontent with economic conditions, the socio-political support-base of radical Islam is shrinking. The government's reaction to the urban unhappiness over austerity measures that surfaced in September 2013 employed unprecedented and lethal repressive measures, which led to divisions within the ruling party and later to a major government reshuffle.

In what follows, Section 8.2 discusses the transition debate and the framework of analysis; Section 8.3 deals with the post-secession context (2011–15); Section 8.4 discusses possible transitions routes; Section 8.5 highlights special factors complicating a Sudanese transition; Section 8.6 concludes.

8.2   The Transition Debate and the Framework of Analysis

An extensive body of literature exists on transition,[7] and for our purposes at least two major perspectives dominate the current debates on the dynamics shaping a transition to democracy. There are cases of authoritarian, autocratic rule where there is no conflict on issues of national identity or of ethnic or regional prejudices. These are autocracies that have not experienced civil conflict and the transition regime is more concerned with democracy, that is, the opening up of state institutions to broad, unfettered participation and the public accountability of government. On the other hand, there are autocratic countries with deep-rooted conflicts around issues of national identity, ethnic prejudice and cultural or religious discrimination. In these countries, which have experienced civil conflict, the transition regime that follows the breakdown of autocracy is likely to place a greater emphasis on a new socio-political order (resolving identity questions), building institutions that support law and order and the security of property rights, rather than any concerns with democracy and a desire to rush into holding elections. However, the two processes are not mutually exclusive, since security of property rights and the rule of law are also elements in democracy and a part of

---

[7] For example, see Huntington (1991, pp. 12–14); Linz (1990, p. 33); Thomas (2002, pp. 6–7); and Levitsky (2002, pp. 51–65).

accountable government. The following discussion explores briefly these two perspectives of transition.

8.2.1   The Transition to Democracy Post-autocracy and Free of Civil Conflict

A number of countries experienced autocracy in their pasts and were able some time ago to resolve questions of national identity, or issues pertaining to national identity were not of major significance in their resistance to their autocratic rulers. Political actors and agents of change in these countries formed broad-based movements or parties not founded on any ethnic, regional or religious basis. For example, in post-authoritarian transitions as in Poland, Brazil, South Korea and, most recently, Tunisia and Egypt, the agents of change fought for a more open political process and basic political rights. As demonstrated in these countries, the process of democratisation following a breakdown of authoritarian rule typically involves an authoritarian government facing a more or less democratic opposition supported by a burgeoning civil society. According to Wantchekon (2004), democracy comes into existence in such an environment when the balance of power within the government shifts in favour of the more moderate elements, which successfully negotiate a political compromise with the democratic opposition (civil disobedience and peaceful consensual elite pact).

In a post-autocracy transition to democracy, the underlying and stabilising sense of national identity in the population is never disputed, and a bond unites the governing and governed, but the demand remains for democracy and holding the ruler accountable to the ruled.

8.2.2   Transition to Democracy in the Aftermath of Civil Conflict

European colonial rule imposed haphazard territorial boundaries on many African states, Sudan included, whereby different ethnic, cultural and religious groups were lumped together as subjects of the colonial regime. During colonial times, in most cases, certain regions and ethnic-national groups benefitted from the concentration of infrastructural and economic projects and they eventually emerged far ahead of the other ethnic and national groups. With calls for independence from European colonialism, national groups that were thus well positioned often took the lead in mobilising the new nation-states for independence, and quite often they surfaced as the new 'nationalist' rulers. However, once independence was achieved, conflicts erupted between regions and ethnic-national groups about who should control the new state. It is not unusual that in ethno-national conflicts, nationalist-factional claims and counterclaims dominate the political discourse of competing ethnic 'national' groups.

The discourse of nationalism in its modern historical expression resides in the fact that it has paradoxically served several conflicting purposes (Pamir 1997). It has acted as the principal ideology which enabled emerging nations to seek independence from colonial authority; later, it also provided the newly created nation-states and their dominant and privileged ethnic-national groups with the ideological justification for holding or for claiming the responsibility of keeping 'the nation' together,[8] much to the dissatisfaction of excluded and marginalised groups who felt they were treated as second- or third-class citizens. In due time, the excluded and marginalised emerged to challenge post-colonial state authority, questioning its claim to legitimacy and calling for 'self-rule' or 'self-determination', a call usually met with condemnation and characterised as secessionist or separatist by the ruling ethnic-nationalities. Leaders of marginalised ethnic or regional groups claiming exclusion, real or perceived, mobilised them in order to demand equal treatment as full citizens or to call for self-determination and their own 'nation-state'.

Hence, ironically, nationalism (and regionalism), in this sense, has contributed to the formation and survival of nation-states following independence, as well as to the dismemberment of nation-states following the emergence of regional-nationalist movements (Pamir 1997; Prazauskas 1998). What is important to stress here is that for ethno-national rebel groups, the ultimate objective of a smooth post-conflict transition is either secession, in order to form their own states, or the restructuring of the 'national' state in order to accommodate marginalised ethnic-national and regional groups as equal citizens. Democracy (as indexed and gauged by the world indicators of Freedom House, the Polity Index and the World Bank) takes a back seat, that is, rebel leaders may be content to share power with the established ruling elites rather than insist on sweeping democratic reforms.[9] Post-civil war, democratisation is primarily motivated by the need for a new political order. But the need to ensure that warring and competing political parties will abandon violence and agree to resolve deep-rooted identity conflicts may dominate over the need for popular representation or even the public accountability of the

---

[8] In Sudan, it was predominantly the Northern elites who benefited from colonial economic projects, took over the state and aligned state resources to the service of their own ethnic-national, regional constituency (Ali and El-Battahani 2011; Khalid 1990).
[9] Despite apparent policy differences between the National Congress Party (NCP) and the Sudan People Liberation Army (SPLM) during the 2005–11 transition, their shared underlined interests as rent-seekers undermined prospects for democratisation during that period.

government. Thus, a post-civil war democracy is Schumpeterian at best; it is essentially means for ensuring elite cooperation in the process of creating a political order (Wantchekon 2004). It is normally different from the process of democratisation following the overthrow of an autocracy in which political institutions exist, albeit on exclusive, undemocratic bases.[10]

To recapitulate, in post-conflict societies, the need is first to create the requisite institutions that guarantee stability and one can worry later about democracy. However, following Sen (1992), the building of the requisite governance institutions cannot be sustained without a democracy. Accordingly, in assessing the prospects for a successful transition in countries where civil conflicts have followed uprisings (e.g. Syria, Yemen and Libya), we should not rule out democratic build-up as part of the transition process that will follow the settlement of these conflicts, even in the nearer term. The same may apply to other countries that are candidates for change, such as Algeria and Sudan. The challenge they will face is how to work out a synthesis between a 'united' nation-state and democratic governance, that is to say, how the forces leading the transition process will implement a viable plan that simultaneously addresses security concerns and the protection of citizens' basic civil and political rights. Despite its shortcomings, consociational democracy may provide a workable model, but only given that certain conditions are set with a view to curbing excessive corruption and the neglect of the public interest, which elements, sadly, the converse has demonstrated in the cases of Lebanon and Iraq.

8.2.3   The Imperative of Democracy during Transitions: Towards a Synthesis

This chapter attempts a synthesis in order to underscore the need for democracy, not only in a transition from authoritarian rule, but also in countries experiencing civil war (where identity conflict features prominently). Democracy is an essential ingredient in both forms of transition. Therefore, we concur with Sen's formulation in addressing both forms of transition simultaneously; in other words, institution building by nation-states and a post-conflict and citizen-centred democracy can be strengthened in a post-autocracy situation; not only can both be strengthened simultaneously, but a citizen-centred democracy is essential for nation-

---

[10] For a discussion on the relation between effective political order and the liberal-democratic state, see Huntington (1968); Tilly (1990). Huntington (1968) considers any form of liberal democracy simply unattainable in the absence of political order, and Tilly (1990) suggests that warlords can create a state, but does not suggest it would necessarily be a democratic state.

state building itself. To use Amartya Sen's dictum, 'a country does not have to be deemed fit for democracy; rather, it has to become fit through democracy' (Sen 1992, p. 2).

In a number of cases, the two transition processes are not and should not be seen as mutually exclusive; in fact, the two are intermeshed in a complex, multi-varied, multi-level process, the dynamics of which keep shifting, in terms of emphasis but not in terms of virtual exclusion, from one dimension to another, that is, if law and order is given top priority, this should not undermine citizens' basic rights. So, in this proposed synthesis, a transition in combined post-conflict–post-autocracy where the assets of political order (national unity, property rights, rule of law, etc.) are weak, cannot be taken to rule out the possibility of democratisation (e.g. contested public space, free and fair elections, etc.); on the other hand, democratisation should not be regarded as a threat to 'the nation holding together'.

Rephrasing Sen's formulation about the imperative of democracy,[11] and using the E/M model, a full grasp of the dynamics of the Sudanese case requires the highlighting of a number of provisos.

First, a viable transition to democracy requires, inter alia, a degree of 'national unity' between the sections making up the population, with no one group claiming or demanding a privileged status over other groups. Ethnic prejudice and religious fanaticism do not support the formation of a broad-based coalition of forces transcending tribal, ethnic and religious or sectarian bonds. Hence a post-civil war transition should lead to the levelling of the playing field for all ethnic, regional and cultural groups. Territorial disintegration and the dismemberment of states take place when members of particular groups are not treated as equal to those who have presumed to hold power.

Second, there is a need for an agreement to abide by a 'democratic' framework that organises the competition between elites, and to instil in the political classes and elites representing various and competing groupings the understanding that politics is not a zero-sum game. The presence of disunited but peacefully competing elites representing various interests is a sine qua non for a stable democracy (Therborn 1983, p. 268). The challenge here concerns whether the dynamics of an unfolding transition would lead to the instituting and honouring of the 'rules of the game', which would in turn ensure peaceful political competition between the elites making up the political class of the country. Giovanni and Memoli (2012) have shown that the more democracy takes root in a country's political system, the more state institutions are consolidated.

---

[11] Also see Arthur Macewan (2001).

Third, transition to democracy entails, among other things, certain economic conditions. A number of theorists have argued that rentier economies are antithetical to democracy, maintaining that moving decisively from a predominantly rentier to a productive economy is an essential condition for facilitating a transition to democracy. Writing on the relationship between democratisation and the resource curse, Paltseva maintains that: 'If an autocrat's resource rents are low, the country develops under maintained autocracy and becomes democratic only after a period of growth. If rents are medium-sized, the country becomes less autocratic early on and grows into a democracy. Finally, if rents are high, the country stagnates under autocratic rule, thereby suffering from a resource curse' (in Elbadawi 2015).

Giving war-affected areas special attention, enhancing employment opportunities for disenchanted youth and taking measures to bridge the gap between rich and poor will go some way to resuscitate the urban middle class and create a constituency for democracy. For genuine democratic transformation to take root, Therborn stresses the need for 'feverish development of the productive forces [and] elasticity and expansive capacity' of the economy in order to provide necessary services and employment for the exploited majority (Therborn 1983, p. 269).

Now that this chapter has defined the framework of analysis and set out the conditions necessary for a transition to democracy in a country such as Sudan, this section considers the extent to which these conditions exist in post-secession Sudan.

8.3   The Post-secession Context

In the foregoing section on the transition debate and the framework of analysis, we drew on the E/M model and on Sen's work in addition to what is referred to as imperatives for ensuring an effective transition to democracy: the absence of endemic ethnic and regional fractionalisation; disunited but peacefully competing elites representing various interests; and a moving away from rentier economic policies to a productive economy. This section of the context post-secession Sudan will be viewed through the lens of these imperatives; the following section will examine the extent to which competing agents of change will heed them.

8.3.1   *Sudan Remains a Highly Diverse Society*

The current post-secession context in Sudan bears on factors that the E/M model identified as shaping the transition process: namely, (i) the formation of a viable multi-ethnic, regional, broad-based coalition of forces in order to indicate a clear shift from divisive politics to a consensus on what constitutes a national identity; (ii) a democratic framework organising competition between the elites; and (iii) a decisive move from a predominantly rentier to a productive economy.

Since independence in the 1950s, Sudan has been and remains a diverse, multi-ethnic, multicultural, multi-religious society and country. According to the much referred to census of 1955/56, the main ethnic groups are Arabs (39 per cent), Southerners (30 per cent), West Darfur (9 per cent), Beja (6 per cent), West Africans (6 per cent), Nuba (6 per cent), Nubia (3 per cent) and Funj (1.7 per cent) (Government of Sudan, 1955/56 Census). Other descriptions of the ethnic composition of Sudan classify these groups in terms of nineteen main nationalities (*majmu'a gawmiyya*) and 597 ethnic groups (*majmu'a irgiyya*) (Beshir and Salih 1984; Beshir 1988). One hundred and fifteen dialects are reported, of which twenty-six are actively spoken languages, each used by more than 100,000 people (Ahmed 1988). About 52 per cent of the population speaks Arabic while 48 per cent speaks other languages. Both Islam and Christianity claim the support of significant sections of the population, Islam in the North and Christianity in the South, with local (indigenous) religions in some regions. Religious heterogeneity is further sustained by the prevalence of sectarian cleavages within Islam. Population censuses taken subsequently, in 1973, 1983 and 2008, did not make any reference to ethnic identification.

When the Islamists took power in June 1989, their main declared objective was the establishment of an 'Islamic state', the threat to which was perceived to lie in the (ethnic, religious) diversity of the country. A jihad was launched with the objective of defeating the rebel movement led by the SPLM and Islamising the entire country. In 2005, the NCP and the SPLM signed a Comprehensive Peace Agreement (CPA), which provided for a transition period from 2005 to 2011 during which (i) either the North and South would sort out the root causes of conflict and see if they could coexist and remain at the end of the transition in a united Sudan, or if South Sudan would exercise self-determination (via a referendum) to decide its own fate; (ii) both the NCP and the SPLM would take measures to ensure democratic reforms. The Interim National Constitution (INC) of 2005, a quasi-secular, liberal document, was seen by and large as one of the most democratic constitutions in Sudan, which, for the first time, included a bill of rights.

The two ruling parties, the NCP and the SPLM, spent most of the transition period from 2005–11 on squabbles and infighting over the distribution of oil revenue (Sid-Ahmed 2013; Young 2012), paying little attention to nurturing an 'attractive unity'. With the end of the transition period in 2011, it was evident that the South would opt for independence, and the ruling Islamists in the North seemed relieved that *mishkilat al-janoub* – 'the Southern Problem' – would no longer exist and they could now govern a homogenous state.[12]

The Islamists thought that, with South Sudan gone, it would be easy to rule Sudan by means of Sharia law: that is to say, to have an Islamic state with Sharia as the supreme law of the land. The president asserted this in a major policy speech in September 2011 which emphasised the point that ethnic-religious-cultural diversity should no longer be regarded as an excuse or stumbling block for not fully implementing Sharia law in all regions of Sudan.[13]

Post-secession Sudan is still highly diverse; ethnic and religious-sectarian diversities seem to have staying power despite persistent efforts to 'Islamise' society. The Islamist political project, called *al-mashru'a al-hadari* (the Civilising Project), was meant to do away with regional, cultural and ethnic identities. Ironically, Islamism in Sudan has had the effect of strengthening these identities (El-Affendi 2015). These developments demonstrate that, even after the secession of the South, not only is diversity still a structural feature of Sudanese society, but the dynamics of conflict are changing, with the rebels fighting Khartoum calling for greater autonomy and for self-rule and self-determination in what is called the 'New South' (see Abdelghaffar Ahmed 2013), threatening further dismemberment of the state.

8.3.2   Sudan's New-Born Autocracy in 2011

From the time the radical Islamists took power in a coup d'état until the signing of a peace agreement with Southern rebels in 2005, Sudan was effectively a one-party state ruled by the NCP. Yet, in 2005, the CPA was hailed as a major political achievement due to its success in ending the civil war and establishing peace between the two parts of the country and a renewed opportunity for the elites to rectify the failures of past transitions and undertake democratic reform. In theory, if properly interpreted and implemented, the INC could have catered for a democratic transition in the old Sudan. In practice, this has not been the case. The period since the signing of the CPA, including its incorporation into the INC and up to 9 July 2011, did not witness any such transformation (thus reinforcing the institutional legacy of failed transition). The end of the transition period

---

[12] For a succinct analysis, see Young (2012).
[13] There he implied that the days of *dagmasa* (fudging issues over the application of Sharia) are over.

of 2005–11 saw the strengthening of the executive and security state organs at the expense of the legislative and judiciary ones.[14]

The consolidation of the 'new-born autocracy' of the NCP during 2011–15 continued unabated in a series of legislative projects and presidential decrees. Clauses referring to South Sudan were dropped from the INC in 2012, and constitutional amendments were passed in January 2015. Not only was the constitution amended to secure a new term for the president, but enormous powers were placed in his hands, such as the appointing of *walis* (governors of states) and complete authority over the disposal of land resources and investment policies (*al-Sudani* newspaper 2015).[15] More important, constitutional amendments also upgraded the Sudan Revolutionary Front (SRF), making it part of the National Intelligence and Security Service (NISS), and also empowered the latter, giving its members sweeping powers and the ability to act with impunity.

The consolidation of autocracy set in motion a series of setbacks as far as democratic reform was concerned. First, dashing hopes for reform and then instituting constitutional amendments, inter alia, led to a series of splits among the ruling Islamists. In the post-secession years, calls for reform came from within the ruling Islamic Movement when about 'one thousand brothers' drafted a memo[16] that openly called for reform, which was followed by an alleged attempted coup by middle-ranking army officers in 2012. A tense struggle ensued between three major factions at the top of the regime, ending with the triumph of the president, who tightened his grip on power and removed his civilian rivals (Ahmed 2013).

When it became plain to moderate Islamists in the government that the leadership was not genuine in its declared intention to lead the reform process, a number of prominent leading Islamists left the ruling party and formed their own political parties.[17] These were the visible signs of a narrowing of the autocracy's support base, even among the Islamists.

Second, al-Bashir's leadership managed to maintain a convenient (though at times tenuous) relationship with the main opposition parties,

---

[14] Laws empowering the security forces were passed at the end of the transition period with the SPLM complicit in returning the NCP's endorsement of the Referendum Act to facilitate secession of South Sudan afterwards. Failure to implement the CPA's democratic components, however, did not draw the attention of any of the parties charged with guaranteeing the agreement and monitoring its implementation.

[15] For coverage of the constitutional amendments, see the archive of the *al-Sudani* newspaper, January–February 2015.

[16] Muzakirat al-Alif Akh (the memo of 1,000 brothers).

[17] Two well-known leading Islamists broke away from the NCP, Ghazi Salah ed-Din established the Reform Now Party and El-Tayeb Mustafa formed the Just Peace Party.

the Umma National Party and the Democratic Unionist Party, thus undermining and effectively removing any potential threats from the opposition.[18]

Third, sustaining violent attacks, scorched earth tactics against armed rebels and maintaining repressive forms of security in urban centres meant diverting resources to the military and security forces, putting a severe strain on the fiscal resources of the government, as will be shown later in this chapter.

After the secession of South Sudan and the loss of much of the oil revenue, the Khartoum government sought to balance the books. When government measures to 'ration' rent handouts to its core groups failed, no option was left to it except removing fuel subsidies. This was an unpopular measure that led to major youth-led urban unrest posing a serious challenge to Islamist rule. To deter political parties from joining the protests, the government responded with unprecedentedly ruthless brutality by employing paramilitary troops. This heavy-handedness by what was widely perceived as a corrupt government caused splits within the ranks of the Islamists and allegations of coup attempts by Islamist army officers (viz., the Wad Ibrahim case). Aware of its limited control over the army and the need to prevent armed rebel groups (which had now come together under the Sudan Revolutionary Front (SRF) in 2012) from building up their strength, the government upgraded its tribal militia, known as the Janjawid, to border guards and then to the Quwwat al-Da'm al-Sariyyi (QUDS; Rapid Support Force). Reports claimed that the SRF was used to ruthlessly crush the youth groups who came out in protest against austerity measures in September 2013, which was seen as public humiliation for the regular army and the police force. The Annual Congress of the Islamic Movement that followed in November 2013 paved the way for limited change at the top of the ruling party, and calls for a national dialogue came in President al-Bashir's major policy speech in January 2014, as will be explained later in this chapter.

Running short of oil revenues after 2011, the autocracy found that its total dependence on the distribution of rents to subsets of the regime's constituency fuelled infighting, with some factions distancing themselves by raising the banner of reform. These moves, however, were met with dissent and resentment among the leading Islamists of the NCP. Indeed, there were signs that Islamist businessmen were beginning to see that the Inqaz autocracy could be a liability vis-a-vis their long-term interests and

---

[18] The symbolism of the representation of sons of the two religious sectarian families in the presidency reveals the steadfastness of their opposition to the Islamist regime.

therefore they would not oppose a 'political' settlement with the Northern opposition and a 'degree of accommodation' with armed rebel groups. The main hurdle to such a settlement remained the head of the autocracy who would fight for his political survival.

Adding to the already existing ethnic-regional tensions, the NCP's inner circle is confined to a narrow minority oligarchy standing at the apex of the political machine, the ethnic-tribal and social base of which is increasingly being eroded.

8.3.3   Sudan's Staggering Economy: 2011–2015

This section builds around Elbadawi and Makdisi (2014), in terms of presenting the *tamkin* strategy as an instrument for generating and appropriating 'rents' which would thus be a means of building a powerbase for the Islamist autocracy, as in fact happened. As a result, the regime was substantially reinforced by oil rents after 1999 (i.e. soft rent combined with hard rent). Further economic measures taken in the post-secession period in 2011 have reinforced the rentier character of the economy and the clientelistic nature of the political regime. Rather than addressing the structural and root causes responsible for economic stagnation, al-Bashir's autocracy is more concerned with short-term interests, securing the financial flows necessary to maintain rent-based patronage networks. When South Sudan went its own way, 85 per cent of the country's oil production – which was concentrated in the southern region of the country – went with it, thus denying Khartoum the rent revenue it used to rely on. How then did Khartoum deal with this situation?

The government put into effect a three-year economic programme, in 2011–14, designed to make up for the loss of oil revenue and to continue with reforming the economy. The policy elements of this programme were based on:

– Intensifying oil exploration efforts and gold mining
– Inviting foreign investment in mining and agricultural sectors
– Privatisation of any remaining government companies and sales of public assets
– Curbing public expenditure and downsizing expanding government bureaucracy

These policy measures were not meant to structurally reform the economy (by investing in productive sectors such as agriculture, livestock and industry), but to ensure that finance was available to spend on an elaborate military-security apparatus, so as to ensure the support of clientelistic networks and to buy off splinter opposition parties and rebel groups.

This co-option strategy demonstrated that the rents at the disposal of the regime could be an effective instrument for impeding or even preventing a democratic transition.[19] This is mainly because the interests of these co-opted groups were narrowly based, focusing on their close-knit upper levels and their middle-ranking ringleaders to the exclusion of the broad mass of the support base they purportedly took power in order to serve. So, as long as the government had sufficient rent resources to satisfy its political allies, it could be sure of securing their support for its autocratic methods of governance. But this strategy had limits, given the dwindling of rent resources, the economic hardship and the increasing levels of unemployment among the educated youth, and the deteriorating living conditions for most low-income groups.[20]

This section demonstrates the corrosive effects of economic hardship and high unemployment levels on Sudan under the present regime, along with its corrupt manipulation of resources. Ironically, certain events in 2014 and 2015 connived to work in favour of the regime. As will be shown later, the first two years, that is 2012 to 2013, were particularly challenging, but things eased somehow in 2014 and 2015.

As mentioned earlier, a three-year economic programme was put into effect. As a result, Sudan intensified its oil exploration and gold mining, as well as the leasing out of land to foreign investors.[21] The curbing of public expenditure and downsizing of an expanded government bureaucracy also continued, as did the privatisation (sale) of government-owned assets, whilst the government further undertook to remove energy and food subsides.

Sudan intensified the extraction of crude oil from its existing fields, signed a number of oil concessions and provided incentives for the exploration of new fields, all in order to raise crude production in the North. The plan was to raise oil production from about 125,000 barrels per day in 2012 to about 325,000 in 2017.[22] In the meantime, the state would need to make immediate and significant fiscal and external account adjustments in response to lower fiscal revenues and export receipts from oil (IMF Sudan IPRS 2013). In this regard, incessant efforts have been made to substitute gold for oil (see table on Sudan: Structure of Export, 2008–16).

---

[19] However, since the regime could not hand out the profits from rents to everybody, in particular after the secession of South Sudan in 2011, it had to confine them to a subset of its constituency and suppress the others, including by promoting a military agenda for resolving political conflicts; again, the recourse to political repression and conflict – which was found quite important in impeding democracy – became a 'rational' strategy for such a regime.

[20] Tanneberg, Stefes and Merkel (2013, p. 115–29).

[21] Africa Development Report for 2014.

[22] In 2014, oil production was 150,000 barrels per day.

Table 8.1: *Sudan: Structure of Export, 2008–2016 (US$ Million)*

	2008	2009	2010	2011	2012 Est	2013 Proj	2014 Proj	2015 Proj	2016 Proj
Oil	12,628	8,087	12,700	11,063	5,174	5,378	6,091	6,760	6,802
Oil/total export %	12,052	7,067	10,991	8,679	2,012	2,576	3,256	3,817	3,780
Gold	112	403	1,018	1,442	2,158	2,104	2,150	2,238	2,290
Gold/total export %	0.9	5.0	8.0	13.0	41.7	39.1	35	33.1	33

Source: IMF Sudan country report, October 2013, p. 11.

According to the minister for minerals in 2014, "Sudan was the third largest African country in gold mining, and, furthermore, he projected that, by 2018, Sudan will have overtaken South Africa as the country with the largest share in the mining and export of gold".[23] In the last quarter of 2014, the government benefited from a fall in oil prices; and the 2015 budget showed no signs of a change in economic policies.

Policies designed to bring quick returns, such as privatisation and the sale of public assets, together with leasing land to foreign companies and states, took precedence over long-term economic measures (ADB 2014). Much of the economic and financial gains from these policies went to the nouveaux riche, the crony capitalists and the military-security. Though officially subscribing to a market economy, government policies have had little to do with levelling the playing field as regards participation in the market. Economic and business ventures owned by members of the political class receive favourable and preferential conditions when it comes to exemption from taxes, granting of loans and access to lucrative business contracts. The auditor general's annual reports abound with documented cases of so-called government companies, ministries and institutions that have refused to be audited (Auditor General 2014). In a conference for national investors organised by the Business Federation of Sudan, the Sudanese business class claimed that almost 70 per cent of transactions were managed by members of the political class.[24]

Observers have noted how these economic measures have benefited regime loyalists and have not served as a genuine attempt to reform the economy. An IMF report referred to what it called 'a shallow and undiversified financial sector', which it said 'creates macro-financial vulnerabilities that affect the macroeconomy, and its ability to sustain growth and reduce poverty' (IMF 2013). Not only did the private sector not receive adequate levels of credit, but the amount received was allocated to those with political connections (El-Mahdi 2012). Inflation stood at 43 per cent in June 2014 and reached 46 per cent by October of that year,[25] bringing further economic hardship to low-income groups and poor families.

On the other hand, the policies designed to curb public expenditure and downsize an expanding government bureaucracy were failing. Strongly entrenched power networks (military, security, crony capitalists and co-opted politicians) opposed any serious measures to undermine their interests. Instead of reducing government expenditure by 25–30

---

[23] *al-Sudani* newspaper, 7 July 2014.   [24] *al-Tageer Daily*, 8 July 2014.
[25] *al-Sudani* newspaper, 29 October 2014.

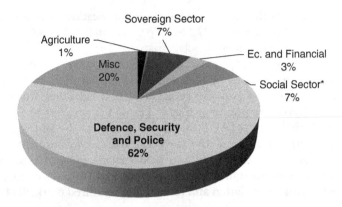

Figure 8.1: Government Expenditure 2012 Budget
Source: Ministry of Finance and National Economy, 2012.

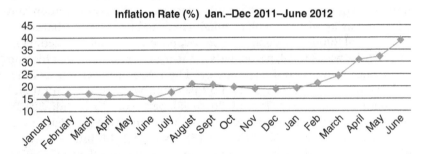

Figure 8.2: Inflation Rate December 2011 to June 2012
Source: Abda El-Mahdi, Impact of Post-secession Economic Crisis,
November 2012.
Inflation now stands at 43 per cent by June 2014.

per cent, actual expenditure for 2013 increased by 45 per cent, from
27.2 billion SDG in 2012 to 39.3 billion in 2013 (Auditor General
2014, p. 10). The annual reports of the auditor general are littered with
cases of tax exemption, embezzlement of public funds, off-budget expenditure and the side-lining of revenue (*tagneeb*) (Auditor General 2014,
p. 24). The so-called *sharikat al-hukumiyya* (government companies),
owned by regime cronies, the Ministry of Defence and the NISS, are
notorious for taking the law into their own hands when doing business,
and the justification has always been that they are defending the national
interest.

Expenditure on the military-security sector steadily increased in the budget, from 62 per cent in 2012 to 78 per cent in 2013 to 88 per cent in 2014 (*al-Sudani* newspaper, article, August 2014).

In September 2014, austerity measures were introduced as a supplement to the 2013 budget, including the devaluation of the currency by 29 per cent and the removal of fuel subsidies worth SDG 3.6 billion (Sudanese pounds), that is, about 1.2 per cent of GDP, the result of which was riots (ADB 2014). In contrast to the lenient attitude towards the nouveaux riche and the powerful, the government showed determination in removing fuel and food subsidies in 2013, provoking violent urban demonstrations in September and October of that year. Economic hardship, inflation and poverty thus featured markedly following 2011.

The rollback of the state, which the Inqaz regime had ruthlessly adopted since the early 1990s, not only contributed to the impoverishment of the majority of the urban and rural low-income groups, it continued to contribute, along with other factors, to the pauperisation and withering away of the secular, enlightened middle class (El-Battahani 2000; Sahal 2000). As Figure 8.3 shows, poverty was and, indeed, continued to be widespread, particularly in the regions and states that took up arms against the central government. The levels of poverty in conflict regions averaged between 56 and 69 per cent, while in the central and northern states, it was around 26 to 44 per cent (El-Mahdi 2012). According to an IMF report for 2013, 47 per cent of the population was now below the poverty line (IMF 2013). By June 2014, inflation was at 43 per cent, and the United Nations and USAID said that 6.9 million people in Sudan were in need of humanitarian assistance (USAID 2014).

Unemployment, particularly among the youth, has been a major problem facing policymakers. Agriculture continued to be the main source of employment for the greater part of the labour force, particularly for people in the rural areas. However, a lack of investment in agriculture lies behind the flight of people from rural districts to urban centres. Increasing unemployment and low levels of productivity in agriculture and industry have been core factors in the high and persistent levels of poverty (IMF 2013). The youth have been particularly affected by high levels of unemployment. In general, young people – the age group from twenty to forty-five years old – make up about 45 per cent of the total population. But, despite their numbers, they are largely excluded from political processes in Sudan and cannot contribute to political debates and policymaking. Unemployment is a major problem in Sudan with enormous apparent potential for destabilising society, and, furthermore, it has increased significantly, from 14.2 per cent in 1990 to 21.6 per cent

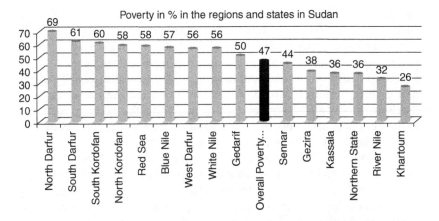

Figure 8.3: Poverty in Percentage in the Regions and States in Sudan
Source: Central Statistical Bureau, Household Survey for 2010, quoted
in Abda El-Mahdi (2012).

in 2010, making Sudan one of the thirty-five countries in the world with
the highest rates of unemployment.

Contrived employment opportunities for youth and deteriorating services in marginalised regions formed ideal conflict-triggering factors,
meaning either the youth were taking up arms as bandits or they were
a potential target for recruitment into armed militia groups.

Overall, the repercussions of the July 2011 secession have continued to
aggravate the problems of managing the economy. The resulting high
external and internal deficits, coupled with the continuing sanctions
imposed by the United States, and the security concerns in Darfur, as
well as in South Kordofan and the Blue Nile, continued to threaten
macroeconomic stability; but on top of this, the austerity measures introduced to supplement the budget led to urban unrest and threatened the
government.

With no sign of change, the 2014 budget continued to implement the
fiscal consolidation in order to maintain macroeconomic stability.[26] Low
world prices for oil in 2014 seemed to favour the government and further,
there was a partial lifting of American sanctions. In foreign policy,
President al-Bashir moved away from Iran towards the Arab regimes
following recent political developments against the Islamists in Egypt

---

[26] The budget for 2015 was not fundamentally different, focusing on macroeconomic and
financial stabilisation. Minister of Finance and National Economy addressing
Parliament, December 2014.

and Sudan, joining the intervention of the Saudi-led coalition in Yemen, all of which was designed to lure Arab investment to Sudan (Ismail 2015). But it was not a question of money pouring into the government's coffers; rather, the government's economic priorities were shaped by the imperative of the survival of the autocracy and the political insecurity of the ruling elites: resources would be put into financing the war against the rebels in marginalised regions and maintaining the security networks against possible urban protests, and what remained of the rent resources was parcelled out between the competing power circles.

In summary, and in line with the E/M model, by 2014, Sudan's dependent economy had become more vulnerable to outside volatile economic and financial changes; its rentier and dependent economy meant that it was not able to provide the economic prerequisites for a democratic transition. At the top of the economy, the elaborate military-security apparatus and various clientelistic networks made up the core support-base of the autocratic regime. Other beneficiaries of the regime included a myriad of social groups and newly formed political parties that had begun to identify themselves as reformed Islamists and so distance themselves from government policies, but it was not clear if and in what fashion their internal economic drive would prompt them to stand with other opposition forces calling for democratic reform and change.

8.4   Possible Transition Routes

Past transitions in Sudan have oscillated between post-autocracy (1964, 1985) and post-civil conflict (2005) and neither of these successfully addressed the root causes of conflict and autocracy. Currently, contending political blocs – Inqaz, that is the incumbent regime, the opposition forces and the rebel groups – are negotiating three different routes or scenarios for transition to post-conflict–post-autocracy democratisation. Though each political bloc has its own 'road-map' for change, these competing routes for (democratic) change are not mutually exclusive, meaning that one element of a scenario may prove to have a triggering effect on another, for example the success of the rebels in the war zone may prompt the army to take over, embolden youth movements to go onto the streets, force the government to reach a peaceful solution or prompt the leadership of the regime to lead the process of change itself.

8.4.1   *Regime-Led Transition*

The South Sudan self-determination referendum in 2011 led to two one-party states: Sudan, under the NCP, and a new state, the 'South Sudan

Republic', under the SPLM. South Sudan's secession effectively ended the jurisdiction of the Interim National Constitution (INT) of 2005 and both regimes had to find new forms of legitimacy.[27] While South Sudan was celebrating its independence, Sudan's ruling elite in Khartoum were arguing over what direction they should take. A leading Islamist figure vying for power raised the label of 'the Second Republic',[28] but this did not go down well with the Islamist ruling groups and did not appeal to the general public; the debate was more about the political contest than anything of a legal constitutional nature; in short, it was about the vested interests of core ruling groups.

The NCP core constituency consists of an alliance between the Islamist movement, army officers, the security forces and the networks of cronies and the middle-ranking business class. President al-Bashir sits at the centre, maintaining a balancing act, though of late he has been much more dependent on the army-security network than on political support from the Islamists. The NCP post-secession strategy has four principal aspects: (i) maintaining control over the disposal of rents (*tamkin*), primarily for the mainstream Islamist constituency but also with a view to bringing in other defected Islamists;[29] (ii) making marginal concessions to co-opt political allies: continuously drawing and redrawing boundaries of patronage networks; (iii) continuing the show of force and the use of repression against the opposition and in the war against the rebels; (iv) manoeuvring carefully in the murky environment of regional and international politics.

The power struggle within the upper ranks of the leadership and the heavy-handed response to urban unrest that led to breakaway factions and the formation of rival Islamic parties has already been referred to. Bowing to pressure and calls for change and reform, the ruling Islamic Movement in its annual conference in October 2013 approved a document calling for reform in the NCP ruling party and the government. To placate critics and to reassure the broad Islamist constituency, President al-Bashir sacked top NCP leaders and opened the door to new young replacements; President al-Bashir also presented an initiative for a national dialogue called 'The Leap' on 27 January 2014,[30] to bring

---

[27] This has led to debates between constitutional experts and political scientists on the efficacy and legitimacy of the 2010 elections: Should both governments continue in office until 2015?

[28] This was coined by First Vice President Ali Osman Taha, who was removed shortly afterwards.

[29] This was in anticipation of reprisals following anti-Islamist sentiments in Egypt and the region generally.

[30] Ironically, the concept underlying the national dialogue the president called for concerns the issues of identity, peace, democracy and development, about which most political forces are in general agreement.

together opposition parties, rebel groups and civil society organisations in comprehensive talks designed to reach agreement on a framework for national dialogue. Yet, rather than providing an environment conducive to dialogue, the government did exactly the opposite, rendering the whole process illusory by arresting opposition leaders, curbing press freedom and cracking down on civil society organisations.[31]

The measures the government took throughout 2014 have alienated pro-national dialogue parties like the Umma Party. Indeed, recent constitutional amendments in early 2015 have further confirmed the consolidation of the autocracy: for example cancellation of elections for state governors; enhancing the power of the president through his appointment of them; elevating and empowering the NISS as an organised force comparable to the army; and giving the president a free hand in the allocation of natural resources across the country, thereby undermining federal arrangements.

Despite a boycott by the main opposition parties and rebel groups, the NCP invited a number of political parties and breakaway rebels to the national dialogue, the proceedings of which are still in progress at the time of writing. While it is difficult to gauge the extent to which this will contribute to an inclusive political settlement, a number of observations can be made: (i) the government has failed to put an end to the warfare and violent conflict in various parts of the country; (ii) it is apparent that the elections in April 2015 did not deliver legitimacy for the government; and (iii) the economy did not benefit from the regime's realignment with the Saudi-led coalition against the Houthis in Yemen. To fend off calls for change increasingly coming even from among Islamists, and to counterpressure exerted by the government and regional and international actors, the ruling party seems to have been forced to make an effort to reach out to political opponents and rebels. Up to the time of writing, the opposition parties are holding out, refusing to join the national dialogue. Those taking part view it from different perspectives, and often take conflicting positions, but non-NCP participants seem to agree that there should be a transition period leading to new political and constitutional dispensations; on the other hand, pro-NCP elements are divided on the outcome, some of them stressing 'reconciliation' and 'accommodation', while others see the affair as an exercise in window-dressing.

It is too early to tell whether the national dialogue will trigger a credible regime-led reform process that may, all things equal, dismantle one-party government or whether al-Bashir's leadership will outmanoeuvre both internal Islamist factions and the fragmented opposition-rebel front and

[31] Atta El-Battahani, SDFG, 2014.

end up by co-opting new allies, thereby buying yet more time for a vulnerable one-party state navigating its way through uncertainties.

The balance of power between the government and the opposition can be described as one of stalemate: neither can score a decisive move against the other. In view of this deadlock, the dynamics for regime-led change should now be seen as a function of the balance of power between competing networks of influence inside the regime (El-Battahani 2016) rather than of the balance of power between the regime and the opposition.

8.4.2 Opposition-Led Transition

During the transition period from 2005 to 2011, the opposition parties in the North benefited from the considerable margin of freedom the CPA ensured and played an active role as opposition parties. However, with the end of the transition period, the autocracy returned with a vengeance.

The opposition parties standing against the Islamist government of Sudan were weak and fragmented. But, given their mercurial and fragmented nature, they did not pose a serious and systematic challenge to the NCP regime; rather, the latter managed to make in-roads into these parties and co-opt influential figures from them. For years, the main concern of the ruling Islamists in Sudan was to neutralise, if not win over, the followers of the main political parties: the DUP and Umma,[32] these being the main forces of opposition to the regime. Three approaches dominated the attitudes of the forces opposed to the Islamist regime: the first, that of the Umma Party, called for the 'peaceful' dismantling of the NCP regime; the second, put forward by the Quwwa al-Ijma'a al-Watani (the Forces of National Consensus), a coalition of opposition parties, called for a peaceful transition leading to the uprooting of the regime; in contrast, the Sudan Revolutionary Forces (SRF) called for violent change as the only possible means of overthrowing the regime.

The Umma National Party (UNP) and Democratic Unionist Party (DUP) are religious-sectarian parties functioning through patronage networks, and they played a central role in Sudan's progress towards independence and in the politics of the country afterwards. The DUP under El-Mirghani's leadership seemed determined to persist in its coalition with the NCP and ceased to be considered an effective opposition to the NCP-led government.

---

[32] When the Islamists took power in 1989, both parties were specifically targeted by a deliberate government policy of infiltration and fermentation of internal splits, and given these parties loose organizational structure they have become prone to further fractures and internal factionalism.

The UNP has also suffered from internal splits and factionalism under the leadership of Sadiq al-Mahdi. Both government and opposition forces realise the political weight and moral authority of Sadiq al-Mahdi, as a descendent of the Mahdi of the Sudan, and so have vied to win him over.[33] Nonetheless, some leaders in the opposition have mixed feelings over Sadiq al-Mahdi's leadership against the Islamist regime. He has kept changing his position and tactics, initially calling for and endorsing a 'national dialogue' as a means of peacefully transforming the autocracy, but then moving to a radical position aligning the Umma Party with the SRF in the 'Paris Declaration' and the 'Sudan Call'.[34]

The National Consensus Forces, the broad coalition of forces working to bring regime change and install a democratic government,[35] continued to be a steadfast source of opposition to the NCP. When the Umma and Sadiq al-Mahdi moved closer to al-Bashir's government, the SCP and PCP[36] seemed to bury their ideological differences and be determined to coordinate their tactics and activities so as to provide an effective leadership for the National Consensus Forces. As we have seen, in the aftermath of the popular discontent of September–October 2013 and the government's lethal repression of peaceful demonstrations, and with the effects of the Arab Spring in mind, President al-Bashir began to remove key Islamist figures and, in January 2014, called for a national dialogue to bring all the political parties and armed rebel groups together to negotiate an end to conflict and to move forward to set up new political and constitutional dispensations to bring opponents on board.

A number of youth and students movements have emerged during the past few years. This was because they detested the mercurial and shifting tactics of the opposition parties, and by benefiting from social media and building on their accumulated experience as students activists, these organised youth groups emerged as an opposition to the government; they are many in number, and it is difficult to gauge their influence. Unlike similar groups in Egypt, the Sudanese youth groups are fragmented. The government was initially able to infiltrate the inner circles of

[33] Reflecting one of the paradoxes of Sudanese politics, despite all this inaction and the mercurial position of its leadership, the UNP remains the principal opposition party and is not greatly affected by internal disputes.

[34] These were important points in the process of bringing together the Northern opposition parties and the armed rebels on a single platform against the Khartoum regime.

[35] These are made up of the Communist Party, Ba'thists, Nasserites, the Sudan Congress Party and the Confederation of Civil Society Organisations; however, the People's Congress Party (PCP) led by Hassan al-Turbi has moved away from the opposition and is now closer to the NCP.

[36] However, later on, fearing a backlash against the Islamists in Sudan, the PCP moved away from the Forces of National Consensus towards President al-Bashir, fully embracing the initiative for national dialogue even when its success was not guaranteed.

these groups, then it clamped down on the ringleaders inside the country and eventually sought, though without success, to close down all the Internet facilities they used.

Rebellion among the youth is not confined to non-partisan youth. A rebellion of the youth within the political parties came as a result of elderly senior and mid-ranking party members dominating policy-making offices for decades, resulting in the political parties having stagnant power structures. However, the youth groups within political parties lacked communication and leadership skills, as well as experience in political management conducted through the prism of policy rather than power, so they found it hard to participate constructively on political issues (a common feature of politics in Sudan). In the Umma National Party and the NCP, younger party members put forward their own initiatives for political reform and, at times, there was direct confrontation with the leadership in almost all parties and, in particular, in these two parties. Almost all these forces – political parties, women's organisations, civil society organisations and youth groups – embrace, to varying degrees, a concept of democratic transition that leans more to the post-autocracy pole rather than to the post-conflict pole.

8.4.3   Rebel-Led Transition

After the secession of South Sudan in 2011, the military threat to the Khartoum government greatly diminished and violent conflicts were confined to skirmishes led by the SPLM-N in the Nuba Mountains and Blue Nile regions, as well as sporadic activity instigated by a number of rebel groups in the Darfur region. To close ranks and coordinate their anti-government activities, the SPLM-N and the Darfur rebels, together with other elements from the North, formed the Sudan Revolutionary Front (SRF).

The SRF called for the total dismantling of the NCP regime and in its place the institution of a secular-democratic state in which members of marginalised ethnic groups would enjoy full citizens' rights equal to those the Northerners enjoyed. The SPLM/A-north sector and the Darfur rebels form the backbone of the SRF. The SPLM-N called for a 'New Sudan', the principles of which were couched in somewhat broader terms in the 'New Dawn' charter designed to include other rebel groups in Darfur and other opposition forces. From the point of view of this chapter, the New Dawn Charter embraces a concept of post-conflict transition because it insists on creating a new political order as a means to settle questions of national identity and to restructure state power.

Although the government succeeded in confining the SRF to the war zone in the aforementioned regions, it nonetheless failed to crush the SRF militarily, as it had promised to do. Using the tactics of war by proxy as a cheap form of counterinsurgency (El-Affendi 2013), and entertaining the notion of a 'final solution' along the Sri Lankan model, all government efforts to mobilise local communities and turn them against the rebels failed. All the government succeeded in doing was to co-opt leaders from these groups, luring them with jobs from the dwindling resources of an impoverished political marketplace (De Waal 2012).

Realising that its chances of toppling the regime by itself were remote, the SRF changed tactics and sought to work with Northern opposition forces. Following the 'New Dawn' charter, rebel leaders moved to reconcile with the Northern opposition and signed the Paris Declaration in August 2014, followed by the Sudan Call in December 2014. The latter was endorsed by the opposition parties, civil society organisations and rebel groups. Observers felt that a rebel-led scenario for toppling the government was not feasible for the time being, which is why the rebel leaders intensified diplomatic and political efforts while at the same time defending their military powerbases in their respective regions and calling for the urban population to rise up against the Islamist government. Whatever their assessment of their own strength and their rivals' relative power, all internal political forces ranging from the regime of the NCP, to both opposition parties and the rebel groups, could not ignore the dynamics of regional and international politics to which we now turn.

8.5   Country-Specific Factors Complicating Sudan's Transition

The following two sections discuss the impact of external factors on Sudan's prospects for a transition to democracy. These factors are grouped into three categories: (1) relations with South Sudan; (2) regional geopolitics and Islamist links (Saudi Arabia and the Gulf, Egypt, Libya, Iran); and (3) international involvement (Western countries, China and Russia, amongst others).

8.5.1   *Relations with South Sudan*

Relations with South Sudan were and will be for the foreseeable future of critical significance to the Khartoum government, not least because a considerable number of the troops who fought for the South Sudan secession are natives of the two regions of the Nuba Mountains and Blue Nile, and are currently fighting under the banner of the SPLM-N for autonomy from central control. The fact that regions of South Darfur, South Kordofan and the Blue Nile are adjacent to South Sudan increased tensions on the border between the two countries, one which is anyway difficult to control. Ideological and military ties, and political sympathies between the SPLM in the South and the SPLM-N and the Darfur rebels, lie behind Khartoum's fears that the border could be used to supply the rebels with arms and ammunition. The violent rebellion that flared up in December 2014 between the South Sudan government in Juba and rebels led by Riak Machar (the former vice-president) provided the necessary pretext for both governments to accuse each other of supporting rebels operating across borders. The significance of the borders, however, goes beyond the long-standing and intricate security issues and threats posed to both of them.

Ironically both governments, in Sudan and South Sudan, stand to benefit from stable and peaceful movement across borders. The flow of oil (and revenue) northwards, shared resources between tribal and ethnic communities, cross-border movements of tribes on both sides, all have inevitably an important neighbourhood impact on their respective domestic situations (Zain al-Abdin 2012). Recurrent violent conflict between the government in Juba, armed rebels near the oil fields and reports of both Northern and Southern rebels crossing borders add to the sensitivity and uncertainty of the Juba–Khartoum relationship. The violence in South Sudan is providing Khartoum with a new means of pressurising Juba on many (security, political, economic) issues and, in doing so, it poses at times as a peacemaker and at other times as a warmonger in order to extract concessions from South Sudan.

8.5.2   Geopolitics and Islamist Networks

During its first decade in power (in the 1990s), the radical Islamic regime in Sudan did not conceal its systemic efforts to export revolution and, in effect, destabilise neighbouring countries, as well as other Islamic countries in North Africa and the Middle East (El-Agib 2011). Countries bordering Sudan in the Horn of Africa were directly affected, but intra-ideological changes in Khartoum and the removal of Hassan al-Turabi from power in 1999 softened the ideological drive and subsequent relations with radical Islamic movements. Relations with radical Islamic groups in the region were not given top priority though not entirely severed.

Equally sensitive, and of vital significance to Khartoum, were its relations with Qatar. In the wake of the South Sudan secession and Khartoum's subsequent loss of oil revenue and the economic and financial crisis, it was the Qataris' financial assistance that rescued the Khartoum government. But the Qatari role is not confined to financial and economic assistance; it has to do with the role of political tutelage it wishes to assume, which is based on supporting radical Islamic movements in the sub-Saharan region, North Africa and the Middle East generally. In all Qatar's moves in these regions, Sudan is seen as a strategic player.

Over the years, Sudan has also cultivated special relations with Iran and Turkey. Iran was instrumental in assisting Sudan's arms industry. Press reports referred to incidents in which Sudan was implicated in arms transfers to Hamas in Gaza,[37] the Houthis in Yemen and jihadist groups in Libya.[38]

However, after the Arab uprisings and the subsequent rapid rise and demise of Islamic movements, particularly in Egypt, Khartoum's ideological affinity, organisational networks and security links with Middle Eastern Islamists, not to mention relations with Qatar, Turkey and Iran, posed a new challenge for the Islamists in Sudan. As mentioned earlier, reports had it that the Khartoum government had facilitated the logistics and delivery of arms, money and safe shelter to groups that Qatar supports, such as Hamas and the Islamists in Libya, with their potential threat to the new anti-Islamist regime in Egypt. But while effective in relieving fiscal pressures on the government, Qatar's financial assistance could not solve the economic problems of the country. And the government's economic and financial problems were further compounded by the tightening of international boycotts and the fact that the Sudanese banks were barred from borrowing or lending as a means of facilitating the importing of basic necessities such as foodstuffs and medicine (Ismail 2015).

However, with new developments in the region after the Houthis stormed their way to power in Yemen and Saudi-Gulf military intervention there, Sudan seemed to move away from Iran and closer to the Saudi-led coalition, even going so far as to send troops to fight the Houthis. Yet, Sudan's shift of positions has raised doubts.

According to *The Economist*:

Yet Western diplomats question whether Mr Bashir has really changed his spots. His regime has long been close to radical causes. It has cosied up to the Saudis over Yemen only after angering them by apparently helping Iran supply the

---

[37] *Times of Israel*, 21 July 2014, quoted in *al-Rakoba* electronic newspaper: http://www .alrakoba.net/news-action-show-id-157312.htm.

[38] President al-Bashir boasted that Sudan contributed to the overthrow of Muamar Qaddafi. The BBC, World Service, 26 October 2011, http://www.bbc.com/news/world-africa-15471734.

Houthis. One reason for Sudan to switch sides is that Saudi money may rescue its floundering economy, as it did Egypt's. The loss of oil revenues after the secession of South Sudan has drained its coffers; the phasing out of subsidies has pushed up prices. (The Economist, *18 April 2015*)

The repercussions and aftereffects of this change were still unfolding in 2015. Initially, though, observers were baffled, posing numerous questions: How would al-Bashir walk through the minefield of the competing and conflicting Arab and Iranian political agendas?[39] Was financial assistance promised in return for Sudan's bold move? Would al-Bashir's autocracy go all the way to distance Sudan from its long-held ideological affinity, organisational networks and security links, with Middle Eastern Islamists? Would those Islamists close to Iran hinder, or even prevent, the new turnabout in Sudanese–Middle Eastern relations?[40]

8.5.2   The Global War on Terror and Sudan

Following the secession of South Sudan, an objective in the realisation of which Western countries had invested heavily, the international community seemed to have lost interest in following through with an agenda for democratic reform as stipulated in the CPA. Relations between Sudan and the West remained in limbo: Western states led by the United States did not want to normalise relations with Sudan and yet, at the same time, they did not want to pressurise the government to a breaking point. Yet it is a fact that the ICC indictment hanging over its leadership was a source of frustration and a stumbling block in the way of the normalisation of relations.

Relations were strained, characterised by ambivalence: on one hand, Western countries valued intelligence cooperation with Sudan in tracking the activities of radical Islamists and assisted in stemming the tide of migration to Europe, but, on the other, they were not yet ready to allow Sudan to join the international community. The regime wanted desperately to integrate into the international community, but with minimal concessions. The international community also appeared keen to work with the regime as a partner, in spite of mutual indictments and mistrust (El-Effendi 2010).

But with the unexpected aftermath of the Arab Spring and the upsurge in the activities of *salafi* jihadist groups in Sub-Saharan Africa and the Middle East, the gathering momentum of the Global War Against Terror (GWAT), the Sudanese authorities now had a role to play. Sudan sought

---

[39] See Ismail (2015) on 'The Many Faces of al-Bashir'.
[40] Arab circles in the Gulf are not sure if Sudan's move closer to the Saudi-led coalition against the Houthis in Yemen is a genuine one. Eric Reevs, "Kleptocracy in Khartoum: Self-Enrichment by the National Islamic Front/National Congress Party", The Enough Project, December 2015, www.enoughproject.org.

to present itself as an indispensable bulwark for peace and stability and a credible ally against non-state fanatical religious groups. Yet, at the same time, it raised the threat that its removal would lead to chaos and instability throughout Sub-Saharan Africa. In Sub-Saharan Africa, where security is fragile at best, Sudanese tactics seemed to have won a sympathetic hearing, and some observers believed that a collapse in Sudan would affect Nigeria, Mali and every country in the East and the Horn of Africa, especially the new South Sudan (*The Economist*, 12 April 2014). Contenting itself with the rhetoric of support and the national dialogue for peaceful democratic reform (Booth 2014), the West seems to have no intention of putting too much pressure on al-Bashir's autocracy in order to make it open up, a point not missed on the Sudanese side. When the regime decided to ignore calls to proceed with the 'national dialogue' and continue with the April 2015 general elections, the West, represented by the Troika (United States, Britain and Norway), issued a statement regretting the failure of the Sudanese government to create an environment conducive to free and fair elections. Restrictions on political rights and freedoms, in contrast to the rights enshrined in the Sudanese constitution, the lack of a credible national dialogue and the continued armed conflict in Sudan's peripheral regions, are among the reasons for the reported low participation and very low voter turnout. The outcome of these elections cannot be considered a credible expression of the will of the Sudanese people.[41]

Following fraud elections, al-Bashir's autocracy has celebrated its 2015 electoral victory and the West seems likely to engage with and persuade the government, the opposition and the rebels to come to the negotiating table with the object of reaching a comprehensive solution to Sudan's ongoing conflicts.

8.6   Conclusions: Islamist *Tamkin*: Political Forces at Dead End?

The radical Islamists in Sudan overthrew a democratically elected, multi-party government in 1989; installed a one-party authoritarian regime; and immediately adopted the aggressive *tamkin* strategy to control soft and hard rent sources. Over time, repressive measures were taken to undermine the opposition, Islamist cadres were installed in all government posts, and a relatively efficient patronage network was put in place to neutralise politicians in the rebel groups and placate tribal and sectarian leaders in rural areas. Furthermore, in other parts of the country, violent conflicts in

---

[41] *Sudan Tribune*, 21 April 2015.

marginal regions, movement of populations and economic hardship, combined with political and social changes, have contributed to making the traditional political parties increasingly less effective at leading the confrontation with the Islamist autocracy. Many of the politicians defecting from the opposition parties, as well as the rebels who signed peace agreements, have been incorporated into an expanded state-run patronage network.

The war against the rebel movements in resource-rich South Sudan turned into a jihad, with the result that the rebels were driven to call for self-determination, which they eventually achieved when South Sudan seceded after the transition period of 2005–11. The limited democratic opening-up (2005–11) was short-lived, and with South Sudan going its way in 2011, autocracy reasserted itself in Sudan under the leadership of al-Bashir. However, the post-secession period had its own dynamic for autocracy: dwindling rents and internal dynamics pushing for change, augmented by pressures from outside that were partly a result of the neighbourhood effect of the Arab uprisings, all forced the NCP to express its intention to change and to promote a national dialogue.

The prospects for a transition in Sudan are still uncertain: the NCP rhetoric of leading the change itself, as well as the fragmentation of the political elites, particularly in the opposition, are overshadowed by the emergence of two opposing socio-economic blocs underlying the political scene. On one hand, there is the formation of the 'new' urban middle class and the nouveaux riche who have benefited from the economic policies of the government over the past quarter of a century, that is from 1989 to 2014, and are supportive of the regime on its own instigating a degree of political change. It is likely that a number of business networks that benefited from the Inqaz regime (and have some confidence in their ability to survive in a relatively competitive economic environment) do not mind a degree of reform being undertaken in order to avoid regime collapse. Yet the question these 'moderate' Islamists in government positions are confronted with is what amount of power they are prepared to release to make the participation of the newcomers (opposition parties and rebel groups) meaningful but not threatening to the interests of the ruling Islamists. However, on the other hand, there are those rent-seeking groups whose interests are inextricably linked with the survival of the autocracy. In sharp contrast to pro-regime forces stand the opposition groupings, albeit with different stances towards autocracy: some do not mind meeting the regime halfway while others call for radical change. These latter groups are drawn from the urban poor, rural producers and hundreds of thousands of university graduates who find themselves out of work for many reasons. This is further complicated by the intersection of the interests and positions of the regional and international actors.

Thus taking all these factors into consideration, instead of assuming a zero-sum relationship between autocracy and democracy, one may visualise the possibility of a symbiosis between the two, mediated by a government–opposition synergy during a period of transition, being put into effect to resuscitate the agents of change and level the playing field for all political forces. During this transition, and whatever the outcome, the democratic transition regime may be seen as *moving away from* authoritarianism rather than *moving towards* democracy, at least as far as the transition period is concerned.[42] One reformed Islamist is already calling for 'consociational democracy' and a relatively long period of transition (Zain al-Abdin 2012).

In contrast to other instances in North Africa and the Middle East, the case of Sudan reveals a number of special findings. From the time it took over, the radical Islamic movement in Sudan adopted a strategy of *tamkin* involving a number of elements:

First, the Sudanese autocracy mastered the 'instrument for the rentier-authoritarian bargain strategy', combining repression with patronage and benefiting from geopolitics and the idiosyncrasies of political Islam taking hold in an Afro-Arab country for a quarter of a century.

Second, the deteriorating standard of living and high unemployment in Sudan, particularly among the youth, were not, and are still not so far, supporting factors for democratic transition. Perhaps, as the E/M model suggested, the ruling elites in this case can provide other forms of transfer beyond the provision of public sector employment in order to secure an effective authoritarian bargain.

Third, following the failed popular uprisings of 2012 and 2013, one may cautiously infer that 'medium to high political repression impedes democratic transitions'. Yet the Sudanese government has been more repressive in the war zones and has managed to push back armed rebel groups, particularly those operating in Darfur. Consequently, the government's aggressive military campaigns in marginalised regions has deterred any 'potential' popular uprising in other areas of the country.[43] This is in line with the E/M analysis that in less endowed societies political repression might be unavoidable for lack of any better alternative in terms of resource transfers (Elbadawi and Makdisi 2014, p. 31).

Fourth, the 'democratic neighbourhood effect' in the Sudanese case expressed itself in two ways, both having a corrosive effect on democratic

---

[42] This gives room for the synthesis between two modes of transition: post-autocracy and post-civil war transition.

[43] Calls for *al-Intifada al-Mahmiyya* (protected popular uprising) have been rejected by opposition parties since this will give the autocracy the pretext to unleash its massive military arsenal against civilian demonstrations, as was the case in September 2013.

transition: provoking a fear that the Islamists inside and outside Sudan might lose their strategic hold on an important region (in the light of recent events in Egypt, Libya, etc.) and bringing about the Sudanese Islamists' involvement in regional Arab wars, most notably the Arab–Israeli conflicts. The E/M model is cognizant of the likelihood that the neighbourhood effect may work either way – to reinforce the incumbent regime's determination to hold on to power and resist any substantive political reform that might weaken their position, or to encourage democratic reform.

Fifth, despite the many setbacks the regime has experienced, splits in 1999, civil war, coup attempts, the secession of South Sudan, popular discontent and protests, dissent and factions breaking away from the ruling party and, above all, harsh economic conditions and fiscal crisis (insolvency), the autocracy of Sudan, thanks to favourable regional and international circumstances, managed to survive by means of the collective action of the elite, the result of which was a strong authoritarian state underpinned by durable coercive institutions. Al-Bashir's autocracy may claim to have succeeded in isolating and confining the rebels to certain geographical zones, and it can also pride itself on containing the sporadic rural and urban unrest, and on having neutralised regional international factors that might call for radical change, yet it has failed to be a national leadership capable of resolving deeply rooted conflicts, or of maintaining the territorial integrity of the country and winning over the support of the various regions and communities in it.

Sixth, although the E/M model has weighted economic hardship and the drying up of rents as an important variable, the model also allows for non-economic variables such as repression and co-optation. The regime used both skilfully: the former shielded Sudan's authoritarian rule from vertical threats such as mass demonstrations, as tragically shown during September–October 2013, while to some degree it addressed horizontal threats in the form of elite splits. Furthermore, infighting and dissent (leading to a narrowing of the support base of the regime) and the visible signs of economic hardship were compensated for through the neutralising of regional and international support for change. Hence, the conclusion that permitting a degree of liberty, within selective restrictions, serves autocrats better than infringements on personal integrity or co-optation (Tanneberg, Stefes and Merkel 2013, pp. 115–29).

Last, but not least, however, a number of interlocking factors, ranging from the economic to elite fragmentation, state dismemberment, political Islam and external intervention, are currently playing out to shape an expected transition, with an uncertain outcome, from an autarchic, conflict-ridden Inqaz regime to a post-Bashir regime. Will Sudan 'slide back into obscurantism and violent rhetoric' (Satti 2012), and through further disintegration turn into a series of mini-Rwandas (Taisier 2014), or can the Sudanese 'learn from a failed Islamist experience and chart a course towards emancipation, enlightenment and prosperity? The survival tactics of al-Bashir's autocracy ranged from co-option and patronage and divide-and-rule to the use of repression; it remains to be seen how long these recombinant and survival tactics will last and whether a post-Bashir Sudan is a post-autocracy or a post-conflict transition; or an ambiguous mixture of both.

Part III

Concluding Observations

9 Resistance to and Prospects for Democracy

Ibrahim Elbadawi and Samir Makdisi

The popular uprisings that swept through parts of the Arab world in 2011 have, no doubt, transformed its political landscape. They have led to the demise of three long-reigning Arab autocracies in Tunisia, Egypt and Libya and given rise to a new era of popular mass protests as well as to large-scale violence, civil wars and terrorism that have attracted, or in some cases were triggered by, regional and global power interventions. But indeed, though this new 'Arab awakening' has been late in coming, it has shattered the mantra of 'Arab exceptionalism' long associated with the region. Yet now, five years since its inception, the so-called Arab Spring is defined more by violence than by democratic transitions. This raises new questions about the future of democracy in this region, most notably: why have the initially peaceful mass movements become so violent? Is 'Arab exceptionalism' reinventing itself in a new guise in terms of violence 'induced' by internal and external forces that stand to lose from more stable forms of transition? Are we witnessing a halt to democratic transitions in the Arab world? And what are the requisite transformations that would improve the prospects for democracy in the region?

The transition experiences of countries in other parts of the world shed light on factors that influence the democratic transition process, its success and potential reversals. Empirical work points out three instructive findings.[1] The first is that the nature of the prevailing autocratic regime can influence the probability of its collapse. Looking at regime types, Geddes and colleagues (2014) concluded that the probability of a monarchy failing is only 2 per cent in a given year; similarly, for dominant party regimes, it remains at the very small ratio of 2.6 per cent. For 'personalist' regimes, the failure rate is a little higher, standing at 6.7 per cent. Military regimes are the least stable, with

---

[1] The review of the evidence provided in the following three paragraphs draws heavily on N. Kearney and A. Kubrusi, 'Democracy in the Arab World: Lessons from Abroad', working paper (July 2015) prepared for the project on 'Transition from Autocracy to Democracy in the Arab World' housed at the Institute of Financial Economics at the American University of Beirut.

a 13.1 per cent probability of failure. While Gandhi and Przeworski (2007) find that civilian (personalist) regimes are more fragile than military ones, the two studies agree on the resilience of monarchies that, as Hadenius and Teorell (2007) observe, have stubbornly resisted change, comprising roughly 15 per cent of all regimes throughout the period 1972–2002.

Second, whatever the case, the collapse of an autocratic regime does not necessarily bring about a democracy, as the process of democratisation is often uneven and not infrequently suffers from reversals (See, for example Kapstein and Converse 2008). Similarly, democratic reversals or backward transitions in the Arab region, with a rejuvenated autocratic order dominated by the military, or a form of partial democracy, or, following North, Wallis and Weingast (2009), a mature LAO (limited access order) are all possible outcomes. Between 1946 and 2010, there were only 102 autocracy-to-democracy transitions in the world as compared to 112 autocracy-to-autocracy regime changes (Geddes et al. 2014). This latter phenomenon is especially true with regard to monarchies overthrown: in the vast majority of cases, they were followed by another military-dominated autocracy. Furthermore, it should be noted that autocracies which allow controlled elections may be driven to introduce measures of political liberalisation should a united and mobilised opposition emerge (Howard and Roessler 2006), possibly opening the door for further moves along the path to democracy.

Third, successful post-uprising economic policies greatly reinforce the unfolding democratic process. However, this requires a broad-based socio-economic contract beyond a mere agreement on the principles and institutions of electoral democracy. Experiences from past transitions suggest that this is a major challenge, because more often than not post-transition elites tend to either confine themselves to the task of consolidating the electoral process, or, worse still, attempt to capture control of state resources through corrupt practices. On the latter subject, the experience of Eastern Europe and the former Soviet republics is instructive: in a number of them, the so-called oligarchs have combined wealth with substantial political influence and captured resources, thereby contributing to a highly distorted transition process (Vujčić 2012).

The experience of Latin America epitomises the other challenge regarding the failure of the new elites to go beyond the national agenda of institutionalising the electoral process. Emerging from the shadows of military dictatorship in the 1970s, major Latin American countries (Argentina, Brazil, Chile) entered into a phase of liberal democracy that focused initially on democratising the political and judicial spheres to the neglect of the socio-economic domain. In consequence, high levels of inequality persisted. Subsequently, greater attention was paid to the questions of income distribution and the promotion of an internal market based on mass consumption. This ongoing shift in the politico-economic trajectory of these countries is expected to lead to the democratisation of education, culture and the media, and so to the effective stabilisation of the democratic process (Sader 2012).

The Arab region's resistance to democracy, therefore, is not unique or specific, and can be ascribed to the same elements that have, to varying degrees, helped to maintain different forms of autocracy in other regions as well as the Arab world (i.e. oil, conflicts, neighbourhood effects and external interventions by both regional and international powers). However, perhaps due to the intensity of these factors, what is special about the Arab region is the almost immediate emergence of what appears to be a region-wide authoritarian counter-revolution in response to the uprisings. Shortly after the collapse of the regimes in Tunisia, Egypt and Libya, potentially vulnerable authoritarian regimes in the region responded by deploying a massive degree of violence that has so far either stifled incipient or nascent uprising, as in Sudan, or transformed essentially peaceful mass movements into armed conflicts or outright civil war, as in the cases of Libya, Yemen and Syria. Especially the struggle for Syria has become a violent and tragic contest between radical fundamentalist Sunni groups and the regime supported by transnational Shi'i militias, intertwined with regional and external interventions in support of opposing sides of the conflict.

The rise of strict fundamentalist groups in the Arab region has commonly been attributed to a variety of factors, including their promotion by the so-called Deep State, which uses them as a pretext for its counter-revolution (Filiu 2015); a response on the part of the poorer segments of the population to political and economic exclusion; the desire of certain fundamentalist regimes and/or foreign powers to use them for their own political ends; a response to past Western colonialism and continued interventions in the affairs of the region; the failure to build a nation-state; or the breakdown of the central concept of Arab nationalism. However, the rising sectarian divide fuelled by regional power-plays and of the direct military involvement of external powers, primarily the United States and Russia, has to be the most alarming underlying cause or catalyst behind the prominence of the fundamentalist-sponsored violence that engulfed the region. Indeed, even the most senseless type of violence and terrorism, such as that of Daesh, could very well be explained, though by no means justified, by the political manipulation of the sectarian divide within Islam. No doubt this divide has manifested, first, in the emergence of factional sectarian democracy in Iraq;

and, second, in the violent response of the essentially sectarian minority regime in Syria to the initially peaceful democratic movement that swept through the country for almost six months before turning into a militarised opposition dominated by fundamentalist groups.

Whatever the reason for their rise, should fundamentalist groups succeed in establishing their control of the political scene as a consequence of the ongoing conflicts, rather than being fully contained, then we submit that the question of democratic transition would, at best, have to be evaluated in a radically different context, a matter that we do not take up in this volume as we consider it a highly unlikely development.

Even if the question of fundamentalism in the region had not arisen, it remains a fact that some countries will still experience a difficult and/or violent transition process, if not an authoritarian counteroffensive that may take hold at least temporarily. The respective experiences of the countries where uprisings have taken place demonstrate clearly how transition experiences can vary. The outcome of the ensuing brutal civil conflicts in Syria, Yemen and Libya will determine the nature of the political regimes to follow, and to what extent, if any, these future regimes will come to reflect the attributes of democratic governance rather than those of new autocratic orders. The delay so far of a substantive democratic move in Egypt is associated with the persisting political dominance of the military elite and the continued political divisions in the country, not to mention the expanding conflicts in the region with all their corrosive effects on the transition process. Thus, save for Tunisia, a region-wide transition to genuine democracy following the initial uprisings remains more an aspiration than a concrete reality.

Admittedly, the move towards democracy in individual Arab countries may be hesitant and uneven. This is especially true in that a relatively large number are monarchical autocracies, though with varied political institutions, ranging from the total absence of elected representative bodies in Saudi Arabia to an elected parliament in Kuwait, whatever the circumstances governing the elections may be.[2] Moves in the direction of democracy may go through various types of partial democracy as a prelude to more advanced forms. Thus, some system of electoral representation may initially be introduced and only later will the checks and balances commonly associated with mature democracies be put in place, for example the rule of law that sets constraints on the power of the

---

[2] During the period 1946–2010, there were nineteen monarchies in the world, of which eleven were in the Arab region. Of the non-Arab monarchies, five were overthrown by military coups, but only one experienced a democratic transition (Nepal, twice in 1991 and 2006). Of the eleven Arab monarchies, three were also overthrown by military coups (Egypt, Iraq and Libya), all in the 1950s when the oil factor had not yet become dominant.

executive branch and ensures accountability, an independent judiciary and gender equality.

Accounting for the devastating violence that had so great an impact on the new Arab awakening and with the lessons from the transition experiences of other regions in mind, we respond to the fundamental question we posed at the opening of this chapter regarding the future of democracy in the Arab world in the context of three brief concluding observations.

First, while developments reveal major obstacles facing the transition to democracy in most of the countries concerned, we hold to the view that the evolving socio-economic and political processes in the various countries will yet put an end to the so-called Arab exceptionalism, and pave the way for a change, whether gradual or not, towards democratic governance. As some of the case studies point out, factors pushing in this direction include a building up of modernising influences (e.g. a growing middle class and improving levels of education), an increasing incompatibility between exclusive political institutions and the increasing openness of economic institutions and an expanding popular demand for freedom, equal political rights and social justice.

Second, the observed resiliency of oil-rich Arab autocracies, especially the super-rich monarchies, is in large measure attributable to the influence of their oil wealth reinforced by foreign support. However, the corrosive political effects of relatively abundant oil resources will, in the passage of time, be countered by the influences forcing change, such as mounting socio-economic inequities, a growing middle class, the weakening rentier effect due in part to changing internal economic conditions and a growing democratic neighbourhood as more and more countries move to partial if not full democracies. Moreover, the seeming structural changes in the global oil market and the potential long-term deceleration of prices towards low 'equilibrium' prices will likely further threaten the sustainability of the authoritarian bargain, even in the highly endowed Arab Gulf societies. And what is more, the more countries succeed in moving towards a consolidated democracy the less is the potential threat of reversal (e.g. see Poast and Urpelainen 2015).

Third, the violence and the post-transition relapse that afflicted the Arab democracy movement is also precipitated by the post-transition collapse of the broad democracy coalition that brought secular and moderate Islamist forces together (see El-Affendi, Chapter 2, this volume). For both sides the future will be an opportunity for learning from and reflecting on this painful experience, as both have lost out to the ensuing authoritarian counter-revolution. Moreover, accumulated experiences suggest that in socially diverse countries, the pursuit of a fundamentalist agenda will only create failed or non-developmental states, as illustrated by the collapse of the racial and religious supremacist agenda in Serbia and, even closer to home, the failure of the factional 'sectarian' democracy of Iraq. It follows that socially diverse Arab states should implement non-exclusive economic and political agendas in order to avoid failed developmental outcomes.

Whatever the motivation behind them, fundamentalist agendas will fail to build viable modern states and eventually will succumb to the forces of progress. Following the argument in this vein, despite their tragic costs, the violent discourses currently engulfing the Arab world may eventually become the most effective educators of both the elites and the people of the Arab region.

A final word: in various Arab countries, resistance to substantive democratic change may still be strong, but the findings of this volume lead us to believe that the dynamics of transition unleashed by the uprisings of 2010–11 are resilient and durable. We believe these events will yet result in significantly expanding the Arab democratic space despite all the challenges of consolidation. This, it seems to us, is the logic of history.

Bibliography

Abbas, Hassan. 2011. 'The Dynamics of the Uprising in Syria', 19 October. Available at: www.jadaliyya.com/pages/index/2906/the-dynamics-ofthe-uprising-in-syria

Abdel Khalek, Gouda and Al Sayyid, Mustafa K. 2011. 'Egypt: Development, Liberalization and the Persistence of Autocracy', in Elbadawi and Makdisi (eds.), pp. 256–81

Abdel Kouddous, Sharif. 2014. 'Does Egypt's Resurgent Labour Unrest Pose a Threat to Sisi's Power?' 8 May. Available at: www.europesolidaire.org/spip .php?page=article_impr&id_article=31837

Abdel Salam, Al-Mahboub. 2010. al-Haraka al-Islamiyya al-Sudaniyya (The Sudanese Islamic Movement). Khartoum: Madarik Publishing House

Abdelrahim, Muddathir. 1978. Changing Patterns in Civil–Military Relations in the Sudan. Uppsala: The Scandinavian Institute of African Studies

Aboulenein, Soheir, El-Laithy, Heba, Helmy, Omneia, Kheir-El-Din, Hanaa and Mandour, Dina. 2010. 'Impact of the Global Food Price Shock on the Poor in Egypt', Working Paper 157. Cairo: Egyptian Center for Economic Studies

Abu-Ismail, Khaled and Sarangi, Niranjan. 2015. 'Rethinking the Measurement of the Middle Class'. WIDER Working Paper #023, February

Acemoglu, Daron and Robinson, James. 2012. Why Nations Fail: The Origins of Power, Prosperity and Poverty. New York: Profile Books

Acemoglu, Daron, Johnson, Simon, Robinson, James and Yared, Pierre. 2009. 'Reevaluating the Modernization Hypothesis', Journal of Monetary Economics 56:8, 1043–58

Acemoglu, Daron, Johnson, Simon, Robinson, James and Yared, Pierre. 2008. 'Income and Democracy', American Economic Review 98:3, 808–42

Acemoglu, Daron, Johnson, Simon, Robinson, James and Yared, Pierre. 2005. 'From Education to Democracy?' American Economic Review Proceedings, 95, May, 44–49

Achy, Lahcen. 2011. Tunisia's Economic Challenges. The Carnegie Papers. Carnegie Middle East Center, Beirut. December

AfDB, OECD, UNDP. 2014, Sudan, Available at: http://www.african economicoutlook.org/

Africa Development Bank. 2014. Sudan, http://www.africaneconomicoutlook .org/

'Afifi, Mohamad. 2008. al-Mustabid al-'Adil: al-Za'ama al-'Arabiyya fi'l-Qarn al-'Ishrin. Cairo: Supreme Council of Culture

Ahmari, Sohrab. 2012. 'The Failure of Arab Liberals', Commentary, May. Available at: www.commentarymagazine.com/article/the-failure-of-arab-liberals/

Ahmed, Abdel Ghaffar M. 2008. 'One Against All: The National Islamic Front (NIF) and Sudanese Sectarian and Secular Parties', Sudan Working Paper, no. 6. Bergen: Chr. Michelsen Institute (CMI)

Ahmed, Abdel Ghaffar M. 1988. Gadaya lil Nigash: fi itar ifregiyat al Sduan was oroubatih (Issues for Debate within the Sudan Afro-Arab Context). Khartoum: University Press, Khartoum, pp. 17–18

Ahmed, Abdel Ghaffar M. 2013. 'Changing Dynamics in the Borderlands: Emergence of a Third Sudan', in G. Sorbo, and Abdel Ghaffar Ahmed (eds.), Sudan Divided: Continuing Conflict in a Contested State. London: Palgrave

Ahmed, Enas. 2013. 'The National Congress Party and the "Second Republic": Internal Dynamics and Political Hegemony', in G. Sorbo and Abdel Ghaffar Ahmed (eds.), Sudan Divided: Continuing Conflict in a Contested State. London: Palgrave

Aldashev, Gani, Platteau, Jean-Philippe and Sekeris, Petros. 2013. 'Seduction of Religious Clerics and Violence in Autocratic Regimes – with Special Emphasis on Islam', unpublished paper

Alexander, Anne. 2013. 'Workers and the Arab Revolutions'. December. Available at: http://socialistreview.org.uk/386/workers-and-arab-revolutions Al-Hayat Daily Newspaper, Various Issues

Ali, Ali Abdel Gadir. 2012. 'Governance', in Kuwait: The National Report on Human Development (in Arabic). Kuwait: The Arab Planning Institute

Ali, Ali Abdel Gadir and El-Battahani, Atta. 2011. 'Sudan: Colonial Heritage, Social Polarization and the Democracy Deficit', in Elbadawi and Makdisi (eds.), pp. 282–310

Ali, Hayder Ibrahim. 2004. Skoutt al-Mashroua' al-Hadari (The Demise of the Civilizational Project). Khartoum: Sudanese Studies Centre

Ali, Omer and Elbadawi, Ibrahim. 2012. 'The Political Economy of Public Sector Employment in Resource Dependent Countries', ERF Research Working Paper # 673. Cairo: The Economic Research Forum

Al Marousa Center for Socioeconomic Development. Egypt's Struggling Labour Movement. Available at: http://muftah.org/egypts-struggling-labour-movement/#.VMN2gGSUemE

Al-Marzouqi, et al. 2008. 'al-Hiwar al-Qawmi al-Islami'. Beirut: Centre for Arab Unity Studies

Alnasrawi, Abbas. 1991. Arab Nationalism, Oil, and the Political Economy of Dependency. Contributions in Economics and Economic History, Number 120. New York: Greenwood Press

Al-Shalakany, Amr. 2013. Izdihar wa Inhiyar al-Nukhba al-Qanuniyya fi-Misr 1805–2005 (The Rise and Fall of the Legal Elite in Egypt 1805–2005). Cairo: Dar al-Shorouq

Al Shazli, Heba F. 'Where Were the Workers on the Days before and after 30 June 2013?' Available at: www.jadaliyya.com/pages/index/13125/where-were-the-egyptian-workers-in-the-june-2013-p

Altayib, Aicha. 2011. 'The Socio-economic Background of the Tunisian Revolution: A Sociological Reading'. [In Arabic]. Paper presented at the conference 'Revolutions, Reform and Democratic Transition in the Arab World' organised by the Arab Center for Research and Policy Studies, Doha (Qatar), 19–21 April 2011

Alterman, Jon. 2004. 'The False Promise of Arab Liberals', *Policy Review* 125, June/July, 77–86

Amin al-Din, Nadeem (ed.). 2014. *Al-'Ihtigagat al-'umaliyya fi Masr 2012 (Workers' Protests in Egypt 2012)* (Cairo: Egyptian Centre for Economic and Social Rights. ECESR). Egypt: Annual Protests Report 2013. http://ecesr.org /wp-content/uploads/2014/07/Protest-report-2013-Web.pdf

Amin, Galal. 2011. *Egypt in the Era of Hosni Mubarak: 1981–2011*. Cairo: American University in Cairo Press

Amin, Magdi, et al. 2012. *After the Spring: Economic Transitions in the Arab World*. Oxford: Oxford University Press

Amin, Mohammad and Djankov, Simeon. 2009. 'Democracy and Reforms'. CEPR Discussion Paper No. 7151

Andersen, Jörgen Juel and Ross, Michael. 2014. 'The Big Oil Change: A Closer Look at the Haber-Menaldo Analysis', *Comparative Political Studies* 47:7, 993–1021

Andeweg, Rudy. 2000. 'Consociational Democracy', *Annual Review of Political Science* 3:1, 509–36

Arab Reform Initiative. 2012. The State of Reform in the Arab World: Arab Democracy Index, 2011, pp. 9–10

Arendt, Hannah. 1963. *On Revolution*. New York: Penguin

Art, David. 2012. 'What Do We Know about Authoritarianism after Ten Years? Review Article', *Comparative Politics* 44:3, 351–73

Assaad, Ragui and Roushdy, Rania. 2007. 'Poverty and the Labor Market in Egypt: A Review of Developments in the 1998–2006 Period'. *Background Paper for Arab Republic of Egypt: Poverty Assessment Update*. Washington, DC: World Bank

Assessment and Evaluation Commission, Final Report & Others, 2009–11. AUHIP, Reports, Statements and Proposals

Atallah, Sami. 2011. 'The Gulf Region: Beyond Oil and Wars – the Role of History and Geopolitics in Explaining Autocracy', in Elbadawi and Makdisi (eds.), pp. 166–95

Auditor General. 2014. Auditor General Addressing the Parliament in Sudan, Parliamentary Records, October 2014

Awad, Mohamad Hachem. 1967. al-Istiglal wa Fasad al-Hukum fi al-Sudan (*Exploitation and Corrupt Rule in Sudan*), Khartoum

'Badau al-Tareek', *al-Ahram*, 8 August 2012, p. 13

Banque du Liban. *Quarterly Bulletin*. Various Issues and Website. Available at: www.bdl.gov.lb

Barany, Zoltan. 2012. The 'Arab Spring' in the Kingdoms. Research Paper, Arab Center for Research and Policy Studies, Doha, Qatar: September

Barro, Robert. 2015. 'Convergence and Modernization', *Economic Journal* 125:585, 911–42

Barro, Robert. 2013. 'Democracy, Law and Order and Economic Growth', Chapter 3. 2013 Index of Economic Freedom. The Heritage Foundation

Barro, Robert. 2012. 'Convergence and Modernization Revisited'. Paper prepared for presentation at the Nobel Symposium on Growth and Development, Stockholm, 3–5 September 2012

Barro, Robert. 1999. 'Determinants of Democracy', *Journal of Political Economy* 107:2, 158–83.

Bashshur, Munir. 2003. 'The Deepening Cleavage in the Educational System', in Theodor Hanf and Nawaf Salam (eds.), *Lebanon in Limbo*. Baden-Baden: Nomos Verlagsgesellschaft

Bayat, Asef. [1963] 2007. *Making Islam Democratic: Social Movements and the Post-Islamist Turn*. Stanford, CA: Stanford University Press

Bayat, Asef. 'Paradoxes of Arab Revolutions', *Jadaliyya*. Available at: www .jadaliyya.com/pages/index/786/paradoxes-of-arab-refo-lutions

Bayat, Asef. On the Post-Islamist Alternative. Available at: https://openaccess .leidenuniv.nl/bitstream/handle/1887/17030/ISIM_16_What_is_Post? sequence=1and

Bellin, Eva. 2012. 'Reconsidering the Robustness of Authoritarianism in the Middle East: Lessons from the Arab Spring', *Comparative Politics* 44:2, 127–49

Bellin, Eva. 2004. 'The Robustness of Authoritarianism in the Middle East: Exceptionalism in Comparative Perspective', *Comparative Politics* 36:2, 139–57

Benin, Joel. 2013. Workers, Trade Unions and Egypt's Political Future,18 January, www.merip.org/mero/mero011813

Benin, Joel. 2010. 'The Struggle for Workers' Rights in Egypt', in Solidarity Center (ed.), *Justice for All*. Washington, DC: Solidarity Center. www1.umn .edu/humanrts/research/Egypt/The%20Struggle%20for%20Workers%20righ ts.pdf

Berman, Paul. 2003. *Terror and Liberalism*. New York: W. W. Norton

Beshir, Mohamad Omer, Mohammed Salih and Mohamed Abdel Rahim (eds.). 1984. *The Sudan: Ethnicity and National Cohesion*. African Studies Series, Bayreuth

Beshir, Mohamad Omer. 1988. On the Unitary State Optimum in Sudan, Proceedings of the Arkawit Eleventh Conference on Nation Building in Sudan, Institute of Extra-mural Studies, University of Khartoum, November

Besley, Tim, Pande, Rohini and Rao, Vijayendra. 2005. 'Participatory Democracy in Action: Survey Evidence from Rural India', *Journal of the European Economic Association* 3:2–3, 648–57

Binder, Leonard. 1988. *Liberalism*. Chicago: University of Chicago Press

Binningsbo, Helga Malmin. 2005. 'Consociational Democracy and Post Conflict Peace. Will Power-Sharing Institutions Increase the Probability of Lasting Peace after Civil War?', Paper prepared for presentation at the 13th Annual National Political Science Conference, Hurdalsjøen, Norway, 5–7 January 2005

Boix, Charles and Stokes, Susan. 2003. 'Endogenous Democratization'. *World Politics* 55: 517–49

Booth, Donald (US Special Envoy for Sudan and South Sudan). 2014. 'U.S. Policy on Sudan and South Sudan: The Way Forward'. Washington, DC: The Atlantic Council, 9 October

Boustany, Hareth. 2008. *Histoire du peuple Libanais du Ier au XXe siècle, Une histoire de culture et de dialogue*. Lebanon: Aleph

Brisson, Zack and Krontiris, Kate. 2011. 'Tunisia: From Revolution to Institution'. Washington, DC: World Bank

Brown, Nathan J. 2014. 'Why Do Egyptian Courts Say the Darndest Things?' *Washington Post*, March 25 www.washingtonpost.com/blogs/monkey-cage/wp/2014/03/25/why-do-egyptian-courts-say-the-darndest-things

Brumberg, Daniel. 2014. 'Reconsidering "theories of transition",' in Marc Lynch (ed.). *The Arab Uprisings Explained: New Contentious Politics in the Middle East* (Columbia Studies in Middle East Politics)

Bushra, Mahfouz. 2013. 'On Urban Disparity between Affluent "Arabised" Residential Urban Quarters and Poor "Africanized" Residential Urban Neighbourhoods', *al-Yawm al-Tali*, 27 July

Cabannes, Yves. 2004. 'Participatory Budgeting: A Significant Contribution to Participatory Democracy', *Environment and Urbanization* 16:1, 27–46

Calhoun, Craig, Juergensmeyer, Mark and Van Antwerpen, Jonathan. (eds.) 2011. *Rethinking Secularism*. Oxford: Oxford University Press

Camacho, Adriana and Conover, Emily. 2011. 'Manipulation of Social Program Eligibility', *American Economic Journal: Economic Policy* 3:2, 41–65

Carbone, Giovanni, and Memoli, Vincenzo. 2012.'Does democratization Foster State Consolidation?: A Panel Analysis of the "Backward Hypothesis"', a research paper in a project on 'The economic, social and political consequences of democratic reforms. A quantitative and qualitative comparative analysis' (COD). Available at: http://www.sociol.unimi.it/papers/2012-04-19_G.%20Carbone%20e%20V.%20Memoli.pdf

Carnegie Papers. 2006. 'Reform in Syria: Steering between the Chinese Model and Regime Change', no. 69, July

Carothers, Thomas. 2002. 'The End of the Transition Paradigm', *Journal of Democracy*, 13 (2002), pp. 6–7

Carothers, Thomas. 2015. 'Democracy Aid at 25: Time to Choose', *Journal of Democracy* 26:1, 60–76

Casey, Katherine, Glennerster, Rachel and Miguel, Edward. 2011. 'Reshaping Institutions: Evidence on Aid Impacts Using a Pre-analysis Plan', Abdul Latif Jameel Poverty Action Lab Working Paper, MIT: Cambridge, MA

Central Bureau of Statistics (CBS). 2011. *The 5th Population Census*. Khartoum: CBS

Central Bureau of Statistics (CBS). 2010a. *Key Findings: National Baseline Household Survey 2009*. Khartoum: CBS

Central Bureau of Statistics (CBS). 2010b. *Poverty in Northern Sudan: Estimates from the NBHS 2009*. Khartoum: CBS

Chai, Winberg. 2006. *Saudi Arabia: A Modern Reader*. Indianapolis, IN: University of Indianapolis Press

Chaib, Andre. 1979. 'The Export Performance of a Small Open Developing Economy: The Lebanese Experience, 1951–1974', unpublished PhD thesis, University of Michigan

Chamie, Joseph. 1977. *Religion and Population Dynamics in Lebanon*. Ann Arbor: University of Michigan, Population Studies Centre

Chaney, Eric. 2012. 'Democratic Change in the Arab World, Past and Present', unpublished mimeo, Department of Economics, Harvard University, March

Cheibub, Jose Antonio and Gandhi, Jennifer. 2004. 'Classifying Political Regimes: A Six-Fold Measure of Democracies and Dictatorships', Paper read at American Political Science Association, 2–5 September, Chicago, IL

Cheibub, Jose Antonio, Przeworski, Adam, Papaterra, Neto, Fernando Papaterra Limongi and Alvarez, Michael M. 1996. 'What Makes Democracies Endure?', *Journal of Democracy* 7:1, 39–55

Chemingui, Mohamed Abdelbasset and Dessus, Sebastien. 2003. 'Non-Tariff /Barriers in Syria,' unpublished paper. Washington, DC: World Bank

Cingranelli, David and Richards, David. 2008. Cingranelli-Richards (CIRI) Human Rights Dataset 2008. Available at: www.humanrightsdata.org

Cleveland, William. 2000. *A History of the Modern Middle East.* Boulder, CO: Westview Press

Coleman, Isobel. 2012. 'Reforming Egypt's Untenable Subsidies', Council on Foreign Relations. Available at: www.cfr.org/egypt/reforming-egypts-untenable-subsidies/p27885. Accessed 11 February 2013

Collins, Robert. 2008. *A History of Modern Sudan.* Cambridge: Cambridge University Press

Concordis International. 2010. *More than a Line: Sudan's North–South Border,* September 2010. Government of Sudan, Reports on the Negotiations, 2010–12

Corm, George. 1994. 'The War System: Militia Hegemony and the Re-establishment of the State', in D. Collins (ed.), *Peace for Lebanon? From War to Reconstruction.* Boulder, CO: Lynne Reinner Publishers

Crystal, Jill. 1995. *Oil and Politics in the Gulf: Rulers and Merchants in Kuwait and Qatar.* Cambridge: Cambridge University Press.

Currie-Alder, Bruce, Kanbur, Ravi, Malone, David and Rohinton, Medhora (eds.). 2014. *International Development: Ideas, Experience, and Prospects.* Oxford: Oxford University Press. https://global.oup.com/academic/product/international-development-9780199671663?cc=ae&lang=en&

Desai, Raj, Olofsgård, Anders and Yousef, Tarik. 2009. 'The Logic of Authoritarian Bargains', *Economics & Politics* 21:1, 93–125

De Waal, Alex. 2012. 'North and South Sudan Are at War', http://africanarguments.org/2012/04/24/alex-de-waal-currently-it%E2%80%99s-war-for-north-and-south-sudan/

Dhillon, Navtej and Yousef, Tarik (eds.). 2009. *Generation in Waiting: The Unfulfilled Promise of Young People in the Middle East.* Washington, DC: Brookings Institution

Diamond, Larry. 2008. 'The Democratic Rollback', *Foreign Affairs* 87:2

Díaz, Naomi Ramirez. 2011. 'The Syrian Revolution through the Eyes of the Demonstrators', Toledo International Center for Peace, Madrid, Spain

Diwan, Ishac. 2012. 'Understanding Revolution in the Middle East: The Central Role of the Middle Class', ERF Research Working Paper # 726, The Economic Research Forum, Cairo

Doornbos, Martin and Markakis, John. 1994. 'Society and State in Crisis: What Went Wrong in Somalia?', *Review of African Political Economy* 21:59, 82–88

Doran, Michael. 2004. 'The Saudi Paradox', *Foreign Affairs* 83:1, 35–51

DRDC 2010. '5th Population and Housing Census in Sudan – An Incomplete Exercise', www.darfurcentre.ch

Eichengreen, Barry and Leblang, David. 2008. 'Democracy and Globalization', *Economics and Politics* 20:3, 289–334

El-Affendi, Abdelwahab. 2015 (ed.). *Genocidal Nightmares: Narratives of Insecurity and the Logic of Mass Atrocities*. New York: Bloomsbury Academic

El-Affendi, Abdelwahab. 2014. 'The Sectarian Menace in the Middle East: The Other "Samson Option"', Keynote Speech Delivered at the International Congress of Civilisations, Istanbul Medeniyet University, January. Available at: www.academia.edu/9034495/The_Sectarian_Menace_In_The_Middle_East_The_Other_Samson_Option_

El-Affendi, Abdelwahab. 2012a. 'A Trans-Islamic Revolution?', *Critical Muslim* 1:1, 61–84

El-Affendi, Abdelwahab. 2012b. 'Revolutionary Anatomy: The Lessons of the Sudanese Revolutions of October 1964 and April 1968', *Contemporary Arab Affairs* 5:2, 292–306

El-Affendi, Abdelwahab. 2011a. 'Constituting Liberty, Healing the Nation: Revolutionary Identity Creation in the Arab World's Delayed 1989', *Third World Quarterly* 32:7, 1255–71

El-Affendi, Abdelwahab. 2011b. 'Political Culture and the Crisis of Democracy in the Arab World', in Elbadawi and Makdisi (eds.), pp. 11–40

El-Affendi, Abdelwahab. 2010. 'The Modern Debate(s) on Islam and Democracy', in Ibrahim M. Zein (ed.), *Islam and Democracy in Malaysia: Findings from the National Dialogue*. Kuala Lumpur: Institute of Islamic Thought and Civilization (ISTAC), pp. 3–68

El-Affendi, Abdelwahab. 2002. *For a State of Peace: Conflict and the Future of Democracy in Sudan*. London: Centre for the Study of Democracy (CSD).

El-Affendi, Abdelwahab. 2013. 'Islamism and the Sudanese State after Darfur: Soft State, Failed State or "Black Hole State"?', in Sorbo, G. and Ahmed, Abdel Ghaffar (eds.), *Sudan Divided: Continuing Conflict in a Contested State* (London: Palgrave, 2013), pp. 54–69

El-Agib, Fatima O. 2011. 'Sudan's Strategic Relations with its Neighbouring States with a Special Reference to the Horn of Africa', unpublished paper presented to a conference on Sudan's Relations with Neighbouring States, organised by the Centre for African Research and Studies, International University of Africa, Khartoum, October

El Amrani, Issandr. 2012. 'Olivier Roy and Post-Islamism', *The Arabist* 7. Available at: www.arabist.net/blog/2012/1/7/olivier-roy-and-post-islamism.html

Elbadawi, Ibrahim and Makdisi, Samir. 2007. 'Explaining the Democracy Deficit in the Arab World', *Quarterly Review of Economics and Finance* 46:5, 813–31

Elbadawi, Ibrahim and Makdisi, Samir. 2012. 'Understanding Democratic Transitions in and outside the Arab World', paper presented at a Workshop on Democratic Transition in the Arab World, held at the American University of Beirut, Beirut, 28–29 September

Elbadawi, Ibrahim and Makdisi, Samir (eds.). 2011. *Democracy in the Arab World: Explaining the Deficit*. London: Routledge

Elbadawi, Ibrahim, Makdisi, Samir and Milante, Gary. 2011. 'Explaining the Arab Democracy Deficit', in Elbadawi and Makdisi (eds.), pp. 41–82

Elbadawi, Ibrahim, Schmidt-Hebbel, Klaus and Soto, Raimundo. 2011. 'Why Do Countries Have Fiscal Rules?', Paper presented at the Catholic University of Chile conference 'Economic Policy in Emerging Economies', Santiago, Chile, 27–28 October

Elbadawi, Ibrahim and Soto Raimundo. 2015. 'Resource Rents, Institutions and Violent Civil Conflicts', Defense and Peace Economics, 26: 1, 89–113

Elbadawi, Ibrahim, and Makdisi, Samir. 2014. "Understanding Democratic Transitions in the Arab World", paper presented at a workshop on Transition from Autocracy to Democracy in the Arab World, held at the American University of Beirut, 8–9 November.

El-Battahani, Atta. 1995. 'Ethnicity and Economic Development in Federal Sudan: 1989–1994', in H. M. Salih et al. (eds.), Federalism in Sudan. Khartoum: Khartoum University Press

El-Battahani, Atta. 2000. 'Economic Liberalization and Civil Society in Sudan: 1989–1995', in Kwesi K. Prah and Abel Ghaffar M. Ahmed (eds.), Africa in Transformation. OSSREA, Addis Ababa, pp. 145–160

El-Battahani, Atta. 2003. 'Political Transition in Sudan: Which Way', in Hassan Abdel Atti et al. (eds.), Civil Society Dialogue on Peace, Democracy and Development. Khartoum: Henrich Voll Foundation and National Civic Forum, pp. 175–96

El-Battahani, Atta and Woodward, Peter. 2012. 'Sudan: Political Economy and the Comprehensive Peace Agreement, in Sudan', in Mats Berdal and Dominik Zaum (eds.), Political Economy of Statebuilding: Power after Peace. London: Routledge, pp. 277–92

El-Battahani, Atta. 2016. 'Civil–Military Relations in Sudan: Negotiating Political Transition in a Turbulent Economy', in Grawert, Elke and Zeinab Abul-Magd (eds.), Businessmen in Arms: How the Military and Other Armed Groups Profit in the MENA Region. Lanham: Rowman Littlefield

El-Battahani, Atta. 2014. National Dialogue in Sudan: Past Experiences and Current Challenges. Sudan Democracy First Group (SDFG) Nairobi, Kenya

El Beblawi, Hazem. 2012. Four Months in the Government Cage. Cairo: Dar al-Shorouq

El Beblawi, Hazem. 2008. Economic Growth in Egypt: Impediments and Constraints (1974–2004). Commission on Growth and Development. Working Paper No. 14. Washington DC: World Bank

El Beblawi, Hazem and Luciani, Giacomo (eds.). 1987. The Rentier State: Nation, State and Integration of the Arab World: London: Croom Helm

El-Ghobashi, Mona. 2011. 'The Praxis of the Egyptian Revolution', Middle East Report: People Power 258, 3–6

El-Khalil, Youssef. 1996. 'Les facteurs de développement industriel dans une petite économie ouverte en voie de développement: Le secteur des biens capitaux au Liban', unpublished PhD thesis, Université d'Auvergne

El-Mahdi, Abda. 2012. 'Impact of Post-secession Economic Crisis', memo (November)

El-Mahdi, Rabab. 2011. 'Labour Protests in Egypt: Causes and Meanings', *Review of African Political Economy*, 38:129, 387–402 http://econpapers.repec.org/article/tafrevape/v_3a38_3ay_3a2011_3ai_3a129_3ap_3387-402.htm

El-Mikawy, Noha. 1999. *Consensus Building in Egypt's Transition Process*. Cairo: AUC Press

El Shimi, Rowan. 2011. 'Best of Egyptian Media Propaganda', February, Available at: rowanelshimi.wordpress.com/2011/02/20/best-of-egyptian-media-propaganda/

Epstein, David, Bates, Robert, Goldstone, Jack, Kritensen, Ida and O'Halloran, Sharyn. 2006. 'Democratic Transitions', *American Journal of Political Science* 50:3, 551–69

ESCWA Working Paper E/ESCWA/ECRI/2014/WP.1, November 2014 'Beyond Governance and Conflict: Measuring the Impact of the Neighborhood Effect in the Arab Region'. Available at: www.escwa.un.org/divisions/ecri_editor/Download .asp?table_name=ecri_documents&field_name=id&FileID=272

Estrin, Saul. 2005. 'Developing the Private Sector in Kuwait'. Kuwait Institute for Scientific Research, unpublished report

European Union. 2012. Rapport de Diagnostic sur la Société Civile Tunisienne. March

Faria, Hugo, Montesinos-Yufa, Hugo and Morales, Daniel. 2014. 'Should the Modernization Hypothesis Survive Acemoglu, Johnson, Robinson, and Yared? Some More Evidence', *Economics Journal Watch* at econjwatch.org

Fearon, James D. 2004. 'Why Do Some Civil Wars Last So Much Longer than Others?', *Journal of Peace Research* 41:3, 275–301

Filiu, Jean-Pierre. 2015. *From Deep State to Islamic State*. Oxford: Oxford University Press

Fish, Steven. 2005. *Democracy Derailed in Russia*. New York: Cambridge University Press

Forum Euroméditerranéen des Instituts de Sciences Économiques (FEMISE) 2011, Annual Report

Galal, Ahmed. 2003. 'Social Expenditure and the Poor in Egypt'. Working Paper No. 89. Cairo: ECES

Gallab, Abdullahi. 2008. *The First Islamist Republic: Development and Disintegration of Islamism in the Sudan*. Aldershot: Ashgate

Gallopin, Jean-Baptiste. 2015. 'Machiavelli in the Twenty-First Century: Sudanese Security Leaks in Perspective', *Jadaliyya*, 2 February. Available at: www .jadaliyya.com/pages/index/20721/machiavelli-in-the-twenty-first-century_ sudanese-s

Gandhi, Jennifer and Przeworski, Adam. 2007. 'Authoritarian Institutions and the Survival of Autocrats', *Comparative Political Studies* 40: 1279–301

Gates, Scott, et al. 2012. 'Democratic Waves? Global Patterns of Democratization, 1800–2000', PRIO Working Paper. Available at: http://aca demic.research.microsoft.com/Paper/11278020.aspx

Gellner, Ernest. 1994. *Conditions of Liberty: Civil Society and Its Rivals*. London: Allen Lane

General Auditor. 2014. General Auditor addressing the Parliament in Sudan, Parliamentary Records, October 2014

Geopolicity. 2011. 'Rethinking the Arab Spring: A Roadmap for G20/UN Support'. October

Ghabra, Shafeeq. 1991. 'Voluntary Associations in Kuwait: The Foundation of a New System', *Middle East Journal* 45:2, 199–215

Ghazouani, Kamel. 2011. 'Evaluation des incitations à l'investissement privé'. Institut Arabe des Chefs d'Entreprises. Tunis

Ghalioun, Burhan and Costopoulos, Philip J. 2004. 'The Persistence of Arab Authoritarianism', *Journal of Democracy* 15:4, 126–32

Ghoneim, Wael. 2012. *Revolution 2.0.* Cairo: Dar al-Shorouq

Giavazzi, Francesco and Tabellini, Guido. 2005. 'Economic and Political Liberalizations', *Journal of Monetary Economics* 52, 1297–30

Giugale, Marcelo. 2012. 'Analysis of the Likely Economic and Social Impact of the Shutdown of Oil in South Sudan', March. Available at: www.sudantribune.com/IMG/pdf/WB_SS_Analysis.pdf

Giuliano, Paola, Prachi, Mishra and Spilimbergo, Antonio. 2010. 'Democracy and Reforms: Evidence from a New Dataset'. IMF Working Paper WP/10/173

Gleditsch, Kristian and Choung, Jinhee. 2004. 'Autocratic Transitions and Democratization', a paper presented at the 45th Annual Meeting of the International Studies Association, March, Montreal, Quebec

Gleditsch, Kristian and Ward, Michael. 2006. 'Diffusion and the International Context of Democratization', *International Organization* 60:4, 911–34

Government of Sudan. 1955/56. First Population Census, Department of Statistics, Khartoum

Gurr, Ted Robert, Marshall, Monty G. and Jaggers, Keith. 2010. Polity IV Project: Political Regime Characteristics and Transitions, 1800–2010. Dataset. Available at: www.systemicpeace.org/polity/polity4.htm

Haber, Stephen and Menaldo, Victor. 2011. *American Political Science Review* 105:1, 1–26

Haddad, Bassam. 2012. 'Syria, the Arab Uprisings, and the Political Economy of Authoritarian Resilience', *Interface* 4:1, 113–30

Hadenius, Axel and Teorell. Jan. 2007. 'Pathways from Authoritarianism', *Journal of Democracy*, 18:1, 143–56

Hamdan, Kamal. 1997. *Le conflit Libanais: Communautés religieuses, classes sociales, et identité Nationale.* Paris: Garnet

Hamdy, Naila. and Gomaa, Ehab. 2012. 'Framing the Egyptian Uprising in Arabic Language Newspapers and Social Media', *Journal of Communication* 62:2, 195–211

Hamilton, Kirk and Ruta, Giovanni. 2008. 'Wealth Accounting, Exhaustible Resources and Social Welfare', *Environmental Resource Economics* 42, 53–64. Published online

Ḥammūdah, Adil. 1995. *Adil Hammudah yuhawir Muhammad Hasanayn Haykal.* Cairo: Shorouk

Huntington, Samuel. 1991. 'Democracy's Third Wave', *Journal of Democracy*, 2 (1991), pp. 12–14

Hanieh, Adam. 2011. *Capitalism and Class in the Gulf Arab States.* New York: Palgrave Macmillan

Harir, Sharif Harir and Tvedt, Terje (eds.). 1994. *Short-Cut to Decay: The Case of Sudan*. Uppsala: Nordiska Afrikainstitutet

Hartshorn, Ian M. 2013. 'Worker's Revolutions and Worker's Constitutions: Egypt and Tunisia in Comparison'. Available at: www.sas.upenn.edu/dcc/sites/www.sas.upenn.edu.dcc/files/uploads/HartshornPennDCC.pdf

Khair El-Din, Haseeb. 2013. 'The Arab Spring Revisited', in Khair El-Din Haseeb (ed.), *The Arab Spring: Critical Analyses*. Centre for Arab Unity Studies. London and New York: Routledge, pp. 4–16

Hashem, Amr and El-Mikawy, Noha. 2002. 'Business Parliamentarians as Locomotives of Information and Production of Knowledges', in Noha El-Mikawy and Heba Handoussa (eds.), *Institutional Reform and Economic Development in Egypt*. Cairo: American University Press, pp. 49–60

Henry, Clement and Springborg, Robert. 2001. *Globalization and the Politics of Development in the Middle East*. Cambridge: Cambridge University Press

Herb, Michael. 1999. *All in the Family: Absolutism, Revolution, and Democracy in the Middle Eastern Monarchies*. Albany: State University of New York Press

Herzog, Christoph and Sharif, Malek (eds.). 2010. *The First Ottoman Experiment in Democracy*. Wurzburg: Ergon Velag

Heydemann, Steven. 2004. *Networks of Privilege in the Middle East: The Politics of Economic Reform*. London: Palgrave, MacMillan

Hibou, Beatrice, Meddeb, Hamza and Hamdi, Mohamed. 2011. 'Tunisia after 14 January and Its Social and Political Economy: The Issues at Stake in a Reconfiguration of European Policy'. Euro-Mediterranean Human Rights Network. June

Hinnebusch, Raymond. 2012. 'Syria: From "Authoritarian Upgrading" to Revolution?', *International Affairs* 88:1, 95–113

Hinnebusch, Raymond. 2006. 'Authoritarian Persistence, Democratization Theory and the Middle East: An Overview and Critique', *Democratization* 13:3 June, 373–95

Hon, Kristina Marie. 2013. 'Oil as a Silent Factor in the Responses to the Arab Spring Uprisings', *Student Scholarship* Paper 351

Hourani, Albert. 1962. *Arabic Thought in the Liberal Age, 1798–1939*, Cambridge University Press

Howard, Marc Morjie and Roessler, Philip. 2006. 'Liberalizing Electoral Outcomes in Competitive Authoritarian Regimes', *American Journal of Political Science* 50:2, 365–81

Hudson, Michael. 1977. *Arab Politics: The Search for Legitimacy*. New Haven, CT: Yale University Press

Human Rights Watch. 2010. 'Sudan Flawed Elections Underscore Need for Justice'. Available at: www.hrw.org.

Huntington, Samuel. 1991. *The Third Wave: Democratization in the Late Twentieth Century*. Norman: University of Oklahoma Press

Hurwicz, Leonid. 1950. 'Least-Squares Bias in Time Series', in Tjalling C. Koopmans (ed.), *Statistical Inference in Dynamic Economic Models*. New York: Wiley, pp. 365–83

Ibrahim, Abdullahi Ali. 2011. 'Inglab 19 Yulu 1971: min Yawmiyyat al-Tahari illa Rihab al-Tarikh (19 July coup d'etat: from Interrogation Diary to History Records)'. Available at: www.sudanile.com/index.php?option=com_content&view=article&id=30456:c1-Ab2C&catid=56&Itemid=55

Ibrahim, Saad Eddin. 1982. *The New Arab Social Order: A Study of the Social Impact of Oil Wealth*. Boulder, CO: Westview Press

Ibrahim, Saad Eddin. 2004. 'An Open Door', *The Wilson Quarterly* 28:2, 36–46

Idzalika, Rajius, Martinez-Zarzzoso, Immaculada and Kneib, Thomas. 2015. 'The Effect of Income on Democracy Revisited: A Flexible Distributional Approach', Georg August Universitat Gottingen, Discussion Papers, No. 247, June

ILO-World Bank. 2010. The Challenge of Informality in MENA. Promoting Job Quality and Productive Employment in the Middle East and North Africa: What Works? Turin: October. Available at: siteresources.worldbank.org/INT LM/Resources/390041-1141141801

ILO. 2011. Statistical Update on Employment in Informal Economy. Dept. of Statistics. June, PDF

International Monetary Fund (IMF). 2013. Sudan Country Report

Information International. 2007. *Iimonthly*. No. 56, February–March

Inglehart, Ronald and Welzel, Christian. 2009. 'How Development Leads to Democracy: What We Know About Modernization', *Foreign Affairs*, March/April: 33–48.

Institut Arabe des Chefs d'Entreprises. 2013. Les effets de perturbations post révolution sur la croissance économique. Tunis, October. www.iace.tn/articles/les-effets-des-perturbations-post-revolution-sur-la-croissance-economique/)

Institut National de la Statistique. 2012a. *Premiers résultats de l'enquête nationale sur le budget, la consommation et le niveau de vie des ménages en 2010*. Tunis

Institut National de la Statistique. 2012b. *Enquête Population et Emploi 2012*. Tunis

International Monetary Fund (IMF). 2006. *Selected Issues: Syria*. Washington, DC: IMF

International Monetary Fund (IMF). *World Economic Outlook*, various issues. Washington, DC: IMF

IRFED (Institut International de Recherche et de Formation en vue du Développement integral et harmonisé). 1962. *Besoins et possibilités de développement du Liban*. 2 vols. Beirut: Ministry of Planning, Lebanese Republic

Ismail, Omer. 2015. 'The Many Faces of al-Bashir: Sudan's Persian Gulf Power Games', Enough Team, 3 June. Available at: www.enoughproject.org/blogs/new-report-many-faces-al-bashir

Jamal, Amaney A. and Robbins, Michael. 2015. 'Social Justice and the Arab Uprisings', Issam Faris Institute for Public Policy and International Affairs, American University of Beirut, Working Paper 31, April, 2–22

Jessop, Bob. 1983. 'Capitalism and Democracy: The Best Possible Political Shell', in David Held (ed.), *States and Societies*. Oxford: Martin Robertson and The Open University, pp. 272–89

Kabbani, Nader and Kamel, Noura. 2009. 'Tapping into the Potential of Young Syrians during a Time of Transition', in Dhillon and Tarik (eds.), pp. 189–210

Kandil, Magda. 2012. Reforms of Public Finance in Egypt: Energy Subsidies in Egypt. Meeting on Price Subsidies in Egypt: Alternatives for Reform. Cairo: ECES. PowerPoint presentation. Available at: http://www.eces.org.eg/Media Files/events/%7B219C5298-73DE-43DD-9260-4E7E82E04D5E%7D_Subs idies%20Pres%20_1Feb_En.pdf

Kapstein, Ethan and Converse, Nathan. 2008. 'Why Democracies Fail', *Journal of Democracy* 19: 4, 57–68

Kursany, Ibrahim and Kameir, Wathig. 1986. 'Corruption as a Fifth Factor of Production', Discussion Paper, Development Studies and Research Centre, University of Khartoum

Kassir, Samir. 2003. *Histoire de Beyrouth*. Paris: Librairie Arthème Fayard

Kearney, Norman and Kubursi, Atif. 2015. 'Democracy in the Arab World: Lessons from Abroad', Working Paper prepared for the project on 'Transition from Autocracy to Democracy in the Arab World' housed at the Institute of Financial Economics, the American University of Beirut, July

Kedourie, Elie. 1992. *Democracy and Arab Culture*. Washington, DC: Washington Institute for Near East Policy, reprinted 1994; London: Frank Cass and Company

Kerr, Malcom. 2007. *The Arab Cold War 1958–1964: A Study of Ideology in Politics*. London: Oxford University Press

Khalid, Mansour. 1990. *The Government They Deserve: The Role of the Elite in Sudan's Political Evolution*. London and New York: Kegan Paul International

Khamees, Akram. 2012. *Thawrat Jil Ultrass*. Cairo: Arab Organization for Human Rights

Khondk, Habibul Haque. 2011. 'Role of the New Media in the Arab Spring', *Globalizations* 8:5, 675–67

Kienle, Eberhard. 2001. *A Grand Delusion: Democracy and Economic Reform in Egypt*. I.B. Tauris Publishers: London, New York

Kuru, Ahmet T. and Stepan, Alfred. 2012. *Democracy, Islam, and Secularism in Turkey (Religion, Culture, and Public Life)*. New York: Columbia University Press

Lam, Ricky and Wantchekon, Leonard. 1999. Political Dutch Disease. Working Paper. Available at: www.nyu.edu/gsas/dept/politics/faculty/wantchekon/research/Ir-04-10.pdf

Lebanon, Central Administration of Statistics. 2012. 'Education in Lebanon'. Available at: www.cas.gov.lb

Lebanon, Central Administration of Statistics. 2009. 'The Multiple Indicators Cluster Survey'. Available at: www.cas.gov.lb

Lebanon, Central Administration of Statistics. 2007. 'Population and Housing in Lebanon'. Available at: www.cas.gov.lb

Lebanon, Presidency of the Council of Ministers. 2010. 'Economic Accounts of Lebanon 1997–2009'. Available at: www.cas.gov.lb/index.php/national-accounts-en

Lebanon, Central Administration of Statistics, Ministry of Planning (PAL). 1972. *L'Enquête par Sondage sur la Population Active du Liban*, November 1970, vol. 2, Beirut

Leenders, Reinoud. 2012. *The Spoils of Truce: Corruption and State-Building in Postwar Lebanon*. Ithaca, NY: Cornell University Press

Levitsky, Steven and Way, Lucan A. 2002. 'The Rise of Competitive Authoritarianism', *Journal of Democracy*, 13:2, 51–65

Lijphart, Arend. 1969. 'Consociational Democracy', *World Politics*, 21:2, 207–25

Linz, Juan. 1990. 'Transition to Democracy', *The Nairobi Law Monthly*, 27 (1990), 33

Lipset, Seymour. 1959. 'Some Social Pre-requisites of Democracy: and Economic Development and Political Legitimacy', *American Political Science Review* 53:1, 69–105

Luciani, Giacomo. 1987. 'Allocation Versus Production States: A Theoretical Framework', in Hazem Beblawi and Giacomo Luciani (eds.), *The Rentier State*. London: Croom Helm

Lust-Okar, Ellen. 2006. 'Syria: Prospects for Reform', lecture given on 27 April. Available at: kb.osu.edu/dspace/bitstream/handle/1811/30188/1/Ellen%20Lust-Okar%204-27-06.pdf

Macewan, Arthur. 2001. *Neo-Liberalism or Democracy: Economic Strategy, Markets, and Alternatives for the 21st Century*. London: Pluto Press

Mahmoud, Fatima N. 1984. *The Sudanese Bourgeoisie: Vanguard of Development*. London and Khartoum: Zed Press and Khartoum University Press

Maitre, Benjamin R. 2009. 'What Sustains Internal Wars? The Dynamics of Violent Conflict and State Weakness in Sudan', *Third World Quarterly* 30, 53–68

Makdisi, Samir. 2015. 'On Transition, Democracy and Socio-economic Justice in the Arab World', Institute of Financial Economics, Lecture and Working Paper Series, no. 1

Makdisi, Samir. 2011. 'Autocracies, Democratization and Development in the Arab Region', in *Politics and Economic Development, Selected Papers from Economic Research Forum Annual Conference*, Antalya. Turkey, March

Makdisi, Samir. 2004. *The Lessons of Lebanon, the Economics of War and Development*. London: I.B. Tauris

Makdisi, Samir, Kiwan, Fadia and Marktanner, Marcus. 2011. 'Lebanon: The Constrained Democracy and Its National Impact', in I. Elbadawi and S. Makdisi (eds.), pp. 115–41

Makdisi, Samir and Sadaka, Richard. 2005. 'The Lebanese Civil War, 1975–1990', in P. Collier and N. Sambanis (eds.), *Understanding Civil War: Evidence and Analysis, Vol 2*. Washington, DC: World Bank, pp. 59–85

Makdisi, Ussama. 2000. *The Culture of Sectarianism, Community, History and Violence in Nineteenth-Century Ottoman Lebanon*. Los Angeles: University of California Press

Maoz, Zeev. 1985. 'The Evolution of Syrian Power, 1947–1984', in Moshe Maoz and Avner Yaniv (eds.), *Syria Under Assad*. London: Croom Helm, pp. 69–82

Marshall, Monty, Jagger, Keith and Gurr, Ted Robert. 2010. 'Polity IV Project. Political Regime Characteristics and Transitions'. Dataset Users' Manual

Marshall, Monty, Gurr, Ted Robert and Jaggers, Keith. 2014. *Polity IV Project Dataset Users' Manual: Political Regime Characteristics and Transitions: 1800–2013*. Center for Systemic Peace, www.systemicpeace.org/polity/polity4.htm

Maseland, Robert and Van Hoorn, André. 2011. 'Why Muslims Like Democracy yet Have so Little of It', *Public Choice*, Springer, 147(3), 481–96, June

Masetti, Olivier, Körner, Kevin, Forster, Magdalena and Friedman, Jacob. 2013. Two Years of Arab Spring: Where Are We Now? What's Next? Frankfurt-am-Main: Deutsche Bank AG DB Research, 25 January

Mazrui, Ali. 1993. 'Islam and the End of History', *The American Journal of Islamic Social Sciences* 10:4, 528–30

Mitchell, Timothy. 2002. *Rule of Experts: Egypt, Techno-politics, Modernity.* London: University of California Press

Ministry of Finance and National Economy (MFNE). 2011. *Sudan: Interim Poverty Reduction Strategy Paper.* Khartoum

Ministry of Finance and National Economy (MFNE). 2010. *Budget Proposal for the Financial Year 2010.* Khartoum

Ministry of Regional Development. 2011. 'Le Livre Blanc'. Tunisia

Mishler, William and Rose, Richard. 2001. 'What Are the Origins of Political Trust?: Testing Institutional and Cultural Theories in Post-communist Societies', *Comparative Political Studies* 34:1, 30–62

Mkandawire, Thandika and Soludo, Charles. 1999. *Our Continent, Our Future: African Perspectives on Structural Adjustment.* Dakar: CODESRIA

Mohieddin, Mohamed. 2011. 'Social Policies and Poverty in Egypt'. The Second Arab Development Challenges Report. Vol. 2: Country Case-Studies. Background paper. Cairo: UNDP

Mukand, Sharun, and Rodrik, Dani. 2015. 'The Political Economy of Liberal Democracy'. Manuscript

Munck, Gerardo L. 1994. 'Democratic Transitions in Comparative Perspective' *Comparative Politics* 26:3, 355–75

Munck, Geraldo and Verkuilen, J. 2002. 'Conceptualizing and Measuring Democracy Evaluating Alternative Indices', *Comparative Political Studies* 35:1, 5–34

Nabli, Mustapha K and Silva-Jauregui, Carlos, 2007. 'Democracy for Better Governance and Higher Economic Growth in the MENA Region?', chapter 5 in Mustapha Nabli, *Breaking the Barriers to Higher Economic Growth, Better Governance and Deeper Reforms in the Middle East and North Africa*, The World Bank, pp 103–133

Nassar, Heba. 2011. Growth, Employment Policies and Economic Linkages: Egypt. Employment Sector Employment Working Paper No. 85. Geneva: ILO

Nasr, Vali. 2009. *The Rise of the New Muslim Middle Class and What it Will Mean for Our World.* New York: Free Press

Nehmeh, Adib. *Al-Fiqr fi Madīnat Tarāblus, al-Kitāb al-Awal.* Lebanon: ESCWA, 2010. http://css.escwa.org.lb/ECR I/Docs/UNTripolibook1

Nickell, Stephen. 1981. 'Biases in Dynamic Models with Fixed Effects', *Econometrica* 49, 1417–26

North Douglas, Wallis, John and Weingast, Barry. 2009. *Violence and Social Orders: A Conceptual Framework for Interpreting Recorded Human History.* Cambridge: Cambridge University Press

Osman, Mohamed Mahjoub. 1998. *al-Jayshwa al-Siyasa fi al-Sudan (The Army and Politics in Sudan).* Cairo: Sudanese Studies Centre

Osman, Tarek. 2006. 'Mahfouz's Grave, Arab Liberalism's Deathbed', openDemocracy, November. Available at: www.opendemocracy.net/conflict middle_east_politics/egypt_mahfouz_4025.jsp

Ottaway, Marina and Muasher, Marwan. 2011. *Arab Monarchies' Chance for Reform, Yet Unmet*. Washington, DC: Carnegie Endowment for International Peace

Owen, Roger. 1988. 'The Economic History of Lebanon, 1943–1974: Its Salient Features', in H. Barakat (ed.), *Toward a Viable Lebanon*. London: Croom Helm, pp. 27–41

Paleologou, Suzanna-Maria. 2015. 'Income and Democracy: The Modernization Hypothesis Re-visited Via Alternative Non-linear Models', *Empirical Economics* 48:2, 909–21

Paltseva, Elena. 2010. Autocracy, Democratization and the Resource. Available at: www.paltseva.com/rev_oct2010.pdf

Pamir, Peri. 1997. 'Nationalism, Ethnicity and Democracy: Contemporary Manifestations', *The International Journal of Peace Studies* 2:2. Available at: www.gmu.edu/programs/icar/ijps/vol2_2/pamir.htm

Paxton, Pamela. 2000. 'Women's Suffrage in the Measurement of Democracy: Problems of Operationalization', *Studies in Comparative International Development* 35:3, 92–111

Pease, Bob. 2010. *Undoing Privilege: Unearned Advantage in a Divided World*. London: Zed Books

Pew Forum on Religion & Public Life. 2009. Global Restrictions on Religion. Washington DC: Pew Research Center, December

Picard, Elizabeth. 1996. *Lebanon, a Shattered Country*. New York: Holmes and Meier

Pickering, Jeffrey and Kisangani, Emizet N. F. 2006. 'Political, Economic, and Social Consequences of Foreign Military Intervention', *Political Research Quarterly* 59, 363–76

Poast, Paul and Urpelainen, Johannes. 2015. 'How International Organizations Support Democratization: Preventing Authoritarian Reversals or Promoting Consolidation?', *World Politics* 67:1, 72–113

Polity IV Project: Political Regime Characteristics and Transitions, 1800–2014. Dataset. Available at: www.systemicpeace.org/polity/polity4.htm

Prazauskas, Algis. 1998. 'Ethnicity, Nationalism and Politics', ISS Working paper, International Institute of Social Studies of Erasmus University (ISS), The Hague

Pronk, Jan. 2006. 'Current Situation in Sudan'. Available at: www.un.org/press/en/2006/sc8607.doc.htm

Prunier, Gerard and Gisselquist, Rachel M. 2003. 'The Sudan: A Successfully Failed State', in Robert I. Rotberg (ed.), *State Failure and State Weakness in a Time of Terror*. Washington DC: Brookings Institution Press, pp. 101–27

Przeworski, Adam. 2009. 'The Mechanics of Regime Instability in Latin America', *Journal of Politics in Latin America* 1, 5–36

Przeworski, Adam. 2004. 'Economic Development and Transitions to Democracy', unpublished paper

Przeworski, Adam (ed.). 1995. *Sustainable Democracy*. Cambridge: Cambridge University Press

Przeworski, Adam, Alvarez, Michael, Cheibub, Jose Antonio and Limongi, Fernando. 2000. *Democracy and Development: Political Institutions and Well-Being in the World, 1950–1990*. New York: Cambridge University Press

Putnam, Robert. 1993. *Making Democracy Work: Civic Transitions in Modern Italy*. Princeton, NJ: Princeton University Press

Quinn, Dennis. 2000. 'Democracy and International Financial Liberalization', mimeo, Washington, DC: Georgetown University

Rabie, Amr Hashem. 2012. *Entekhabat Majlis Al-Sha'b 2011/2012*. (*The People's Assembly Elections of 2011/2012*). Cairo: Al-Ahram Center for Political and Strategic Studies

Ramadan, Tarek. 2012. *The Arab Awakening: Islam and the New Middle East*. London: Allen Lane

Ratta, Donatella Della. 2012. 'Dramas of the Authoritarian State', Middle East Report Online, February. Available at: www.merip.org/mero/interventions/dra mas-authoritarian-state

Reid, Donald M. 1982. 'Arabic Thought in the Liberal Age Twenty Years After', *International Journal of Middle East Studies* 14:4, 541–57

Republic of South Sudan. 2012. Presidential Statement on the Current Crisis, 13 April

Rodrik. Dani. 2000. 'Institutions for High Quality Growth: What They Are and How to Acquire Them', National Bureau of Economic Research, February

Rodrik, Dani and Wacziarg, Romain. 2005. 'Do Democratic Transitions Produce Bad Economic Outcomes?' *American Economic Review Papers and Proceedings* 95:2, 50–55.

Roessler, Philip. 2011. 'Political Instability, Threat Displacement and Civil War: Darfur as a Theory Building Case' (1 August). Available at: ssrn.com/abstrac t=1909228 or dx.doi.org/10.2139/ssrn.1909228

Roessler, Philip. 2011. 'The Enemy Within: Personal Rule, Coups, and Civil War in Africa', *World Politics* 63:2, 300–46

Ross, Michael. 2015. 'What Have We Learned about the Resource Curse?', *Annual Review of Political Science* 18, 239–59

Ross, Michael. 2009. 'Oil and Democracy Revisited', unpublished mimeo. Los Angeles, CA: UCLA Department of Political Science, March

Ross, Michael. 2008. 'But Seriously: Does Oil Really Hinder Democracy?', unpublished mimeo, Los Angeles, CA: UCLA Department of Political Science, March

Rothstein, Bo and Broms, Rasmus. 2011. 'Why No Democracy in the Arab-Muslim World? The Importance of Temple Financing', paper given at the Annual Meeting of the American Political Science Association, Seattle, WA

Roy, Olivier. 2012. 'The Transformation of the Arab World', *Journal of Democracy* 23:3, 5–18

Rustow, Dankwart. 1963. 'The Military in Middle Eastern Society and Politics', in Sydney Nettleton Fisher (ed.), *The Military in the Middle East: Problems in Society and Government*. Columbus: Ohio State University Press

Sacks, Jeffrey. 2012. 'Reply to Acemoglu and Robinson's Response to My Book Review', December. Available at: jeffsachs.org/2012/12/reply-to-acemoglu-and-robinsons-response-to-my-book-review/

Sader, Emir. 2012. Latin American Critical Thought: Theory and Practice, compiled by Alberto L. Bialakowsky. Ciudad Autónoma de Buenos Aires: CLACSO

Safadi, Raed, Munro, Laura and Ziadeh, Radwan. 2011. 'Syria: The Underpinnings of Autocracy – Conflict, Oil and the Curtailment of Economic Freedom', in Elbadawi and Makdisi (eds.), pp. 142–64

Sahal, Ibrahim G. 2000. 'Pauperisation of the Middle Class in Sudan: Adjustments to Structural Adjustments', in Kwesi K. Prah and Abel Ghaffar M. Ahmed (eds.), Africa in Transformation. Addis Ababa: OSSREA, pp. 145–60.

Said, Rosemarie. 1998. The Making of the Modern Gulf States: Kuwait, Bahrain, Qatar, the United Arab Emirates, and Oman. Reading, NY: Ithaca Press

Sajoo, Amyn. 2012. 'A Win for "Secularists" in Libya? It's not What You Think', Christian Science Monitor, July. Available at: www.csmonitor.com/Commentar y/Opinion/2012/0719/A-win-for-secularists-in-Libya-It-s-not-what-you-think

Salamé, Ghassan. (ed.). 1994. Democracy Without Democrats: The Renewal of Politics in the Muslim World. London: I.B. Tauris

Salem, Paul. 2007. Kuwait: Politics in a Participatory Emirate. Carnegie Papers, 3. Washington, DC: Carnegie Endowment for International Peace

Salih, Mahgoub M. 2001. 'The Outstanding Issues and the Future of North–South Relations', unpublished article (Arabic), March

Salih, M. A. Mohamed and Harir, Sharif. 1994. 'Tribal Militias: The Genesis of National Disintegration', in Sharif Harir and Terje Tvedt (eds.), Short-Cut to Decay: The Case of the Sudan. Uppsala: Nordic Africa Institute, pp. 186–203

Salih, M. A. Mohamed. 2003. African Political Parties: Evolution, Institutionalization and Governance. London: Pluto Press

Satti, Nureldin. 2012. 'Quo valid: Sudan at Crossroads', in United We Stand, Divided We Fall, the Sudan after the Split, Working Group Series Paper 2, Washington, DC: Wilson Centre

Schmidinger, Thomas. 2009. 'Tyrants and Terrorists: Reflections on the Connection Between Totalitarianism, Neo-liberalism, Civil War and the Failure of the State in Iraq and Sudan', Civil Wars 11:3, 359–79

Schmitter, C. Philippe. 2010. 'Twenty-Five Years, Fifteen Findings', Journal of Democracy 21:1, 17–28

Seale, Patrick. 1990. Assad of Syria, the Struggle for the Middle East. Berkeley: University of California Press

Sen, Amartya. 1992. Inequality Reexamined. Oxford University Press.

Shafik, Nemat. 1995. Claiming the Future: Choosing Prosperity in the Middle East and North Africa. Washington, DC: World Bank

Sidahmed, Alsir. 2013. The Oil Years in Sudan. Khartoum: Madarik Publishing House

Sinkainga, A. Alawad. 1980. 'Sudan Defense Force', unpublished MA dissertation, Institute for Afro-Asian Studies, University of Khartoum

Slocum, Brian. 'The Left and the Workers Movement in Egypt's Democratic Revolutions', Available at: www.thenorthstar.info/?p=7986

Soroush, Abdolkarim. 2002. *Reason, Freedom and Democracy in Islam: Essential Writings of Abdolkarim Soroush*, translated with a critical introduction by Mahmoud Sadri and Ahmad Sadri. New York: Oxford University Press

Spinks, Todd., Sahliyeh, Emile. and Calfano, Brian. 2008. 'The Status of Democracy and Human Rights in the Middle East: Does Regime Type Make a Difference?', *Democratization* 15:2, 321–41

Stampini, Marco and Verdier-Chouchane, Audrey. 2011. 'Labour Market Dynamics in Tunisia: The Issue of Youth Unemployment'. Working Paper no 123. African Development Bank. February

Strand, Havard, Hegre, Havard, Gates, Scott and Dahl, Marianne. 2012. 'Democratic Waves? Global Patterns of Democratization, 1816–2008', unpublished mimeo. Oslo: Center for the Study of Civil War, PRIO

Sudanese Government. 2006. *Constitutions of Sudan; 1953–1998.* Khartoum: Council of Ministers General Secretariat

Taisier, Mohamed Ahmed Ali. 1990. *The Cultivation of Hunger.* Khartoum: Khartoum University Press

Taisier, Mohamed Ahmed Ali, 2014, Personal communication

Tanneberg, Dag, Stefes, Christopher and Merkel, Wolfgang. 2013. 'Hard Times and Regime Failure: Autocratic Responses to Economic Downturns', *Contemporary Politics*, 19:1 (2013), pp. 115–29

Tétreault, Mary Ann. 2011. 'The Winter of the Arab Spring in the Gulf Monarchies', *Globalizations* 8:5, 629–37

Tétreault, Mary Ann and Al-Mughni, Haya. 1995. 'Gender, Citizenship and Nationalism in Kuwait', *British Journal of Middle Eastern Studies* 22:1–2, 64–80

The Comprehensive Peace Agreement between the Government of the Republic of the Sudan and SPLM/A. Nairobi, 9 January 2005

Therborn, Goran. 1977. 'The Rule of Capital and the Rise of Democracy', *New Left Review* 103, 3–41. Reprinted in David Held (ed.), *States and Societies.* London: The Open University

The Economist. 2015. https://ecolearnings.wordpress.com/2015/04/17/econo mist-4172015/. May 2015

The Syrian Centre for Policy Research. 2013. 'Socioeconomic Impact and Roots of the Syrian Crisis', January

Tilly, Charles. 1975. *The Foundation of National States in Western Europe.* Princeton, NJ: Princeton University Press

Ulfelder, Jay. 2007. 'Natural Resource Wealth and the Survival of Autocracies', *Comparative Political Studies* 40:8, 995–1018

Ulfelder, Jay and Lustik, Michael. 2005. 'Modeling Transitions to and from Democracy', Prepared for delivery at the 2005 Annual Meeting of the American Political Science Association, 1–4 September

Umbadda, Sidig. 1990. 'Education and Mismanagement of Sudanese Economy and Society', Discussion paper no. 83, Development Studies and Research Centre, University of Khartoum

UNCTAD. 2011. World Investment Report 2011. Geneva, Switzerland

United Nations Development Program (UNDP). 2012. The New Civicus Civil Social Index Rapid Assessment tool. February

UNDP. 2011. Pathways to Democratic Transitions 5–6 June

UNDP. 2008. Poverty, Growth and Income Distribution in Lebanon

Van Hoorn, André and Maseland, Robert. 2013. 'Does a Protestant Work Ethic Exist? Evidence from the Well-Being Effect of Unemployment', *Journal of Economic Behavior & Organization*, Elsevier, 91(C), 1–12.

World Bank Database, World Development Indicators, 2014

UNDP/INP. 2005. Egypt Human Development Report, 2005. Cairo: UNDP. Available at: hdr.undp.org/sites/default/files/egypt_2005_en.pdf

UNDP. 1998. *Lebanon: National Human Development Report*

United Nations High Commissioner for Refugees (UNHCR)

United Nations Office for the Coordination of Humanitarian Affairs (UNOCHA)

UN Security Council. 2012. 'Resolution 2046 (2012) on Sudan & South Sudan'. New York, 5 May

USAID. 2014. Sudan – Complex Emergency, FACT SHEET #6, FISCAL YEAR (FY) 2014. Available at: www.usaid.gov/sites/default/files/documents/1866/sudan_ce_fs06_09-30-2014.pdf

Valbjørn, Morten and Bank, André. 2007. 'Signs of a New Arab Cold War: The 2006 Lebanon War and the Sunni-Shi'i Divide', *Middle East Report* 242, 6–11

Vujčić, Boris. 2012. 'Transition Experiences in Eastern Europe, Any Lessons to be Learned?', PowerPoint presentation at a panel titled: 'The Road to Democracy: the Arab Region, Latin America and Eastern Europe Compared', organised by AUB and GDN, 18 May at AUB

Wahba, Jackline. 2009. 'The Impact of Labour Market Reforms on Informality in Egypt. Gender and Work in The MENA Region' Working Paper Series, No. 3. Cairo: The Population Council

Wahba, Jackline. 2000. 'Informality in Egypt: Stepping Stone or a Dead End?' Working Paper #456, Cairo: Economic Research Forum

Walter, Barbara. 1999. 'Designing Transitions from Civil War', *International Security* 24, 38–72

Wantchekon, Leonard. 2004. 'The Paradox of "Warlord" Democracy: A Theoretical Investigation', *American Political Science Review* 98:1, 17–33

Waterbury, John. 1994. 'Democracy Without Democrats?: The Potential for Political Liberalization in the Middle East', in *Democracy Without Democrats? The Renewal of Politics in the Muslim World*. G. Salamé (ed.), London: I.B. Tauris, pp. 23–47

Wedeen, Lisa. 1999. *Ambiguities of Domination: Politics, Rhetoric, and Symbols in Contemporary Syria*. Chicago, IL: University of Chicago Press

Woodward, Peter. 1987. 'Is the Sudan Governable? Some Thoughts on the Experience of Liberal Democracy and Military Rule', British Society for Middle Eastern Studies. Bulletin 13:22

Woodward, Peter. 2008. 'Sudan Past Transitions', Sir William Luce Fellowship Paper No. 9, Durham Middle East Papers No. 83, September, pp. 1–14

World Bank. 2014. World Development Indicators. Washington, DC: World Bank

World Bank. 2011. Doing Business 2011: Making a Difference for Entrepreneurs. Washington, DC: World Bank.

World Bank. 2010. Egypt's Food Subsidies: Benefit Incidence and Leakages. Washington, DC: Social and Economic Development Group, Middle East and North Africa Region

World Bank. 2005. Egypt – Toward a More Effective Social Policy: Subsidies and Social Safety Net. Report No. 33550-EG. Washington, DC: World Bank

World Investment Report. 2014. Sudan, Foreign Direct Investment (FDI) Overview, selected years, World Investment Report, Available at: unctad.org/wir

Wright, Joseph, Frantz, Erika and Geddes, Barbara. 2014. 'Oil and Autocratic Regime Survival', *British Journal of Political Science* 45:2, 287–306

Young, John. 2012. *The Fate of Sudan: The Origins and Consequences of a Flawed Peace Process*. Chicago, IL: Zed Books

Zain Al-Abdin, Al-Tayib. 2013. 'The Outstanding Issues Between the Two Sudans: A Way to Peace or Conflict', paper presented at the Sudanese Programme's Conference, Oxford University. Available at: www.sudantribune.com/spip.php?article43062

Zakaria, Fareed. 1997. 'The Rise of Illiberal Democracy', *Foreign Affairs* 76:6, 22–43

Index